The Johns Hopkins University Studies in Historical and Political Science
124th series (2006)

1. BENJAMIN EHLERS, *Between Christians and Moriscos: Juan de Ribera and Religious Reform in Valencia, 1568–1614*

2. ERIC R DURSTELER, *Venetians in Constantinople: Nation, Identity, and Coexistence in the Early Modern Mediterranean*

Between Christians and Moriscos

Juan de Ribera and Religious Reform

in Valencia, 1568–1614

BENJAMIN EHLERS

The Johns Hopkins University Press

Baltimore

This book has been brought to publication with the generous assistance
of the Program for Cultural Cooperation between Spain's
Ministry of Culture and United States Universities.

2 4 6 8 9 7 5 3 1

The Johns Hopkins University Press
2715 North Charles Street
Baltimore, Maryland 21218-4363
www.press.jhu.edu

Library of Congress Cataloging-in-Publication Data
Ehlers, Benjamin.
Between Christians and Moriscos : Juan de Ribera and religious reform in
Valencia, 1568–1614 / Benjamin Ehlers.
p. cm.
Includes bibliographical references (p.   ) and index.
ISBN 0-8018-8322-9 (hardcover : alk. paper)
1. Juan de Ribera, Saint, 1532–1611. 2. Valencia (Spain)—Church history.
3. Moriscos—Spain—Valencia. I. Title.
BX4700.J739E35   2006
261.2′7′0946763—dc22   2005021648

A catalog record for this book is available from the British Library.

Frontispiece: Pere Oromig, *Embarque de los Moriscos en el Grau de Valencia* (1612–13). Colección Bancaja, Valencia, Spain. At the moment of his exile from Valencia, a kneeling morisco father bids farewell to his daughter, who has been adopted by an Old Christian family. Detail from Pere Oromig, *Departure of the Moriscos from the Port of Valencia* (1612–13). *La Expulsión de los Moriscos del reino de Valencia*, 51–53. Valencia: Fundación Bancaja, 1997. Photographed by Juan García Rosell and Gil Carles.

To my family

Contents

Preface ix

Acknowledgments xv

Prologue. The Formation of a Tridentine Bishop 1

1 Two Flocks, One Shepherd: *Christians and Muslims in Valencia* 9

2 The Limits of Episcopal Authority: *The Pasquinades of 1570–1571* 36

3 Reform by Other Means: *The Colegio de Corpus Christi* 58

4 From Moriscos to Moros: *Ribera and the Baptized Muslims of Valencia* 80

5 Disillusionment and Its Consequences: *Ribera, Philip II, and the Valencian Moriscos* 106

6 Justifying the Expulsion: *Ribera and Philip III* 126

Conclusion. The Ideal Bishop and the End of Spanish Islam 151

Notes 159
Bibliography 215
Index 237

Illustrations appear following page 79

Preface

In February 1610, the archbishop of Valencia, Juan de Ribera, petitioned King Philip III to close the schools in the capital city dedicated to educating the children of moriscos, or baptized Muslims, in the Christian faith. Founded nearly a hundred years earlier, these schools represented the hope that the children among this religious minority could be induced to lead Christian lives despite the widespread survival of Islamic practices among their parents. Early in his tenure as archbishop (1568–1611), Juan de Ribera had demonstrated his belief in the possibility of conversion by supporting these schools and reorganizing the parish system to place priests in morisco areas throughout the diocese. Over time, however, Ribera despaired of these projects and came to advocate instead the wholesale expulsion of Spain's three hundred thousand moriscos to North Africa, an event that came about in 1609–14. His request of 1610 emerged from the ensuing debate over the fate of the morisco children. Doubting that even four-year-olds separated from their parents and immersed in Spanish society could be truly remade as Christians, Ribera attempted to at least free himself of this financial burden by asking that all the children from the morisco schools be placed in private homes.[1] His cynicism on this score in his last years of life reflected his belief that only total expulsion could free Spain of any lingering morisco practices.

Ribera had another motive as well: closing the schools would allow him to divert their rents to his prized foundation in the city of Valencia, the seminary and chapel he christened the Colegio de Corpus Christi. Ribera's relationship with the Catholic majority in his diocese followed a very different trajectory from his increasing hostility toward the moriscos. The so-called Old Christians, who claimed to be untainted by Jewish or Moorish blood, distinguished themselves from the baptized descendants of these other faiths, whom they referred to as New Christians. After stumbling through an initial series of obstacles in the capital city, Ribera caught his stride among the Old Christian community, modifying his program of reform to accommodate the religious impulses of the Valencian laity. Through his patronage of local holy figures and his acquisition of paintings and relics of Valencian saints, Ribera attracted worshippers to the Colegio, where he promoted the Eucharistic sacrament after which it was named. Comprising a seminary, chapel, library, and mausoleum, the Colegio illustrates that in his reforms Ribera did not simply attempt to enforce Tridentine dogma and morality. On the contrary, he mounted many of his initiatives in response to the desires of the people, and as he built up a network of supporters in Valencia he engaged rather in a process of exchange, or interplay, between official activity and popular religion. Ribera strove to eliminate all trace of the moriscos in 1610, but he hoped to leave the Colegio as a monument to his inclusive program of reform among Old Christians.

Ribera's creation of a Tridentine seminary and his role in the evangelization and then expulsion of the moriscos established him as a major figure among the reforming bishops in the decades after the Council of Trent, a Spanish counterpart to Carlo Borromeo of Milan. His unusually long tenure provides an excellent opportunity to examine in detail the activity of a bishop in the process of reform. The prosperous Mediterranean archdiocese of Valencia included more than ninety thousand moriscos, most of whom continued to practice Islam despite their forced baptisms during the sixteenth century and who lived alongside a majority Old Christian congregation accustomed to practicing their local devotions in the absence of the higher clergy.

The extensive documentation still housed in the Colegio de Corpus Christi sheds light upon not only the archbishop Ribera's practical efforts to reform the dual communities he encountered in Valencia but also his inner spirituality. His collected sermons, personal library, correspondence, and financial records illustrate how Ribera's spiritual world and his reforms influenced each other, as when he dedicated the Colegio de Corpus Christi to the Host, or when he altered his initial views on the morisco question in response to the changing reality of the situation. In addition, rich collections including the Royal Archive in Valencia, the National Historical Archive in Madrid, and the British Library provide a valuable counterpoint to Ribera's perspective. Local chronicles and journals, secular court cases, viceregal correspondence, and inquisitorial records illuminate both the situation that greeted Ribera upon his arrival and the varying effects of his policies on the ground. Combined with the scholarship of modern Spanish historians, much of which remains inaccessible to a broader audience, these documents provide the basis for a new appraisal not simply of Ribera but also of this critical era in Valencian history.

The present volume thus is not a biography of the archbishop Ribera but rather a study of his episcopate in Valencia and his evolving relationship with both the Old Christians and the moriscos in his diocese. To understand how these two reform

projects could have diverged so dramatically, this book brings into dialogue two his-
toriographical traditions that have traditionally remained separate: Catholic Reformation studies and scholarship on Spanish Islam. In the first historiography, the
particular importance of bishops in Christian history has varied with shifting perspectives on the institutional Church as a whole. Ecclesiastical histories going back
as far as the Venerable Bede link the health of the Church to the capabilities of its
higher clergy. Leopold von Ranke gave a modern expression to this view in 1834,
when the publication of his grand synthesis *The History of the Popes* established the
Counter-Reformation as a field of historical inquiry.[2] Like the nineteenth-century
political historians who wove their narratives around the deeds of great men, Ranke
focuses on the relative merits of the titular heads of the Church and reckons time in
accordance with episcopal and papal succession. Ranke employs this approach to
refute the claims of apologetic Spanish Catholic historians on their own grounds, by
reassessing the history of the Church from an institutional perspective. His tendency
to extrapolate the state of the Church as a whole from the state of the higher clergy
leads him to neglect the great diversity that existed among the lower clergy, the regular clergy, and especially the laity of early modern Europe.

In the twentieth century, historians of religion have advanced the field beyond
the Catholic-Protestant polemics that marked its beginnings and expanded the focus to include the wide range of experiences and practices existing beneath the
level of episcopal activity.[3] H. Outram Evennett finds the "spirit of the counter-
reformation" not in bishops but in the Jesuit order founded by Ignatius of Loyola in
the mid-sixteenth century. Jesuit teachings showed "almost all the characteristic
counter-reformation marks to the highest degree," precisely because, upon closer examination, they bear neither the reactionary tendencies that Protestant historians assigned to them nor the saintliness seen in them by apologists.[4] John Bossy's *Christianity in the West, 1400–1700* develops the idea that the Protestant and Catholic
Reformations can be seen as parallel movements with many similarities, particularly
the depersonalization of Christianity brought about by the Church; in this period
religion changed from a communal phenomenon to an "ism," from fraternal soli-
darity to doctrinal abstraction.[5] The historian William Christian proposes a very different perspective in his highly influential work *Local Religion in Sixteenth-Century
Spain*. Applying an anthropological model to popular religion in early modern
Castile, Christian argues that rural devotions, shrines, and holy days formed a timeless response to environmental threats to the collective well-being, such as drought
and plagues of locusts.[6] Unlike Bossy, Christian detects less of an impact of the institutional Church upon the laity.[7] As diametrically opposed as they may seem, both
Bossy and Christian have exerted an influence on the study of Spanish Catholicism:

several scholars have examined the process of reform largely from the perspective of the people, while tracing a shift away from communal forms of devotion and toward a more official religion governed by the institutional Church.[8]

The historiography of the moriscos of Spain follows a similar pattern in that the detailed regional studies of the twentieth century breathed new life into a field dominated by confessional battles in the nineteenth. In other respects, however, the Christian-Muslim axis differs from Western studies of Christianity.[9] Sixteenth-century disputes over the exact nature of the moriscos framed the question for historians well into the modern era. Responding to the second morisco rebellion in Granada (1568–70), the soldier-historian Luis de Mármol Carvajal characterized the moriscos as a fifth column, a ravening horde of heretics given to looting churches and murdering Christians.[10] The diplomat and humanist Don Diego Hurtado de Mendoza, by contrast, lamented the persecution that left the moriscos between two worlds, "treated as Moors among the scornful Christians, and as Christians among the distrustful Moors."[11] This debate was mirrored in discussions among Muslim scholars as well: whereas some moriscos insisted that they remained legitimate Muslims despite the constraints of their situation in Spain, Islamic scholars abroad questioned whether a Muslim could pay tribute to a foreign king and dissimulate so amply in the question of religion.[12] After the expulsion of the moriscos in 1609–14, this divide persisted in officially sponsored celebrations of the decree and the sometimes subtle criticisms offered by artists, fiction writers, and the exiled moriscos themselves.[13]

In the modern era, the expulsion of the moriscos emerged as a key piece of evidence in the debate over the causes and nature of the decline of seventeenth-century Spain.[14] Spain's slow and halting transition to modernity, marked by a failure to embrace democracy and industrialization as rapidly as other Western nations, led many historians to comment upon the concerns of their own times in works ostensibly dedicated to the Habsburg era. The nineteenth century, in particular, witnessed a resumption of morisco studies in conjunction with the renewed Spanish presence in North Africa and the emergence of purportedly scientific definitions of race. The Spanish contributions of this period have traditionally been denominated "liberal" or "conservative" according to their view of the expulsion as intolerant or justified, but all of these works cited immutable laws of history to explain the failed attempt to draw together two essentially opposed races.[15] Pascual Boronat y Barrachina, a Valencian cleric, marshals an array of previously unpublished materials to "scientifically" defend Ribera's advocacy for the expulsion of the moriscos, characterizing the New Christians as unified in their apostasy and uniformly hated among Old Christians.[16] The American historian Henry Charles Lea, in the first

major contribution to the subject by a foreigner, disagrees that racial differences in-
evitably led to the expulsion.[17] Focusing rather on the beliefs and decisions of the
Spanish officials, Lea argues that the complicity among kings, seigneurs, and vassals
perpetuated a long-standing coexistence, disrupted only by a Church that followed
up its abject failure to convert the moriscos with an equally futile effort to secure
conformity through persecution.

Twentieth-century historians share Lea's sympathy for the plight of the moriscos
without perpetuating his view of the Spanish as dogmatic and intolerant. In the succinct words of Fernand Braudel, "We are not here concerned with judging Spain in
the light of present-day attitudes: all historians are of course on the side of the
Moriscos."[18] Seeking to understand rather than to praise or blame, a generation of
historians inspired by Braudel have illuminated numerous aspects of the morisco
question. Books and articles dedicated to the moriscos now number well into the
hundreds, the vast majority of them in Spanish or French. If a general trend can be
discerned from the recent literature, it is an increasing sensitivity to distinctions
among morisco communities and to changes over time. Nearly fifty years ago, a disciple of Braudel characterized Christian-Muslim relations in Spain as a conflict between two nations fundamentally divided by culture and religion.[19] While most
moriscologists would still accept this thesis at the level of policy—Old Christian officials and morisco leaders did speak of each other in polarized terms—the work of
the last few decades has striven to nuance this stark dichotomy, focusing on moriscos
and Old Christians who dissented from the dominant view of the Other. The field
has also benefited from the greater inclusion of other disciplines, including linguistic studies drawn from Arabic sources.[20] Recent research has enhanced our understanding of the discussions, twists, and turns that characterized the Habsburg
morisco policy, as well as the diversity and vitality of the moriscos themselves.[21]

The present study of Ribera and his divided congregation in Valencia draws from
both Catholic Reformation studies and the historiography of Christian-Muslim relations and seeks to make a contribution to both fields. On the one hand, it offers
the first sustained assessment of Ribera as a reformer, arguing that he was neither in-
cidental to the religious life of Old Christians in Valencia nor hostile to their unique
forms of expression. The debates that led to the formulation of the decrees at the
Council of Trent were mirrored in the diverse patterns of implementation across the
Catholic world.[22] Ribera's initial attempts to reform his Old Christian congregation
drew from Tridentine principles, but over time he adapted his methods in response
to changing priorities among his parishioners. In this sense, the archbishop's relationship with the laity did not follow the shift from communal practices to doctrinal
religion traced by Bossy elsewhere in Europe. Ribera used available opportunities to

promote aspects of official religion such as the Eucharist, but he did so as part of an ongoing conversation with the laity, incorporating rather than stifling their own local devotions. Despite his initial status as a "foreigner" from Castile and the limitations on his formal powers as archbishop, Ribera came to identify with the interests of his diocese so closely over the course of forty-two years that it would be impossible to imagine early modern Valencia without him.

Restoring human agency to Ribera brings the moriscos of Valencia into sharper focus as well. Ribera's attempts to entice the New Christians to punctuate their lives in accordance with the liturgical rhythms of the Church provoked responses ranging from enthusiasm to disdain, from accommodation to resistance. As the moriscos evolved, in his vision, from potential converts to irredeemable heretics, Ribera continued to pursue evangelical programs even after he no longer believed that they could lead to conversion. In this context a measure that might seem gentle or harsh on the face of it takes on new shades of meaning, and the conventional categories of "rigorous" or "gradualist" cease to apply. The religious practices of the moriscos affected Ribera as well, to the point where the perpetuation of Islam among the majority blinded him to the assimilation of the minority. Faced with ambiguity, Ribera divided his flock in the search for clarity. His attempt to shut down the school for morisco children and direct its revenues to the Colegio de Corpus Christi in 1610 underscores Ribera's ultimate loyalties and the divergent consequences of the process of reform in early modern Valencia.

Acknowledgments

I would like to thank the following people and institutions for their support of this project: the Fulbright Commission; the Program for Cultural Cooperation between Spain's Ministry of Culture and United States Universities; the Center for Humanities and Arts of the University of Georgia; Richard Kagan and the history department of the Johns Hopkins University; Jorge Catalá and the history department of the University of Valencia; the Erasmus Institute of Notre Dame; the Office of the Vice President for Research and the history department of the University of Georgia; and the editors and readers of the Johns Hopkins University Press. Don Ramón Robres Lluch generously provided me with access to the holdings of the Colegio de Corpus Christi, Valencia. I am especially grateful to Kathleen Dawson for the laptop computer with which I first began my archival research in Spain.

Between Christians and Moriscos

The Formation of a Tridentine Bishop

Juan de Ribera lived most of his life in the kingdom of Valencia, but his roots were firmly planted elsewhere. Born in Seville around 1532, Ribera grew up among the well-laid gardens and classical statuary of the Casa de Pilatos, home to the prestigious Enríquez de Ribera lineage. His ancestors on the Enríquez side of the family descended from King Alfonso XI (r. 1312–50), making Ribera a distant cousin of Ferdinand the Catholic and thus of the Habsburg monarchs.[1] This house was merged with the Ribera clan in the marriage of Ribera's great-grandparents, Pedro Enríquez (d. 1492) and Catalina Ribera (d. 1505), consolidating two of the more expansive landowning families in Andalusia. His famous great-uncle, Fadrique Enríquez de Ribera (1476–1539), took the habit of the Order of Santiago at the age of nine and began fighting Muslims at age fourteen. Fadrique also participated in the suppression of an uprising of Granadan Muslims in 1500, and in 1514 Philip I named him 1st Marquis of Tarifa.[2] In 1519–20 he undertook a pilgrimage to the Holy Land, accompanied by Juan de Encina, a Spanish classicist who served as master of the chapel for the pope.[3]

While in Jerusalem, Fadrique followed the path of Christ from the house of Pontius Pilate to Golgotha, recording in his journal a distance of 1,580 paces.[4] In the 1530s he decided to recreate the Way of the Cross in Seville, beginning at his newly constructed palace (hence the name Casa de Pilatos) and terminating at a cross in the countryside, on the road to Granada. Juan de Ribera scarcely knew his great-uncle, but he spent his childhood in an environment built by Fadrique, a world of Roman coins, religious artwork, and hundreds of books ranging from Seneca to Boccaccio to Augustine. The boy also lived to see this complicated man's vision of a Vía

Crucis in Seville grow from a rite observed by a few penitents to a popular civic event.[5]

Fadrique's brother having died years before, his titles devolved upon his nephew, Per Afán de Ribera III (1509–1571), 2d Marquis of Tarifa, 6th Count of Los Molares, and—subsequently—1st Duke of Alcalá de los Gazules. None of these titles, however, would be passed on to Per Afán's only son. Juan de Ribera, the illegitimate off-spring of Per Afán and a local noblewoman, knew that despite his father's open recognition of paternity he would never inherit the Casa de Pilatos. Upon the premature death of his mother, his sister Catalina took over the responsibility of caring for him; years later he would reward her for this act of kindness with a regular stipend for the rest of her life.[6] Although his father continued the family's centuries-old tradition of royal service as viceroy of Catalonia (1554–58) and Naples (1558–71), Ribera chose another path at an early age. In 1543 he received the clerical tonsure at the parish church of San Esteban, and in 1544, with his father's blessing, the twelve-year-old and a retinue of six servants set out for the University of Salamanca.[7]

At the university Ribera studied canon law and Thomist theology under disciples of the famous neo-scholastic Francisco de Vitoria.[8] Despite his noble pedigree and his house filled with servants, Ribera did not follow the example of those young gentlemen who used their time in Salamanca as an opportunity to lead an "easy, pleasurable student life."[9] He did associate with fellow students Fernando de Toledo, brother of the Count of Oropesa, and Antonio de Córdoba, brother of the Duke of Feria, but these men turned down more lucrative offers to become a humble priest and a Jesuit, respectively. The hagiographers of Juan de Ribera have presented testimony to his studiousness and parsimony, claiming that at one point his father had to intervene to compel him to return from a hermitage to his appointed house.[10] In 1554 he matriculated as a theologian with a bachelor's degree in arts, and in May 1557 he earned his master's degree in theology.[11] By this time he had already expressed a desire to take holy orders as a priest, an event that took place shortly thereafter.

In 1562 Philip II nominated the young and inexperienced Ribera to the bishopric of Badajoz, a modest see on the Portuguese border. Philip II had inherited from his father the power to name bishops in Spain, and his appointment of Ribera mirrored the common Renaissance practice of promoting second sons and illegitimate children of noble clans to ecclesiastical office. This gesture of gratitude to Per Afán also served as a means of collecting royal fees and shaping a nobility beholden to the Crown.[12] But whereas Charles V had used bishops to combat Protestantism in his realms, Philip II sought rather to renovate the Church within Spain, through the promotion of a new generation of pious, educated prelates.[13] This shift in emphasis was influenced by an international gathering of churchmen then in its final sessions in Trent, a mountain town north of Italy. The Council of Trent, which convened on three occasions between 1545 and 1563, attempted to restore the unity of the Christian Church in the West, clarify Catholic doctrine, and lay out a program of religious reform. The first of these objectives fell by the wayside after Protestant leaders declined to participate in the council, and so the Catholic fathers who traveled to Trent turned instead to the restoration of their own flock within this newly divided world.

Through twenty-five sessions and hundreds of debates, the assembled fathers in Trent produced a series of decrees addressing the Church's position on contentious theological issues and setting guidelines for clerical reform. In the matter of doctrine, the Council reasserted the validity of Catholic beliefs and practices that came under fire in the Protestant Reformation, such as the cult of the saints, relics, artwork, and purgatory. In contrast to Martin Luther's views, the decrees insisted on the legitimacy of all seven sacraments and defended the real presence of Christ in the Eucharist, one of the most divisive issues of the Reformation era. At the same time, the fathers attempted to prevent abuse of Catholic traditions by warning, for example, that masses sung in honor of the saints are offered not to them "but to God alone who crowned them."[14]

The Council's program for Church renewal decisively empowered the bishop as the locus of reform, rather than granting leadership to religious orders or cathedral chapters, institutions that had grown in power during a medieval era of episcopal absenteeism and corruption. Taking the diocese as the unit of analysis, the decrees authorized bishops to curb abuses and promote exemplary behavior among the secular clergy, cathedral canons, monasteries, and convents. Episcopal responsibilities to the laity included eliminating pagan practices and enforcing proper worship and observance of the sacraments. Toward these ends the decrees ordered bishops to reside in their dioceses and deliver sermons regularly, hold periodic councils and synods, carry out frequent visitations to their parishes and churches, and review existing educational institutions, as well as found diocesan seminaries. Amid the welter of competing ecclesiastical institutions and jurisdictions that characterized early modern Catholicism, the Council of Trent placed the responsibility for ensuring doctrinal purity and enacting Church reform on the shoulders of its bishops.

The omissions and occasionally ambiguous language of these decrees, however, belied the heated disagreements that marked their creation in Trent. That the council came into being at all was a testament to the reforming spirit of Pope Paul III, who overcame his predecessors' reluctance to call a gathering that could potentially circumscribe the power of the Vatican. Although the decrees skirted the issue of papal authority by taking no direct stance on the matter, the struggle for control appeared in other guises. The Spanish contingent, led by the archbishop of Granada, Pedro Guerrero, disagreed among themselves on some points but on the whole sought to focus on the issue of reform, central to Charles V and Philip II. The majority Italian party usually steered the discussion toward matters of doctrine, where the pope could more effectively assert his supremacy.

These divergent approaches collided over the matter of episcopal residency. All of the councilors agreed that bishops should ideally remain in their dioceses to carry out reform, but two camps divided over the question of the source of this obligation. Was the requirement a function of the office itself, as consecrated by the papacy, or did the obligation to reside derive from God alone, as the Spanish contended? The suggestion that bishops answered to a higher power than the pope led to a crisis, one ended only by a compromise that asserted the obligation without detailing its origins.[15] These unresolved tensions persisted after the conclusion of the council: in 1563 the pope was careful to ratify the decrees to affirm that their validity depended on his authority. Philip II's rapid promulgation of the decrees in Spain reflected not an endorsement of the papal view but rather a counterclaim that reform in his lands would unfold under his authority. Recognizing the Tridentine focus on episcopal powers, the king set out to effect reform in Spain through bishops who enjoyed the spiritual imprimatur of the Church Universal but answered to the Crown in practical matters.

Not all Catholic bishops were quick to embrace the reform movement after the closure of the final session at Trent. Given Ribera's background, one might reasonably have expected him to resemble Bishop Marquard von Hattstein of Speyer (1560–81), a well-educated nobleman who concerned himself more with business and politics than with his spiritual duties: "Marquard's career was not altogether unusual for a talented, hard-working young nobleman, but his success had nothing to do with his personal piety or a commitment to Church reform."[16] Over his six years in Badajoz (1562–68), however, Ribera established his reputation as a committed reformer. He published the Tridentine decrees in his own diocese in 1564, and in the following year he held a diocesan synod and participated in the provincial council of Santiago de Compostela.

At this latter council Ribera offered a formal report outlining his program of reform, drawn not only from Trent but from previous councils as well.[17] In this wideranging document Ribera called for a number of reforms, from curbing clerical luxury and absenteeism to enforcing respect for the Sacrament. Not all of his proposals appeared in the official decrees of the council, but the scattered documentation from his time in Badajoz indicates that he made every effort to live by his own rules. He made regular visitations to his diocese to preach and reform abuses and gained fame for personally taking the Sacrament to those too ill to attend church. Although Ribera's retinue consisted of more than fifty officials and pages, he maintained a strict budget and oversaw diocesan expenditures such as charitable donations of wheat.[18] According to his hagiographers, Ribera attracted such a following in his diocese that when the time came to leave, he did so at midnight, so as not to have to witness the tears of the people.[19]

Ribera's reforms in Badajoz drew suspicion as well as adulation, however, in both cases because his fervent desire to engage the religiosity of the laity led him to embrace controversial practices such as mental prayer and interior piety. On Christmas Day in 1563, standing before his new congregation in Badajoz, Ribera delivered "the first sermon I preached in all of my life."[20] The thirty-year-old bishop offered the following commentary on the star of Bethlehem: "The clarity of God illuminated [alumbróles] all who saw it, because the light that had come into the world would illuminate all. The Bible says, 'they were filled with fear.' Man is afraid because the sacraments of God do not fit in his understanding: after the splendor, comes the fear. Fear is not an evil thing; it is not as perfect as love, but it is a beginning."[21]

In his other sermons and pastoral letters through the 1560s, Ribera continued to develop the theme of illumination, emphasizing the role of silent prayer. "Prayer illuminates the soul. Prayer and meditation remove blindness, and act as a torch for the soul."[22] His sermons in this period reflected the influence of works by Franciscan spiritualists such as Francisco de Osuna and Bernardino de Laredo. Laredo's The Ascent of Mount Sion, for example, outlined a series of spiritual exercises designed to mortify the passions and annihilate the self as a means of attaining knowledge and ultimately union with God.[23] Like Osuna and Laredo, Ribera underlined the importance of mental prayer and silence, rather than limiting one's devotion to spoken prayers in formal liturgies: "Man cannot seek divine remedy amid the evil and tumult of the day. Come the quiet night, and amid this silence God will arrive, not in a whirlwind, but in a delicate zephyr. He who seeks God, seek Him in silence."[24] Ribera's admonitions to his congregation in Badajoz echoed the sentiment of Laredo that achieving unitive love with God depended on the abnegation of one's self, the ability to "think nothing at all."[25]

As Ribera was aware, such forms of devotion had come under attack in Spain in recent years, owing to the apparent similarities between individual union with God and the Protestant focus on personal piety rather than worship mediated by the Church. His former professor, the Dominican Melchor Cano, oversaw the prosecution of suspected Protestant heretics in Seville and Valladolid in the years after 1559. In his final will and testament, Ribera thanked God for three *mercedes*, or gifts, that he had received over the course of his life. On each of these occasions, his father, Per Afán, considered placing Ribera under the tutelage of a well-respected scholar who was subsequently exposed as a Protestant heretic.

Seemingly innocuous circumstances ultimately prevented the young student from coming into contact with the licentiate Manso, who shortly thereafter fell into the hands of the Inquisition, and Dr. Constantino Ponce de la Fuente, a former preacher to Charles V and leader of the so-called Lutherans of Seville.[26] Ribera interpreted the fact that none of these events came to pass as a sign of "the particular care and paternal providence that God has always had for this miserable sinner. Because these people held such esteem, and I was so young in age, with no knowledge of the heresies they propagated, they might have taught me some evil doctrine against our holy faith."[27] In his view, the Erasmian thought of Constantino and his circle would have corrupted Spain had it not been checked by the Inquisition, and for this reason the archbishop supported the royal ban on study abroad (in 1559) and the restrictions on the English residing in Spain.[28]

Although Ribera supported the suppression of those who strayed from the Church, as bishop of Badajoz he nonetheless defended the orthodoxy of the silent meditation practiced by his own congregants. According to one investigator of heresy, Ribera even warned the group of people under his spiritual direction, prophesying their persecution at the hands of the Inquisition. Such thoughts may well have informed a sermon he delivered on Easter 1567: "He who wants to know the path to heaven, ask. The man who walks on the path of God, what does he see, what does he do, without fearing that ignorant and foolish followers of the devil will murmur and contradict him? Only the good man can see."[29] Not even resistance from his former mentor Cano prevented Ribera from implementing a program that he believed would allow him to establish more meaningful points of contact between the institutional Church and the spiritual development of the laity. Ribera's willingness to promote interior piety in Badajoz reflected his growing ability to interpret and expand upon the prescriptive decrees of the Council of Trent in his reform projects.

The year 1568 brought two signal honors to the young prelate. Within the space of a few months, Philip II nominated him to the position he would hold for the rest of his life, and Pius V gave him the name by which he would be known. Both of these titles, archbishop of Valencia and patriarch of Antioch, had been vacated in April upon the death of Fernando de Loaces, the eighty-five-year-old who had held the see briefly in 1567–68. Ribera's appointment represented a departure from standard practice, both for Philip II and for the archdiocese of Valencia. Most bishops of this era climbed the ladder more slowly, beginning their careers in third-tier dioceses and working their way up to more lucrative posts. Bernardo de Rojas y Sandoval (1546–1618), nephew of the bishop of Oviedo, served as a cathedral canon in Seville before his appointment as bishop of Ciudad Rodrigo (1586), Pamplona (1588), Jaén (1596), and finally Toledo (1599). Aided by his powerful nephew the Duke of Lerma, Rojas y Sandoval saw his annual rents increase almost thirtyfold to 220,000 ducats in Toledo, the principal and wealthiest see in Spain.[30]

Bishops in the most prominent dioceses often served at the highest levels of government as well, as royal councilors and grand inquisitors, a practice that led to absenteeism: Ribera's correspondent Cardinal Gaspar de Quiroga (1512–1594), for example, attempted to reform his archdiocese of Toledo even though his responsibilities as grand inquisitor required his presence at court.[31] The mobility and gradual advancement of Spanish bishops also led to an ecclesiastical "gerontocracy" like that of the Spanish bureaucracy as a whole, in which the long tenure of the most senior councilors inhibited innovation.[32] In northern Castile, the average age of a bishop upon nomination under Philip II was fifty-five; in Valencia, the five years between 1563 and 1568 witnessed the deaths of four elderly archbishops of Valencia.[33]

In an effort to break this cycle and open a path for sustained projects of reform, Philip II decided not to appoint yet another senior prelate when the Archdiocese of Valencia again found itself without a bishop in 1568. The king turned instead to Juan de Ribera, who at thirty-six years of age was much younger than the typical nominee for a post as lucrative and important as Valencia, which ranked in the highest tier just behind Toledo. The king was drawn by Ribera's growing fame as a reformer in Badajoz, a reputation that inspired the pope to call him "a luminary for all of Spain."[34] Ribera initially tried to turn this post down; all false modesty aside—to lust after honors and benefices ran counter to the humility expected of a Tridentine bishop—he was evidently concerned that the reform projects he had initiated in Estremadura would not bear fruit in a diocese that contained so many moriscos. Philip II insisted, and Ribera's formal transfer by the College of Cardinals set the stage for his remarkably long tenure in Valencia.

By declining to relocate Ribera again or appoint him to a post at court, furthermore, the king provided the archbishop with the opportunity to develop his programs across a lifetime. This decision would have profound effects for Ribera, for his divided congregation, and ultimately for all of Spain. Whereas Ribera succeeded in engaging the religiosity of the Catholic laity, adapting his Tridentine vision of reform to existing spiritual impulses, the radically different trajectory of his interactions with the moriscos led him to advocate their expulsion. The chapters that follow explore the dynamism and multiplicity of relations between Christians and baptized Muslims in the final days of pluralist Spain, demonstrating that the greatest achievements of the Catholic Reformation in Valencia remained intimately bound to its darkest tragedy.

CHAPTER ONE

Two Flocks, One Shepherd

Christians and Muslims in Valencia

In March 1569 Juan de Ribera traveled eastward across Spain and took possession of the archdiocese of Valencia. In this new post he discovered a deeply divided flock, with Old Christians and moriscos separated by economic status, language, race, and religion. Ever since the Islamic conquest of Valencia more than eight centuries earlier, Christians and Muslims had engaged in a struggle for control of the region's abundant resources of water and land. The Christian Reconquest of the thirteenth century shifted the balance of power but did not end coexistence in Valencia, for many Muslims chose to remain as Mudejars, vassals to the new Catholic king. This situation persisted through the crisis of the fourteenth century and the prosperity of the fifteenth, until a changing political climate saw the forced baptism of all Spanish Muslims in the 1520s under Charles V. The nominal unity of sixteenth-century Valencia, however, belied the continuance of Islamic practice among "new converts" (as the moriscos were known), and this disparity contributed to increased suspicion of moriscos in connection with the rising Turkish menace in the Mediterranean. An examination of Old Christian and morisco religious practices at the time of Ribera's arrival reveals the incongruity of his two flocks: whereas Old Christians embraced the pageantry and spectacle of the Corpus Christi procession, the ceremony that provided the standard for urban rituals, moriscos withdrew to their homes on Friday evenings to observe Muslim rites to the greatest extent possible in this hostile world.

According to the Gospel of John, the good shepherd brings all his sheep into one fold, just as Jesus exhorted his followers to reach out to the Gentiles among them: "I am the good shepherd; I know my own and my own know me, as the Father knows me and I know the Father; and I lay down my life for the sheep. And I have other sheep, that are not of this fold; I must bring them also, and they will heed my voice. So there shall be one flock, one shepherd" (John 10:14–16). In his efforts to draw the Valencian people to heed his voice, Ribera encountered resistance from both halves of his congregation. The seeming harmony and majesty of the 1569 Corpus Christi festival masked deep-seated tensions within the Valencian capital, where the confraternities and local officials who organized and enacted the rituals were not accustomed to following the lead of the archbishop or other royal appointees. By the same token, the third of the kingdom's residents excluded from the Corpus Christi celebrations also defined their spiritual world in opposition to official religion. The moriscos who conducted Islamic ceremonies in that same summer weekend owed nothing at all to the institutional Church, drawing inspiration rather from the beliefs of their Mudejar ancestors.

ISLAMIC VALENCIA AND THE TRANSFER TO CHRISTIAN RULE

Islamic Valencia, established with the Muslim conquest of Visigothic Spain in 711–18, occupied a prominent position within the shifting world of Al-Andalus, or Muslim Iberia. The region prospered in the centuries after the conquest, as Muslim agriculturalists introduced new systems of irrigation to create arable lands beyond the reach of previous Roman canals.[1] These advances made possible a medieval Green Revolution, in which Muslims introduced rice, sugar, cotton, fruits, and vegetables to the varied microclimates of Valencia, establishing the area as an important center for trade.[2] The succession of medieval warlords and immigrants from the Maghreb who reigned over this region, however, ultimately failed to halt the Christian Reconquest. The process of recapturing Valencia from the infidel unfolded in a much less clear-cut and heroic manner than later chronicles might suggest. The frontier between Christians and Muslims in Valencia became blurred over time as Christians adopted the religion of their conquerors, in some cases rising to prominence in a society dominated by Arabs and Berbers.[3]

In the midst of this multiethnic but overwhelmingly Muslim population, small communities of Christian merchants and immigrants known as *mozárabes* continued to practice their faith on the fringes of society. When the conqueror Rodrigo Díaz, better known to posterity as El Cid, took the city of Valencia temporarily in 1094, he encountered a group of Christians headed by a Mozarabic bishop.[4] James I of Aragon (r. 1213–76) definitively instituted Christian rule in Valencia on 9 October 1238, when he led his Aragonese and Catalan troops into the city in triumph. This victory punctuated an ongoing series of alliances, negotiations, and battles through which James pushed the frontier east to the sea and south to the Murcian border.[5] Seeking to keep the nobility among these two groups in check, James created Valencia as an independent kingdom with himself as king, beholden to neither Aragon nor Catalonia.

In the period immediately following the Reconquest, Christians in Valencia remained a numerical minority, an island in a sea of Muslims. Nevertheless, within a few decades, James and his ministers established an array of institutions appropriate to a new, Christian state. By the end of the thirteenth century the kingdom of Valencia boasted its own legal code and currency, a host of new governmental officials and justices, several monasteries, a papal university, and a network of parishes and dioceses centered on the cathedral chapter and bishopric of Valencia.[6] James also set an important precedent shortly after 1238 when he rewarded his Aragonese generals with large parcels of land in Valencia's rural interior, the dry-farming region (secado) where Muslim farmers raised grapes and olives. The Catalan nobility, by contrast, received parcels of the fertile orchard (huerta) and charters to coastal towns. In these latter areas, Christian immigrants from the north gradually displaced the Muslims over the course of the fourteenth century, whereas in much of the interior, the Muslims remained in the majority. The total proportion of Muslims in Valencia fell to roughly one-half by 1350 and one-third by 1450.[7] This pattern of population distribution persisted until the expulsion of the moriscos in 1609, at which time the former Muslims numbered more than one hundred thousand.

Despite the rise of a Christian kingdom in Valencia, the Muslims enjoyed a considerable degree of autonomy, especially in matters of law and justice. Conquerors and conquered alike participated in the creation of Mudejar aljamas, integral surrendered communities existing in parallel with the new Christian society. In negotiating the acquisition of Alzira in 1242, for example, James consulted with Muslim jurists, conceding legal and religious continuity in exchange for permission to "build a wall in order that the Christians should not interfere with the Moors nor the Moors with the Christians."[8] This wall arose not from a mutual respect but from a mutual contempt and a shared desire for separation.[9] Whatever his motives, James I granted charters to the Muslims allowing them the public exercise of their religion, freedom to travel and engage in commerce, and the right to appoint their own tax collectors and Islamic magistrates.[10] Under these concessions, the Mudejars continued to worship in mosques, govern their municipalities, and maintain a diverse economy, but these systems now operated under Christian control and taxation.[11]

The transfer to Christian rule in Valencia frequently brought about the emigration of the aristocracy and the intellectual elite. Once a vital part of Islamic scholarship, the Valencian Muslims played a reduced role in the broader world of Islamic learning after the conquest.[12] Those who remained as Mudejars, however, were not all poor farmers, and in many areas wealthy families assumed greater roles in the new aljama than they had previously held.[13] The conflicted situation of the Mudejars led to a heated debate among jurists as to the legitimacy of their status. In the Islamic world, the question arose whether a true Muslim had an obligation to emigrate from the Abode of War, or non-Muslim part of the world, to the Abode of Islam, in which society was organized in accordance with Muslim law (*shariah*). Whereas some legal scholars in North Africa demonstrated a remarkable sympathy toward the predicament of the Mudejars and pointed out circumstances that could justify persevering in Spain, others took a more rigorous stance, arguing that "a Muslim's willing residence in Christian land was 'manifest proof of his vile and base spirit.'"[14]

The reinstated Catholic Church in Valencia demonstrated a similar diversity of opinion. The first bishops in the diocese, dismayed that this "crusade" had resulted in a majority Muslim population, advocated the expulsion of the so-called Saracens from Valencia.[15] For practical and economic reasons this line of thinking did not carry the day, and Valencian clerics reconciled themselves to the divided nature of their diocese. Some churchmen limited themselves to restricting contact between the two faiths, while others actively sought the evangelization of the Muslims. The Catalan missionary and writer Ramón Lull (ca. 1232–1316) implemented a tactic of confrontation, preaching against Islam and in favor of Christianity in mosques and Muslim areas.[16] In keeping with his belief that dialogue and reason would lead to conversion, in the late thirteenth century Lull helped to found a series of schools dedicated to instructing preachers in polemics and the Arabic language.[17] When the predicted mass conversions failed to materialize, however, this millennial optimism dissipated, and by the middle of the fourteenth century most of these schools had folded. The Valencian Church arose from this cycle with a much more circumspect view of the Muslims, a cautious stance that would persist until the time of the archbishop Ribera.

These tensions inherent to the Mudejar arrangement combined with external factors in the late thirteenth and fourteenth centuries to produce a series of crises that threatened to destroy this pluralistic equilibrium. Mudejar rebellions in Castile, Aragon, and Valencia in the later years of the thirteenth century led to a climate of fear in which Christian kings repealed the initial surrender agreements and reduced their Muslim vassals to a seigneurial arrangement through increased dues, services, and restrictions.[18] Furthermore, the Islamic rulers of Granada launched three invasions to liberate their Valencian coreligionists in 1304–32, and Muslim pirates ramped up their attacks on Aragonese interests in the Mediterranean.[19] In response, Christian rulers sought to restrict the movements of the Mudejars, confining them to Moorish quarters in larger cities and to more strictly designated aljamas in rural areas. These policies resulted from the simultaneous desires to protect the Muslims from Christian mobs, segregate them from Muslims abroad, and prevent the loss of workers.[20] This last concern weighed heavily in the fourteenth century, when poor weather and deficient agricultural techniques led to endemic famine, leaving the people more vulnerable to the plague.[21] As Christians in search of more and better land began to encroach upon previously Muslim areas, increased contact led to riots, the enslavement of Mudejars, and criminal activity including prostitution.[22] Thus the economic downturn of the fourteenth century led the Christian authorities to impose tighter economic and social controls on the Mudejars, leading to a deterioration of interfaith relations.

Although the transfer to Christian rule introduced persistent tensions to Valencia, Christian-Muslim relations did not follow a simple downward progression from Reconquest to forced baptisms to expulsion. On the contrary, the Valencian boom of the fifteenth century was a tide that lifted all boats; everyday transactions between Old Christians and Mudejars lowered the barriers between them and brought stability to their arrangement of coexistence.[23] Production of rice, sugar, cereals, textiles, and the famous ceramics of Manises rebounded in the age of Alfonso the Magnanimous (r. 1416–58), a dynamism subsequently immortalized in the majestic Lonja or silk exchange.[24] In the late fifteenth century, with Catalonia facing internal crises and before the discovery of silver in the New World, Valencian shipping in the all-important Italian trade flourished, and her merchants acted as royal financiers to the monarch.[25]

In this era of economic growth, Muslim farmers, muleteers, and artisans benefited in the form of cultural autonomy and relatively benign treatment. The Mudejars typically resolved internal matters and questions of Islamic law within their own communities, but in many situations they made recourse to Christian judicial institutions, with some expectation that they would receive justice.[26] If their position in society left them exposed to attacks from Christian mobs acting on common prejudices, the fact remains that their Christian lords afforded them a degree of protection. This state of affairs resembled the toleration of Mozarabic Christians under Muslim rule in some senses but differed in this important respect: whereas the Islamic rulers could cite the Quran in defense of their tolerance of infidels—"Fight those who do not believe . . . until they pay the *jizyah* [poll tax]"—the Christian monarchs of Valencia received no such support from the New Testament.[27] Acting rather for pragmatic reasons, Christian rulers simply adapted the existing model to the new circumstances. Because this arrangement rested solely upon the will of the king, it could survive outbreaks of anti-Muslim violence, such as the assault on the

Moorish quarter (*morería*) of Valencia by a Christian mob in 1455, but not a change in royal policy.

Such a change occurred in the wake of the marriage of Ferdinand of Aragon and Isabella of Castile in 1479. This Union of the Crowns linked the fortunes of the Valencian Mudejars with those of their coreligionists elsewhere in Spain. In 1502, after a policy of forcible conversion led to a Muslim uprising in Granada, Isabella ordered the baptism, under pain of expulsion, of all Mudejars living under the Crown of Castile. Ferdinand acquiesced to this change but insisted that the policy of forced baptisms not be applied to the Levantine Mudejars.[28] Thus when Charles V succeeded to the throne in 1516, he inherited a realm divided: Castile, owing to the expulsion of the Jews in 1492 and the baptism of the Mudejars, had attained nominal religious unity, but Aragon remained heterogeneous, as the Mudejars continued to enjoy many of the same freedoms as their medieval forebears. The economic and social structures of the kingdom of Valencia, in particular, had long been predicated upon the differences between Christians and Muslims, and Charles hesitated to disrupt this equilibrium with an attempt to convert the Mudejars to Christianity. At the Valencian Cortes (Estates General) in 1518, Charles swore a solemn oath to uphold the promise previously made by Ferdinand never to force the baptism of the Valencian Mudejars.[29]

Over the next decade, however, developments in Valencia forced Charles to break his word. In 1519 an outbreak of plague led most of the nobles living in the city of Valencia to flee to the countryside. In their absence, groups of artisans organized themselves into *germanías*, or armed brotherhoods, ostensibly dedicated to the defense of the coast against the Turks. Charles initially welcomed the artisan militias and even granted them certain ceremonial concessions. But when the germanías began to voice grievances against the wealthier merchants and aristocracy in 1521, the king declared them outlaws and ordered Diego Hurtado de Mendoza (d. 1536), count of Mélito, to mobilize an army against them. These opposing forces quickly came to blows. In the summer of 1521, the germanías successfully laid siege to the town of Játiva, and in the coastal town of Gandía another contingent of artisans defeated royalist troops led by the Duke of Segorbe.[30] After these stunning victories, the artisans experienced a series of setbacks that culminated in the execution of their leaders and the suppression of the germanías.[31]

Despite their defeat, the germanías exerted a profound influence on Christian-Muslim relations in Valencia. Following their victories during the summer of 1521, bands of artisans forced the Mudejars living in Játiva, Cocentaina, and Gandía to receive baptism, executing those who refused. The artisans persecuted the Mudejars for various reasons, including the desire to disrupt the economic stability of the landowning nobility, who relied heavily upon the labor of their Muslim vassals; as a reprisal against Mudejars who served in the royalist armies; and as an act of piety designed to underscore the justness of their cause by association with the Reconquest. An extensive inquisitorial report compiled in 1524 reveals that in the immediate wake of the rebel victories, physical violence often preceded and accompanied the forced baptisms, which in turn affected the character of the ceremonies themselves. One Old Christian laborer of Gandía, describing the aftermath of the battle, testified that he had seen more than 150 dead Muslims between the village gate and his parish church.[32]

Accepting baptism, furthermore, did not spare the Mudejars of Gandía from all violence. "The soldiers took the moros and stripped them, and robbed them, and carried them with great fury to the church to be baptized."[33] Even under these chaotic circumstances the priests attempted to maintain the basic rituals of baptism, but several of them expressed doubts as to the regularity of the sacraments thus administered: "The church was packed, and he saw the chaplains sprinkling holy water, but he does not remember if they used an aspergillum or hyssop, or what words they said, or whether they gave them Christian names."[34] In the ensuing weeks, hundreds of Mudejars in these areas requested and received baptism using the standard liturgy, though these sacraments proved equally problematic. According to the local presbyter in a town north of Játiva, "Shortly before the conversion of the Moors [moros] of Alzira, I heard that the captains of the germanía had gone through the town saying that if the Moors did not become Christians, they would slash their throats and seize their possessions."[35]

After the defeat of the germanías in September 1522, Charles V convened a panel of theologians (junta) to assess the legitimacy of the forced baptisms. The junta recognized the ambiguity of the situation but rejected the idea that the Valencian baptisms could be nullified by the circumstances under which they had been administered, "which did not excuse the converts from remaining Christians."[36] Following the logic of Thomas Aquinas, the panel distinguished between pagans who had never known the law, and thus could not be forced to convert to Christianity, and those who had chosen to receive baptism under any circumstances, who could be obliged to observe Christian practice.[37] That the Mudejars did not resist in the moment of baptism—consciously choosing this option over death—led the committee to conclude that these sacraments were theologically valid: "In the conversion or baptism there was no necessary or absolute force or violence."[38]

Upon receiving the panel's report in 1525, Charles endorsed its findings, thereby confirming the status of the baptized Muslims as moriscos. By the time the king did so, however, word had begun to filter up that after observing Catholic ritual for a few weeks many moriscos in Gandía and Denia had already returned to their previous religious practices.[39] The panel claimed these "simple people" had been "seduced" by Muslims who fled before the germanías and then returned to restore Islamic practices, as well as by Old Christians who encouraged the newly baptized in their apostasy.[40] The Valencian nobility, fearing that any royal or inquisitorial interference in their lands could jeopardize both their jurisdiction and their economic well-being, organized a delegation of nobles to go to Court to complain that the commissioners' powers violated the laws of Valencia.[41]

These legal challenges and the continued presence of Muslims among the new converts created a volatile situation in Valencia, at a time when Charles V found his realms under attack by Ottoman Turks in the Mediterranean. The forced baptisms emerged from a popular rebellion rather than an unfolding royal policy, but they nonetheless presented the king with an opportunity to pursue two of his existing objectives: stability on the eastern coast and control of the Valencian nobility.[42] In September 1525, driven by all these concerns, Charles V issued a new order requiring the forced baptism of all the Mudejars in Spain.[43]

Realizing that securing the baptism of his subjects would require compromise, Charles struck a deal with a group of twelve Muslim leaders. The king granted their communities all of the franchises, exemptions, and liberties of other Christians in exchange for assurances of help in converting their people and a cash donation of fifty thousand ducats. Under this treaty, ratified in 1526, the Holy Office promised to demonstrate leniency with respect to various minor Islamic practices (such as burial rites) for forty years and to permit the use of Muslim dress and language for ten years.[44] The official execution of the baptisms prompted a failed uprising in Benaguacil, followed by the prosecution of dozens of Muslims for "the most nefarious crime of having conspired against our Royal Majesty." Many who took up arms against the forces of Charles V later claimed that they had not believed that their king ordered the forced baptisms and protested their loyalty to him.[45] Taking this debatable assertion at face value allowed Charles to pardon some while making an example of others, thereby securing the nominal religious uniformity of all his Spanish subjects.

In the years after 1526, however, it became clear that the involved parties came away from the treaty with wildly different expectations. The moriscos and their seigneurs interpreted the payments and assurances of gentle treatment as a renewal of the medieval arrangement, in effect, a license to continue the quiet observance of Islam. Given their Muslim heritage, the relative isolation of their settlements, and the support of their seigneurs, the first Valencian moriscos had good reason to think they would be able to return to their prior situation after the inquisitorial commissioners had come and gone. The Holy Office, by contrast, understood the treaty as a means of eliminating Islamic rituals gradually rather than abruptly and continued to prosecute the new moriscos for Muslim practices. These trials underscored the principal change that the forced baptisms brought to communities of morisco, who now found themselves to be parishioners of the Catholic Church and subjects of the Spanish Inquisition (which held no formal jurisdiction over Muslims and Jews). Rather than resolving the tensions between Christians and Muslims in Valencia, the treaty of 1526 initiated a struggle between the rural nobility and the Crown, one that would take place between rival councilors at Court and between moriscos and in-quisitors in the Valencian countryside.

The different interpretations of the treaty of 1526 arose from diverging understand-ings of the baptisms that led to the agreement. Even within the Catholic world the sacrament was neither universal nor uniform, and many rural families anointed their babies at home, using traditional rituals, before proceeding to the church.[46] In the 1520s Charles's empire stretched from Spain to the Netherlands, from Germany to the Americas, and contact between Catholics and peoples of other faiths caused further anxiety over the efficacy of sacraments such as baptism. At this same historical mo-ment, Martin Luther rejected five of the official sacraments and opened questions as to the nature of the remaining two, baptism and the Eucharist. During the conquest of Mexico, which unfolded at the same time as the germanías (1519–21), Hernán Cortés ordered the immediate baptism of the Aztec leader Ixtlilxochitl over the ob-jection that, for all his seeming willingness, he had not been properly instructed.[47]

In Valencia, similar uncertainties plagued the issue of the forced baptisms. All concerned parties recognized that the sacramental act of baptism had improperly preceded the gradual process of persuasion and conversion. The official panel of the-ologians legitimized the baptisms, and Charles V endorsed this view in his search for both religious unity and political stability. The moriscos and their seigneurs ul-timately agreed to the baptisms but also raised doubts that would reappear during the morisco century. These doubts would underpin their defense of continuing Mus-lim practices and their objections to rigorous efforts to bring the moriscos into the Christian mainstream. The façade of religious unity masked a battle between those who would maintain the status quo of effective toleration and those who contended that all Valencians now formed part of one flock.

TOLERANCE, PERSECUTION, AND NEGLECT: 1528 – 1568

In the forty years following the forced baptisms, the task of ensuring the Chris-tianization of these new converts after the fact fell primarily upon ad hoc commissioners endowed with inquisitorial powers. Even after resident archbishops and local inquisitors began to participate somewhat in the evangelization of the moriscos at midcentury, their efforts did little to close the gap between theology and practice. The forced baptisms raised the stakes of Christian-Muslim relations in Valencia, in the sense that the moriscos' continued practice of Islam now represented an act of heresy in an age of nominal religious unity. The role of the New Christians in Valencian society, furthermore, grew to be ever more narrowly defined, in stricter opposition to the place of the Old Christians. Charles V and his son Philip II's increasingly hostile relationship with the Ottoman Turks held important implications for the moriscos, who fell under suspicion of collaborating with their coreligionists in the Mediterranean. The outbreak of violence between Christians and Muslims in Granada created an atmosphere of unprecedented tension at the moment of Ribera's arrival in Valencia.

In 1528 the inquisitorial commissioners responsible for the baptism of the Valencian Mudejars completed their task and returned to Castile. To follow through on instruction, the Council of Inquisition sent a series of ad hoc commissioners to Valencia to build churches, appoint priests, and organize parochial finances.[48] The three principal commissioners who visited Valencia armed with this apostolic authority, however, failed to achieve lasting results. In 1535 Antonio Ramírez de Haro increased the number of morisco parishes by a third, from 123 to 190, and set aside an annual subsidy of two thousand ducats from the archiepiscopal income for their endowment, but these orders remained a dead letter.[49] Bartolomé de los Angeles, a preacher famous for his knowledge of Arabic, inspired protests by the local nobility and the clergy in the 1540s as a result of his campaign to raise funds to ransom North African Muslims imprisoned in Spain.[50] In 1561, furthermore, the commissioner Gregorio de Miranda failed miserably in his attempt to name certain morisco leaders as familiars of the Inquisition.[51] In each case, lack of cooperation from the nobility prevented the commissioners from implementing their plans. By continuing to collect extraordinary taxes and allow labor on Sundays and Christian holidays, the nobles fostered a climate in which Muslim practices could flourish.

·The morisco leaders similarly turned from their commitment to promote Christian practice and belief within their communities.[52] On the contrary, witnesses in New Christian areas complained that the moriscos defiantly practiced Islam and mocked Christian ritual, in one case throwing the bread of the Eucharist out the church door during a Catholic festival.[53] The local tribunal of the Inquisition in Valencia further complicated matters by prosecuting moriscos for offenses such as fasting during Ramadan, prompting objections from nobles who argued that the treaty of 1526 forbade these incursions.[54] The nobility complained incessantly about the

Inquisition, which derived a significant portion of its revenues from the confiscation of morisco goods.[55] Charles V occasionally ordered cessations of inquisitorial activity to allow for instruction, but the Valencian tribunal did not generally comply with these orders, insisting that they proceeded with all "benignancy and mildness."[56] The essentially persecutory and self-interested nature of the Inquisition, combined with noble resistance, prevented the occasional ad hoc commissioners from breaking down the barriers that divided the Old and New Christians of Valencia.

The appearance of resident archbishops in Valencia did not change this cycle of ignorance and neglect. At the time of the forced baptisms, the current archbishop lived in Flanders; the inquisitor general wrote him a letter describing plans for parish reform in 1528, as if to underscore the prelate's absence.[57] In 1538 Jorge de Austria became Valencia's first resident bishop in more than a century.[58] In collaboration with Ramírez de Haro, Austria wrote the *Instructions e Ordinacions per als Novament Convertits del Regne de Valencia*, the first catechismal work directed expressly at the instruction of the moriscos.[59] This brief work, written in Valencian, ordered priests to reside in their parishes, to fulfill their obligations, and to stop charging the moriscos extraordinary fees for the administration of sacraments "so that the new converts will not think that our Christian religion is based in self-interest."[60] Despite these good intentions, however, the *Instructions* were not published until 1566, and they failed to have much impact.

The Augustinian Tomás de Villanueva (abp. 1545–55), who would be canonized in 1688 for his preaching and charitable work, located the responsibility for the morisco question in the hands of the inquisitorial commissioners. In 1547 he wrote to Prince Philip, asking him to replace the departed Ramírez de Haro: "Since the bishop of Segovia left, these new converts dare to perform their morisco ceremonies more publicly with each passing day; because of the commission the bishop had from the Pope, the inquisitors and I have our hands tied to undertake the correction of the moriscos, and there is no one here to address these issues on behalf of Ramírez de Haro."[61] In 1552, reacting to an alleged sighting of the Turkish armada near Mallorca, Villanueva requested troops from Castile and recommended that "these soldiers could also disarm the moriscos once the Turkish threat is past."[62] Villanueva saw the entire morisco project as fundamentally an inquisitorial responsibility, and where he did get involved he focused on enforcing outward observance of Christian ritual rather than delving into questions of interior conversion.[63]

Martín Pérez de Ayala, a churchman who attended all three sessions of the Council of Trent before his appointment as archbishop of Valencia in 1564, redefined the role of the bishop with regard to Old Christians and moriscos alike. He organized a diocesan synod and a provincial council in which he codified Tridentine standards for clerical education and for orthodoxy in lay devotions. In addition, he published a bilingual Arabic-Spanish catechism, *Doctrina Christiana en Lengua Arábiga y Castellana*, designed to help parish priests to communicate with their morisco parishioners. Pérez de Ayala's morisco program combined rigor with moderation. His provincial council banned Islamic customs and ceremonies and specified fines for the failure to observe Christian practices: all morisco children, for example, were to be baptized in the church, dressed in "the shining white clothing of innocence," under pain of a fine of one ducat.[64] On the other hand, Pérez de Ayala sought to limit the role of the Inquisition with regard to the moriscos: "The Inquisition should have nothing to do with them, except for those who sin shamelessly and publicly."[65] Rather, he centered his program of instruction on the secular clergy, and toward this end he worked to raise parochial salaries.[66] Pérez de Ayala applied Tridentine methods to the morisco question and located responsibility for the reformation of the diocese in the secular clergy. His death after only fifteen months in office, however, prevented him from following through on these designs.

These frustrated efforts at evangelization unfolded amid growing fears, both at Court and in Valencia, of the moriscos as an Ottoman fifth column. Ever since the late fifteenth century, Spain's Mediterranean coast had been subject to periodic attacks by Turkish and Berber raiders. By the 1540s Charles V had abandoned his youthful dreams of conquering Jerusalem, but his efforts to maintain peace with the Ottoman Empire failed as the Turks ramped up their support of increasingly well-organized North African corsairs.[67] The rise of Spanish-Ottoman conflicts in the east led to a widespread suspicion of the moriscos, and of those from abroad in particular. A royal decree of 1541 prescribed death for any Granadan, North African, or Aragonese morisco caught in Valencia and fines and lashes for those who harbored them.[68] This law provided a pretext for Christian officials seeking to distinguish between "their" moriscos, born and raised in Valencia, and potentially dangerous outsiders. A North African morisco arrested in 1545 while conducting business in the main plaza of Orihuela was accused of hoarding supplies to set sail from Spain, despite his protestations of innocence.[69]

Moriscos from Aragon, known as *tagarinos*, fell under suspicion on account of rumors that they moved through Valencia rallying support for an insurrection in alliance with the Turkish corsairs. Pedro Conde, an Aragonese morisco with a criminal record, was arrested in 1555 for robbing another morisco on the royal road near Miles. Conde was paraded through the area in a wagon before being beheaded, drawn, and quartered, and his body parts were then displayed along the road where he committed the robbery.[70] The Valencian nobility generally supported the prosecution of outsiders but resisted laws that affected their own morisco tenants. The

Duke of Segorbe, viceroy in the early 1560s and lord of many morisco areas in his own right, was quick to denounce three moriscos from Benimamet who had murdered a saddler in the Valencian capital.[71] Yet he urged Philip II to proceed with "mildness and love" among local moriscos and warned the king that forcing them to abandon their customs and ceremonies could lead to an uprising.[72] Many of the jurisdictional disputes between the viceroy and the Valencian nobility arose from the repeated royal laws against morisco emigration to the coast. The seigneurs complained that these laws abridged their authority, just as the viceroys of Valencia accused the nobles of impeding their efforts to combat violent crime.[73]

In 1563 Philip II set aside the objections of the nobility and ordered the disarmament of the moriscos, a remarkable move designed to prevent a rebellion.[74] The New Christians had long been prohibited from bearing arms, but in 1563 the systematic search for morisco weapons turned up some twenty-five thousand crossbows, firearms, swords, and knives.[75] In practice, the prohibition provided another excuse for officials to question and search any morisco who seemed suspicious.[76] The moriscos risked prosecution by hiding weapons because they believed that turning them in would leave them even more vulnerable in their violent world. The royal order interrupted an ongoing feud between the moriscos of Oliva and Villalonga, and when the group from Villalonga encountered one of their rivals unarmed in 1563, they took the opportunity to avenge a murder of several years earlier.[77] In Sagra, the morisco Joan Rayolet turned in a full set of weapons in 1563 but kept a crossbow and sword on account of a feud with another morisco family. The official who confiscated these arms ended up before the judge himself, for stealing weapons and jewels from Rayolet and instructing the notary not to list them on the inventory.[78] Thus the royal prohibition placed moriscos at risk whether they complied or not, from existing morisco adversaries and from fraudulent government agents.

The seizure of morisco weapons did not eliminate Christian fears of revolt, which rather skyrocketed in 1568 when news of a morisco uprising in Granada reached Valencia.[79] In the Revolt of the Alpujarras (1568–70), the enforcement of laws prohibiting Muslim dress and customs provoked the moriscos of the Granadan Albaicín to rise in armed rebellion. Even though this insurrection was ultimately defeated, it caused a great deal of anxiety in the Levant. The Valencian authorities expressed concern on two levels: first, that their own moriscos might follow suit and rebel, and second, that refugees among the fifty-five thousand expelled Granadan moriscos could contribute to the already significant population of morisco bandits in Valencia.[80] Responding to reports that the moriscos of Segorbe had taken up arms, Philip II wrote an uncharacteristically alarmist letter to the Valencian viceroy, stating that a strong Turkish armada was headed to Spain to rally the moriscos.[81] The king ordered Valencia to inspect coastal fortifications, mobilize the cavalry, and collect provisions in Old Christian areas. Wary of secret communications and hidden weapons among the moriscos, Philip II also instructed the viceroy to quietly remove "those restless and enterprising moriscos who hold the most authority and esteem, who could be made into ringleaders." His corresponding order that the seigneurs temporarily relocate moriscos living near the coast went unheeded but nonetheless spoke to this period of "collective psychosis" following the Granadan revolt.[82]

Juan de Ribera arrived in Valencia in February 1569, at the height of these tensions. The mutual mistrust exacerbated by the rebellion in Granada exerted a profound effect upon the religious practices of Christians and moriscos in his new diocese. Despite the legal fiction, present from the very beginning, that the New Christians would enjoy all of the rights and privileges of Catholic society, Christian authorities continued to treat moriscos as a second class of parishioners. Effectively barred from the priesthood, the religious orders, and the university, moriscos did not evolve into full-fledged members of the Church. The Catholic world of local shrines, veneration of the saints, and perennial festivals remained foreign to them. Rather, the moriscos developed a clandestine spiritual world of their own, removed from the official Church and loosely tolerated by the noble lords who constituted one of their principal points of contact with Christian society. Their religious practices separated them from their fellow Valencians and reinforced their linguistic and cultural connections to Spain's enemies abroad. In the Mudejar period, economic self-interest and long-standing tradition had proved sufficient to guarantee the continued observance of Islam under Christian rule. The forced baptisms of the 1520s led to pressure from the Inquisition and royal officials, which succeeded mainly in driving Spanish Islam underground. After 1569, the moriscos—like their Old Christian counterparts—would find their spiritual world altered dramatically by a resurgent Church under Ribera.

RELIGIOUS PRACTICES IN VALENCIA:
OLD CHRISTIANS AND NEW

"The order and gravity of proceeding with all harmony, accompanied by the immense display of lights, and a thousand other things of outlandish majesty and devotion, make the city appear on that day a heaven; and the streets where they pass a Milky Way, or the road to Santiago," said Gaspar Escolano of the Valencian Corpus Christi procession.[83] The chronicler's description underscores the public nature of this celebration, a lavish expression of both religious fervor and civic virtue. Unlike rituals of inversion such as the charivari, a popular Renaissance celebration ridiculing elites, the Corpus Christi procession represented fundamentally an affirmation of Valencian society.[84] Town councilors, clergymen, artisans, and laborers shared the vivid colors, jubilant music, and pungent aromas that accompanied the Host on its progress through the city. The carefully scripted "majesty and devotion" of the festivities, however, also illuminated the differences between the local dignitaries who organized the procession and the royal officials who held the highest offices in Valencia. Natives of the city professed their loyalty to the king but often challenged the decisions of his appointees, such as the viceroy and the archbishop. Just as Valencians struggled for control of their political institutions, so they attempted to define their religiosity through parish churches and confraternities rather than the Church Universal. The papal bull of 1264 that established the Corpus Christi feast in the period between Easter and Advent dedicated the festival to reflecting upon the events of the Passion and receiving the Holy Spirit, but these theological subtleties could get lost in the music and dancing.[85] Like the city itself, the Corpus Christi celebration had evolved without leadership from the higher clergy, and, despite his nominal authority as archbishop, Ribera began as an interloper within a well-established hierarchy of competing local interests.

The Corpus Christi procession also demonstrated the rift that separated the moriscos of Valencia from Christians throughout the kingdom. The proceedings did not hold out the same sense of community for the moriscos, and on that same weekend fully one-third of the kingdom carried out Friday worship ceremonies in accordance with the Quran. Testimony given at the trial of Damián Doblet, an alfaqui of Buñol, stated that "on many Friday nights the moriscos and moriscas went to Doblet's house dressed in finery and made up. Suspecting that he was preaching the sect of Muhammad, one night we determined to take them by surprise, and finding the main door locked we entered by a false door. We found Doblet seated in a chair with a lute in his hands and one foot unshod, and a morisco held an open book in front of him from which he read and sang."[86]

The private gathering detailed by Doblet's accusers would have been replicated in various forms by the great majority of New Christians irrespective of the ongoing Corpus Christi celebrations. Excluded legally and symbolically from the offices represented in the procession, the moriscos directed their religious impulses inward, maintaining an alternate vision of themselves and their place in society. Hidden in residences and secret worship centers removed from Catholic influence, the moriscos adhered to a form of Islam tailored to their unique situation. The geography of Christian and Muslim Valencia at the time of the archbishop Ribera's arrival in 1569 can be mapped out by examining the Valencian Corpus Christi procession and the ceremonies led by Doblet. The mystery plays, banners, and rituals of the

Corpus Christi procession constituted a highly developed expression of civic identity—an identity very different from that which Ribera had created in Andalusia and
Castile. A great gulf divided the "nations" of Old Christians and New in Valencia,
but in both cases the people of Valencia had long grown accustomed to shaping their
own identity in the absence of archiepiscopal influence.

LOCAL IDENTITY IN THE VALENCIAN
CORPUS CHRISTI PROCESSION

In June 1569, the young archbishop Ribera stood at the altar of the cathedral,
sanctifying the Host at the end of the Corpus Christi celebration dedicated to its
praise. As he intoned the Latin words signifying "This is my body," his bearded face
with its delicate features remained hidden from the congregation that filled the massive church behind him. The assembled dignitaries and commoners saw only the
miter that covered his shaved pate and the glittering brocade of his pontifical robes
as he lifted the Eucharist over his head.

What might seem like a moment of triumph for the Tridentine Church and its
reassertion of the sacraments, however, was only one example of the events that drew
the attention of the people during the festival. The religious theater of the Mass in-
jected a degree of solemnity and doctrinal authority into the proceedings, yet this
message could be overshadowed by the many available forms of entertainment and
by other means of achieving contact with the divine. The worshippers who entered
the cathedral through its Romanesque entrance passed by the sculptured heads of
seven prominent Valencian citizens and their wives; the interior of the domed structure featured chapels dedicated to local holy figures such as the early martyr St. Vincent. Hours earlier, the congregants had participated in a procession organized by
confraternity and parish, long-standing organizations that commanded more loyalty
than a new archbishop could muster. The Church Universal possessed revenues and
ceremonial privileges, but in 1569 its influence paled by comparison with that of local institutions. The particular form of Catholicism practiced by the Valencian people represented one manifestation of the city's struggle to maintain its regional identity in an age of Habsburg absolutism.

The Corpus Christi festival began and ended in the cathedral, but in the interim
the celebration unfolded outside the church, both literally and figuratively, as it advanced through the winding streets and irregular plazas of the city center.[87] The
dozen horse-drawn carriages that led the procession featured actors in elaborate costumes of cloth and carton enacting the traditional Valencian mystery plays. Large
canvases erected at three places along the route—the plaza of the cathedral, the

street Cavallers, and the marketplace—provided a backdrop for plays with religious themes including the opening of Christ's sepulcher, the temptation of Adam and Eve, and the allegory of St. Christopher. The mystery play commemorating the flight from Egypt concluded with a popular scene in which the minions of Herod swept down into the crowd to attack the female spectators with rolled-up pieces of paper. Evolved from the earliest form of theater known to the region, these Biblical dramas continued to be performed in the Valencian dialect decades after the arrival of Castilian political appointees under Charles V.[88]

This fact would not have been lost on Juan de Herrera y Pimentel, the Count of Benavente, who had entered Valencia as viceroy two years earlier. Like the royal judges who shared his balcony high above the procession, Benavente did not hail from the kingdom where he now enjoyed broad political and military powers as the representative of the king.[89] The title of viceroy dated only as far back as Ferdinand the Catholic, and the history of relations between the viceroys and the city was not an especially harmonious one. The reorganization of the Valencian court along humanist lines to modernize the "provincial" Valencian aristocracy augured the imminent decline of the Valencian language in high culture and politics.[90] The actors punctuated their defiant use of the local dialect by enacting the plays in the shadow of the gallows, the symbol of royal justice, thereby reiterating the never-ending negotiation between royal prerogatives and local resistance.[91]

Royal appointees enjoyed a prestigious vantage point, but the events of Corpus Christi remained an expression of Valencia's more permanent residents. The people living along the procession route constructed altars in front of their homes and decorated their windows with torches, religious icons, and artistic inventions in hopes of winning one of the prizes offered by the city council for such adornments.[92] On the appropriately named street Cavallers, home to the local nobility, the organizers constructed a canopy overhead, to provide shade, and "platforms so that the town councilors and other municipal magistrates could attend comfortably the representations of the mysteries."[93] The six town councilors were charged with the governance of the city, including food supply, water management, relief in times of plague, overseeing the guilds, and appointing justices.[94] Over time, the king had gained effective control of most municipal posts in the city, and he awarded them to a relatively small number of influential families in exchange for their loyalty to him.[95] Escolano compared Valencia to a pomegranate, small in size but rich in nobility: "All that is contained in that compact, round globe is seeds, and seeds in quantity: and as such Nature has crowned it Queen of the fruits."[96] In an age of economic stagnation, when Valencian nobles and merchants turned from industry and commerce to safer but less profitable investments in the countryside, the oligarchy turned to the king for support but simultaneously asserted their regional identity through their patronage of the Corpus Christi and other celebrations.[97] By budgeting a significant portion of their annual revenues to acts of local piety, the town council asserted in ceremonial terms an independent streak that did not carry over into acts of rebellion against the monarchy.

In political terms, Valencia may well have deserved its reputation as the obedient younger sibling to the more unruly Catalonia, but the Corpus Christi festival afforded its people the opportunity to establish that they crafted their religious identity with little reference to the center. The procession began with the urban guilds, each accompanied by its standard and a group of musicians, each playing a different melody. The river of gun powderers, basket weavers, porters, glove makers, silk dyers, butchers, fishmongers, locksmiths, cloth shearers, and others, all with lighted candles in their hands, continued for more than two hours.[98] Although the artisans participated in major festivals such as the Corpus Christi, in a given year they directed most of their religious impulses to smaller organizations such as confraternities.[99] These lay organizations, which typically drew their membership from a given trade or parish, functioned as both mutual aid societies and religious groups. The young Valencian nobleman Bernardo Catalá de Valeriola held office in a number of confraternities during his lifetime and once helped the confraternity of Nostra Señora de la Seu organize a relief effort in response to a famine.[100]

Across Spain and Catholic Europe, the mid-sixteenth century marked a tipping point for confraternities, as Tridentine bishops used their powers of visitation to wrest control from town councils. In seventeenth-century Ourense, for example, these conflicts brought changes to civic feasts, supplanting "the purely recreational aspects of communal religion with a more restrained, overtly religious program."[101] In 1569, however, the Valencian town council still oversaw the confraternities through which many among the laity chose their patron saints, marked the passages of life, and participated in large-scale events such as processions and *autos de fe*—public displays of penance designed to dissuade the faithful from sinful behavior. In theory, the Catholic Church held the keys to salvation, and most Valencians did receive baptism and last rites that framed a lifetime of annual confession and participation in the Mass. The priests who administered these sacraments, however, found themselves forced to compete with lay organizations such as confraternities, which offered alternate forms of religious expression. Catalá de Valeriola chose his patron saints, celebrated key moments in his family life, and pursued his civic and charitable duties without relying on the institutional Church.

After the artisans, the next Corpus Christi participants to issue forth from the plaza of the Virgin were the clergy who vied for their attention. Monastic houses and parishes functioned as both religious organizations and urban units, and like the confraternities they had grown accustomed to running their own affairs. Religious orders such as the Franciscans and the Dominicans, both of which appeared in Valencia immediately after the Reconquest of 1238, competed for pride of place within processions as another means of contesting ongoing disputes over the proper form of interior prayer and economic matters.[102] The friars were followed by the secular clergy from the city's fourteen urban parishes. The six oldest parish churches dated to the Reconquest, and several of these were located in converted mosques.[103] Founded in the ongoing effort to reclaim the city from its Islamic usurpers, the parishes grew in wealth and prestige over the centuries. By 1569 some churches, such as San Martín, had received so many bequests and gifts that they were able to support sixty priests, deacons, and curates.[104]

As members of the oldest religious foundation in Valencia, the canons, choristers, archivists, and other clerics of the metropolitan cathedral enjoyed the privilege of proceeding behind the parishes, illustrating the competition that existed among them. According to the historian Escolano, "The innumerable clergy and religious excel, with discoveries of costly and rare crosses, reliquaries, tabernacles, and monstrances [receptacles containing the Host]; and almost all the clerics, who come to more than four hundred, dressed in precious capes of gold and silk."[105] The clergy bore these sacred objects to celebrate the history and character of their individual parishes. In his autobiography, Juan Martín Cordero (d. ca. 1588), a humanist and editor of classical texts who held a benefice in the parish of Santa Catalina, recounted a horrific church fire.[106] Having suffered burns on his head and his hands rescuing the portable monstrance with the Host, Cordero displayed his scars to the people with pride, as a dramatic symbol of his devotion to the parish.[107] The parishes of Valencia formed the lowest rung on the ladder of the Church hierarchy, but in practice their efforts to meet the needs and desires of their urban communities owed little to the dictates of the higher clergy.

Dressed in distinctive costumes, the group following the secular clergy, twenty-four kings, an eagle, and an angel, would have signaled to the Valencian people the impending climax of the procession. Each of these figures represented an entirely orthodox scriptural reference: the twenty-four elders symbolized the twelve patriarchs of the Old Testament and the twelve apostles of the New Testament, and the cardboard eagle, large enough to hide a man inside, stood for the evangelist John.[108] But the onlookers did not need to understand theology to make a request of the tutelary angel of the realm, object of much devotion as an intercessor for the spiritual and material welfare of Valencia.[109] The custodia, or monstrance, protected by a canopy of brocade, required twelve chaplains to bear its weight, and twelve more walked at their side to relieve them. The people standing in the balconies above honored the arrival of the Host with a cascade of flower petals, and those along the procession route—from commoners to the viceroy—showed their devotion by removing their hats and kneeling down before the mystery of the Sacrament. At every point throughout the city, carillons of church and monastery bells greeted the centerpiece of the Corpus Christi, culminating in the thunderous peals of the bell tower as the monstrance returned to the cathedral, now filled to capacity in anticipation of the celebratory Mass.

The archbishop walked directly behind the monstrance, surrounded by the falling petals and the ringing of bells, accompanied by only the four senior canons and a few pages to carry his crosier.[110] As Ribera entered the cathedral, what should have been a moment of triumph and the culmination of Corpus Christi must have seemed an anticlimax. Grand pageantry aside, the higher clergy exerted a limited influence over the laity of Valencia. More so than the visually arresting drama of the Mass, the reassuring presence of neighbors and relatives among the colorful procession lent meaning and continuity to the lives of the people. Archbishops represented a more ephemeral presence in the city, and Ribera played a minor role in a festival organized by the town council to feature confraternities and parishes. Removed from the dimly understood language of the Corpus Christi dramas and the obscure references to local history and geography, Ribera looked at the accreted customs around him and saw the challenge he would face as a reforming bishop. Before implementing any of his ideas concerning clerical exemplarity and proper lay devotion he would need to establish his authority as archbishop among a people with existing means of fulfilling their spiritual needs.

Even if Ribera managed to reassert the Church Universal in the city, the fact remained that his archdiocese extended far beyond the capital where his official seat was located. On an occasion such as Corpus Christi, this city of fifty thousand would have been further swelled by farmers from the outlying areas. Old Christian farmers worked the famous orchard of Valencia, the lush, abundant gardens outside the capital city that inspired the image of Valencia the Beautiful in geographical works such as Pedro de Medina's *Libro de Grandezas*.[111] In 1494 a German visitor marveled at this bounty: "They took us to the garden of the city, which is splendidly planted with lemon trees, orange trees, citron trees, and palm trees. . . . It has very fragrant white flowers, like lily of the valley. It is always green, like the box tree. Easily one is persuaded, one is drawn in, one changes direction and doubles back everywhere."[112] Many agricultural laborers lived farther from the capital, ranging from the Old Christians who dominated the Maestrazgo in the north, so called because much of this land pertained to the royally owned military order of Montesa, to the Spaniards living in coastal and southern towns, most of which were under the jurisdiction of the king or the Church. The Corpus Christi celebration—like Holy Week in the spring—constituted a major festival encompassing Christians from all over Valencia, and rural workers congregated in nearby towns for processions on a much smaller scale. As in the capital, agricultural towns organized their year around local pilgrimages and devotions reflecting the unique needs and histories of their communities.

The rural laborers present at these Corpus Christi processions included only a few representatives of the kingdom's morisco population, and those who came to the capital created a source of concern for the authorities. At the time of Ribera's arrival in 1569, moriscos living in the kingdom of Valencia numbered about eighty-five thousand, most of them small proprietors in dry-farming lands controlled by the nobility.[113] They were scattered about in some four hundred settlements, located primarily in the sierras north and south of the river valleys formed by the Turia and the Júcar.[114] There, subsistence farmers grew vineyards, olive trees, and carob trees, crops well suited to the arid climate. A few sizable concentrations of moriscos, in addition, grew cereals, rice, and sugar in the irrigated coastal lowlands of Denia and Gandía. Back in the fifteenth century, Mudejars flocked to the capital city for the Corpus Christi procession, not to worship but simply to witness the spectacle; no one expected these Muslim observers to kneel before the Host.[115]

This situation had changed by the 1560s in more senses than one. On the one hand, by this time the crowd included a small minority of converts who had chosen acculturation over continued resistance to Christian society. The Valencian cloth worker Ferrando de Gali, accused of bearing illegal arms in 1563, defended his status as a Christian by pointing out that he was married to an Old Christian and "lived as an Old Christian at all times, hearing Mass, confessing, and taking communion at the times instituted by the holy mother Church." An Old Christian neighbor and co-worker vouched for Gali, claiming that the two often went to festivals together and "attended Mass in the churches where they know there are good preachers," establishing themselves as connoisseurs of sacred oratory.[116] Most of the moriscos who attended Corpus Christi festivities, however, evidently did not share Gali's appreciation for its religious content. In the sixteenth century the city employed officials to patrol the procession and enforce the appropriate respect for the Sacrament. Many of the moriscos "did not respect the sanctity of the passage of the procession, stopping to watch it with their caps on their heads, and for this irreverence, when the officials passed by, they reached out with their staves to knock the hats off the moriscos' heads."[117]

THE MORISCO COMMUNITIES: RESISTANCE AND SURVIVAL

These conflicts at the Corpus Christi procession underscored the dichotomy between Old Christian and morisco religious practices in Valencia. No longer welcome as observers at the grand expressions of Christian worship and resentful of their forced participation in local celebrations of the Mass, most moriscos turned toward their own people for spiritual fulfillment. Deprived of their public mosques and *madrasas* (religious schools), the moriscos created a clandestine form of Islam suited to survival in an inquisitorial age. The devotions of the moriscos included many elements common to worshippers throughout the Islamic world, such as the daily cycle of prayer and the fast of Ramadan: that individual Muslims could bear witness to Allah in the absence of an established authority figure facilitated the exercise of these rituals in a Catholic kingdom. Knowledge of Arabic remained strong in Valencia by comparison with other moriscos in Spain, and the written word formed an important element in the perpetuation of traditions and beliefs. The demands of the Inquisition, however, also affected the moriscos in subtle ways. The need for secrecy led them to develop forms of ritual that differed from the practices of their coreligionists abroad, many of whom continued to question whether the moriscos were truly Muslim at all. Paradoxically, the records of the Inquisition provide the best means of reconstructing the religious life of the moriscos on the eve of Ribera's arrival.

On a typical Friday night in Buñol, a dry-farming town twenty-five miles west of the capital city, the moriscos converged on the home of their Islamic teacher and worship leader (*alfaqui*). Like New Christians across Valencia, the moriscos of Buñol worshipped in private space, although in their case the isolation of their community allowed them a wider range of possibilities. The powerful Mercader family, lords of Buñol from the fifteenth to the nineteenth centuries, did not actively prohibit Islamic practices among their vassals. Virtually all of the residents of this area were moriscos, a fact borne out by the near-total depopulation of Buñol after the expulsion of 1609. A morisco arriving at the worship center on Friday, therefore, encountered a relatively bold statement of religious identity. A crowd of fifty or a hundred people, fully half of the town, sat "in an uncovered patio with four pillars, and on two sides there were stone benches arranged as altars." This patio "was built in the manner of the mosques they had seen in the kingdom of Granada," the last bastion of Islamic rule in Spain. In morisco Valencia, the alfaqui sensed that he had enough latitude to reconstruct the architecture and spatial arrangement of a public mosque in the relative seclusion of his home, although he made the concession of calling the people to prayer at night rather than at midday.[118]

Each of the two stone altars "had a conch shell with water and a blue cloth." The shells symbolized the *guadoc*, a ritual ablution performed upon awakening in the morning, before prayer, and on Fridays and holy days. This widespread practice consisted of washing the body parts in a specific order, accompanied by prayers of purification and supplication. The moriscos of Valencia described washing the hands, face, mouth, "shameful parts," feet, arms, and head, praying while cleaning the nose, for example, that they would smell the scents of paradise rather than the acrid odors of the fire.[119] Moriscos in less amenable circumstances carried out this ritual *en seco*, or without water, "scrubbing the palms of the hands with a stone and then washing the face with their hands."[120]

On Friday the New Christians properly followed up this ritual by donning a clean shirt, although the residents of Buñol went a step further, arriving at the alfaqui's house "dressed in finery and made up." Once inside the house, the women sat on cloths and pillows while the men occupied stone benches placed around the patio. They arranged themselves in rows with no gaps, collectively recreating the positioning they assumed each day in their homes for the *zalá*, the traditional cycle of prayer. In observation of the second pillar of Islam, the moriscos knelt on a mat or cloth at dawn ("when the last star fades from the sky"), midday, afternoon, sunset, and at night, to perform an obligatory series of bows toward the East synchronized with prayers derived from the Quran. Circumstances such as work or contact with Old Christians frequently compelled them to modify this schedule, but even these concessions had an Islamic precedent in the interpretive science of *fiqh*, the application of Islamic law to specific cases.[121]

On Fridays, the moriscos of Buñol gathered for a service led by Hali Muceyem Barbero, their alfaqui, also known by his Christian name, Damián Doblet. This day of the week was consecrated for prayer, good works, fasting, alms, and reading the Quran, and by coming to the alfaqui's house the moriscos observed the Islamic obligation to attend the mosque and hear the sermon.[122] Doblet issued first the call to prayer, pronounced in public plazas by muezzins elsewhere in the Muslim world, followed by the Surat al Fatihah, the opening discourse of the Quran: "Praise be to Allah, Lord of the Worlds; the Beneficent, the Merciful; Master of the Day of Judgment. You alone do we worship and from You alone do we seek aid. Show us the Straight Way, the way of those upon whom You have bestowed Your grace, not of those who have earned Your wrath or who go astray" (Quran 1:1–7).[123] After this affirmation of their faith, and of their desire not to join those who have fallen off the path, the alfaqui proceeded to recite a series of suras (chapters from the Quran), followed by a sermon, accompanying himself on a lute. The introduction of musical complement underscored the sacred nature of the Arabic language and the Muslim obligation to commit passages of the Quran to memory.

The moriscos who participated in the Friday rituals had learned these orations from Doblet himself, as the alfaqui ran a school to teach children Arabic and Islamic prayers. Broadly speaking, the scholars (*ulama*) who passed on their knowledge of the Quran and the teachings of Muhammad in the premodern era did so informally in houses, mosques, or madrasas, with no exams or degrees.[124] Thus the destruction of the Valencian mosques that occurred during the sixteenth century did not eliminate the system of religious education but rather shifted it exclusively to private space. In his role as instructor, for which he received "gifts and shoes," Doblet also copied out and sold prayer books. The son of an alfaqui himself, Doblet brought continuity and consistency to the people of Buñol, both as an educator and as a celebrant in worship.

The alfaqui's responsibilities to his community went beyond the Friday ceremonies to include a number of religious observances marking the stages of life. Parents of a newborn brought the child to the mosque (or its equivalent) for a ritual ablution known as *fadas*, which culminated in the naming of the baby and his or her public initiation into the Muslim community. As the doctor to the people of Buñol, Doblet also carried out procedures including circumcision, performed in the waning of the moon while invoking the name of Muhammad. Virtually all morisco boys born in Valencia were circumcised, in contrast to the practice among the relatively more assimilated moriscos of Castile.[125] The alfaqui did not preside at morisco weddings, which were civil acts rather than religious ceremonies, but the couple did perform the guadoc before nuptial festivities, which included candles, musicians, and dancers. Doblet also instructed the moriscos on the proper observance of Ramadan, the Quranic obligation to fast between dawn and nightfall during this month of the Islamic year. Alfaquis determined when the moon of Ramadan had arrived and adjudicated possible exemptions from fasting, such as pregnancy, advanced age, or compulsory attendance at a meal with Christians. Designated moriscos went through the town before dawn, waking up the residents for the *zahor*, or predawn meal, followed by prayers they had learned from the alfaqui. Moriscos marked the end of Ramadan with festivities and the slaughter of animals in the Islamic manner.[126]

Finally, Doblet oversaw the proper rites at the end of life. The dying were encouraged, whenever possible, to utter "There is no God but Allah, and Muhammad is his prophet" as their final words. After death, the body was washed according to the same ritual followed at birth, dressed in a clean shirt, and wrapped in a clean linen sheet. The mourners then buried the body deep in virgin soil, on its side with the face oriented toward the East.[127] In teaching and leading the cycle of prayers for the deceased, the alfaqui maintained the Islamic traditions of the moriscos of Buñol among the survivors.

The written word played a significant role in the retention and dissemination of morisco rituals. Doblet possessed two baskets of esparto grass in which he concealed numerous books, including passages from the Quran, prayer books, and handwritten journals recording the meetings of the morisco leaders.[128] Royal officials arrested Miquel Ciurana of Polop as an alfaqui in 1564, in part because of the suspicious documents in his possession. Ciurana's books and letters included both Arabic works, such as prayers from the Quran, and Spanish writings rendered in Arabic characters, such as an explanation of how to perform the zalá and a collection of Arabic histories and tales.[129] These latter documents formed part of the *aljamiado* literature, which derived its name from the Arabic word for foreign. Orthodox Muslim scholars typically discouraged the translation of sacred texts, but owing to the practical needs of the expanding Islamic world the use of Arabic script in writing the local vernacular became a standard practice.[130] This aljamiado literature testified to both the preservation of Islamic culture and the decline in knowledge of classical Arabic among the moriscos. The alfaqui Ciurana, "a man of great wisdom and letters," was evidently literate in Arabic, but other religious leaders in the morisco era relied upon the aljamiado literature to minister to their communities. This literature included interlineal translations of the Quran, forbidden in orthodox Islam, and in later manuscripts the copyists omitted the original Arabic altogether.[131]

Damián Doblet transmitted morisco culture in the town of Buñol, but in many morisco areas these practices persisted by being passed across the generations through the family or through the activities of traveling alfaquis, who moved from village to village offering instruction in exchange for financial support. Miquel Ciurana confessed to having recently visited numerous morisco communities from Játiva to Segorbe, although he said that his only business was to transport coal. (Had this been the case, it seems unlikely that two different morisco towns would have stepped forward to offer considerable sums of money for his release.) An inquisitorial trial in 1567 brought to light the Barber of Elda, a resident of Cocentaina, who traveled through the kingdom performing circumcisions in exchange for one real.[132]

Alfaquis could also assume some of the judicial functions previously exercised by the Islamic judge (*qadi*) in the Mudejar period, such as settling internal disagreements over land and goods. Testifying before the Inquisition in 1565, a Christian merchant listed numerous alfaquis and noted that the morisco communities held these men in great esteem. The alfaqui Eça of Fansara, for example, "is considered very wise in his law, both in Fansara and in the rest of the kingdom of Valencia, and for this reason many moriscos come to solicit his advice, and he resolves their doubts and disputes. He also knows how to read and write our Castilian language, living in all ways like a true moro."[133] Many morisco men spoke the Valencian language in addition to their native *algarabía* (colloquial Arabic), but Eça's proficiency in written Castilian facilitated his activity as a mediator between the Christian authorities and the Valencian moriscos.[134] Wealthier morisco families also called upon alfaquis to offer legal advice and medical help.[135] By these means, alfaquis throughout the kingdom attempted to re-create the legal and religious autonomy of the fifteenth century to the greatest extent possible.

The beliefs and practices promoted by these leaders also encompassed non-canonical popular devotions that might be compared to the divinations commonly found among Christians in the premodern era. Miquel Ciurana carried a rod and a little book with letters in black and red ink, "a book of fate that the moros have in their law. When they want to go on a trip or something they use this rod," casting it on a piece of paper divided into quadrants with a letter in each one, to foretell the outcome.[136] In 1573 the Inquisition accused Gaspar Faena, a tailor from Turis, of writing and selling "letters with colored Arabic script, which the moriscos placed on their chest when they were about to die, so that they would be cleansed of their sins. . . . In spite of his office as a tailor, he has much of the alfaqui in him."[137] The Inquisition regularly confiscated talismans from putative alfaquis and even illiterate moriscos, such as silver coins inscribed with Arabic letters and *nóminas*, writings used to bring about results, including cures.[138] Just as Old Christians integrated harvest festivals into the liturgical year and recast white magic as the veneration of the saints, so moriscos incorporated fortune-telling and healing rituals into an Islamic framework.

Faena's case and others like it demonstrate that morisco communities found ways to perpetuate their faith in the absence of the formal institutional structures characteristic of Islamic communities located within Muslim polities. Decades after their forced baptisms, the moriscos had not converted to Christianity in the fullest sense of the term. Rather, they had constructed a form of Islam that—even if it did not conform in all ways to orthodox practices in Muslim lands—continued to be defined in opposition to Christianity. When Ribera first visited his morisco parishes, he did not encounter a people on the path to assimilation; rather, the moriscos comprised a nation apart, clinging to the beliefs and practices of their ancestors. But the New Christians also shared certain points in common with the Old Christians: both communities had developed long-standing religious practices independent of any church hierarchy, Catholic or Muslim. The regular clergy, cathedral canons, and laity of Valencia pursued their spirituality with little interference from the higher clergy, crafting their religious identity without reference to the emerging Tridentine Church. The moriscos responded to outside influences, from both Spanish Catholics and North African Muslims, but on the whole they also shaped their spiritual world on their own terms.

In the 1560s, two external sources of pressure—both of which had been mounting for years—came to bear on Valencia, with profound consequences for its dual religious communities. In this decade, Philip II and his officials responded to the perceived obduracy of the New Christians with alarm, adopting stricter royal controls on the moriscos while simultaneously entrusting their instruction to the bishops.[139] Their fears of a Muslim conspiracy to assault Catholic Spain peaked in the Granadan rebellion, when Philip II took the prospect of an Ottoman invasion very seriously.[140] Royal efforts to police the moriscos, including the disarmament of 1563 and the heightened alert of 1568, coincided closely with a separate series of events that would also bring great changes to Valencia: the conclusion of the Council of Trent (1563) and the appointment of Juan de Ribera as archbishop of Valencia (1568). These factors converged to place a great deal of responsibility in the hands of the young prelate, now charged with the spiritual care of an independent-minded Old Christian congregation and a morisco population that embodied a host of potentially dangerous contradictions.

CHAPTER TWO

The Limits of Episcopal Authority

The Pasquinades of 1570–1571

In the early morning hours of 10 August 1570, a thirty-four-year-old priest named Antonio Pineda posted handwritten copies of a broadsheet on the doors of the archiepiscopal palace, the school for morisco children, and the University of Valencia:

> We the students of the famous, celebrated, and illustrious University of Valencia, to you, Mr. Juan Ribera, bastard son of the filthiest, most vile whore and the mangiest, poorest student of Salamanca, though falsely believed to be the son of the most excellent Duke of Alcalá. It has come to our attention that in order to appease the Jesuits, false, disruptive sowers of discord among the people, you have without cause nor reason imprisoned the most reverend rector of our university. With this broadsheet we order that today, Friday, it be made known to the people who you are with bulletins placed around the city, because we know you better than you think.[1]

With these words Pineda and a group of students protested the recent arrest of the rector Pedro Monzón by the newly arrived archbishop Juan de Ribera, suggesting that Ribera had given this order to curry favor with the Jesuit College of San Pablo. A few months earlier, in one of his first initiatives as archbishop, Ribera had carried out a royally ordered visit to the university. Even before he published or attempted to enforce his proposed reforms, which included a provision allowing university students to take courses in theology at the Jesuit college, several members of the university community began to complain that the archbishop had overstepped his bounds. Chagrined by these protests, Ribera imprisoned the rector Monzón together with three of the most outspoken professors on the faculty of theology. In the flurry of broadsheets that followed, Ribera quickly found himself hanging by a thread, wielding his episcopal authority against a tightly knit group of local professors and students with close ties to the native Valencian oligarchy. By exercising his influence with the inquisitor general Diego de Espinosa, Ribera managed to salvage his reputation to a degree, but in the process his reforms of the university fell by the wayside.

The *pasquinades* of 1570–71 illustrate both Ribera's initial position with regard to the Valencian people and the causes behind the rapid and committed opposition to the archbishop's first attempts at reform.[2] Ribera initially hoped to employ the powers and privileges of his office to pursue reforms modeled on the Council of Trent. Ribera's proposed changes to the faculty of theology formed part of his broader effort to improve the level of clerical education in Valencia and curb ecclesiastical abuses. The university community and their supporters, however, regarded Ribera as a foreigner and a meddler, and his actions sparked an immediate and concerted protest that recalled other conflicts between center and periphery in Habsburg Spain. Royal efforts to raise revenues, levy troops, and curtail the autonomy of local institutions met with resistance in Catalonia and even in Castile, the heartland of the monarchy.[3] The endogamous community of prominent Valencian families that dominated the municipal council and the university defended their loyalty to Philip, but only in his capacity as king of Valencia; their objections to Ribera's reforms underscored that this sense of *patria*, or homeland, did not encompass their new prelate, who hailed from elsewhere in the Spanish monarchy. The inquisitorial trials that resulted from this dispute demonstrate that many of the local elite's objections related to the archbishop's wider program of reform as well. The drawn-out controversy over Ribera's visit to the university in 1570 revealed the fault lines of power in the city of Valencia as he encountered it, as well as the tenuous nature of the archbishop's initial position within this network of competing interests.

EPISCOPAL POWERS AND PRIVILEGES

Juan de Ribera took possession of the Valencian see during a contested period in the evolving history of the office of the bishop, during which the papacy and the Council of Trent attempted to define the extent of episcopal authority.[4] On the one hand, the Spanish contingent at Trent had sought to steer the discussion toward reform on the local level and away from the theological disputes separating the Catholic Church from the Protestants of central Europe. In 1563 the reform party succeeded in passing a number of decrees empowering bishops to run the affairs of their dioceses. On the other hand, however, the higher clergy of Spain relied upon the papacy as a spiritual touchstone, an affirmation of their orthodoxy and adherence to Catholic tradition. Like many Spanish bishops, Ribera upheld the theoretical authority of the papacy even as he strove to implement reforms in an atmosphere free of papal interference. Although he occasionally sought papal support to legitimize his efforts, the success or failure of the archbishop's reforms depended much more upon the acceptance or resistance of the Valencian people. The limitations on his powers came principally from below, not from above.

When Ribera traveled to Valencia in February 1569, many of the city's leading figures came out to pay him their compliments, and the town council "announced a procession for the entrance of the most illustrious and reverend Señor Archbishop."[5] Following this entrance, Ribera entered the metropolitan church and assumed the archiepiscopal chair that he would occupy for the next forty-two years. Despite his status as an outsider in Valencia, Ribera wielded a wide variety of powers by virtue of his office. Like all Catholic bishops, Ribera derived his authority ultimately from God, as manifested in his consecration, the laying on of hands that could be traced in direct succession to Christ and the apostles. In terms of his spiritual authority, Ribera had the power to ordain priests, appoint auxiliary bishops, and reform abuses among the lower clergy through visitation and the ecclesiastical court. The archbishop also held the right to approve (or revoke) licenses to administer confession and to preach in the diocese.[6] The Inquisition referred books on religious topics to Ribera for review before publication. The archbishop enjoyed pride of place in processions such as Corpus Christi and the commemoration of the Reconquest of Valencia. At meetings of the Valencian Cortes, Ribera led the ecclesiastical estate, as depicted in a near-life-size portrait of the clerical representatives that still occupies one wall of the historic meeting hall.

As the highest-ranking clerical official in the city, Ribera could also sit under the canopy at inquisitorial autos de fe, hearing the crimes of the penitents read aloud and watching the administration of their punishments. At these public events, so crucial to the regulation of civic life in early modern Valencia, the assembled onlookers would have recognized Ribera immediately by his ornate brocade chasuble, miter, and crosier. Furthermore, wherever he traveled through his diocese, Ribera carried before him a cross with two unequal lines, a shorter one above and a longer one below, "as the Sacred Canons concede to the patriarchs."[7] Well aware of the importance of semantics in his quest for reform, Ribera used these symbols to bolster his authority among the people of Valencia.

Ribera oversaw the disbursement of the enormous revenues that pertained to the diocese of Valencia, which ranked among the three or four wealthiest of the fifty bishoprics in Spain.[8] The diocese collected annual rents from many agricultural settlements, including both morisco towns and Old Christian areas, and the dozens of court cases housed in the Colegio de Corpus Christi demonstrate that Ribera sought to increase these holdings by pursuing through legal means any funds that he believed pertained to him.[9] In addition, Ribera brought with him a considerable private fortune, one that grew even larger upon the death of his father in 1571.[10] Thus the archbishop had reserves even beyond his total annual episcopal income of eighty thousand libras, more than five times the endowments of Spain's poorer dioceses.[11] Ribera's suffragan bishoprics of Orihuela in the south and Segorbe in the north, for example, complained constantly of their poverty, although in practice Ribera exercised little control over the day-to-day finances and operations of these dioceses.[12]

In his own diocese of Valencia, Ribera encountered a divided congregation in which both Christians and moriscos looked to the archbishop for benign neglect rather than leadership. On 1 June 1569, shortly after his arrival, Ribera published a wide-ranging set of norms establishing that his ambitions went far beyond anything the people of Valencia had ever seen. The archbishop ordered his priests to read these directives (which run to fifteen pages in a modern edition) during Mass and to post them in all the churches of the diocese. Among the laity, these norms set penalties for conducting business during religious festivals, disrespecting the name of Christ in church, and dissolving a marriage without the Church's permission. The punishments for repeated instances of blasphemy escalated from a fine of twenty-five ducados, spending an entire day in the door of the church with hands bound, and public whipping to having one's tongue pierced and being banished to the galleys.[13]

Through education, encouragement, and chastisement, Ribera sought to enforce these decrees in Valencia. In his archiepiscopal palace, for example, he organized a school for young members of the local gentry, in an effort to enhance their religiosity and discourage the immoral or violent practices often associated with younger nobles. Within five years of Ribera's arrival, these students numbered more than twenty, and the archbishop attempted to supplement their spiritual education with classical works such as the orations of Cicero and the commentaries of Caesar.[14] He also donated a considerable portion of his income each year to charitable endeavors, including a program under which he provided needy young women with dowries to entice them to marry within the Church.[15] In addition to these efforts, Ribera attempted to reform public morals from the pulpit; in 1570 alone he delivered at least fifteen public sermons in the city of Valencia, in which he placed particular emphasis upon the sacrament of the Eucharist.[16] Through these initiatives and others, in keeping with his Tridentine orientation, the archbishop exhorted the people of

Valencia to conduct their lives according to the sacramental rhythms of Catholicism. His programs formed part of the larger Catholic Reformation initiative to define lay morality and establish the authority of the Church over rites such as marriage.[17]

As his edict of June 1569 makes clear, Ribera dedicated his most aggressive reforms to elevating the piety of the fifteen hundred clergymen of Valencia. The Council of Trent assigned the leadership role to bishops in reform but noted that they could bring lasting change only through the activity of a devout and motivated parish clergy. Sensing the need to begin with the head before proceeding systematically to the members, Ribera attempted a radical reorientation of a local priesthood accustomed to local patronage and a degree of spiritual self-sufficiency. The norms of 1569 consistently held the clergy to a higher standard of behavior than their parishioners, asserting that reform must begin with the institutional Church. Ribera ordered priests to sing Mass and take communion regularly, but his prescriptions went far beyond the Tridentine minimum. Just as the laity must kneel and bow their heads in church, so the priest should avoid the sin of pride by refraining from walking through the congregation, offering his stole for the people to kiss. Priests should not keep dogs or hunting animals or legitimize gambling sessions and drinking parties with their attendance.

Demonstrating a keen sense of early modern priorities, Ribera ordered that blasphemous priests would face the loss of their rents for a year for a first offense, for life for a second, and for further offenses the loss of their office. Finally, in response to common practice, the archbishop forbade priests to hold secular offices, including in this category not only lawyer and merchant but also tutor and healer. Ribera followed up on this edict through his ecclesiastical court, in which he tried and punished priests accused of crimes, and his diocesan synods, which reiterated standards of clerical exemplarity.[18] By these means Ribera strove to elevate the local clergy and distinguish them more sharply from their ambient society.

Prelates across Spain struggled to improve the educational level of the clergy during the Catholic Reformation, through formal and informal instruction. The bishop of Cartagena complained that "when I arrived in my diocese I found the clergy to be both numerous and idiots," reflecting a common misgiving among the higher clergy. In neighboring Cuenca the early modern Church brought about a significant improvement in the knowledge of Latin and liturgy among the clergy, whereas in the Galician diocese of Ourense a century of clerical reform yielded few results.[19] Valencia boasted no diocesan seminary, but the University of Valencia presented a logical choice for an aspiring priest, as one of only seventeen colleges in Spain with a curriculum dedicated to clerical training. In an effort to improve the educational level of the Valencian clergy, the archbishop launched an attempt to modernize and diversify the faculty of theology at the University, which he viewed as both academically deficient and internally corrupt. This initiative, however, brought him into conflict with the students, the professoriate, and the powerful local oligarchy controlling the university from behind the scenes, setting off a crisis that pitted Ribera against both royal officials and his new congregation.

THE UNIVERSITY OF VALENCIA AND THE JESUIT COLLEGE

In the early modern period, the people of Valencia took great pride in the fact that James I had established their kingdom in 1238 as a political entity separate from Aragon or Catalonia. Like other subjects of the Habsburg kings, Valencians tended to identify first and foremost with their region rather than with Spain as a whole.[20] The *fueros* (law code) of Valencia represented the greatest manifestation of this regional sentiment, in both affective and practical terms. These laws not only regulated the internal affairs of the town council and various other municipal organizations but also placed limits upon the authority of royal appointees such as viceroys and archbishops and even upon that of the king himself. Because the king had granted Valencia its legal code, any order that contravened these statutes could be contested as *contrafuero* against the laws of the realm. Thus, for example, in 1570, when the viceroy ordered that all Valencians be prepared to take up arms in the event of an attack by the Turkish armada, the municipal council compelled him to exempt a number of people from this mandate, in deference to the *fueros*.[21] Valencian regional sentiment crystallized as well in the preservation of the language, a distinct dialect of Catalan, and in the population's reverence for its unique past: the celebration of the Reconquest of Valencia on 9 October 1238 still represents one of the longest-standing continuously observed commemorations in Spanish history.[22]

Several of the principal institutions in Valencia limited their membership to native-born Valencians. By means of these restrictions, a relatively small group of prominent families exercised control over the town council, the university, and a significant number of the benefices in the cathedral. Thus the names of Carroz, Pallas, Vich, and Serra appeared again and again in the rolls of municipal offices, the professoriate, and the canons.[23] This native oligarchy sought to retain its influence at every turn, ceaselessly petitioning the king to appoint Valencian officials.[24] At the time of Ribera's arrival, the ranks of the lower clergy were also closed to foreigners, defined here as those not native to Valencia. As a consequence of these restrictions, most of the more permanent officials in the Church and the government were natives who lived out their lives in the kingdom of Valencia. Most viceroys, archbishops, inquisitors, and other royal officials, by contrast, hailed from Castile and moved on to other posts after serving for a few years. Not surprisingly, the Valencian oligarchy generally regarded these transient appointees with suspicion and did everything in their power to weaken the royal officials by preventing unity among them. In 1600, for example, the city of Valencia protested the appointment of one of Ribera's favored canons as inquisitor, because "the Holy Office loses a great deal of authority in having an inquisitor who is subordinate and subject to the archbishop."[25] The royal officials, for their part, often accepted posts in Valencia with great reluctance, hoping that these positions would lead to something better. Vespasiano Gonzaga, appointed viceroy of Valencia in 1575, referred to the post as "the least important of all there are, both inside Spain and abroad."[26]

The particularist sentiments behind these tensions manifested themselves to an unusual degree in the case of the University of Valencia, then located on a plaza not far from the cathedral. Consolidated in 1411 and elevated to university status in 1500–1502, the Estudio General developed under the close protection of the municipal council over the course of the sixteenth century.[27] Under the original constitutions, the town council and a select group of municipal officials elected the faculty of the university on an annual basis. In 1548 the rector Joan de Celaya secured the right to examine the candidates, but the Church remained powerless in the process—despite the fact that Pope Alexander VI had bestowed the honorary title of chancellor upon the archbishop in 1492.[28] This municipal control of academic appointments led to a high incidence of professors allied to the local nobility, especially in the faculty of theology, which between 1540 and 1568 expanded to include additional chairs dedicated to Holy Scripture, the Old Testament, and Thomism.[29] In 1570 the faculty of theology included native Valencians such as Pedro Monzón, Juan Joaquín Mijavila, and Miguel Juan Luviela, all with fierce loyalties to the municipal oligarchy that appointed and continued to support them. By means of this circular progression, the local elite exerted a remarkable degree of influence over the personnel and the intellectual character of the university.

The established leaders of this insular educational system quickly perceived the Jesuits as a threat after the arrival of the Society of Jesus in 1544, despite the role of one of Valencia's most prominent citizens, the Duke of Gandía, in the early history of the order. Francisco de Borja (1510–1572), distraught over the death of his wife, chose to reject his inherited privileges of wealth and rank and join the Jesuits, to serve a master who would never die. Much to the surprise of the court in Madrid and Valencia, Borja traveled to Rome and devoted his life to writing spiritual works and directing evangelical missions, eventually serving as general of the order.[30] Inspired by Borja's founding of the first Jesuit college in Europe, the Jesuits in Valencia instituted the College of San Pablo in 1552.[31] Fifteen years later, in 1567, they opened the doors of the school of theology to the public, primarily for the benefit of Jesuits studying at the university.[32] This brought the Jesuit college into conflict with the university, which had passed a statute in 1561 prohibiting its students from taking classes at monasteries or other outside institutions. The university, undoubtedly aware of the rapid expansion of Jesuit colleges in Cuenca, feared losing its students and thereby its livelihood.[33]

Exacerbating this issue was the fact that many contemporaries held up the College of San Pablo as an exemplary institution, whereas the university's faculty of theology, a bastion of scholasticism by this date, evidently lagged behind the faculties of medicine and ancient languages in terms of prestige.[34] This came about largely through the work of Celaya, who as a student in Paris (unlike the famous humanist Juan Luis Vives) had embraced the nominalism that dominated French intellectual circles in the early 1520s.[35] As rector of the university, Celaya mounted a war against the heretic grammarians, as he termed followers of the Christian humanist Erasmus, and contributed to the formation of a Valencian humanist expatriate community at the Sorbonne.[36] The 1564 execution of the nobleman Gaspar de Centelles, who had cultivated a circle of Erasmians at his palace in Pedralba, solidified the link between Erasmian ideas and Protestant heresy.[37] The eclectic Jesuit program of education encompassed any form of learning that might prove useful in missionary work, including humanist influences. Because the University of Valencia professors enjoyed the protection of the town council, reformers such as the Jesuits found it extremely difficult to introduce their controversial curriculum into the existing system.

In 1569–70 the Jesuit college appealed to the viceroy Benavente, claiming that the university's prohibition on classes outside its walls ran counter to papal decrees and to the practice of other European universities.[38] Their logic notwithstanding, this dispute with the university exemplified the resistance that the growing Jesuit order encountered from existing institutions elsewhere. Whereas Italian detractors sensed a hidden Spanish agenda on the part of the Society of Jesus, Spanish critics of the Jesuits pointed to Loyola's international base to depict the order as foreign. The Society held no guarantee that bishops—even reforming bishops—would support their educational and evangelical projects. Loyola hinted at his reservations with respect to the state of the secular church when he expressly prohibited his followers from accepting benefices and bishoprics, to avoid conflicts of interest and worldly distractions. In Valencia (as in Catalonia), however, the reforming bishop recognized a kindred spirit in the new order.[39] In a letter to the vice chancellor of the Council of Aragon, Ribera sided with the Jesuits in no uncertain terms: "The town councilors of Valencia, in an effort to favor their university, want to prevent their students from taking classes in certain religious houses (where theology is taught with more benefit to the intellect and to virtue). . . . It is a shame that this university is run by men who never in their life learned to read or write."[40] Whether he directed this insult at the faculty or the councilors who appointed them, Ribera clearly believed that the quality of the theologians at the university fell far short of the ideal.

In response to these criticisms, the town councilors petitioned Philip II to appoint an outside visitor to inspect the University of Valencia. More so than his father Charles V, Philip developed an aggressive strategy of university reform, sending visitors around the kingdom to revise curriculum, end internal political struggles, and control academic administration.[41] In keeping with this philosophy, the king chose Ribera, citing his capacity as titular chancellor of the university, as inspector. A royal order of May 1570 empowered the archbishop to "visit, reform, and redress the statutes and ordinations of the Estudio General, striking and adding constitutions as you see fit."[42] Philip further authorized Ribera to review university finances and ordered all royal and municipal officeholders to assist Ribera and comply with his recommendations, under pain of a fine.[43] The town council's scribe noted the reception of this decree succinctly: "The officials responded that they would take counsel with the city's lawyers and take steps in conformity with justice."[44] Three weeks later, on 25 May 1570, the council wrote to Philip II describing the appointment of Ribera as "against the fueros and privileges of this realm and highly prejudicial and harmful to the city."[45] Even before Ribera set foot in the university, the town council sent Jerónimo Climent to Court to protest the visitation.

In July and August 1570, Ribera carried out his review of the Estudio General, accompanied by the canons Don Miguel Vich, Bernardo Gómez de Miedes, and Francisco Escrivá and Francisco Juan Roca, dean of the cathedral.[46] First, the archbishop sought to make provisions for university students to attend classes of theology at the Jesuit college.[47] Second, he attempted to pave the way for the appointment of Jesuits to the faculty of theology. This measure corresponded closely to his third proposed reform, the inclusion of more voices (including, presumably, his own) in the selection of university professors.[48] Given Ribera's opinion of the faculty of theology, it stands to reason that he would attempt to wrest control of university appointments from the hands of the council.[49] These reforms emerged from Ribera's desire to improve the education of the Valencian clergy, the initial focus of his program of spiritual renewal in Valencia. To locals with a higher opinion of the theology faculty, however, the archbishop's actions represented little more than a threat to municipal control of the university.

RESISTANCE TO RIBERA'S UNIVERSITY VISITATION

News of Ribera's proposed changes to the Estudio General provoked a strong re-action from the town council, the professors, and the students. In addition to aggra-vating their existing resentment of the Jesuits, Ribera evidently both insulted the in-tellect of the professoriate and challenged their system of patronage.[50] On 7 August 1570, even as Ribera continued to conduct the visit, the council complained to Philip II of the proposed "novelties and mutations" and sent a professor to Court to defend the existing constitutions.[51] The rector Monzón reportedly referred to Vich and Roca as "those villains, who make war against us in the visit to the Estudio."[52] The student body also "rioted," challenging Ribera's authority and "maltreating" his name, though this event was most likely orchestrated by the professors.[53] Reports of these protests reached Ribera, and on 8 August he imprisoned the rector Monzón along with the professors Luviela, Mijavila, and Gil Cavaller. In a letter to the king, Ribera justified his actions as follows: "I received information that the sole cause of this disruption was four clerics, professors at the university. These men have con-trolled the Estudio up to now, on account of their influence with its officials."[54] He further claimed that the four had stirred up the town council and stated publicly that Philip had overstepped his bounds in ordering the visit, and thus "as a royal servant" he felt compelled to punish them.[55]

Over the next week, Ribera engaged in a series of negotiations with the town council, the university, and the Inquisition, often with the viceroy as an intermedi-ary. The inquisitors Juan de Rojas and Soto Calderón, royal officials charged with prosecuting offenses against the Catholic faith, occupied a contested position in 1570. The Valencian tribunal drew the majority of its inquisitors from the secular clergy of Castile, but over time the institution became enmeshed in local society through a host of native jailers, attendants, and informants (*familiares*).[56] On 9 Au-gust 1570, Rojas and Calderón responded to the brewing controversy by seeking out an escape. They informed Ribera that two of the imprisoned professors, Luviela and Mijavila, held the position of theological consultant (*calificador*) in the Inquisition and therefore were exempt from ecclesiastical jurisdiction. The inquisitors requested their release and an account of the specific charges against them, still unknown out-side Ribera's circle. According to the inquisitorial messenger, "The archbishop re-sponded that he would not give out any information and that the inquisitors could confine the two professors."[57] The inquisitors agreed to this arrangement but then proceeded to allow the professors to return to their own homes.

Ribera took this action as a great affront to his authority, as it suggested that he had imprisoned the professors without cause.[58] Given that the festival of San Lorenzo fell on the following day, Ribera deprived Luviela and Mijavila of their licenses to preach. In theory, the archbishop's right to assign and revoke these licenses stemmed from his responsibility to ensure that the Tridentine requirements on regular sermons did not lead to heresy in the pulpit, but in this case his dissatisfaction with the professors clearly emerged from their opposition to the visitation.[59] Disappointed with the lack of support from his presumptive allies in the Inquisition, Ribera thus attempted to bring his critics to justice through his own powers as archbishop.

This decree immediately polarized the city, and on the night of 9 August a group of students posted a series of anonymous broadsheets on prominent buildings around the city. One, cited at the beginning of this chapter, questioned Ribera's parentage, calling him a "bastard son of the filthiest, most vile whore and the mangiest, poorest student of Salamanca, though falsely believed to be the son of the most excellent Duke of Alcalá." These allegations were untrue but may well have struck a nerve, since Ribera was indeed an illegitimate son of Per Afán de Ribera, a source of embarrassment for him and his apologists.[60] Following up on its contention that the archbishop had "without cause nor reason imprisoned the most reverend rector of our university," this broadsheet concluded as follows: "All of the people are agitated to see that you have so much malice and passion against the learned Valencians, that you have placed in your jail men of such valor, luster, and good example, as are the Reverend Master Luviela and Master Menjavila, senior doctors in theology and masters of our university."[61] Characterizing Ribera's attempt to reorganize the university as simple contempt for its members, the students exploited the cultural divide that separated the Seville native and Salamanca graduate from his new congregation. The language of the broadsheet also contrasts the "passion" of Ribera—arguing that he acted on emotion rather than reason—with the "good example" of the learned men whom he imprisoned. This inversion undercut Ribera's contention that he had acted in the interest of improving the level of education offered by the university.

Two other broadsheets posted at this time expanded upon these criticisms and applied them to the Jesuits and Ribera's allies in the cathedral as well. One posting copied a purported exchange in Latin between Ribera and "magistro Santander Gymnasii Valentini rectoriam desiderante," implying that the Jesuit Santander had hidden designs to seize the rectorate of the university. In Ribera's "reply," the authors imagined him agreeing to the request and lamenting the fact that the uneducated students had turned the people of Valencia against him. Citing the book of Isaiah (29:12–13), the archbishop states, "And the Lord said: 'Because this people draw near with their mouth and honor me with their lips, while their hearts are far from me, and their fear of me is a commandment of men learned by rote.'" An educated passerby seeing this letter posted on the doors of the cathedral would have grasped its implications quickly. On the face of it, the "author" Ribera reiterates his stated disdain for the theology faculty by using scripture to impugn the scholastic training of their students. But this broadsheet was clearly the work of students, suggesting just the opposite: that they understand the Latin Bible much better than the archbishop. The true meaning emerging from the passage is that the "hearts" of the Valencian people remain far from their young and newly arrived prelate, who signs off to Santander, "I am young and despised, your flattery will not be forgotten. And peace to you."[62]

The authors of a third broadsheet demonstrated a similar willingness to alter a collection of Biblical verses as a means of condemning Ribera, the Jesuits, and others sympathetic to the university visitation. One passage drew from Jacob's speech to his assembled sons (Genesis 49:5–7) to compare the visitors Vich and Roca to the two who carried out the massacre of the Canaanites: "Simeon and Levi are brothers; weapons of violence are their swords. O my soul, come not into their council. . . . Cursed be their anger, for it is fierce; and their wrath, for it is cruel!" Thus in this view Ribera's trusted advisers from the cathedral do not deserve his confidence, as they have used their influence to carry out a vendetta against the university.

The broadsheet expressed a similar opinion of the university professor Juan Bautista Caro, a former friend of Monzón who fell out with the rector after supporting the visitation of 1570.[63] Playing off the Latin definition of *caro* (flesh), the authors combined passages from John 6:63 ("It is the spirit that gives life, the flesh is of no avail") and Galatians 5:19 ("Now the works of the flesh are plain") to accuse Caro simultaneously of impiety and a host of worldly sins such as fornication, dissension, and drunkenness. One final passage from Acts 12:3, "Witness Herod, who orders the arrest of Peter to please the Jews," suggested that Ribera had acted on behalf of the Jesuits in jailing Monzón.[64] The association between Ribera and the autocratic ruler responsible for the beheading of John the Baptist depicted the archbishop as a threat to his flock, here equated with the early Christians in an age of persecution. Comparing Santander to the Jews who ordered the arrest of Jesus and his followers connoted both legalism and the possible taint of Jewish blood within the Society. Taken as a whole, these broadsheets tried to marginalize Ribera by associating him with the Jesuits and the more reform-minded members of the cathedral, in contrast to the innocent "learned Valencians" and their supporters among the local population.

Ribera was stung by these attacks but had no recourse against the anonymous authors. Given his openness to the wide-ranging Jesuit curriculum, including its humanist elements, the archbishop may well have seen the broadsheets as an example of scholastic excess, grouping together scattered quotations with little sensitivity for context. As he could not respond directly, he directed his anger against Soto Calderón for releasing the professors to their homes, insisting that "it was necessary for Calderón to carry out the imprisonment that had been ordered, since the professors were natives to Valencia and had many who defended them."[65] The archbishop suggested secluding the *maestros* for a few days in a monastery: such a measure would have allowed him to preserve his authority as well as set a precedent for others who would speak out against his reforms. Calderón, however, insisted repeatedly that Ribera specify the "insolent words" spoken by Luviela and Mijavila.[66] Ribera refused to produce the charges, "because he intended to forward them to the king," and noted that he meant no offense to the Inquisition with the ban on preaching, "which under common law, and according to the Council of Trent, falls under the authority of the bishop."[67] Ribera sent a message to Rojas and Calderón warning them, "if you free the professors, this would be highly contrary to the royal service and to the authority of those of us who carried out the visitation."[68]

This note to the inquisitors hinted at the strategy Ribera would take throughout the remainder of the controversy. In defending his visit to the university he could have appealed to his episcopal authority, as the Council of Trent had empowered bishops to reform academic institutions.[69] Sensing the inadequacy of this mandate in the present context, Ribera instead appealed to the authority bestowed upon him by the king he shared with the people of Valencia.[70]

After the viceroy's attempt at mediation failed, Ribera found himself without an effective ally in Valencia and thus turned to Madrid for assistance.[71] As an opening gambit in a letter to the king, Ribera stated, "Although I am not much concerned with honor, when I consider that I must always guard it in the service of God and Your Majesty, I see that I would sooner part with my life."[72] Ribera explicitly called on Philip II to punish the inquisitor Calderón in a "public demonstration," a request he repeated in a letter to the grand inquisitor Diego de Espinosa: "Through the mercy of God I have done nothing to lose the esteem so necessary for the exercise of this office, of which Dr. Calderón would deprive me for no reason other than his custom of receiving good works with ingratitude. . . . If before it would have been possible to resolve this matter by turning the case over to you, now it cannot be cleared up unless you also order either Dr. Calderón or me to leave Valencia."[73] Finally, as Ribera expressed it in another letter, "For people in the public eye, reputation is more important than life, and thus I would rather the king remove me from this office than allow me to be discredited by these people."[74]

Philip II and Espinosa responded with a call for peace, reprimanding the inquisitors and ordering them to return Luviela and Mijavila to Ribera's custody.[75] The archbishop promptly placed the professors "not in a better prison, nor even in the one they occupied before, but in a much worse one, in rooms beneath the common prison."[76] In September 1570, having made his point, Ribera was instructed to free the rector Monzón and to allow Luviela and Mijavila to resume teaching classes, although the professors were still banned from preaching, hearing confession, or entering the cathedral.[77] In addition, he turned the matter of the visitation over to the Council of Aragon and forwarded the relevant materials to Madrid. On St. Michael's Day, Ribera departed Valencia to visit his family in Seville.

The viceroy Benavente reportedly stated that in the aftermath of the affair Ribera resented three things: "that so many noblemen and other people, both prominent citizens and other sorts, had gone to visit Luviela and Mijavila when these men were confined to their houses by the inquisitors, . . . that Don Luis Ferrer and the lord of Betera had ordered that Mijavila could leave his house to give a nuptial Mass, . . . and . . . that the lord of Buñol and his wife had spoken [badly] of the archbishop."[78] In a letter from Seville, Ribera provided a simpler, and perhaps more optimistic, explanation for his disillusionment: "If it were not for two or three town councilors and six people from the university who are so obstinate in defending their interests, the visit would have been received with much applause. But these people, with the prudence typical of this age, made more of a protest than the many people who desired the visit."[79] The controversy had not yet ended, however, and the events of the next year would demonstrate that the resistance to Ribera's reforms ran deeper than he had come to believe.

RESISTANCE TO REFORM

Based on the series of events up to August 1570, it would be possible to interpret the visitation to the Estudio General precisely as previous historians interpreted it—as a reaffirmation of royal power on the part of Philip II, who wanted to demonstrate that royal representatives and institutions must be obeyed in spite of their internal differences.[80] The king's refusal to indulge the showdown between Ribera and Calderón also reflected the view that as royal appointees, bishops and inquisitors had a shared responsibility to overcome these differences and present a united front before the subjects under their jurisdiction. In August 1571, however, once again in the dead of summer, students from the university posted another series of broadsheets. On this occasion, following instructions from Espinosa, the local inquisitorial tribunal undertook the investigation of the matter and the punishment of those involved—a total volte-face in comparison with their involvement after the pasquinades of 1570. The detailed proceedings of the twelve resulting inquisitorial trials cast light upon the world of the disaffected students, professors, and clerics who rose up against the archbishop and demonstrate that their resistance did not, as Ribera claimed, arise "all on account of the visitation."[81] On the contrary, these trials show that the visit to the Estudio General provided the opportunity for certain elements in Valencian society to voice deeper enmities directed toward Ribera and his reforms.

At the end of September 1570, in accordance with Philip II's wishes, Ribera forwarded his university report to the town council, who were to review it and submit their opinion to the Council of Aragon. On 23 October 1570, having returned to Valencia from Seville, Ribera wrote that "although it has been twenty-five days since the town council received the constitutions, they have not said a word, nor have I, as it seemed to me that the matter might be completed in this manner."[82] As Ribera understood it, however, the local councilors did want to debate his proposed reforms with him, a process that "could go on for infinity, and is not necessary," since they were at liberty to write whatever they wanted in their report to the Council of Aragon.[83] All the while, Ribera refused to lift the restrictions on Luviela and Mijavila, despite repeated protests by the town council and their allies at Court.[84]

This was evidently a sensitive subject: on 16 December 1570, the town council reported to Climent, "The last time we spoke to the archbishop we found him so worked up about this matter that he spoke only of 'my business' and 'my witnesses,' saying the words of the professors had offended his ears."[85] In a letter to Philip II, Ribera countered that the professors "had said and done so many insolent things that anyone trying to uphold justice would punish them severely" and urged the king not to believe "the things that have been publicized about me."[86] Frustrated with these obstacles to his attempt to reform clerical education in Valencia, Ribera decided on a change of both location and priorities. In February 1571, the archbishop traveled to Játiva to commence the pastoral visitation of his morisco parishes, a project he had already delayed on account of his review of the university.[87] Even after Monzón, Luviela, and Mijavila came to Játiva in person, "kissed his regal hands, and made all the appropriate submissions and reparations," Ribera declined to remove the prohibitions on preaching.[88]

Partly as a result of his refusal to reinstate the professors, the anonymous attacks on Ribera's character continued throughout the summer of 1571. The archbishop reported that "they have placed men in women's clothing in the windows of my servants, with others in the street calling out, 'Such beautiful women in the patriarch's house!' so that the neighbors would hear."[89] Ribera referred to a satirical letter he had received in the middle of the night, purportedly written by an anonymous cleric.[90] The author commiserated with the archbishop, describing his congregation as "lost sheep": "These are the most rebellious people in the state. It seems they were taught by the professor Satan, and graduated from the school of pride and envy, with high honors in malice."[91] Tongue firmly in cheek, the writer urged Ribera to run his house as if it were "a castle placed in the middle of Turkey," telling him to forbid his servants "from being seen by the spies of the devil taking presents to women in neighboring houses, though they be good and prominent women."[92] Along the same lines, Ribera interpreted the note that accompanied this letter, asking him to "place a handkerchief in the window of his study," as an attempt to induce him to make a sign that could be misinterpreted as a signal to his friend Doña Beatriz Vich, who lived across the street. The writer marveled at the audacity of the professors and town councilors, who "said that you do not dare speak out against three or four people in this diocese because they are the only ones in your favor, and all the rest wield their poisoned darts. All is lost."[93] Thus the unnamed author depicted Ribera as an interloper, a leader of would-be reformers whose own moral failings undermined their standing in the community.

In August 1571, broadsheets began appearing once again on the doors of the principal buildings in Valencia. One reprised a key theme of the preceding anonymous letter, but without the mock sympathy: "Certain shameless priests and officials in your house keep women publicly. Reform your own first, and do not direct your malice against the theologians who have brought so much honor and benefit to this city."[94] In his first year in office Ribera had incarcerated a chaplain of the cathedral and several other priests for concubinage, to the outrage of local judges who believed that these arrests compromised their authority.[95] The students who posted the broadsheet attempted to deprive Ribera of his moral high ground by redirecting these same accusations of sexual license against his household. The authors also moved beyond the university visitation to denigrate Ribera's camp of reformers in general: "Those who have arrived at the Court tell us that you deal only with villains, traitors, hypocrites, Indians, rebels, and bad men, through whom you have germinated scandal and uproar in this city."[96] By questioning the sincerity, political loyalty, and even racial purity of the archbishop's allies, the broadsheet recast Ribera's crusade to raise the bar for the local clergy as an ill-intentioned infringement upon the upstanding locals and their regional liberties.

A second broadsheet took the allegations of immorality against Ribera himself to a new level. Imitating the style of a theatrical handbill, the posting announced a "farce" to be produced in a local plaza, recounting "the tragedy of the romances of the illustrious patriarch. It is an exemplary work, and consolatory for those with concubines. Arrive early to find out who the woman and the other actors in the romances are."[97] The reference to this play would not have been lost on people passing through the city center. In the preceding decades, the Valencian nobility had gradually abandoned their country residences for life in the capital, giving rise to a florescence of culture including secular dramatic productions. Among the comedies popular at the time figured *Farce in the Manner of a Tragedy*, a five-act play detailing an affair between a rustic shepherd and a married woman, with the consent of her husband.[98] This broadsheet compared the plot of the play to an alleged relationship between Ribera and Doña Beatriz Vich; other (unsubstantiated) rumors identified the sacristan Jerónimo Carroz, Ribera's sworn enemy, as the go-between and spoke of a secret passage into the archiepiscopal palace.[99] The student authors of this announcement equated Ribera with an unlettered and immoral pastor, the embodiment of raw sexual passion, in contrast to his presumed status as a good shepherd to his flock.

A final broadsheet featured a caricature of Ribera kneeling as if in prayer, with passages from several psalms written below in Latin. Three of these excerpts were drawn from prayers for deliverance from personal enemies:

> Remember not the sins of my youth, or my transgressions. . . . Consider how many are my foes, and with what violent hatred they hate me.

> But as for me, I walk in my integrity; redeem me, and be gracious to me.

> Hide not thy face from thy servant; for I am in distress.

A fourth passage, extracted from a psalm of thanksgiving for the ultimate destruction of evildoers, takes on a different meaning as a conclusion to the broadsheet: "The dull man cannot know, the stupid cannot understand this."[100] Like the other pasquinades, this broadsheet represented a "world turned upside down," inverting the values typically associated with the model of the ideal prelate in the early modern period.[101] These charges caused a scandal precisely because so much of the religious literature of the period, including both saints' lives and prescriptive texts, focused on the importance of clerical exemplarity. Ribera's reputation for piety, later celebrated by his hagiographers, was well known in his time; the archbishop arose before dawn for the first of several daily prayer sessions and occasionally complemented his meditations with a scourge to discipline himself. His detractors attempted to expose this devotion as hypocrisy, in a supplicant who roundly deserved the enmity of the people under his pastoral care on account of his sinful nature. In his stupidity the kneeling Ribera misunderstands the Biblical verses he is uttering, thinking himself to be an unfairly persecuted champion of righteousness, whereas his flock recognizes him as a self-righteous hypocrite.

These broadsheets, more so than the ones of a year before, cut Ribera to the quick. On 3 September 1571 he wrote to the grand inquisitor Espinosa, asking him to order the trial and punishment of the libelers.[102] "The first broadsheets, which attacked Ribera by saying that he was not the son of his father and other things, did not bother him. But he cannot ignore the new ones, because they touch upon the honor of God."[103] He singled out in particular one that "prayed to God to remove him from this state of adultery," adding that his antagonists "had chosen the person whom they could most easily disquiet and provoke into firing a shot in response."[104] The dignity of his office prevented him from answering these attacks on the same level, and so Ribera offered an ultimatum: "Anything that is done by means of Valencian officials will come to nothing, because they are all bonded by their hatred of Castilians. If His Majesty does not favor the archbishop in this matter, he will leave it all behind [that is, renounce his position]."[105] As in August 1570, Ribera turned to the king and the inquisitor general, but on this occasion his demands called for action beyond sending letters.

On 29 August 1571 Espinosa ordered the Valencian inquisitors to "use the authority and hand of the Holy Office to procure the reform and punishment of those who are found guilty."[106] Espinosa based this decision upon the gravity of the actions, "so vicious to the authority and estimation of the Church," as well as upon Ribera's nominal status as an official of the Inquisition.[107] Less than a year after demanding Calderón's dismissal, therefore, Ribera solicited and received the assistance of the Valencian tribunal in seeking out and punishing those responsible for the attacks against him. On 20 September 1571 Rojas and Calderón posted edicts around the city requesting information or suspicions regarding anyone involved with the broadsheets and promising absolution for those who came forward.[108] Ribera endorsed these proceedings wholeheartedly: on 10 October 1571, writing from Seville on the occasion of the death of his father, Ribera implored Espinosa to continue his good work, "upon which depends not only my ability to continue living in Valencia but also the faithful exercise of my office."[109] Rojas and Calderón detained, questioned, and in some cases tortured more than a dozen defendants, several of them from prominent Valencian families, all in the name of restoring Ribera's credibility.

The active involvement of the Inquisition crystallized the opposition to Ribera's reforms, and the trial records reveal the activity and motivations of those who were mobilized in response to the visitation of 1570. On the one hand, the rector and the theologians consistently professed their innocence, disputed the jurisdiction of the Inquisition, and called upon their powerful allies in the Valencian oligarchy to assist them. The rector Monzón was placed under house arrest on 8 August 1570 "because he was more outspoken than the others in the matter of the university and the

Jesuits."[110] Ribera initially offered Monzón remission of guilt in exchange for his co-operation, "but as Monzón refused, Ribera silenced him. Monzón has spoken threatening words that clearly demonstrate that he wishes Ribera ill, saying that the archbishop was a madman who should not be allowed to rule and hinting that Ribera might regret his actions."[111]

The roots of Monzón's hatred for Ribera ran deeper than the matter of the visitation, however. By allying himself with Vich, Miedes, and Roca, Ribera tapped into the existing enmity between the theology faculty and the members of the cathedral who wanted to reform the university. Shortly after the posting of the first broadsheets, Monzón reportedly stated that if his fellow professors did not secure his release, "the wickedness of Don Miguel Vich, Dean Roca, and the rest would be known in the plazas, at Court, in Rome, and all the world over."[112] Several of the professors who appeared before the Inquisition expressed similar views with regard to the ecclesiastical visitors. The professor Onofre Serra allegedly dictated "a broadsheet in the vernacular, asking in the name of the students for the patriarch to free the professors, on account of the harm done to the university. The broadsheet spoke poorly of the archbishop and told him not to listen to the advice of canon Vich, Dean Roca, or Santander."[113]

This last example hints at the control exerted by the professoriate over the students, young nobles, and lesser clerics who actually wrote and posted the broadsheets. Ribera's secretary Feliciano de Figueroa testified that the students who posted the broadsheets "are passionately opposed to the patriarch and would do whatever they could to win the favor of Monzón and the other professors under arrest."[114] Many of these young men, however, had reasons of their own for attacking the archbishop. Ribera identified the perpetrators of the broadsheets as the professors he had imprisoned "and with them six or seven young noblemen whom he had confessed and several of the most infamous clerics whom he had reprehended or punished."[115] The cleric Antonio Pineda, responsible for transcribing and disseminating a number of broadsheets, "had been imprisoned by the archbishop for more than a year over his dealings with women."[116] The infamous sacristan Carroz, a resident enemy of reform within the cathedral, figured among the principal "murmurers" who objected to Ribera's treatment of the theologians.[117] Even before his visitation to the university, Ribera's efforts to implement the decrees of the Council of Trent in his new diocese had sparked resentment among the younger nobles and clerics of Valencia. The Council authorized bishops to review lay morality and parish priests, but the priorities of the theologians at Trent did not always match those of the congregation in question. When the professors began to mount a response to the archbishop's proposals in 1570, they found a group of willing accomplices among those whose perceived lack of morality had already brought them into conflict with Ribera.

THE FAILURE OF REFORM

As the inquisitorial trials initiated in 1571 dragged on into the spring of 1572, Ribera's allies in Madrid, having intervened to defend the archbishop's authority, began to assert the need for reconciliation. Encouraged by Philip II, Espinosa decided that the trials themselves had been punishment enough. In this spirit, the Valencian Inquisition gradually loosened the restrictions on the prisoners before releasing them altogether between March and August 1572.[118] Monzón and the professors all received absolution and in several cases even succeeded in having their names stricken from the records.[119] A few of the less well-connected defendants were assigned to the galleys, but even in these cases the sentences were never carried out.[120] The dissipation of these trials speaks to the power of the forces aligned with the professors — as well as to the less-than-total commitment to the cause on the part of the local tribunal.[121] Rojas and Calderón, having fulfilled their obligations to Espinosa, raised no objection to dropping the matter of the pasquinades from their docket.

Amid the chaos of the imprisonments and the inquisitorial trials, the matter of the reform of the university fell by the wayside. Ribera, for his part, dutifully submitted his recommendations to the Council of Aragon, at which point they immediately became a dead letter. One moment from the 1580s might serve as testimonial to Ribera's utter failure to bring change to the personnel and constitutions of the university: On 10 May 1586, the rector of the university appeared before the town council to ask them to review the case of Christopher Gazull, a student in theology. Gazull had been denied his degree because ten or eleven years earlier he had "taken some lessons in the Jesuit college and in other monasteries in Valencia, which is prohibited in the constitutions of the Estudio General." The town council considered the case and ruled that "since the constitution [against study outside the university] remains in force, the present petition cannot be approved."[122] The university did not allow students to take classes in monastic houses until well into the seventeenth century.[123]

On the most basic level, Ribera found the resources at his disposal inadequate to the task entrusted to him by Philip II. The archbishop's low opinion of the faculty of theology may well have been justified, but in 1570 the connections between the university and the oligarchy prevented him from implementing the reforms he believed would remedy the situation. Valencian humanism survived in various forms outside the university, in editions of classical texts and other writings, but the professoriate succeeded in blocking Ribera's efforts to expose students to a broader range of ideas.[124] The endogamy of the Spanish university remains a perennial concern, and Ribera would not be the last reformer to rail against the university system for excluding new and critical approaches to the questions of the day.[125]

Subsequent moments from Ribera's tenure, though not directly related to the visitation, shed light upon the greater importance of the events of 1570. On Friday, 16 December 1580, the clergy of the cathedral led a service in honor of the recently deceased Anne of Austria, Philip II's fourth and final wife.[126] Dressed in the pontifical robes and miter appropriate for such an occasion, Juan de Ribera said Mass, with the assistance, as usual, of the sacristan Jerónimo Carroz. The sermon was given by none other than Juan Joachím Mijavila, the previously imprisoned professor whom the town council had since named official preacher of the city.[127] The death of a queen represented a highly formal occasion, but this scene was typical of the personnel who regularly conducted services at the cathedral. Having endured a bitter dispute with Carroz, Mijavila, and others during the first two years of his tenure, therefore, Ribera found himself forced to contend with these exact people on a daily basis for years to come.[128]

The archbishop even made his peace with Pedro Monzón, after a fashion. When the secular clergy of Valencia selected the former rector as their advocate in a 1578 dispute with the mendicant orders, Ribera dutifully recommended Monzón as "a man of great letters and virtue."[129] This exchange typified Ribera's begrudging acceptance that he would have to coexist with what he saw as a mediocre university. The archbishop did not go out of his way to provide for university professors, and his practice of promoting other candidates for church stipends led the town council to complain that Ribera favored "foreigners" over the impoverished but deserving local faculty.[130] When the town council awarded a series of benefices to four members of the faculty of theology in 1588, however, the archbishop conceded that "they have made a good choice. Although some of the professors are of little benefit to the students, they deserve this compensation for their many years of service to the university."[131]

Ribera's acceptance of his limited powers over the university did not, however, indicate any concessions with respect to either the dignity of his office or the importance of his program of reform. After the unraveling developments of 1570–71, he arguably toughened his position on matters of precedence, against both local and royal officials. In the 1570s, Ribera engaged in protracted disputes with the viceroy and the local Inquisition over the semantics of the Mass and autos de fe, and at the Cortes of 1585 he delivered an exhaustive speech detailing his complaints concerning ceremonial matters.[132] Ribera insisted upon his episcopal authority to the extent that one weary viceroy remarked in a letter to Philip II, "The patriarch is one of the harshest men I have ever met. . . . He involves himself in your royal jurisdiction so much that if he came away with what he wanted, Your Majesty would need neither viceroy nor council here."[133] The Renaissance culture of praise and blame took on particularly acute forms among the Spanish, obsessed as they were with questions of honor and reputation.

Ribera's humiliation at the hands of anonymous satirists at the outset of his episcopate only underscored his existing sense of the esteem owed to a bishop. Along the same lines, the failed visitation of 1570 sharpened the archbishop's desire to improve clerical education in his diocese. Turning from the university, Ribera looked rather to the small group of men who held a higher vision of reform but lacked the means to implement it. The archbishop took up the leading role and revitalized this camp of the reformers, strengthening its position relative to the oligarchy and the laity. Over the next forty-two years, Ribera greatly expanded on this base and provided it with a spiritual and organizational center in the form of the Colegio de Corpus Christi. In this time, Ribera evolved from a headstrong young prelate, vulnerable to scurrilous attacks on his parentage, chastity, and authority and reliant upon the royal will for his very survival, into a bishop capable of working with, around, and sometimes against the local elite.

CHAPTER THREE

Reform by Other Means

The Colegio de Corpus Christi

On 24 October 1591, Juan de Ribera appeared before the civil court of Valencia declaring his desire to be established as a "son and resident" of the city, with all the prerogatives, privileges, and immunities enjoyed by natives of the realm under the kingdom's laws. The archbishop presented several witnesses to attest to his residence in Valencia and to his many contributions to the city.[1] The judges signed his petition, and with this act Ribera became an official *vecino* (legal resident) of the city he had inhabited for the preceding twenty-two years. This moment hardly symbolized Ribera's entrance into the native oligarchy of the city, however. On the contrary, in the eyes of some town councilors, professors, and nobles, the archbishop remained an outsider for the duration of his tenure, a foreigner seeking to bring change where none was needed or desired. But in other ways Ribera's act of 1591 did emblematize his evolving relationship with the city of Valencia. The concept of local identity in early modern Spain went beyond legal and political affiliations to encompass religious devotions and social networks.[2] Like Carlo Borromeo in Milan, Ribera ultimately placed his stamp on his diocese to such an extent that it would be impossible to imagine early modern Valencia without him.

Frustrated in his efforts to reform existing ecclesiastical institutions such as the university and the cathedral, Ribera decided in the early 1580s to create an urban religious center of his own design, where he could pursue the reform of the clergy and the enhancement of lay piety on terms more of his own choosing: the Colegio de Corpus Christi, a Tridentine seminary that also served as Ribera's chapel, reliquary, museum, and mausoleum. He pursued the planning and construction of the Colegio over a period of twenty years, culminating in its official consecration in 1604. By virtue of having built the Colegio from the ground up, writing its constitutions and choosing its personnel, Ribera was able to avoid some of the challenges associated with reforming older institutions that had fallen into more relaxed standards over time. In its architectural character and its adornments, the Colegio reflected the archbishop's inclusive tastes, which ranged from classical statuary to devotional artwork.[3] Ribera sought to raise the profile of the Colegio by promoting the veneration of local holy figures, including people he had known in life and important saints from Valencia's more distant past. Through his acquisition of artwork and relics and his promotion of Valencian holy people, Ribera converted the Colegio into an important center for lay piety and a monument to his vision of the reformed Christian community.

The archbishop's Castilian background and his program of reform often placed him at odds with the native sons of the city, but he did carve a niche for himself within that world, and the Colegio de Corpus Christi became a locus of urban reform in Valencia. Ribera's experiences in Valencia warn against any interpretation of reform in which the role of the bishop is limited to implementing a preconceived set of norms upon a local populace and its existing institutions. The decrees of Trent provided bishops across Europe with a standard of reform, but the debate that characterized their creation was mirrored in the diverse means by which individual prelates pursued their implementation. In Valencia, Ribera recognized the vibrant religiosity of the people, who possessed a number of institutions, rituals, and organizations through which they could mark the passages of life, solicit divine assistance, and seek to understand their world. This religiosity—this spiritual marketplace—both formed the object of Ribera's reforms and influenced the archbishop's efforts to create a reformed community within this shared urban space. Ribera did not become one with the ruling elite of Valencia, but he did come to identify most strongly with the interests of his diocese. This loyalty, bred of his reciprocal relationships with the people of Valencia, demonstrates that the localizing aspect of the process of reform could affect both the laity and the clerics who ministered to them.

RIBERA AND THE CATHEDRAL OF VALENCIA

After his unsuccessful visitation to the university, Ribera turned to the reform of the cathedral. Through edicts, synods, and visitations, Ribera attempted to end long-standing abuses, but though he persisted for decades this project yielded only limited results. On paper, the archbishop headed the metropolitan church, as reflected in his ceremonial privileges during religious processions and occasions such as Philip II's visit to Valencia in 1586, when Ribera exercised his right to travel with the king through the realm as his master of ceremonies.[4] The fathers at Trent, further-more, empowered bishops to review the canons who had assumed so much author-ity in many sixteenth-century dioceses. In practice, however, Ribera exercised little control over appointments to the cathedral chapter or the administration of capitu-lar revenues. The cathedral hierarchy included three distinct levels of preeminence: the twenty-four canons, who held the most prestigious offices in the cathedral; the *dignidades,* laymen typically from the nobility who collected ecclesiastical rents without performing duties for the church; and more than two hundred *beneficiados,* who served as choristers, vergers, and liturgical assistants, for example, in exchange for simple benefices.[5]

At the time of Ribera's arrival, a canon who had been active for just fifteen years would have seen six archbishops of Valencia come and go, with several periods of vacancy in between. The most powerful and long-standing canons owed their prin-cipal loyalties to their families and their allies in the town council.[6] This self-replicating cycle of patronage produced clerics such as Jerónimo Gombau (1536–1597), the illegitimate son of a sacristan, who received a papal dispensation to assume a canonry at the age of twelve. Jerónimo Carroz, Ribera's sworn enemy after the pas-quinades of 1570–71, exercised a great deal of influence over the chapter between 1546 and his death in 1582. The cathedral officials oversaw the collection of their own rents, occasionally leading to squabbles over the coveted sinecures.[7] Ribera, given his limited powers in this arena, could only attempt to reduce the tension between canons and lay dignidades, as when he intervened to resolve disputes over finances or seating arrangements in the choir loft.[8]

As a result of these limitations on his powers, Ribera succeeded only partially in implementing the Tridentine decrees on residence, liturgical uniformity, and cleri-cal exemplarity in the cathedral. The anger of the young priest and broadsheet au-thor Antonio Pineda, whom Ribera had punished for immorality, prefigured the re-sistance that greeted subsequent threats to the autonomy of the local clergy. When Ribera tried to reduce the maximum allowed time a canon could spend away from the cathedral each year from four months to three, the chapter appealed to the Sa-cred Congregation of Rites in Rome, which overturned the new restriction in 1576.[9] Ribera tried to counterbalance defeats such as this one with his diocesan synods, gatherings in which he reiterated strict standards of clerical behavior. More often than not, however, the decrees of these synods demonstrated the ways in which the clergy fell short of his high ideals. Six years after the decision in Rome, for example, Ribera repeated the stricter standard on residence, though the canons had already won their right to ignore it.[10] The archbishop's stipulations that the clerics attend-ing Mass dress appropriately, "sing with devotion and reverence," and refrain from "fighting, yawning, or causing a scandal" give a sense of his opinion of existing practices.[11]

Ribera modified the constitutions of the cathedral, but these innovations did not afford him control of its individual members. In 1584 the Inquisition remanded several clerics to the ecclesiastical tribunal for violating the new order prohibiting the use of firearms, and in 1601 the king, the archbishop, and the canons agreed to appoint an official to curb the abuse of ecclesiastical immunity by clerics who committed crimes.[12] The archbishop's experiences in this respect mirrored those of his contemporaries, in his own suffragan dioceses and across Spain: Cristóbal de Rojas y Sandoval, bishop of Córdoba from 1562 to 1571, failed to improve the relaxed standards of his church despite convening six diocesan synods during his nine-year tenure.[13]

Although Ribera never reformed the cathedral to his own standard, he did succeed in cultivating his cadre of reformers over the years by placing several of his supporters in prominent posts. In many cases, Ribera advanced the careers of his allies by naming them to offices he controlled unilaterally, in his household and diocesan staff, until he could orchestrate their appointment to the cathedral chapter. Miguel de Espinosa, a fellow native of Seville and visitor to the diocese since 1570, was promoted to both cathedral canon and *vicario general* (Ribera's principal assistant) in 1576. Francisco Tudela, another of his visitors responsible for traveling to parishes around the diocese, achieved a canonry in 1582.[14] Ribera's personal secretary, Feliciano de Figueroa (1541–1609), who came with him from Badajoz, joined the ranks of the canons in 1586, and in 1592 he assumed duties as the cathedral cantor as well.[15]

Ribera also endeavored to reward those canons who assisted him in his projects of reform with such influence as he could provide. He consecrated Bernardo Gómez de Miedes (d. 1589), a canon since 1547 and one of the few incumbents who stood by Ribera during the pasquinades, as bishop of Albarracín in 1586.[16] The nobleman Francisco Escrivá (d. 1617), a canon who entered the Society of Jesus shortly after the visitation of 1570, served as the archbishop's confessor and eventual hagiographer. Despite Ribera's efforts to promote the appointment of reformers among the canons, however, the chapter as a whole remained an enclave for privileged members of the Valencian nobility and thus a divided and at times hostile environment in which to pursue reform.[17] The archbishop eventually came to the conclusion that the financial and legal independence of the chapter would make it impossible for him to create a truly reformed spiritual center in the cathedral.

THE COLEGIO DE CORPUS CHRISTI

In a letter to Philip II, dated 31 October 1581, Ribera outlined his new strategy for bringing reform to Valencia. Rather than relying on existing institutions, where his nominal powers as archbishop clashed with long-standing custom, he proposed a new foundation in the city. This diocesan seminary, with twenty-four students and six priests to teach them, would provide a proper education for the future clergy of the diocese. Noting that the Council of Trent ordered bishops to create seminaries, Ribera recognized the difficulties involved with implementing this decree. On the one hand, he stated that "although I have wanted to carry out this project for a long time, the obligations and responsibilities of my office have not allowed me," hinting perhaps at the extraordinary demands of evangelizing quarrelsome locals and recalcitrant moriscos.[18] On the other hand, he pointed out that following the decrees of Trent to the letter would mean relying exclusively on archiepiscopal tithes, which since his arrival had been falling.

Ribera's 1581 letter seized upon several of the impediments to the foundation of seminaries around the Catholic world. Many of the Tridentine decrees concerning bishops' responsibilities repeated earlier councils, but the requirement to build diocesan seminaries was a truly new development. Not surprisingly, wary cathedral chapters and local universities opposed this innovation, and among Spain's fifty-five dioceses only twenty succeeded in founding a Tridentine seminary by 1600. Many of the seminaries founded in the sixteenth century failed within a generation owing to lack of funds or a poor academic reputation in comparison with other colleges.[19] Seeking to avoid this pattern of obstruction and decay, Ribera asked the king for permission to "alienate" fifty thousand ducats from his other sources of revenue to fund the construction and maintenance of the seminary.

Philip II agreed, and on 14 March 1583, Ribera declared his resolve to build a "seminary and college under the invocation and name of the Holy Sacrament of the most precious body of our Lord and Savior Jesus Christ." Echoing the Tridentine decree on seminaries, he argued that "the manifestation of the Word of God and the use of the holy sacraments are most certain and necessary for the souls of the faithful and provide bishops with the surest means of banishing ignorance, both among the clergy who administer them and the people who receive them." Lamenting the fact that "many parishes in this diocese lack priests, and others do not have the service they ought to have," Ribera envisioned his seminary as a means of attacking the problem at its root.[20] Although parish visitations and diocesan synods could address immediate problems, only an institution dedicated to training a new generation of clerics could lay the groundwork for a truly reformed clergy. Like his contemporary (and occasional correspondent) Carlo Borromeo, Ribera hoped that the ability to groom priests in his own school would mitigate his lack of control over many ecclesiastical appointments in Valencia. That both these prelates constructed lasting seminaries set them apart in an age when only a few bishops followed through on this Tridentine decree.[21] Ribera achieved this feat through a potent combination of determination, longevity, and personal wealth; his eventual expenditures far exceeded the initial sum authorized by Philip II to create an endowment for the institution.

The new seminary's name, the Colegio de Corpus Christi, reflected Ribera's theological priorities. In processions and sermons, he consistently took every opportunity to promote "the Most Holy Sacrament, in which we are given not only grace, as in the other sacraments, but also the author of grace Himself. Thus the Eucharist is the most principal of all, and worthy of greater reverence and admiration."[22] By placing the Eucharist as the centerpiece of Catholic devotion, Ribera advanced the larger Tridentine program of defining the sacraments and asserting their value and efficacy in the face of their Protestant and humanist critics. In naming his seminary, Ribera focused on the one sacrament that was available to all believers, could be taken on a regular basis, and formed part of the Mass, the Church's grandest and most imposing setting for religious theater. In his sermons and liturgies Ribera attempted to define the Eucharist carefully, to combat popular beliefs that focused on the object of the Host without recognizing the significance of the Mass as a ritual.[23] Many of the archbishop's subsequent initiatives, such as the acquisition of artwork and relics, would be designed to draw the laity to the Colegio so that he could use these opportunities to promote the Eucharist as the key to salvation.

In choosing a site for the seminary, Ribera decided upon an area in San Andrés, a large parish in the southeastern part of the city populated primarily by merchants, booksellers, and functionaries.[24] His choice of this location was no accident. The parish bordered upon the former Jewish quarter, and after the expulsion of 1492 many *conversos* had settled in this area; Ribera may well have intended that the seminary contribute to the Christianization of the parish. More important, for more than a hundred feet along the south side the proposed site abutted directly upon the university. The implications of this geographic proximity would not have been lost on Valencians. Having failed to alter the constitutions of the university in 1570, Ribera decided to undertake the reform of ecclesiastical education by other means, as an example and a challenge to the faculty of theology.[25] In a 1589 letter to Philip II, the town council complained that more than two hundred houses had been torn down recently in the city center "for the seminary the patriarch is building, as well as for the Jesuit house and other monasteries."[26] The councilors warned the king of the need to avoid crowding in the expanding city and the threat to public health, but beneath these concerns lay a fear of competition from the archbishop's foundation.

Over the next eighteen years, Ribera and his officials carefully supervised the work of the army of builders, laborers, and artists who gradually completed the construction of the Colegio. The complex of the Colegio, built around a Renaissance cloister, included the main chapel to the west of the main entrance, a smaller chapel to the east, and two stories of libraries and dormitories wrapping around to the north. Ribera based the design for the cloister on the patio of the Casa de Pilatos, the palace in which he had lived as a child in Seville, and furnished it with marble columns and classical statues from his private collection. In contrast, he based the chapel of the Colegio upon the Escorial, a building he had visited on previous trips to Madrid. To emulate the large, multitiered retable that Philip II constructed in the basilica of the Escorial, the archbishop hired the Genoese mannerist Bartolomé Matarana (1550?–1606) to design the retable of the Colegio, which featured religious images painted on wood set among jasper columns.[27] Matarana also painted the interior of the chapel, including the spacious cupola, which he decorated with frescoes featuring the miracles of St. Vincent Ferrer.[28] Integrating these images of Valencia's principal patron saint reflected Ribera's desire to establish the Colegio as a uniquely Valencian spiritual center.

For other adornments in the chapel Ribera drew upon the talents of Valencian artists. In his first years in the city, he commissioned local artists on a limited basis, principally to create works for his collection in the archiepiscopal palace and his nearby houses in Alboraya and Burjasot. These acquisitions placed him in the company of other noble collectors around Spain, many of them women, who purchased art for private homes and chapels.[29] Ribera aspired to a much broader audience in the Colegio, and his patronage of a new generation of Valencian painters, notably Francisco Ribalta (1565–1628) and Juan Sariñena (1545–1619), reflected both his tastes and the existing devotions in his congregation. Ribalta, a Catalan by birth, relocated from Madrid to Valencia after the death of Philip II in 1598. Over the next ten years Ribera commissioned him to paint a series of works for the chapel, including the famous *Apparition of Christ to St. Vincent Ferrer* (1604) and *The Last Supper* (1606). Sariñena, a Valencian painter who had studied in Rome, provided Ribera with several portraits for the four chapels, including images of local saints and holy figures.[30] The archbishop adjudicated the orthodoxy of all works of art in the diocese, and the Colegio provided him with the opportunity to set an example of local figures in theologically sound representations. With these commissions, Ribera promoted the work of a resurgent school of Valencian artists and channeled their efforts toward enhancing the dignity and aesthetic appeal of his foundation.

In January 1604, capitalizing on the presence of King Philip III in Valencia for the Cortes, Ribera announced the completion of the Colegio de Corpus Christi. He paid a bugler to spread the news throughout the city that the following week the Host would be carried from the cathedral to the Colegio in a triumphant procession.[31] The participation of Philip III virtually guaranteed a large turnout for the proceedings, but the archbishop left nothing to chance. In the announcement he promised sizable cash prizes for the best crosses, tabernacles, and altars constructed along the procession route.[32] To complement the triumphal arch commissioned by Ribera, parishes responded by installing a multitude of adornments between the cathedral and the Colegio. A torrential downpour before the procession, however, led the parishes to dismantle almost all of these creations. Undaunted, Philip III asserted that the march would go on "even if it rains cats and dogs" and settled into a balcony on the central plaza to watch. At the appointed hour a procession including "all the guilds, all the monasteries, all the parishes, and all the priests from twenty miles around," each with a large candle provided by Ribera, began to slog through the mire.[33] When the Host reached the balcony, the king descended to accompany Ribera and the town councilors to the Colegio.[34] Unfortunately, "fifteen minutes before the end of the procession the skies opened again, and thus the proceedings were hurried and ended in disorder."[35] Nevertheless, true to his word, Ribera disbursed more than four hundred libras in prize money for altars that had been washed away and dances performed in the mud.[36]

The events of this rain-soaked day might serve as a metaphor for Ribera's longstanding efforts to establish a diocesan seminary in Valencia. Twenty years after its conception, the Colegio opened its doors. The constitutions of the seminary entrusted the direction of the college to six permanent *colegiales*, priests who served as rector, vice rector, choir director, sacristan, quartermaster, and treasurer.[37] These men, assisted by a master of studies, were to oversee the academic progress of the twenty-four seminarians toward a bachelor's degree in either theology or canon law.[38] The requirements for incoming students included intellectual preparation but also focused on their background and character: twenty-one places were reserved for native Valencians, and all seminarians "must be Old Christians, unstained by Moorish and Jewish blood through either parent."[39]

Many seminary constitutions addressed the moral rectitude of the students, who were to hear Mass daily, confess monthly, and comport themselves with gravity at all times. These constitutions corresponded with Ribera's decision to allow—and even encourage—his students to take classes at the adjoining University of Valencia and to dispute publicly with members of its school of theology. In the constitutions, Ribera stated that "it is our intention that our college conform in all things with the

Estudio General and regard the university as its mother, treating her with great respect." Although the Council of Trent did not require university degrees for priests, Ribera and other bishops around Spain preferred that the secular clergy receive a higher education.[40] The archbishop's enthusiasm for maintaining close relations with the university also suggests that having failed to reform this institution directly in 1570–71, he sought after 1604 to elevate the level of discussion in the faculty of theology by other means. In his vision for the Colegio, Ribera expected the irreproachable seminarians and colegiales to set a higher standard for the university community while reaping the benefits of a higher education.

The seminary, however, constituted only one facet of the Colegio de Corpus Christi. The constitutions for the chapel called for a staff of eighty attendants, including thirty priests, fifteen secondary chaplains, and a host of other officials.[41] Ribera's instructions for the running of the chapel may be seen as a reassertion of the reforms he had been unable to implement to his satisfaction in the cathedral. In his effort to create "an example to other churches, in this kingdom and beyond," the archbishop sought to eliminate "the many faults and abuses that occur in most churches."[42] Placing particular emphasis on the need for gravity in the liturgy, he ordered the priests of the Colegio to lead the services "with deliberation and decency, and much silence, and devotion; this is an extremely important responsibility."[43] Ribera devised a new liturgy for Thursdays "to awaken the people to the supreme and most humble devotion owed to the infinite majesty of the Holy Sacrament."[44] During this intricate ceremony, which involved an array of attendants and bell ringers, the Host remained on display throughout the morning and evening services.[45] Like Albrecht V of Bavaria, who promoted the feast of Corpus Christi as "a more effective way of cultivating orthodoxy and religious allegiance than laws," Ribera sought to bring clarity and purity into the ritual practices of the Valencian people by enticing them to worship in an institution dedicated to the Eucharist.[46]

These *jueves del Patriarca*, or Thursday services designed by Ribera, represented only the first of the patriarch's efforts to attract the Valencian people to the Colegio de Corpus Christi. By means of the acquisition of relics and artwork, the archbishop sought to establish an alternative to the cathedral as the spiritual center for the urban laity. In the period preceding Ribera's death in 1611, the Colegio played a central role in his efforts to foster the veneration of both local holy figures and patron saints.

CREATING INTERCESSORS: LOCAL FIGURES
AND PATRON SAINTS

The opening section of this chapter evokes the metaphor of a spiritual market-place, in which Ribera had to compete to attract the Valencian populace to forms of devotion mediated by the Church. This is not to suggest that the religiosity of the Valencian laity can be reduced to purely functionalist terms, in which economic motives underlie all acts of devotion. On the contrary, this religiosity was expressed within a rich and vibrant arena of exchange in which official Catholic forms of worship promoted by the archbishop coexisted and competed with a host of other options. The Colegio de Corpus Christi, like the sacrament after which it was named, provided a point of contact between the human and the divine, between the people of Valencia and Ribera's vision of reform. In the latter part of his tenure, Ribera tailored his Tridentine program of reform to the unique needs and concerns of the Valencian community. By drawing upon spontaneous popular impulses and promoting the veneration of local saints and holy people, Ribera strove to attract attention to his newly founded seminary and chapel and to the sacrament after which it was named. This dynamic, in turn, held important implications for the evolving role of the bishop in the process of reform.

In October 1581, Fray Luis Bertrán (1526–1581) became deathly ill. A former prior of the Dominican monastery, Bertrán was known as the Apostle of the Indies for his missionary work in the New World during the 1560s. Upon hearing of Bertrán's condition, Juan de Ribera rushed to his bedside, where he prayed for his friend's health and "fed Bertrán from his own hand." On 9 October 1581, Bertrán passed away, causing a remarkable outpouring of devotion in his native city. The Catholic Reformation concept of "dying well" included both private absolution and public funeral rites; in the case of a revered figure such as Bertrán, these rituals took on broader significance.[47]

In the days leading up to his burial, the Dominican friars placed Bertrán's body on public display atop a catafalque in their church, provoking a near riot. According to one source, "A multitude of people came to witness and adore his body, kissing his hands and feet and leaping to touch him."[48] The bereaved citizens tore off so many pieces of Bertrán's robe that his brothers were compelled to dress him in a new one for his burial. "So great was the fervor of the people that the friars were afraid to place the body in the ground."[49] Four days later, when Ribera returned to the monastery to deliver the eulogy, the crowds remained a force that could not be contained: "Already at three o'clock in the morning the concourse of people was so great that no one could enter the church. When the archbishop mounted the pulpit to give the sermon, the disorderly crowd could not be quieted, and he was forced to step down without preaching. This was unprecedented, that such a great prince and prelate stood up to preach and the multitudes would not allow him."[50]

Rather than fleeing from or attempting to suppress this outpouring of devotion, Ribera sensed an opportunity to foster a new Valencian cult. Toward this end, Ribera supported the Dominican order in pursuing the beatification of Bertrán. As early as 1582, the archbishop sanctioned an annual *fiesta* to commemorate the Apostle of the Indies and approved the publication of a hagiography of Bertrán.[51] In addition, he commissioned Juan Sariñena in 1584 to paint a portrait of Bertrán adoring a crucifix in his left hand, with his right hand over his heart.[52] Later, in 1608, Ribera celebrated the beatification of Bertrán by leading a *Te Deum* in the cathedral and then a general procession that wound its way to the Dominican monastery.[53] On this occasion, Ribera ordered Sariñena to paint yet another portrait of Bertrán, which he placed in a special chapel in the Colegio.[54] Through these efforts, Ribera both promoted the cult of Fray Luis Bertrán and channeled these devotions toward the symbolic capital that he was trying to create in the Colegio.

In several other cases, Ribera took a leading role in creating new religious cults in honor of deceased local figures. The example of Margarita Agullona, both in life and in death, illustrates several key aspects of his reform project and his use of the Colegio to promote his vision. Under the archbishop's protection, Agullona practiced recollection (*recogimiento*), a silent, contemplative form of prayer often characterized by raptures and visions. Unlike some of his contemporaries, Ribera embraced recollection as a way of fostering the mystical impulses present among the laity, to the mutual benefit of both the practitioner and her patron. Given the tense atmosphere of the later sixteenth century, in which several spiritual women confessed to having fabricated their raptures before the Inquisition, the archbishop ran a tremendous risk in adopting this strategy—a strategy that brought him and his supporters under suspicion on more than one occasion. Inquisitors rooting out heresy in Badajoz condemned Ribera as a "wet nurse who reared the illuminists of Estremadura" and ordered him to extradite a servant he had brought with him to Valencia.[55] In 1588 Ribera's correspondent and confidant Luis de Granada suffered the condemnation of his spiritual charge, the Portuguese abbess Sor María de la Visitación, for falsifying miracles.

In the same year, the Valencian Inquisition condemned the African former slave Catalina Muñoz, a visionary and stigmatic whom Ribera had evidently endorsed before the accusations were made against her.[56] Such was the dilemma of the Counter-Reformation clergy, trapped between the official fear of hazardous impulses from be-

low and the need to engage the common people to prevent them from turning to
other forms of expression not mediated by the Church. When Agullona's detractors
brought her before the Inquisition, Ribera not only stood by her but also used the
opportunity to articulate his openness to recollection. After her death, Ribera emphasized the most controversial aspects of her spiritual activity in promoting her cult
in the Colegio de Corpus Christi, thereby continuing to benefit from his association
with this local holy figure.

Margarita Agullona was born in 1536 to a humble family in Játiva, the second-
largest city in the diocese. According to her hagiographer, she resisted her parents'
pressure to marry, choosing rather to take up the habit as a *beata* (tertiary) in the order of St. Francis. Around 1575, her ardent displays of public devotion, such as her
fervent reenactment of the Passion in going through the stations of the cross, attracted the attention of Ribera. She also claimed to receive visions and miracles from
God, who had once healed a blind child when she made the sign of the cross. By
means of these vivid and visible demonstrations of faith, Agullona began to accu-
mulate a following that included members of her order, the nobility, and the urban
laity.[57] When she went to pray in the chapel of Nuestra Señora de la Esperanza in
the cathedral, it was reported that many people surrounded her in the hope of receiving some benefit through her intercession.[58]

Drawn by her sanctity and her popularity, Ribera took Agullona under his wing,
both spiritually and financially. Upon her death he testified that he had "assisted with
her costs of living and provided her with a house and dwelling in the city of Valencia."[59] The archbishop also encouraged Agullona to write letters and brief treatises
addressing her spiritual exercises. On the whole, her brand of mysticism fell within
the larger tradition of Franciscan recollection. Writing of the knowledge of God and
self, Agullona compared them to two flaming arrows: "The more they burn, the
clearer is this knowledge, until the fire is so great that only one with experience can
believe it. Without hearing or speaking, but rather through signs, one discovers the
abyss of marvels never comprehended, that exhaust the understanding; the will is
burnt up, the heart is unburdened, so much that all of creation seems to be truly inside of you."[60]

Like Teresa of Avila, who lamented the insufficiency of language to capture such
an ineffable experience, Agullona used vivid imagery to approximate her mystical
retreat from the physical toward union with the divine.[61] Some of her writings, such
as a letter concerning her preparation for the Eucharist, suggest more clearly the theological influence of Ribera. Agullona expressed anxiety over taking communion,
for fear that her soul was not clean, as well as reverence for the sacrament. In one
letter to Ribera, she described a vision of doves soaring through a sky of fire; when

the priest approached her she thought she saw a beautiful cloud in his hand, and fire emanating from the son Jesus when she received the Host. In Agullona's meditations, her concerns over her own unworthiness—she signs this letter "your worthless little sheep"—are ultimately resolved by the power of the Eucharist and the reassuring figure of Ribera.[62]

Although Agullona used the kind of metaphorical language that brought many spiritual men and women into disrepute in the sixteenth century, she did so under the direction of her Franciscan confessor and the archbishop. Despite Ribera's protection, Agullona's ecstasies and raptures prompted "murmurs" regarding the beata's sanctity. Some of her Franciscan sisters, whom her biographer described as jealous, expressed doubts concerning Agullona's fervent displays of piety. "The calumniators of recollection and persecutors of spiritual exercises withdraw their wives and daughters from her company, persuading them of the danger of being exceptional in the service of God and of the danger that threatened Agullona on account of her singularities."[63] In 1582 Agullona, her Franciscan confessor Jaime Sanchis, and another friar found themselves before the Inquisition, accused of a host of crimes against the faith. The witnesses against them, most likely other Franciscans, testified that the three of them were engaged in an elaborate scam to deceive the people, and worse: some took these charges to their logical conclusion, maintaining that the three had engaged in sexual relations during Agullona's supposed spiritual ecstasies.[64] Although the Inquisition never convicted Agullona, even some of her supporters encouraged her to cease her raptures or to return to Játiva.[65]

With Ribera's support, however, Agullona remained in Valencia and continued to practice her "singular" form of mysticism, maintaining a following that included members of Valencia's elite. The Council of Trent ordered bishops to cloister female religious in convents, although in practice many Spanish women and their patrons continued to define their vocation in such a way as to retain their connections with the broader community.[66] Ribera, for his part, celebrated Agullona's ability to relate to people from all walks of life: "Though she had been raised in the house of a laborer, she respected the decency of the people she dealt with and treated each one according to his estate, just as if she had been raised in the royal house."[67] These skills evidently served her well. On 18 April 1598, for example, Agullona and a prominent clergyman served as godparents at the baptism of Otger, son of the noble councilor Bernardo Catalá de Valeriola.[68] When she fell deathly ill in 1600, "the viceroy the Count of Benavente visited her, as did a great many titled nobles."[69]

The outpouring of devotion among both the masses and the nobility on the occasion of Agullona's death speaks to the nature of her relationship with Ribera. The archbishop lent her the authority of his support, encouraged her to explore the sacramental dimensions of her spirituality, and brought her private meditations to the attention of the higher clergy. Through her ability to appeal to the higher nobility as well as the lower classes, Agullona aided Ribera in establishing and maintaining contact with all levels of Valencian society. Ribera sometimes observed Agullona in her extended raptures, during which she would name "under her breath several public necessities."[70] Ribera did not specify the exact nature of these "necessities." This crucial detail, however, suggests that through his most famous spiritual charge, the archbishop kept his finger on the pulse of the Valencian laity. In a nation with more shrines to the Virgin Mary than to any male saint, it stands to reason that a woman such as Agullona would be able to fulfill the spiritual needs of the community in ways inaccessible to male representatives of the institutional Church.[71] This symbiotic relationship allowed Agullona and Ribera to pursue their intersecting goals: she brought her vivid form of mysticism to the working class and the nobility alike, and he drew upon her popularity both to exhort the Valencian people and to learn about their religious impulses.

After Agullona's death in 1600, Ribera sought to perpetuate her popularity and channel it toward the Colegio de Corpus Christi. Although he never succeeded in securing her beatification, he did promote her veneration through publications, ceremonial, and art. Given the controversy aroused by Agullona and her practice of recollection, Ribera might well have decided to recast her posthumously as a less controversial figure. On the contrary, emphasizing the more problematic dimensions of her piety, he used the legacy of Agullona to defend his openness to lay mysticism. Shortly after her death, Ribera selected her longtime confessor, the Franciscan Jaime Sanchis, to write a hagiographical *vida* of the beata "as an example for the people, and to pay the debt that the living have to the dead."[72] In this biography, dedicated to Ribera and bearing his license for publication, Sanchis devoted more than a hundred pages to an exploration of Agullona's inner piety. If on the one hand Sanchis underlined Agullona's extreme obedience and her stated fear of falling into error, he also detailed the conflicts between her and other members of her order, the Inquisition, and other "calumniators of recollection and persecutors of spiritual exercises."[73] Far from reducing Agullona to an innocuous or nonthreatening figure, this hagiography rather sharpened the polemical edge of her mysticism and prophecy, often drawing upon her letters to the archbishop, which survive only through their inclusion in this biography.[74] Through this work, Ribera extended the campaign he had mounted before her death to promote Agullona as a viable and orthodox example of a Catholic female mystic.

Ribera promoted the cult of Agullona within the context of the Colegio, where he built a chapel to express his support of her brand of mysticism. In 1605, when he moved her body to the Colegio, he commissioned Ribalta to create a painting of her in ecstasy and placed it above the beata's tomb in the chapel.[75] In this work, the artist depicts Agullona kneeling before a cross with her eyes uplifted, arms folded across her chest. The painting bears the seal of Ribera at the top and the words *si compatimur i conglorificavimur* (If we suffer together, we will be glorified together) scrolling upward from her mouth. The word *compatimur* shares the same root as "passion" and thus could be taken to connote the emotion characteristic of recollection as well as suffering. This portrait formed a crucial part of Ribera's effort to cultivate the use of Agullona as an intercessor.[76] As the archbishop expressed it, "The devotion that she awakened in the people was considerable; this continues at her sepulcher, where many people realize benefits from God with her help."[77] Just as Agullona had mortified her body in life, through the intense physicality of her spiritual exercises, to intercede on the behalf of her community, so her body served as a locus for similar petitions in death.[78] In this manner, Ribera drew upon the cult of Agullona to establish the Colegio as a pilgrimage site uniquely suited to the spiritual needs and historical memory of the Valencian people.

In his use of artwork to foster devotion, Ribera took part in the wider Catholic movement to defend the role of images in the practice of faith. In 1597 the Valencian theologian Jaime Prades published his *History of the Adoration and Use of Holy Images*, a response to the iconoclasm of the Protestants in the Netherlands and elsewhere in Europe. Prades argued that images can serve as a book, depicting virtues, temptations, and the mystery of redemption even more clearly than words. Just as God imposed order upon nature in Creation, so artists create images to "represent and make present that which they signify." Prades then spelled out the implications of this Aristotelian, representational view of art for a Christian context, maintaining that exterior reverence to images constituted a kind of public confession through which the viewer gives life to his interior faith.[79] The art historian Miguel Falomir has suggested that Prades's work captured in prose the governing ideas behind the archbishop's patronage of art.[80] Ribera put this philosophy into practice by commissioning paintings such as Ribalta's portrait of Agullona. By combining word and image, this painting represented the fulcrum of her cult, drawing together the sentiment of her hagiography and the visual representation of the body that lay beneath the floor. By these means Ribera sought to provide a focal point for the many supporters of Agullona in the wider community, to foster his understanding of her significance, and to entice the laity to attend services in the chapel of the Colegio, where he could continue to draw upon her popularity in Valencia to promote the Eucharist through sermons, liturgies, and her own writings on the subject.

RELICS AND THE COLEGIO DE CORPUS CHRISTI

Relics played a role in the veneration of recently deceased local figures such as Agullona, but they were absolutely crucial in the cult of saints who had passed from living memory. Ribera's efforts to secure relics for his new foundation in the years around 1600 took place against the backdrop of a controversy perhaps even more heated and acerbic than the dispute over religious images. At the Council of Trent, the assembled fathers placed the responsibility upon bishops to uphold the proper use of relics: "Those are altogether to be condemned, who assert that no veneration of honour is owed to the relics of the saints, or that it is futile for people to honour them and other sacred memorials, and that they rehearse the memory of the saints in vain when seeking to gain their help." At the same time, the council sought to obviate Erasmian criticisms by ordering that "all superstition must be removed from invocation of the saints, veneration of relics and the use of sacred images; all aiming at base profit must be eliminated."[81]

In some senses, therefore, the defenders of the cult of relics demonstrated a greater sensitivity to the role of these sacred objects within their social context.[82] Ribera was well aware of this debate and kept abreast of contemporary developments within Spain. In 1598 he received a letter from Pedro de Castro, bishop of Granada, concerning the ongoing struggle to certify the recently "discovered" lead tablets of the Sacromonte, through which Castro hoped to establish the Christian heritage of the last city to be reconquered.[83] Ribera defended the thaumaturgical powers of relics, through which "the faithful can achieve positive spiritual and temporal benefits."[84] As in other areas of his ministry, he asserted his beliefs more through actions than through words. Through his acquisition and promotion of relics, Ribera tapped a rich vein of spirituality in the city of Valencia. By seizing the initiative in the struggle both to advance and to benefit from the popularity of Valencia's patron saints, the archbishop further established the position of the Colegio in the religious cityscape.

In 1600, as the result of a bitter dispute with the Dominicans and the town council, Ribera became aware of another fervent devotion among the laity and another possibility for the promotion of his seminary. At this time the nobleman Juan de Aguila decided to give the city of Valencia a relic he had acquired in France, a rib of St. Vincent Ferrer.[85] Interestingly, despite the preeminent role of the Dominican preaching friar and his annual procession in urban ceremony and religiosity, Valencia at the time could claim no relic of its patron saint. The arrival of the relic in Valencia generated an overwhelming public response: after the governor's wife and the head of the town council received miraculous cures by virtue of the rib, "all the people of Valencia came to beg for Ferrer's auxiliary in obtaining the mercy of God."[86]

The popularity—and profitability—of the rib, in turn, inspired a controversy among the Dominicans, the nobility, and the cathedral canons as to where the relic should come to rest. In this case, acting as the primate of Valencia, Ribera was compelled to argue in favor of the cathedral rather than the Colegio. In the end, the aggrieved parties turned to Philip III, who granted the archbishop's request but also reminded him of his obligation "to procure the spiritual quietude of the city" by "putting an end to the litigation and differences that you and the canons have with the town council."[87] Ribera did make an effort at conciliation: on the following 15 October the Dominican monastery organized a procession for "the finger of the glorious St. Vincent Ferrer, which they said was the one he used to signal the Final Judgment."[88] The parish priest and diarist Joan Porcar offered an interesting analysis of the rather sudden appearance of this relic:

> There have certainly been murmurs among the patriarch [Ribera], other orders, and the rest, because for two hundred years it has never been known that the Dominicans had a relic of Ferrer. On the contrary, these same friars have been heard to preach that the Valencians were unfortunate to have no relic of this saint. . . . Many believe this to be the relic that the friars used to venerate as the finger of St. Mark, or St. Thomas. . . . I do not know what inspired them to this innovation, except the desire to divert the people from the cathedral, because they know that our people are very fond of new things. But I am confident that through the merits of this glorious saint, my patron, the truth will be known.

Whatever his private doubts as to the authenticity of the object, Ribera set them aside in the interest of harmony. The archbishop lent his authority to the procession by carrying the reliquary in his own hands before placing the finger in the chapel of the Dominican monastery.[89]

Ribera did not begrudge the Dominicans their finger, in part because he had already initiated plans to "divert the people from the cathedral" and the Dominican convent alike by bringing another relic of St. Vincent Ferrer to Valencia for placement in his nearly completed seminary. An avid collector, the archbishop had developed an extensive network of contacts across Europe to assist him in purchasing relics. He was a distant relative of his principal agent, Doña Margarita de Cardona, who used her position as the wife of Adam von Dietrichstein, Baron of Odenburg, to send many relics from central Europe to Spain.[90] In the early seventeenth century, Ribera mobilized his agents and allies to gather sacred objects with which he

could compete in the religious environment described by Porcar. In 1601, shortly after the controversy over the rib, Ribera sent a team of his own to France, where Vincent Ferrer was buried. These men arrived in Vannes armed with a letter from Cardinal Pierre de Gondi, exhorting the canons of the cathedral to "give the best part of
the body."[91] The cardinal's nephew Henri Gondi, bishop of Paris, was traveling in
Brittany at the time and lent his support as well.[92] The canons provided the agents
with a femur, "one of the largest, most intact, and most beautiful bones among the
relics of Ferrer," and a piece of the saint's burial shroud, along with the all-important letter certifying the items as genuine.[93] Ribera spared no expense in celebrating the entrance of the relic into the city in a general procession with all the traditions of the festival of St. Vincent Ferrer.[94] According to the historian Gaspar
Escolano, the magnitude of the event "caused the sun to stop in its course for a
time."[95]

Even before installing this relic in the Colegio, Ribera actively promoted its veneration by gathering testimony regarding the miracles that accompanied the entrance of the leg of St. Vincent Ferrer. One Franciscan friar testified that when the
relic arrived, "he was in his deathbed, with a leg that had been crippled for years."
He made his way to the church with a cane, and as he kissed the relic Ribera said to
him, "Have faith in St. Vincent Ferrer, and you will be healed," which he was.[96] In
1604, when Ribera brought the Host to the Colegio in the presence of Philip III, he
also transferred his considerable personal collection of relics to its final destination.[97]
Once the principal relics were ensconced in the chapel of the Colegio, he sought to
present these objects to the greatest effect. He complemented his prized possession,
the leg of St. Vincent Ferrer, with a painting by Ribalta, and in 1609 he secured a
papal brief allowing him to build a special altar to the saint. The Duke of Lerma,
royal favorite of Philip III and a frequent and genial correspondent of Ribera in this
period, assisted him in obtaining this privilege, which he described as "one of the
most ample that His Holiness has granted."[98] Ribera also established a new fiesta in
honor of Ferrer on the fourth Sunday of October, for which he composed much of
the liturgy himself.[99]

In addition to securing a relic of Valencia's most important patron saint, Ribera
also procured another relic that led to the creation of a new patron. In 1578 the discovery of catacombs in the vicinity of Rome led to a brisk trade in many relics believed to be the remains of early Christian martyrs.[100] In 1599, sensing an opportunity, Ribera "asked and supplicated His Holiness Clement VIII with much insistence
to give him a blessed body for the Colegio."[101] Ribera enlisted the aid of several powerful advocates in Italy, including the Count of Olivares, viceroy of Naples, and Cardinal Fernando Niño de Guevara, future inquisitor general and archbishop of

Toledo.[102] Despite his apparent reluctance "to allow relics to be removed from Rome," the pope eventually relented and granted Ribera the body of the early martyr St. Maurus, found in "a complete sepulcher adorned with three palms" and inscribed "Mauri in pace." Sailing to Valencia with the body in a lead box, Guevara evidently survived a storm at sea through the intercession of Maurus.[103] Guevara entered the city on 16 November 1599, but on account of heavy rain he and Ribera waited until the next day to transfer the reliquary to its temporary quarters in the Capuchin convent.[104]

On 12 December, in a ceremony delayed once again by rain, the archbishop brought the city together in a rare moment of harmony to celebrate this acquisition of an important relic. Posting large, colorful proclamations announcing the general procession of the body of St. Maurus, the town councilors asked all along the route to place lights in their windows and prohibited carriages in the streets between noon and one o'clock under pain of a fine.[105] On the appointed day, the archbishop and the viceroy preceded a group of chaplains and canons carrying the ornate reliquary aloft like a monstrance. Followed by the governor, justices, town councilors, and all the orders, this procession passed under an arch with "Maurus Martir Rome" inscribed in silver letters to welcome the city's newest treasure.[106]

Through Ribera's efforts, the cult of St. Maurus gradually took root in Valencia. In 1600 Ribera solicited and received permission from the pope to organize a major fiesta for St. Maurus on 3 December and disseminated a letter to his clergy exhorting them to promote the veneration of the saint among their congregations.[107] In 1609 the archbishop printed and distributed a brief *Historia Beati Mauri Martiris*, detailing the saint's martyrdom and acquisition, to be inserted into the liturgy of the Colegio chapel.[108] Ribera's campaign to promote St. Maurus received help from the elements. That torrential downpours seemed to accompany each presentation of the body was not lost on the people; in the early seventeenth century, St. Maurus became the intercessor of choice in times of drought. In the two decades after Ribera's death, the city requested the procession of the relic on numerous occasions, and evidently these ceremonies consistently brought results. On 7 June 1631, the general assembly of the town council voted St. Maurus an official patron of the city.[109]

The adoption of St. Maurus by the city of Valencia complemented perfectly the principal role of St. Vincent Ferrer and Margarita Agullona in the Colegio de Corpus Christi. These phenomena illustrate well the localizing nature of the process of reform. The early modern chronicler Gaspar Escolano marveled at the religiosity of the Valencian people, as demonstrated by "the adornment of sacred places and the great number of ecclesiastics. The general populace has such a natural propensity for devotion and worship that the entire city seems a church or monastery of religion."[110] This metaphor may have been more apt than Escolano knew. The people did indeed seek to express their devotion through a variety of means, but in the absence of a strong episcopal presence they developed these forms of expression on their own terms.

Ribera came to Valencia with a vision of a reformed community of believers, in which the people would manifest their religiosity according to the sacramental and liturgical rhythms of the Church. In implementing this vision, he engaged in a dialogue with the laity, building upon existing forms of devotion in an effort to infuse them with elements of his own Tridentine program of reform. Over the course of four decades, this process brought change to both Ribera and his congregation. By coming to the Colegio as an important center of religiosity, the urban laity engaged in grand ceremonies and venerated intercessors promoted by the archbishop. Tailoring his activities and liturgies to compete with the other devotions available to the people, Ribera inserted moments such as sermons on the Eucharist to promote the official doctrines of the Church. Although he did not succeed in all of his reform projects, his willingness to engage the laity enhanced his influence among them and solidified his position within Valencian society—certainly in comparison with the thirty-seven-year-old bishop who found himself hanging by a thread after the controversial university visitation of 1570.

The Colegio de Corpus Christi also provided Ribera with an institutional and symbolic base of operations where his authority was not compromised, as it was in the cathedral. Ribera did not succeed in reforming all the clergy in Valencia, but from the Colegio he oversaw the careers of his supporters and rewarded them with promotions, building upon what he had accomplished in his household. The Toledan doctor in theology Alonso de Avalos entered the archbishop's service in 1576 as a teacher for Ribera's nephew, before his appointment as visitor to the diocese and then auxiliary bishop of Corón.[111] Miguel de Espinosa, whom Ribera named as auxiliary bishop of Morocco in 1579, was a close confidant who assisted at the death of Fray Luis Bertrán and helped to initiate the campaign for the friar's beatification. After serving Ribera as his overseer of almsgiving, Espinosa subsequently took office as the first rector of the Colegio, where both he and Avalos were ultimately buried. His nephew Tomás de Espinosa, who began as a page in the archiepiscopal palace, rose through the ranks as an episcopal visitor, accountant, and principal assistant to Ribera. In 1607 the archbishop compensated him for his service by appointing him as auxiliary bishop of Morocco.[112] A university-trained theologian, Tomás de Espinosa consulted on the thorny question of the morisco children, and in 1610 he led the procession to celebrate the expulsion of the moriscos from Spain.

By the end of his forty-two years in Valencia, Ribera's circle of pages and servants had also produced twelve bishops, two archbishops, and a cardinal, in addition to the dozens of followers who remained in Valencia. These prelates did not always share Ribera's position on a given issue, and the morisco question, in particular, divided the archbishop from several former pages who later held the suffragan bishopric of Segorbe. But the fact remains that the graduates of Ribera's circle committed themselves to Church reform, and the differences that arose among them spoke to the difficulty of implementing the decrees of Trent on the ground. Philip II's decision to place Ribera in Valencia and keep him there led to a generation of clergymen trained in a laboratory of reform centered on the Colegio.

In the summer of 1610, Ribera participated in the citywide Corpus Christi procession for the final time. Portraits of the now elderly prelate suggest that he no longer needed to shave his pate to achieve a tonsure, as he had done when he first arrived in the city. In his last rounds of Valencia, the Biblical dramas, decorations, processants, and plazas seemed familiar rather than daunting. In 1569 the Corpus Christi procession had represented a rare moment during the year when the archbishop and the Eucharist encroached upon the religiosity of the Valencian people, accustomed as they were to ordering their lives through confraternities and other means. By the time Ribera elevated the Host above his head in the Mass that concluded the 1610 procession, he had succeeded in integrating the message of the Church Universal into the daily lives of the laity to a much greater degree. His detractors notwithstanding, Ribera was no Castilianizer, bent on stifling local traditions in favor of arid, theologically correct displays of the power of the Church. On the contrary, the archbishop's projects demonstrated an innovative spirit reminiscent of the most famous reformers of his time, Ignatius of Loyola and Teresa of Avila. Like these two members of the regular clergy, who responded to the needs of early modern Catholicism by creating a new order and a distinctly reformed branch of an older order, Ribera did not limit himself exclusively to the reform of existing institutions.[113]

The experiences of Ribera speak to the broad range of possibilities available to reform-minded Catholic bishops in the early modern period. As a royal appointee and a foreigner, Ribera faced a series of challenges in Valencia, where his nominal authority did not extend far. Unlike a political official charged with governance, furthermore, as archbishop his position required him to speak to the spiritual concerns of his congregation, opening questions of morality and belief. Rather than confining himself to what little he was able to accomplish through the university and the cathedral, Ribera created a new institution, an example of creativity and exchange in reform, rendered in stone, marble, and tile. The people of Valencia did not simply reject or adapt to his reforms; rather, they contributed to their development by expressing their devotion to a given relic or intercessor. In this sense, the Colegio itself stands as a monument to the archbishop's willingness to engage new and existing local customs, propelling his reforms far beyond the decrees of Trent. Ribera augmented the main altar, the focal point for the sacrament of Holy Communion, with side chapels designed to appeal to the nobility, clergy, and artisans alike. The vivid artwork and reliquaries of the Colegio, promoting popular local figures such as Margarita Agullona and Vincent Ferrer, testify to the strong collaborative dimension of the process of reform in Valencia.

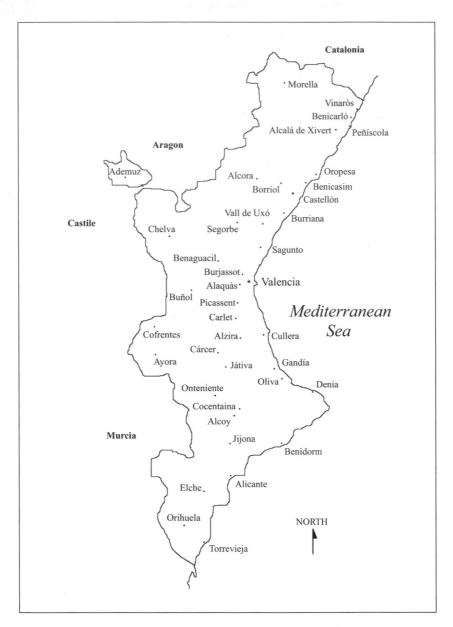

Map of Valencia, Spain, in the sixteenth century. Prepared by the author.

Juan Sariñena, *El Patriarca Juan de Ribera* (1607). Colegio de Corpus Christi, Valencia, Spain. Fernando Benito Domenech, *Pinturas y Pintores en el Real Colegio de Corpus Christi*, 325. Valencia: Federico Domenech, 1980.

Bartolomé Matarana, Retablo Mayor. Colegio de Corpus Christi, Valencia, Spain. Principal altarpiece in the chapel of the Colegio de Corpus Christi, designed by Bartolomé Matarana. Fernando Benito Domenech, *Pinturas y Pintores en el Real Colegio de Corpus Christi*, 227. Valencia: Federico Domenech, 1980.

Francisco Ribalta, *Aparición de Cristo a San Vicente Ferrer* (1604–5). Colegio de Corpus Christi, Valencia, Spain. Francisco Ribalta, *The Apparition of Christ to St. Vincent Ferrer* (1604–5). Fernando Benito Domenech, *Pinturas y Pintores en el Real Colegio de Corpus Christi*, 298–99. Valencia: Federico Domenech, 1980.

Francisco Ribalta, *Sor Margarita Agullona* (1606). Colegio de Corpus Christi, Valencia, Spain. Fernando Benito Domenech, *Pinturas y Pintores en el Real Colegio de Corpus Christi*, 302–3. Valencia: Federico Domenech, 1980.

Within the image: LOS ESCŌDIDOS EN / LAS CVEVAS HAZIAN GRĀ / DES DAÑOS ROBANDO PORLŌ / CAMINOS YMATANDO:YPARA / RENDIRLOSENBIOSVMAGESTD / ADO GARCIA BRAVO ELQVALLES / PERSIGVIO CŌLOSSOLDADOS / YBAXARO:AENBARCARSE / MAS DE MIL.

JÚCAR

ROAYA

CORTES.

REY TVRYGI. PRESO.

DOJVAN PACHE. CO. CABO DE LA CAVA LLERIA:

Vicent Mestre, *Rebelión de los Moriscos en la Muela de Cortes* (1613). Colección Bancaja, Valencia, Spain. Moriscos committing suicide at Muela de Cortes, site of a rebellion during the expulsion of the moriscos. Detail from Vicent Mestre, *Morisco Rebellion in Muela de Cortes* (1613). *La Expulsión de los Moriscos del Reino de Valencia*, 62–63. Valencia: Fundación Bancaja, 1997. Photographed by Juan García Rosell and Gil Carles.

Pere Oromig, *Embarque de los Moriscos en el Grau de Valencia* (1612–13). Colección
Bancaja, Valencia, Spain. Two moriscas bid farewell to their Old Christian mistresses at the
port of Valencia. Detail from Pere Oromig, *Departure of the Moriscos from the Port of
Valencia* (1612–13). *La Expulsión de los Moriscos del Reino de Valencia*, 51–53. Valencia:
Fundación Bancaja, 1997. Photographed by Juan García Rosell and Gil Carles.

Vicent Mestre, *Embarque de los Moriscos en el Puerto de Denia* (1612–13). Colección
Bancaja, Valencia, Spain. Moriscas dance to music on the beach at Denia, followed in their
steps by Old Christian women. Detail from Vicent Mestre, *Departure of the Moriscos from
the Port of Denia* (1612–13). *La Expulsión de los Moriscos del Reino de Valencia*, 58–61.
Valencia: Fundación Bancaja, 1997. Photographed by Juan García Rosell and Gil Carles.

CHAPTER FOUR

From Moriscos to Moros

Ribera and the Baptized Muslims of Valencia

In 1583 the elderly morisco Francisco Zenequi appeared before the Inquisition of Valencia, accused of practicing Islam. As a resident of the coastal region of Gandía, Zenequi hailed from a particularly independent New Christian community. Despite his relative isolation from the centers of Valencian society, however, Zenequi had experienced years of evangelization, including baptism, forced attendance at the Mass, and countless sermons by preachers explaining the rudiments of Catholicism. For all this, he remained as Muslim as ever. One witness against him reported, perhaps with a hint of irony, that "in spite of his advanced years" Zenequi had not eaten at all during Ramadan. Another testified that Zenequi had said, "The reason we're having bad weather is that, unlike the Turk, who recognizes the three laws of Moors, Jews, and Christians, the king of Spain does not allow each one to live by his own law." On the subject of his own conversion, Zenequi added, "I don't care how much the patriarch pressures me. I will not be a good Christian."[1]

By 1583, Zenequi's declaration would not have surprised the patriarch in the least. When Juan de Ribera assumed command of the sprawling archdiocese of Valencia fifteen years earlier, he confronted a large population of morisco parishioners—more than in any other region of Spain. As an idealistic young prelate in the 1570s, Ribera attempted to adapt his ideas on reform to a unique set of circumstances different from those confronted by other Tridentine bishops: François de la Rochefoucault in France and Carlo Borromeo in Milan faced many challenges, but these did not include the task of converting sizable communities of baptized Muslims residing within their own dioceses. In the first decade of his tenure in Valencia, Ribera maintained his belief that he could succeed where previous prelates and inquisitors had failed and bring about the "true conversion" of the moriscos. This early optimism gradually gave way to disillusionment, however, and by the 1580s he had become convinced of the impossibility of effecting the religious and cultural assimilation of this segment of his flock. In this sense his experiences with the moriscos followed a very different trajectory from his relationship with the Old Christians of Valencia. Ribera's attempts to reorganize the morisco parishes and provide them with competent priests represented the first concerted campaign of evangelization since the forced baptisms of the 1520s. By the early 1580s, however, the continued apostasy of the moriscos and resistance from the Valencian clergy and nobility led Ribera to change his perspective radically. His writings of 1582 demonstrate clearly that by this point his prior optimism in the expansion of the Universal Church had given way to a much more pragmatic point of view.

RIBERA'S MORISCO POLICY

"Reform [in early modern Spain], as in most parts of Catholic Europe, was essentially an urban phenomenon."[2] Like other bishops in the Tridentine era, Ribera struggled to reach the great many members of his congregation who lived in rural areas, often far removed from his base of operations. The Colegio de Corpus Christi provided a constant point of contact for Valencians living in the capital, but the archbishop could maintain only an occasional presence in the countryside, despite his Herculean efforts in this area. Ribera dedicated three or four months each year to the personal visitation of his diocese, traveling to parishes across the kingdom to inspect churches and their ornaments, preserve orthodoxy in the liturgy, and review the conduct of priests and laymen alike. During his tenure, Ribera and his diocesan visitors carried out more than twenty-seven hundred visitations of the churches and monasteries of Valencia, compiling some ninety thousand folio pages of records detailing their observations and instructions. Unfortunately, all of these documents were burnt to a crisp, along with the rest of the archdiocesan archive, by Communist soldiers in 1936.[3] On account of this loss, Valencia lacks many of the sources that have made possible the careful study of popular religion in Cuenca, Galicia, and Catalonia. The fragmented papers that survive in other Valencian collections, however, suggest that like his contemporaries, Ribera found his influence muted in rural areas. In Picanya, an Old Christian farming town to the south of the capital, Ribera's officials recorded thirteen visitations between 1570 and 1600, during which they ordered improvements to the fabric and oversight of the church. The intervening absences of several years, however, limited their ability to follow up on these reforms, mirroring the experiences of visitors to other peripheral areas in Spain.[4] Ribera's aspirations for Valencia encompassed his entire diocese, as evidenced by his extensive visitations, regular synods, and frequent circulars to all of his priests. But his ability to influence the lives of his parishioners remained strongest in the city, where he exerted his personal authority over ecclesiastical institutions, religious processions, and devotional practices.

In the end, paradoxically, the rural morisco populations of Valencia proved the glaring exception to this rule. Ribera's reform programs met with the most resistance and the least success among the New Christians, and yet the archbishop ultimately affected the moriscos more than his rural Old Christian parishioners, through his eventual support of expulsion. His final views on the subject constituted the end point of a long evolution, however, and Ribera's initial response to the challenge presented by Valencia's morisco population was to decline Philip II's nomination to the archbishopric.[5] After the king insisted, Ribera shifted to a different strategy, adapting his education and Tridentine program to the task at hand. His previous experiences and studies afforded him a limited knowledge of the moriscos and a framework for his subsequent attempts to evangelize them. As a boy in Seville, even one raised in the rarefied environment of the Casa de Pilatos, Ribera almost certainly came into contact with the morisco communities that abounded in the Triana and other peripheral parishes in the city.[6] At public functions such as processions, autos de fe, and ritual punishments of criminals, Ribera would have encountered a people apart, separated by clothing, customs, and often language, and yet living among the Old Christians. During his studies in Salamanca, as his extensive notebooks demonstrate, Ribera learned the Thomist system within which he would attempt to bridge this gap. In his *Summa Theologica*, Thomas Aquinas insisted that the process of conversion must begin with God: "God being the prime mover, his motion causes all beings to turn (*convertantur*) toward him, following their general tendency toward the good, and each tends to become similar to God in his own fashion."[7] In translating the Greek term επιστρεφειν as *convertere*, Aquinas retained the multiplicity of meaning this word could have in the New Testament: to turn toward, to orient oneself, to direct.[8] By the same token, Aquinas also captured the reciprocal nature of conversion, in which man turns toward God through faith. Aquinas added that the nonsacramental act of conversion should be followed by a period of demonstrated good works, reflection, and instruction before the formal initiation of the proselyte into the Church through baptism.

The moriscos of Valencia, unlike the ideal convert described by Aquinas, had received baptism without conversion, and in fifty years they had demonstrated little desire to turn toward a Christian God. In the first decade of his tenure Ribera attempted to overcome these challenges, and his early efforts and writings reflect a vision of the moriscos as fallen from the path but still perfectible. Ribera implemented his initial optimism with regard to the New Christians in three areas of his morisco policy: his support of the 1571 treaty between the Inquisition and the moriscos, his efforts to restructure the morisco parishes, and his faith in preaching as a means of conversion.

LIMITING INQUISITORIAL PROSECUTION OF MORISCOS

Ribera assumed the see of Valencia at a time of great tensions between Old Christians and New, tensions that threatened to reach the boiling point shortly after his arrival. The initial forty-year treaty between the moriscos and the Inquisition expired in 1568, amid reports that moriscos had abused Christian officials in the Vall de Uxó of the northern sierra. The Valencian Inquisition took a more aggressive line in response, prosecuting morisco leaders and their seigneurs in a series of dramatic autos de fe.[9] These punishments led to rumors in Valencia and abroad. In June 1570, Don Guerau de Spes reported to Philip II from London that the English planned to assist the King of Fez with "ships, weapons, and munitions to transport his Moors to Spain," to help the moriscos in their rebellion against the Spanish.[10] An Englishman recently returned from imprisonment in Valencia delivered "reports current in that town about the war with the Moriscos. Many daily repair to their camp for avoiding of the great vexations and troubles done by the Inquisition, which the Moriscos demand to have taken away."[11] In these crucial months before the final defeat of the Revolt of the Alpujarras and the victory over the Turkish armada at Lepanto (1571), the Valencians lived in fear of an uprising among the moriscos of their own realm. Circumstances beyond Ribera's control seemed to conspire against his plans to instruct and integrate the moriscos.

Despite this atmosphere of distrust, the moriscos of Valencia did not rise up in arms. In fact, a series of negotiations between the king, the Inquisition, the nobility, and a group of representatives from certain morisco communities (aljamas) produced the most lenient and wide-ranging treaty to date.[12] On 12 October 1571, the king and the grand inquisitor Gaspar de Quiroga signed a royal order granting specific immunities to the twelve morisco communities in exchange for an annual subsidy of fifty thousand sueldos. Under the terms of this new *concordia*, the Inquisition extended immunity from the confiscation of goods to those moriscos condemned of "crimes of heresy or apostasy in observing the sect of Muhammad and its rites and ceremonies." This immunity also applied to "dogmatizers, alfaquis, circumcisers, and any other person," including relapsed heretics and those presently incarcerated in the inquisitorial prisons.[13] Other clauses in the concordia set a limit of ten ducats on fines imposed upon the moriscos and ordered the Valencian tribunal to direct these revenues either to the parish church of the morisco in question or to feed poor morisco prisoners.[14] Quiroga agreed to this treaty because he believed that "the moriscos are delinquent through ignorance and lack of instruction rather than out of malice. It would be overly rigorous if we were to execute the maximum penalties under the law on those who have apostatized."[15] On the surface, Quiroga's edict resembled the previous edicts of grace extended to the moriscos, but it also reflected the shift in responsibility among the Christian authorities in the time around 1570. By acknowledging that the Inquisition had achieved little by punishing the moriscos, Quiroga tacitly admitted that the Valencian tribunal was ill suited for education, opening the way for the resurgent secular clergy to assume the task of catechizing the New Christians.

Ribera, for his part, shared Quiroga's vision of the moriscos as an uninstructed and perfectible people and believed that given the opportunity to evangelize in an environment free of inquisitorial persecution, he would succeed in convincing them to abandon their Islamic practices and beliefs. During the negotiations, Ribera endorsed the idea of a treaty with the Inquisition while expressing reservations about both the nobility ("The seigneurs care less about the religion and peace of their vassals than they ought to") and the moriscos, predicting that "great drawbacks" would result were the New Christians to be given responsibility for collecting the subsidy.[16] No surviving letter records Ribera's immediate reaction to the concordia of 1571 as it emerged, but his sardonic comments in a letter to Philip II written more than ten years later suggest that he threw his weight behind the morisco cause: "The spirit of the moriscos can be seen in the fact that they search for someone who does not know them and has not dealt with them, so that they can bring a greenhorn into the matter and deceive him. I can speak from experience in this, given what they did with me shortly after I arrived in this kingdom. They came away with what they wanted, because they tricked me, and I believed them, and wrote to Your Majesty in their favor."[17] Ribera may have viewed his cooperation with the moriscos as yet another example of misplaced trust in the later years of his tenure, but in 1571 his approval of the initiative reflected his willingness to take up the morisco problem as his own.

PARISH REFORM IN MORISCO COMMUNITIES

Ribera supported an agreement with the Inquisition in 1569–71 so that he would be able to carry out the instruction of the moriscos through the institutional Church. All earlier efforts to endow the morisco communities with a church and a qualified priest had failed.[18] Ribera established the parish as the basis for his morisco policy and mounted the first sustained, systematic effort to effect the conversion of the New Christians through instruction at the parochial level. In July 1573, Ribera began to collect information on which parishes had insufficient churches and priests and how to secure funding to remedy the lack.[19] After his first ad hoc committee on the moriscos fell apart in disagreement over finances, Ribera convened a new panel including the canon Miguel Vich, Dean Roca of the cathedral, and Juan Bautista Caro, all allies from the controversial university visitation of 1570. Working with this handpicked committee, Ribera determined that many parishes had "one, two, three, or more annexes," reflecting the population growth within morisco communities. This profusion of annexes led the panel to question whether one priest could give adequate instruction to so many scattered settlements. The committee thus decided to create new parishes in areas where large numbers of moriscos lived apart from their "mother church," providing them with priests and new church buildings.[20] In this way Ribera hoped to obviate the common complaint by the moriscos that the inconvenience of walking to the next town kept them from attending Mass.

The committee then turned to the greater challenge of funding these new parishes. Ribera's panel acknowledged that the low salaries set in the 1530s had failed to attract qualified priests in an age of rampant inflation, leading to widespread absenteeism.[21] The committee resolved to raise the priestly salaries to one hundred libras, drawing the necessary funds from the rents previously directed to Muslim mosques as well as from an additional annual contribution from the archiepiscopal rents and tithes.[22] Ribera and his assistants conducted a thorough review of the funds contributed to the morisco parishes by the archbishopric, other ecclesiastical institutions, and the members of the laity who had gained control of ecclesiastical revenues. In 1577 Ribera's treasurer compiled a report adjusting the expected contributions upward to account for increases in these rents over time.[23] Although Ribera assumed the lion's share of the burden, this reassessment represented an aggressive attempt to compel those persons and institutions deriving money from the morisco parishes to contribute to the sustained evangelization of the vassals generating these revenues.[24]

Drawing upon these funds, the committee declared its intention to build suitable churches in all of the morisco parishes and their annexes, together with rectories to house the priests. Ribera, for his part, consistently met or exceeded his commitments, supplementing priestly salaries and creating 22 new morisco parishes, raising the total number to 212.[25] To offset the costs of construction, ornaments, and vestments, the archbishop also placed substantial sums from his own episcopal income in a new morisco fund.[26] In the late 1570s, Ribera used this account to purchase chalices, chasubles, and prayer books as well as to subsidize the construction of churches in morisco areas such as Mirarrosa, a coastal town near Denia.[27] The archbishop also drew upon these resources to revitalize an existing school for morisco children in the capital. Like the municipal schools designed to divert Old Christian orphans and vagabonds from a life of crime, the morisco school operated on the belief that children were more open than adults to receiving a religious education. When the Old Christian rector of the Valencian school retired in 1575 after thirty years of service, Ribera replaced him with a more activist leader committed to instructing the morisco students in theology and sending them to preach and set a positive example in morisco parishes.[28]

Ribera's financial commitment to the morisco parishes reflected his optimism that a resident secular clergy could bring the moriscos firmly within the Christian fold. The parish constituted "a critical intersection of local and official religion in Europe," and in this area Ribera combined his Tridentine programs of clerical reform and evangelization of the laity.[29] The archbishop established special morisco accounts, but these were designed to provide the moriscos with the services of Catholic priests, such that the differences between the two communities might be erased over time. Along these same lines, Ribera's edict of 1 June 1569 regulating morality among the clergy and laity of Valencia contained only one specific reference to moriscos, in his decree concerning marriage in prohibited degrees. The penalties for blasphemy and other infractions did not discriminate between Old Christians and New. Similarly, at his diocesan synod of 1578, though some chapters discussed issues that provoked controversy in morisco areas, such as the proper respect for the Eucharist, the observance of Christian burial rituals, and the monitoring of midwives, the decrees of the synod as a whole applied equally to priests and believers in all areas.[30] In contrast to the *Instructions y Ordinacions* of Jorge de Austria, the synod of 1578 did not target morisco parishes or dictate specific restrictions on Islamic practices. The edict and the synod formed part of a program of instruction, devotion, and administration of the sacraments that could be applied to any diocese in Valencia, thus underscoring Ribera's hope that the Tridentine tools at his disposal could inspire the true conversion of the moriscos.

PREACHING TO THE MORISCOS

Sacred oratory represented one of the most important means of evangelization, and one of the most problematic. Ribera arrived in Valencia at a critical juncture within the history of preaching in Catholic Europe. The fifth session of the Council of Trent decreed that "since the preaching of the gospel is no less necessary than instruction for a christian state, and this is the chief task of the bishops, the same holy council has decided and decreed that all bishops, archbishops, primates, and all others who preside over the churches are personally bound, unless legitimately impeded, to preach the holy gospel of Jesus Christ."[31] In the wake of this council, a generation of churchmen devoted themselves to the task of rescuing sacred oratory from what they saw as its medieval decline into abstract disquisitions and bawdy anecdotes. A historian of late-sixteenth-century Rome describes the Eternal City as "the center of a vibrant, assertive, if often uncompromising Roman Catholic culture that learned to broadcast this message loudly and skillfully wherever it could throughout Europe and the new worlds."[32] Jesuit scholars led the way in this revival, adapting the epideictic genre of classical rhetoric (associated with speeches assigning praise and blame) to a new, Christian vision of the dignity of man.[33] Fray Luis de Granada, one of Ribera's many confidants, made the greatest Spanish contribution to this literature with his *Ecclesiasticae Rhetoricae* (1575). In this work, Granada argued for the Christianization of classical rhetoric, as well as for the dignity of the office of preacher, and the spiritual preparations necessary to fulfill this duty properly.[34] Inspired by these Christian humanist treatises, bishops such as Carlo Borromeo wrote and disseminated practical handbooks on preaching, emphasizing the need for concise, lucid homilies on Biblical texts to instruct the people and dissuade them from straying from the path.[35]

The Flemish bishop Mathius Hovius (1542–1620) recorded in his daybook the challenges involved in reforming the Spanish Netherlands, but Ribera kept no such diary.[36] Nor, in the period before 1582, did Ribera write detailed letters to the king, as he would later in his tenure. The contents of the archbishop's library and the character of his numerous sermons, however, corroborate the thesis that he set out on his initial preaching tours of morisco Valencia with a great deal of evangelical optimism. Ribera ultimately accumulated some two thousand books, shelved in his archiepiscopal palace, the Colegio de Corpus Christi, and his two houses in the neighboring towns of Alboraya and Burjasot.[37] In addition to the classic work on preaching, Augustine's *De Doctrina Christiana*, Ribera also possessed chronicles of the spread of Christianity and the collected sermons of many preachers in history. His modestly appointed private rooms in Burjasot, which overlooked the local church and a sprawling pasture, featured the Venerable Bede's account of pagan conversions in late antiquity. In his small study in Alboraya, "with two windows overlooking the pool of swans and another opening onto the fountain in the garden," he could contemplate Antoni Beuter's chronicle of the triumph of Christianity in ancient and medieval Valencia. Ribera's collections also included numerous works by and about the most famous preacher in Valencia's past, the patron saint Vincent Ferrer. The hagiographer Justiniano Antist celebrated Ferrer's excellence in oratory, claiming that

his two- to three-hour sermons, all delivered in the Valencian dialect, inspired thousands of Jews, Waldensians, and other heretics across Europe to convert to Christianity.[38] Audiences such as the Bretons and the English court were able to understand Ferrer because he was purported to possess the gift of tongues, one of the many
miraculous powers attributed to him. These providential histories of conversion often overlooked the complexities and limitations involved in the Christianization of
the West, neglecting the persistence of pagan beliefs beneath a Christian veneer and
the socioeconomic factors that influenced conversion in times of change.[39] Nevertheless, sixteenth-century historians such as Francisco Diago continued to celebrate
these histories and preachers as an inspiration and example to be followed, illustrating their relevance in the early modern period.

In Ribera's own time, Catholic preachers also carried their message around the
globe, acting on the belief that Christianity would continue to rise from its humble
origins in the ancient Near East to dominate the great empires of the world. After
the discovery of the Americas, the Dominican friar Bartolomé de las Casas assigned
a unique role to Spain in this process, urging Philip II to promote the gathering of
all peoples under Christ as a prelude to the Second Coming and the end of time.[40]
Ribera's library reflects a keen curiosity about Catholic evangelization in the wider
world. His many geographical works included the classic treatises of Ptolemy as well
as more recent studies, such as Francisco Alvares's description of Ethiopia, drawn
from the Portuguese expedition of 1520. The archbishop also owned numerous accounts of Jesuit missions to China and Japan and polemical works addressing the
evangelization of Protestants in Europe. These wide-ranging collections, which included banned works by the Dutch humanist Erasmus, mirrored the Jesuit practice
of making use of any available means to propagate the faith. Beyond his library walls,
Ribera attempted to bring these ideas to bear in Valencia. He drew upon the morisco
fund to send preachers from the monastic orders, Jesuits in particular, to evangelize
morisco areas. In 1578 Ribera paid one hundred libras to "four fathers of the Society
[of Jesus] of this city, who went to preach and instruct the New Christians of this
archdiocese," as part of a mission he had organized.[41] Ribera found a kindred spirit
in the Jesuits of Valencia, who supported him during the firestorm after his visitation to the University of Valencia in 1570. The archbishop developed this positive relationship with the Society over the years, hiring Jesuit preachers, extending loans
to the order, and choosing a Jesuit as his confessor (and eventual hagiographer).[42]
In the 1570s Ribera employed Jesuit preachers because he believed their evangelical philosophy would bridge the cultural differences that divided Christians and
moriscos.

This confidence in the power of the Word is borne out in Ribera's own sermons as well. The archbishop devoted three months each year to the personal visitation of his diocese, and on many occasions he included morisco parishes in his travels. His collected sermons include fifty delivered in New Christian areas in the period before 1588.[43] Early in 1571, Ribera and his entourage of priests, diocesan officials, and porters embarked southward on a journey to Játiva, Valencia's second-largest city and home to a significant morisco population. Ribera encountered a tense situation there, as illustrated by a series of events that had taken place just months before at the sprawling castle on the hilltop overlooking the city. In February 1570, the lieutenant of the castle wrote to the viceroy in urgency, reporting that three prominent morisco leaders, descended from the Turks, had attempted to infiltrate the castle to survey the ongoing construction. Subsequent sightings of signal fires in nearby morisco areas portended an attack upon the castle, the culmination of "these times of the moro peril."

The detailed testimony of these moriscos and other Old Christian witnesses, however, suggests that these ominous predictions arose from a comparatively mundane incident. The moriscos in question denied that they were conspirators, or even close friends. One had gone into the city to buy a donkey, another to get some financial documents from a man in the castle. An Old Christian friend invited them to see the castle, and when the gatekeeper objected they left peacefully. Their friend, a tanner who knew the moriscos "very well," testified that at first they all stood outside the castle joking around. He confirmed that when the gatekeeper denied them entry the moriscos complied, adding that they later complained to the local judge. Even the gatekeeper conceded that he had stopped the moriscos primarily because of the recent rebellion in Granada, and his wife (who spoke colloquial Arabic) stated that the moriscos had not said anything treasonous.[44] After reports of these events spread, however, the bailiff arrested the three moriscos and searched their houses, discovering writings including account books, Islamic prayers, and passages from the Quran. In such a charged atmosphere, the simple possession of such documents— even in the absence of any observed Muslim practices—was enough to transform a benign misunderstanding into a conspiracy to assault the castle.

Undaunted by the threat of violence, Ribera preached in Játiva and the surrounding area for several months before congregations of both moriscos and Old Christians. In these sermons, Ribera followed the classical structure detailed by Luis de Granada in his manual for preaching, from exhortation to narrative to a conclusion applying the scriptural passage to the present context. The archbishop also took advantage of specific moments in the liturgical calendar to explain the rudiments of Catholic faith and worship in a plain manner, assuming no prior knowledge on the part of the listener. On Ash Wednesday, he began his sermon, "Today marks the beginning of Easter. Let us talk about the intention the Holy Church had in instituting Easter." The teachings of Matthew 6:16 ("And when you fast, do not look dismal, like the hypocrites, for they disfigure their faces that their fasting may be seen by men") afforded Ribera the opportunity to discuss penitence, fasting, and the meaning of the ashes. Using simple examples drawn from daily life, such as his description of penitence as "medicine for one's sins," he emphasized the importance of focusing on God while performing rituals.[45] Two weeks later, Ribera noted the appropriateness of Matthew 5:43–44 to the assembled listeners: "You have heard that it was said, 'You shall love your neighbor and hate your enemy.' But I say to you, Love your enemies and pray for those who persecute you." Applying this text to the history of interfaith hostility in Játiva, Ribera underscored the need for mutual forgiveness. The archbishop acted upon this desire to bring Christians and moriscos together, leaving the confines of the cathedral church in Játiva to deliver sermons in the morisco towns that dotted the interior of this agricultural sector. In Benigánim, Ribera took as his text the words of Jesus to his disciples, foretelling his death and resurrection: "Truly, truly, I say to you, you will weep and lament, but the world will rejoice; you will be sorrowful, but your sorrow will turn into joy" (John 16:20). The divinity of Jesus constituted one of the most contentious points in Christian-Muslim polemics of the era, but this sermon did not back down from the implications of the passage: on the contrary, Ribera patiently explained that belief in the resurrection was necessary for salvation. At the same time, however, he stressed the universality of the resurrection and the desire of the Church to bring all together as one.[46]

Ribera's early sermons, in keeping with his support of the concordia of 1571 and his efforts to reform the morisco parishes, demonstrate his faith that through the power of the Word the Valencian clergy would eventually bring about the conversion of the moriscos. His optimism on this score placed him within an evangelical tradition in Spain stretching from the apostles to medieval preaching friars to the messianic universalism that accompanied the discovery of the New World. In this providential vision of human and divine history, the Spanish occupied a unique role as the means by which heretics and infidels would gain access to salvation. As the archbishop of Valencia, Ribera would play his part by using the Tridentine methods at his disposal to renew the Church in head and members, enticing Christians and moriscos alike to embrace his reformed brand of Catholicism.

FROM OPTIMISM TO DISILLUSIONMENT

Through the 1570s, all three of these projects—the concordia of 1571, the reform of the parishes, and the attempts at preaching—failed to achieve the desired results, and this failure led to a deep-seated disillusionment on the part of Ribera. Information from several sources contributed to this increasing pessimism. In addition to his own travels through the diocese, Ribera received reports from his diocesan visitors and his parish priests in morisco areas. The archbishop furthermore occupied a conspicuous place in the regular dramas that brought the affairs of the heterogeneous countryside into the heart of the capital, the inquisitorial autos de fe. These "acts of faith," public displays of penance designed to dissuade the faithful from sinful behavior, evolved into elaborate representations of inquisitorial power over the course of the early modern period. Every year or two, following a proclamation, crowds gathered in the main plaza by the cathedral to witness a long procession of notables, followed by those who had been sentenced by the Inquisition. The penitents wore robes reflecting the nature of their crimes and listened as their offenses were read aloud for all to hear. The litany of transgressions, which could take hours to read, was followed by a penitential Mass, a sermon, and the reconciliation of the guilty. The sacraments and exhortations of the preachers gave examples of piety as a counterpoint to the negative exemplarity of the blasphemers, sodomites, and other criminals against the faith. Through religious ceremony, as well as punishments ranging from lashes to burning at the stake, the inquisitors attempted to define the boundaries of orthodoxy for the Valencian people.

In September 1581, Ribera attended an auto de fe much like the others he had witnessed during his first decade in Valencia. Climbing the stairs to assume his customary place on the temporary platform reserved for dignitaries, Ribera must have wondered whether the supposed leniency of the Inquisition or the activism of the Church had affected the moriscos at all. The endless line of New Christians who filed by him for their cosas de Mahoma, or "Muhammad activities," included a sixty-year-old morisca sentenced to prison for fasting, performing Islamic ceremonies, and maltreating a daughter who wanted to marry a Christian and convert.[47] An unrepentant morisco from Corbera, a town to the south of Valencia, received a year's reclusion for asking his parish priest for permission to slaughter a calf in the morisco manner in exchange for "a nice part" of the meat. This reputed teacher of Islamic ceremonies also offered his opinion of Philip II's ongoing efforts to inherit the crown of Portugal, vacated by the death of King Sebastian in 1578: "If His Majesty wants to win Portugal he should arm the moriscos and let each live according to his own law; they would win it for him."[48] Heretical statements such as this one—which netted a fine of only ten ducats under the concordia—led Ribera to question the idea that the moriscos were simply unaware of his campaign. In these cases, as in many others, the moriscos demonstrated an understanding of the expectation that they would convert and of the unacceptability of their beliefs and practices in the eyes of the authorities. A decade of witnessing similar cases at autos de fe, coupled with his frustrated attempts at parish reform and his increasingly troubled visitations, convinced Ribera that evangelization was failing because the moriscos and their seigneurs refused to embrace the message he had promoted so assiduously.

In the first place, the concordia did not accomplish its stated goal of improving relations between the Inquisition and the moriscos, and in some areas the agreement may well have made matters worse. Although the moriscos' representatives recognized that this period of reduced sentences was designed to allow for instruction, their communities saw in the concordia of 1571 a tacit renewal of the arrangement that had bound Christians and Muslims in the time of their grandfathers: like the Mudejars, they would subsidize the Christian authorities with annual payments and occasional fines in exchange for de facto permission to practice Islam. The inquisitors, on the other hand, observed the stipulations of the concordia in individual cases but did not halt their prosecution of the moriscos as a group. On the contrary, the tribunal processed between twenty and forty moriscos a year in the 1570s, a figure that rose to seventy to eighty a year by the 1580s. In the half century after 1571, the Valencian Inquisition tried approximately thirty-nine hundred moriscos, and New Christians accounted for three-quarters of the defendants receiving sentences.[49] Thus disagreement over the intent of the concordia led to a subtle battle of wills between inquisitors seeking to regulate (and profit from) New Christians, despite the limitations of the agreement, and moriscos resentful of the continued incursions of authorities, whom they considered paid in full.

Not all morisco areas in Valencia ratified the concordia, and everywhere the edicts of grace by which the Inquisition attempted to gather penitents under the promise of leniency were mutually recognized as a farce. The inquisitors hated conducting visitations in morisco areas and devoted a disproportionate amount of their attention to communities near Old Christian settlements.[50] Their forays into more isolated areas often came in the wake of a murder investigation. In both cases the moriscos and their seigneurs engaged them in a game of cat-and-mouse designed to promote the idea that they had not received instruction—while simultaneously preventing any such dialogue. When the Count of Fuentes wrote asking for an edict of grace for Gea, a morisco town on the Aragonese border, the tribunal greeted his request with cynicism, given his history of obstructing the Inquisition.[51] The inquisitor Diego de Haedo's edict of 1573 drew few confessants but rather insults and threats against the Inquisition and anyone suspected of testifying.[52] After Haedo complained to the Count of Fuentes, the moriscos of Gea wrote to say that they failed to embrace the edict "not out of disrespect but because they did not understand what it was."[53] According to Haedo, the moriscos also feared that those who had been reconciled by the Inquisition before, who numbered more than two hundred, would be burned as relapsed heretics. The Inquisition agreed to reissue the edict, but in 1575 the inquisitor Rojas doubted that the result would be any different: "The New Christians here are so secret and cautious."[54]

The moriscos' reluctance to testify arose in part from a fear of the consequences, in the inquisitorial cells and in their own towns. A morisco from Borriol, imprisoned for fasting during Ramadan, twice resisted torture before confessing that "his companions in the inquisitorial prison told him that if he confessed he would be ruined."[55] The concordia limited the fines levied upon moriscos for certain common offenses but did not protect them from torture or from harsher penalties if they were found guilty as relapsed heretics. The Council of Inquisition, in reviewing an account of the auto de fe of 1577, repeatedly questioned the Valencian tribunal as to why Islamicizing moriscos had not been sent to the galleys in addition to their lighter sentences.[56] Fear of corporal punishment colored the testimony of moriscos in more ways than one. The New Christian officials of Chelva, a western farming town along the banks of the Turia, evidently warned a morisca that "if she told the truth, that she had lived as a mora, the Inquisition would burn her." As an enticement not to testify against them, the officials promised her alms.[57] This seemingly benign offer hints at a darker alternative, suggesting an explanation of why many moriscos were willing to undergo torture despite their hatred of the process: as much as they feared the Inquisition, they feared reprisals in their own communities even more. The case of four moriscos from Cortes, in the western highlands, burned at the stake in 1577 for their involvement in the death of a man who testified before the Inquisition, was indicative of a widespread resentment against witnesses for the state.[58] Pedro Tallón of Segorbe, who claimed that many moriscos wanted to confess but did not dare, begged the Inquisition for three things: that he be released, that they not torture him, and that it not become known that he had testified against anyone.[59] These cases illustrate that the threat of physical violence, administered through legal or extralegal means, loomed over morisco witnesses whether or not they chose to testify to the Inquisition.

Rather than providing an atmosphere conducive to instruction, the concordia of 1571 sharpened existing tensions between and within the Old and New Christian communities. Most moriscos resisted the Inquisition, revealing as little as possible and designing their testimony to avoid torture and punishment. Some used the institution as a means of settling old scores, risking the wrath of their neighbors and aggravating divisions in morisco towns. The inquisitors, for their part, distrusted the moriscos and questioned the effectiveness of evangelization: in a letter of 1581, the Valencian tribunal noted that "in our experience with the moriscos of this kingdom, even if they are well instructed in Christian doctrine they remain moros as if they had never been indoctrinated."[60] The task of instruction, they added, fell to the bishops. Ribera and Quiroga's hopes for the concordia went unfulfilled: inquisitors and moriscos alike came to regard the treaty as a façade, breeding disillusionment and suspicion on both sides.

OBSTACLES TO PARISH REFORM

Just as the arrangement between the moriscos and the Inquisition failed to meet its goals, Ribera's plan to revitalize parish reform in Valencia met at first with limited success. From the beginning, the archbishop found it difficult to persuade other Old Christian individuals and institutions to support the proposed endowment of the morisco parishes. Although Ribera had secured papal approval of his plan in 1576, many of the seigneurs and even ecclesiastical institutions refused to contribute the required sums.[61] Ribera found himself compelled to devote a substantial part of the morisco fund to costs associated with his efforts to enforce compliance, including hundreds of "mandates to the people who have to contribute the amounts stipulated by his Holiness [Gregory XIII]," ordering them "not to impede the exaction of the said endowment."[62] Ribera also initiated legal proceedings against the monastery of Valldigna for "payment of tithes," the notary Pedro Sancho for fraud in assessing the tithes, and even his own treasurer.[63] The troublesome litigation over the rents of the former mosques led Ribera to contract the services of Tomás Cerdán de Tallada, the famous legal scholar.[64] Despite his diligent efforts, revenues that should have pertained to him—including the escusado, "a subsidy imposed upon ecclesiastical rents . . . to offset the costs of the war against the infidel"—remained out of his reach.[65]

Predictably, these financial setbacks inhibited Ribera's ability to combat the existing problem of priestly absenteeism in morisco areas. In later years, Ribera staffed the morisco parishes with clerics from other dioceses and members of the regular clergy, but in the 1570s, he found himself confronted with a serious shortage of parish priests. Between a rate of absenteeism of at least 15 percent in "mother churches" and the many communities designated as annexes of other parishes, roughly half of the morisco towns lacked the services of a resident priest.[66] The archbishop's inability to follow through quickly on his goal of manning all morisco parishes provided uninstructed moriscos with a readily available explanation for their ignorance of Christian doctrine and practices. Unlike in Cuenca, where more than half of the moriscos questioned by the Inquisition could recite the basic prayers of the Church, the vast majority of Valencian moriscos showed a limited or entirely deficient grasp of the Apostles' Creed, the Lord's Prayer, and the sign of the cross.[67] In 1579 Pedro Barcaco, a fifty-year-old morisco from Parcent, a small town inland of Denia, confessed to having fasted during Ramadan and attendance at a wedding conducted according to a morisco rite but denied that he attached religious importance to these acts: "He fasted because they told him that this is what moriscos do." Barcaco furthermore claimed that he had begun fasting at the age of twenty-six and continued up until recently, when "he heard a Christian play in the church of Parcent and determined to live the life of a Christian." He evidently confessed for the first time that Easter, "and he began to learn his prayers, marking a little set of cards for this purpose." If Barcaco did not yet know his prayers, he insisted, "it was because the rector did not reside there."[68]

Barcaco's refusal to assume full responsibility for his ignorance mirrored the defense of Pere Bodol, a morisco of Antella (a town in the fertile region around Alzira) accused of circumcising his son in the morisco manner. The persistence of this practice led the Inquisition to declare in 1581 that fathers of circumcised sons could be whipped on that evidence alone, because the moriscos always concealed the identity of the circumciser.[69] Virtually all of the moriscos examined by the Inquisition were circumcised, and Christian officials sought in this physical sign the objective certainty that so often eluded them in witness testimony of Muslim rituals.[70] They did not always find it: some moriscos confessed to allowing the circumcision of their sons but claimed that this was a medical procedure rather than a Muslim ceremony, while others simply denied that they were circumcised despite the opinion of the inquisitorial "experts."[71] In his testimony, Bodol protested that he had not circumcised his son, stating that "the midwife told him that his son was born like this, but when he ran to get the priest he could not find him."[72] In the absence of a permanent clerical presence, moriscos such as Barcaco and Bodol could shift the burden of proof from their shoulders by citing the failure of the Church to reciprocate their efforts.

The residence of a priest in a morisco parish did not guarantee that the moriscos would adopt even a veneer of Christianity. In Gea, the new rector painted a grim portrait of his parishioners: the moriscos conducted Muslim burial rites, supported an alfaqui, and dug a tunnel with a secret entrance "to hide in when the authorities come to arrest them."[73] The rector knew that a pair of Gascon emigrants had converted to Islam simply because the moriscos provided for them and taught them their trades: "If they had been good Christians, the moriscos would not trust them nor help them as they do."[74] The village maintained one special table for the dead, used for washing and shrouding the body before a series of obsequies in Arabic. One woman in the village ran a school, where more than forty girls typically studied the Quran in Arabic; the school for boys had been suspended only when the alfaqui they had brought in from Valencia fled before a visit from a Christian official.[75] On the outskirts of town, the moriscos maintained "a house they call the *ravita*, in which they have a well full of water. They go there once a year on the appointed day, and anyone who wants to can go more often out of devotion," to pray and bathe. "In this ravita the rafters are inscribed in Arabic, with no other images."[76] That the moriscos named their place of worship (*ribat*) after the military fortresses that once marked the Christian-Muslim frontier in medieval Spain reflects their hostility to the intervention of the Church.

In many instances the presence of a priest sparked open defiance on the part of the moriscos. In Chiva, the priest's attempt to conduct Christian funeral rites for a female New Christian failed after a morisco disrupted the ceremony and "verbally abused the rector."[77] Miguel Muça of Chiva was arrested "for having disinterred a morisca who had received a Christian burial and burying her again in a morisco ceremony." A few years later, Muça appeared in an auto de fe again, convicted of teaching morisco children to read Arabic and turning the cross of the local justice upside down.[78] This inversion of Christian ritual resembled an "old game" played by two moriscos of Gea "in which one of them was seated and the other knelt before him, washing his face with a dampened cloth and saying 'I adore you, father saint savior.'"[79] Misbehavior in church and blasphemous humor represented a problem throughout Catholic Europe, but in morisco areas these issues took on a different hue. Just as the burial of a Muslim in an Old Christian cemetery represented a desecration of Islamic practice, these moriscos used such knowledge as they had of Christianity to mock the priests sent to instruct them.

Ribera also discovered the limits of his ability to effect change through the parish system in his attempt to bring the morisco diet into conformity with Old Christian practice. Old Christian officials had always regarded practices such as fasting during Ramadan and refusing pork and wine to be evidence of Islamicizing, although in these cases the Inquisition usually sought corroborating evidence as well: that these prescriptions involved abstinence rather than visible participation in a Muslim ritual led to a problematic ambiguity.[80] In 1579, for example, the Old Christians of Alcodar accused several moriscos of observing Ramadan because they worked all day without eating "nor snacking on sugar cane as they are accustomed to do."[81] In prosecuting a morisca mother and daughter for fasting in 1581, the Inquisition added that they had also celebrated "Easter *de moros*," with fried eggs and crullers (*buñuelos*, today a staple of the springtime festival of Las Fallas).[82] In a 1578 circular to his priests in the New Christian areas of the diocese of Valencia, Ribera similarly focused on morisco feasts rather than fasts, lamenting the fact that the moriscos, "among other rites and ceremonies of the reprobate sect of Muhammad, butcher *al alquible* [in the Muslim manner] the cattle they kill to eat." According to a book of ceremonies seized by the Inquisition, this practice included "facing the animal toward the kiblah [that is, Mecca] and intoning the name of Allah Akbar at the time of slaughter." Ribera ordered that all butchers must be Old Christians and that in exclusively morisco areas the rector or bailiff must oversee the slaughter of animals. Less than two months later he issued another general letter rescinding this exception and barring all moriscos from butchering animals.[83]

Ribera's decree concerning butchers failed to achieve its objective of bringing the morisco diet into line with Old Christian practices, regardless of the level of compliance in a given area. Some morisco butchers continued to slaughter animals as they always had: Miguel Obeyt of Olocau was arrested in 1579 "because he slaughtered several goats, piercing their gullets and skinning them, leaving only the nose on the head," in accordance with morisco practice.[84] In 1581 several Old Christian butchers from Gandía were flogged and deprived of their offices for preparing meat in the morisco manner. Their sentences might have been more severe had not the Inquisition concluded that they "committed these crimes out of poverty, and for the benefits the moriscos gave them."[85] An Old Christian from Valencia city, whose grandmother had been reconciled for practicing Judaism, lost his position as administrator of the butcher shops in Buñol for striking a deal with the morisco leaders to set up a special room in his house there for preparing goats *a la morisca*.[86] Even in areas where the moriscos largely complied with the decree, the inquisitors reported that the New Christians had simply stopped purchasing and eating meat, "except in three or four places where their temporal seigneurs have ordered it." These seigneurs represented the exception to the rule, since the noble estate as a group complained to Philip II in 1579 that the prohibition would bring "little or no benefit for the reformation of the new converts."[87] Under the circumstances, most moriscos chose rather to "sustain themselves for many days on eggs and fish."[88] The Inquisition attributed this reluctance to a precept in the confiscated morisco book of ceremonies: "Do not eat anything hunted by a person of another law, except that which they fish from the sea." Ribera's edict of 1578 demonstrated that his network of priests could bring about change in morisco practices, especially when reinforced by the specter of inquisitorial prosecution. On the whole, however, the archbishop failed to eradicate the culinary differences that separated Old Christians and New, manifestations of the broader disparities between the two communities. Under coercion, morisco communities abandoned more controversial and easily verifiable practices and restricted their diet to staples common to all. A morisco consuming eggs and fish still fulfilled the mandates of their ceremonial: "Do not eat an animal slaughtered by the hand of one who does not practice the *zalá*."[89]

The response to the decree on butchers also illustrated the importance of seigneurial support—or opposition—to the process of parish reform among the moriscos. A lawyer writing to Philip II in 1581 stated an opinion that Valencians took as a given: "Morisco towns in this realm, because they work harder than Old Christians and content themselves with less, pay much higher rents to their seigneur than Old Christian vassals."[90] Clearly, economic self-interest underlay the tendency among noble lords to allow or even profit from unorthodox practices among their morisco vassals. Don Sancho de Cardona allowed the New Christians of Guadalest, Benaguacil, and Adzaneta to maintain mosques and charged itinerant moriscos on their way to the Maghreb (an illegal traffic) a fee for safe conduct.[91] Don Francisco de Castelvi, seigneur of Carlet, ruled with the philosophy, "In my lands, I am king and pope." He recognized that the moriscos in his holdings to the south of the capital "lived as moros, and that one of these days they would be ordered to live as Christians, but in the meantime he would secretly favor them and dissimulate." This favor took the form of allowing (at a price) remarriages among moriscos who had separated from their spouses, without telling the rector and the bailiff. On one occasion Castelvi referred a legal question over remarriage to an alfaqui who happened to be present in his house to hear cases from the moriscos, indicating the seigneur's desire to preserve internal Islamic authority as well as his own. Castelvi also sold licenses to hold morisco dances and sometimes attended these in person.[92] These practices did not receive close scrutiny until Ribera sent episcopal visitors to Carlet in 1570. At this point the bailiff and the rector described Castelvi's arrangements with the moriscos and testified that they had not dared say anything out of fear, given the way in which the seigneur maltreated the Old Christians in his territory.[93]

Thus de facto tolerance of morisco rituals could go beyond simple economic self-interest, to respect for Islam and adoption of Muslim practices. Sancho de Cardona argued that the baptisms of the moriscos had been forced, that attempts to compel them to live as Christians "ran counter to all justice . . . [,] and [that] the prelates who defended the legitimacy of the baptisms to the king were great villains, who did this to achieve greater dignities." The seigneur reportedly planned to send a morisco agent to the Ottoman sultan "to procure that he write to the Pope, saying that since in his lands he allowed the Christians to live as Christians, it stood to reason that in Christendom they should leave the Moors to live as Moors."[94] Don Luis Pallás, the noble lord of Cortes and the son of a mora, spoke the morisco language and learned to read and write in Arabic. Stating that "the moros have a better life and live better than anyone," he took part in morisco ceremonies such as weddings and told his vassals that if the royal judge came the moriscos would kill his bailiffs and lead a revolt from the mountains of Cortes (prefiguring an actual revolt during the expulsion of

1609–14).[95] These seigneurs' objections to evangelization went beyond profits and jurisdictional disputes. Their desire to perpetuate the long-standing arrangement with their moriscos resulted from a relativism that complicated mightily the efforts of clerics seeking the "heartfelt conversion" of the moriscos.

RIBERA'S RESPONSE TO LIMITED PROGRESS

In a letter to Philip II in 1582, Ribera demonstrated a keen awareness of the obstacles to evangelization, which he ascribed to the moriscos and their seigneurs. A statement concerning moriscos who lived in parochial annexes hinted at his growing pessimism: "The moriscos say that their priests do not reside in their communities, but rather in neighboring towns populated by Old Christians, because the clergy do not trust them. But Mass is said and Christian doctrine is taught everywhere, and no one is allowed to be married who does not know his prayers. If from time to time there is no Mass, it is because none of them comes to hear it unless the priests and bailiffs force them to come. The priests find themselves alone and out of favor with the other ministers of justice, who sometimes threaten them if they insist too much in this."[96]

Although Ribera's goal in this document was to answer those who claimed that the moriscos lacked instruction, he nonetheless identified another key factor contributing to absenteeism: the reputation for hostility in morisco areas. Priests found themselves surrounded by morisco parishioners, who resented their presence on religious grounds, and Old Christian governors, who resisted the encroachment upon their jurisdiction. The failure of the other members of Valencian society, lay, clerical, and morisco alike, to support Ribera's plan for parochial reform seriously impeded his efforts to redress this situation. As Ribera expressed it in a 1582 letter to the grand inquisitor Quiroga, "The seigneurs have a great affection for these people. You would be shocked to see the material benefit they derive from the moriscos, through means both just and unjust. The moriscos suffer it all gladly, in order to be favored in the retention of their customs."[97]

These failures took their toll on the archbishop. If in 1569 he arrived with a great deal of optimism about the conversion of the moriscos, a decade later he was much more cynical in this regard. In 1577 the Jesuits Ribera hired to preach in morisco areas reported that their own mission had been a failure.[98] In his mounting frustration over the morisco question, Ribera requested a transfer from Valencia, turning down an appointment to Córdoba only because it would have constituted a demotion.[99] If pride kept him in Valencia, the changing tenor of his sermons reflected his growing dissatisfaction with the moriscos in his diocese. On an extensive tour that took him from the southern sierras to the Costa Blanca, Ribera foreshadowed the antagonistic tone that gradually replaced his earlier, straightforward explanations of scripture and Catholic doctrine.[100] On 23 June 1577, Ribera delivered a sermon in Alcoy explicating a Bible passage concerning the Jewish authorities' response to the company Jesus kept: "And the Pharisees and the scribes murmured, saying, 'This man receives sinners and eats with them'" (Luke 15:1–2). On the one hand, Ribera argued that no sin is too horrible to close the door on God. "We are all sinners, but through God we will be accepted, and can even live together."[101] But the archbishop also underlined the distinction between the faithful and the Pharisees: "The first thing to consider here is the difference between true virtue and seeming but false virtue." Ribera introduced a psalm to illustrate his point: "No man who practices deceit shall dwell in my house; no man who utters lies shall continue in my presence" (Psalm 101:7). In the archbishop's view, this passage demonstrated that "it is true that men must avoid dealing with evil men, because their customs can be transmitted." Ribera did not cite the following verse in this psalm, probably used in ancient coronation ceremonies: "Morning by morning I will destroy all the wicked in the land, cutting off all the evildoers from the city of the Lord" (Psalm 101:8). Yet the psalm as a whole captured a recurrent theme he developed in his sermons after this point, the opposition between the righteous and those who presented a threat to the godly community.

In subsequent sermons Ribera clarified the distinction between the godly and the wicked, focusing on the question of free will and man's role in his own salvation. The fathers at Trent had disagreed over some subtle aspects of justification, but they joined together to refute the Protestant doctrine of predestination and uphold the validity of good works in salvation. Seizing upon this idea, Ribera drew a contrast between those who actively embraced the gospel and those who refused it. On 1 February 1579, preaching in Játiva before an audience that may have included both moriscos and their lords, Ribera offered a thinly veiled critique in his analysis of the famous parable of the sower (Matthew 13:24). "Sowing is a difficult and uncertain task. The Bible tells us how much it pained Jesus Christ to preach doctrine and sow the seed of the Evangel. And what a difficult task this is for preachers, and how uncertain, because the good people who want to take advantage of this great benefit are so few." Preaching before the unreceptive moriscos, in this view, is akin to casting seeds upon thorns or rocky ground. "If the seed does not bear fruit, it is not the fault of the seed nor the sower, but of the earth that is not prepared to ripen it."[102] During a visit to Bocairente, a southern town famous for its textiles, Ribera reiterated the reciprocal nature of the process of religious instruction. In a sermon on John 3:16, Ribera emphasized "two things: the first, how God demonstrated His love in giving His son, and the second, what man must do on his own behalf to make use of this important act."[103] Preaching in Xixona, Ribera spoke of the need to "seek out the one who can remedy our miseries," not simply with words but also with deeds.[104] In these sermons Ribera reproached both the moriscos, for failing to seize the opportunity presented by their pastors, and the nobility, for tacitly encouraging the apostasy of their vassals.

Ribera foreshadowed the effect of this perceived obstinacy upon his morisco policy in Játiva, on 15 February 1579. In the parable of the vineyard (Matt. 20), a householder hires several groups of laborers over the course of a day and then pays them all the same amount, even though some had worked less time than the others. Reprising the theme of good works, Ribera argued that the master did not buy the workers but hired them: "God does not want you bought, and forced, but hired and free." Even those who come to the law later than others can earn the same eternal reward. The archbishop tempered this message of inclusion, however, with a further comparison between preaching and viniculture. Both require many hands, and suffering on the part of the workers. "Consider also what the workers and masters of the vineyard do, removing the vine shoots and leaving only the trunk. Likewise ministers of the gospel, who must remove everything within evil men."[105]

Rather than leaving the comparison at this point, with the implication that preachers should exhort all men to withdraw from sin, Ribera returned to the Old Testament to establish a connection between vine shoots and irredeemably wicked people: "God compares evil men to a vine shoot, 'it was good for nothing.'"[106] The reference was to a spoiled garment in Jeremiah 13:7; the expanded quotation that must have been in the back of Ribera's mind reads, "'Thus says the Lord: . . . This evil people, who refuse to hear my words, who stubbornly follow their own heart and have gone after other gods to serve them and worship them, shall be like this waistcloth, which is good for nothing.'" This passage illustrates how far Ribera's thinking had evolved since his earliest sermons before the moriscos. Rather than explaining the rudiments of Catholicism in simple language, he used elliptical references to little-known scriptural verses to voice his growing cynicism. Believing that the moriscos had chosen not to embrace his message, Ribera shifted focus to the challenges involved in preaching and the possible explanations for obstinacy. The objective of these latter sermons was not so much to instruct the moriscos as to assign them the blame for their apostasy, as well as hint at his own responsibility to save the healthy trunk by cutting away worthless vine shoots.

Ribera's frustration with respect to the moriscos provided the inspiration for a scene in the play *El Gran Patriarcha Don Juan de Ribera* (1616), by Gaspar de Aguilar.[107] This play featured several of the classic elements of Spanish Golden Age comedies, such as the tribulations suffered by the young Roberto before finally winning the hand of his love in marriage (with the help of Ribera). Aguilar also provided moments of low comedy, including a scene in which Ribera attempts to preach to a group of moriscos. When he first arrives at the parish church, accompanied by Fray Domingo Anadón and a Franciscan friar, Ribera finds that the moriscos have all sneaked away under various pretexts ("Since I hurried here, I forgot to water my donkey"; "I left a shirt on the door of my house"; "I have to get some vine water from my seigneur to cure this belly-ache").[108] Ribera takes this in stride—"although they are bad, they must be treated with love"—and eventually the bailiff rounds them up again.[109] Once Ribera begins to preach, however, he is amazed at the moriscos' seeming lack of understanding and proceeds to quiz them on their knowledge of basic Christian prayers:

> *Ribera.* You don't know the commandments of the law? Have you nothing to say? Surely you don't know them, since you have become so pale.
> *Farachino [a morisco].* Sir, my priest never taught me this.
> *Ribera.* Is it possible?
> *Bailiff.* The priest teaches them every day, sir, and none of them emerges any wiser.
> *Ribera.* Do you know the Lord's Prayer?
> *Ronquillo [a morisco].* I will know it, sir.
> *Ribera.* When?
> *Ronquillo.* In ten or twelve years. I have a bad memory.
> *Fray Domingo Anadón.* His shamelessness is notorious.
> *Franciscan friar.* Even he knows it.
> *Ribera.* And you?
> *Boamit [a morisco].* I know the prayers very well.
> *Ribera.* Then on my life, say if you will the Ave Maria.
> *Boamit.* You say it first, sir, and I'll repeat after you.
> *Anadón.* Could there be greater folly?
> *Franciscan.* They mock us, sir.
> *Ribera.* So I see. You, child, can't you make the sign of the cross?
> *Boy [a morisco].* I've never been able to, sir. I have a crippled arm.
> *Ribera.* You will know your wickedness well.

This scene, although a product of Aguilar's imagination, undoubtedly captured Ribera's eventual disillusionment with the morisco parishes. In 1602 Ribera complained that the moriscos had to be bullied into coming to church under the threat of fines and that once they arrived they disrespected the holy water, refused the Host, and plugged their ears during the service.[110] Aguilar imagined a single episode that pushed Ribera over the edge: Ribera arrives at the morisco parish hoping to teach the moriscos the basic catechism and departs convinced of their damnation. The

surviving documentation suggests rather that Ribera came to this conclusion gradually over the years, as a result of consistently meager returns on repeated visitations,
sermons, and parochial reforms. Faced with a congregation that he perceived to be
not only unwilling but also actively hostile and skilled in the arts of deception, Ribera's thought on the morisco question underwent a profound and radical change.

IN SUPPORT OF EXPULSION: 1582

After more than a decade of failed attempts at the conversion of the moriscos, Ribera gradually became convinced of the impossibility of the task. In 1582 his evolving views crystallized when it seemed that the moment had arrived to take more dras-
tic measures. In March of that year, wild rumors circulated of a morisco arriving in
Segorbe with secret letters promoting an uprising in Valencia.[111] Furthermore, Ribera received a report that the galleys of Captain Juan Andrea Doria had been
sighted off the coast of Denia. Many explanations could have accounted for the arrival of this fleet; Ribera, perhaps optimistically, chose to interpret it as a preparation
for the wholesale expulsion of the moriscos from Spain.[112]

On 9 March 1582, Ribera wrote to the grand inquisitor Quiroga, urging him to
use his influence with the king to promote this measure. Referring to the moriscos
as "enemies," Ribera emphasized the need to remove them from the peninsula; lest
they carry out their conspiracies to rebel against the king: "For the great benefit it
would bring to the service of Our Lord and the good of this kingdom and all the kingdoms of Spain, I am compelled to supplicate your Illustrious Lordship (as insistently
as I can) to inform His Majesty how necessary this provision would be to secure his
kingdoms." Ribera expressed his fear that those with a financial stake in preventing
expulsion would gain Philip's ear: "If His Majesty listens to what many of his ministers tell him, I do not think he will do anything, because of their self-interest in this
matter."[113] The archbishop also alluded to the precarious nature of his own position,
given his pastoral responsibilities toward the moriscos. "I have not written His
Majesty because it would not be appropriate for him to hear from me in this matter." He asked Quiroga to represent to Philip that "I am very convinced that God has
ordered this novelty [novedad]."[114] Ribera's use of this word—usually an epithet in
early modern Spain, used to describe unprecedented and illegal innovations—
speaks to the fact that in this letter, his first known writing in which he promoted expulsion, he recognized the precipitous nature of this proposed change in policy and
that on some level he felt this departure would leave him open to attack.

Ribera did not rely upon interlocutors for long. In Quiroga's enthusiastic reply
the grand inquisitor issued a pointed request for another letter to be given to the king,

imploring that "such a dangerous situation be remedied all at once, and quickly."[115] In his reply to Philip II, Ribera took expulsion as a given: "First of all, given that His Majesty is resolved to expel the Moors from all of Spain, it would not be expedient to do it all at once."[116] Ribera was in fact quite wrong—the king had made no such resolution, nor had Quiroga suggested that he had—but this opening did allow the archbishop to maintain the fiction that Philip II had first proposed expelling the moriscos and that he wrote his recommendations out of obedience.

Ribera insisted that expulsion could be carried out without remorse and offered several ideas concerning its proper execution. He repeatedly urged Philip II to carry out the expulsion in stages, beginning with the moriscos of Valencia, on account of their demonstrated propensity for violence ("We know for a fact that they have many weapons, hidden in caves and secret places, to use on the occasion they are awaiting") and their proximity to the coast. Thus Ribera exploited the current rumors of a morisco rebellion to justify expulsion and to equate this measure with the future security of the realm. Responding to the nobles' counterclaim that the expulsion decree itself would lead to open warfare, Ribera argued that this could be prevented if troops could be mustered, commenting dryly, "Now would be a good time to take the nobles up on their offer to guard the realm."[117] Finally, he acknowledged that noble and ecclesiastical rents would fall in the wake of the expulsion but noted that Christians could come from the mountains of Aragon and from Castile to repopulate Valencia. "We have to sustain ourselves with what we can, and even if we do not have as much, we will be safer. This small loss will prevent the total ruin that this realm and its people will suffer if the moriscos revolt."[118]

In a gesture toward the inherent theological difficulties in expelling baptized, nominally Christian subjects of the king, Ribera followed these pragmatic concerns with the bare beginnings of a theological defense of expulsion. "Well I know that many with the appearance of piety will want to defend this people [the moriscos], and I, by the grace of God, am not so devoid of mercy that this step would not touch my soul. I hold many of these people to be my parishioners."[119] Without directly faulting those who would oppose expulsion, Ribera argued that anyone without first-hand knowledge of "the obstinate souls of this people" and "their public shamelessness before God and king" should have no vote in the matter. Anticipating the criticism that sending the moriscos to Muslim lands would generate, Ribera pointed out that the moriscos already lived among Muslims: "They fast and live according to their law publicly and openly declare themselves vassals of the Turk. In my time I have seen them make a demonstration of sorrow when His Majesty achieved victory with the armada of the Holy League [Lepanto, 1571] and celebrate when La Goleta was lost [1574]."[120]

That subsequent chroniclers of the expulsion celebrated Ribera for his defense of this "memorable and most just exile" should not blind us to the magnitude of the decision to advocate the measure in 1582 in such vivid terms. After devoting considerable sums of money and years of his life to parochial reorganization, to litigation with the Valencian laity and clergy, to an effort to alter the very structure and character of Valencian society, all in the name of catechizing the moriscos, Ribera had come to see "these people" as a foreign nation, as "moros." "It would do much less damage to let them to go to limbo than to allow the name of God to be blasphemed by so many heretics, in a province which God through his mercy has kept [otherwise] free of infidelity."[121] By 1582, the archbishop believed that the eternal salvation of the moriscos could legitimately be sacrificed to prevent the corruption of the Christian community through coexistence with heretics.

Francisco Zenequi, the elderly morisco who appeared before the Inquisition the following year, sought nothing more than that: to coexist with heretics, to "allow each one to live by his own law." The local Inquisition refused to support this view, and Zenequi was convicted and sentenced to three years' reclusion. Zenequi's willingness to testify against his morisco enemies as well did not reduce his sentence, but it did lead to his murder after the moriscos of Gandía took up a collection to hire an assassin.[122] Although Zenequi died before his penance could be carried out, the inquisitorial scribe announced his crimes at the auto de fe of 19 June 1583 nonetheless, as an example of the fate of heretics. Those assembled in the main plaza of the city of Valencia on that day included the patriarch himself. By this point he had witnessed the failure of Tridentine methods of evangelization among the moriscos of Valencia; the reform of the clergy and the preaching of the Word had not brought about the kind of conversions related in Christian chronicles and the lives of the saints. These histories proved impossible to re-create.

Ribera placed the blame not on the messenger or the message but on the moriscos themselves and thus could only pursue his desire to build a reformed Christian community by arguing for their exclusion. The moriscos had not converted in Ribera's sense of the term, stubbornly refusing to turn toward God and thereby render possible their own salvation. But Ribera now placed the morisco question in a political rather than religious context. Characterizing the moriscos as apostate, violent conspirators against the Spanish state, he dissociated them from the history of conversion and situated them rather within the legend of the Reconquest. Seen from this angle, the expulsion of the moriscos would represent not the failure of a campaign of evangelization but rather the triumphant culmination of a centuries-long march toward religious unity.

CHAPTER FIVE

Disillusionment and Its Consequences

Ribera, Philip II, and the Valencian Moriscos

On 14 May 1582, the grand inquisitor Gaspar de Quiroga wrote to Archbishop Ribera expressing his optimism that Philip II would heed his advice and follow through with the expulsion of the moriscos from Spain. Quiroga stated that he had forwarded Ribera's report to Philip II "so that he will see the many excellent reasons that you give for remedying without delay the damage caused by the moriscos, bad neighbors to this realm."[1] In his response, Ribera reciprocated Quiroga's sentiments: "When I think of the experience that His Majesty has in these matters, I am persuaded that he will not pay attention (as some people zealous in the service of God and king fear) to the obstacles that have been pointed out to him."[2] Ribera also expressed concern that "if God is not served (for our sins) to expedite the measure now under consideration," Philip II would call for further deliberation, "even though it will not serve any purpose other than to grant treaties to our enemies, so they can better pursue their ends with vituperation of our Christian religion and universal harm to us."[3]

Ribera's fears proved to be well founded. Philip II had ordered Andrea Doria to transport troops by ship from Murcia to Valencia as a simple precaution, in response to reports of morisco conspiracies. On 19 June 1582, the Council of State asked the viceroy of Valencia for a report on the "artillery, arms, and munitions" held by the morisco population. In September, the council recommended the expulsion of the moriscos of Valencia but argued for the retention of the New Christians in Castile and Aragon. The councilors cited proximity to the coast as the determining factor in their decision to limit the extent of the expulsion, but there were other forces at work.[4] A faction of nobles led by the Marquis of Denia presented the king with a series of briefs emphasizing the potential economic consequences of expelling tens of thousands of Spain's most productive workers. In the end, Philip II decided to suspend the council's resolutions. A less-than-coincidental subsidy of one hundred thousand libras from the Valencian nobility, ostensibly for the "peace and security of the realm," illustrated the nobles' desperation to retain their New Christian vassals at a time of economic uncertainty.[5] Philip II's motives, however, went beyond crass materialism. In the decade since the battle of Lepanto in 1571, the king had engaged in a series of truces with the Ottoman Turks and shifted his foreign policy ambitions toward northern Europe and the Atlantic. As part of this turn away from the war against Islam, Philip II rejected the clear recommendations of his most senior ecclesiastical and secular advisers and determined to retain the moriscos of Spain, insisting more than ever on the necessity of their true conversion.

This series of events left Ribera in a tenuous position, one that he would occupy for the following twenty-five years. Having already expressed his opinion, in a formal letter to the king, with regard to the obstinate nature of the moriscos and the futility of instruction, he found himself entrusted with their spiritual welfare once again. This difference of opinion between the king and his senior religious official in Valencia placed a strain on their relationship. During the pasquinade of 1570, Philip II had demonstrated his willingness to defend the reputation of his appointed visitor to the university as well as a subsequent desire to bring the matter to an end and foster harmony with the Old Christians of Valencia. In the matter of the moriscos, by contrast, the king's hopes for reconciliation through education coincided more closely with the recurring pleas for instruction voiced by the moriscos and their noble lords. For these reasons, Ribera's morisco policy between 1582 and 1609 was characterized by a host of ironies and paradoxes.

In the first months and years after Philip's 1582 decision, Ribera criticized the proposals of others and pointed out the futility of alternatives other than expulsion. His radical and incongruous proposals of this period underscored his disillusionment with the prevailing situation and his skepticism that change could arise without a major alteration in the status quo. As the Colegio de Corpus Christi took form in the capital, however, the archbishop decided to curry royal favor by taking on a less antagonistic tone. Rather than blaming the king for proposing an impossible objective and neglecting to support the enterprise, he determined a new course of action.

In the 1590s, despite his reservations, Ribera mounted the most systematic catechical campaign of his tenure. Historians have traditionally categorized officials in charge of morisco areas as either "assimilationist" or "rigorous." Hernando de Talavera, the archbishop of Granada (1492–1507) who attempted to convert the Muslims through persuasion, and Francisco Jiménez de Cisneros, the archbishop of Toledo (1495–1517) who implemented rather a policy of forced baptisms in Granada, usually provide the extreme ends in this dichotomy.[6] Viewed in detail, Ribera's morisco policy does not conform to straightforward categories of gentle and rigorous. Even after he grew disillusioned with the moriscos in the 1570s, he continued to borrow elements from many of the available approaches to instruction. In the 1590s Ribera devoted a great deal of money and attention to the effort to endow and man the morisco parishes, and he achieved more success in this area than anyone who had preceded him. He presided over a number of committees dedicated to the morisco problem, and he republished or reedited several of the treatises and decrees written by Martín Pérez de Ayala, Jorge de Austria, and others.

Ribera also maintained close relations with the Jesuits and continued to employ them as preachers in morisco areas. Ribera remained open to various methods of instruction, however, not because he believed in them but rather because he believed that they were all doomed to fail. In the period after the 1580s, Ribera mounted an aggressive campaign of evangelization—not to achieve the true conversion of the moriscos so much as to prove their apostasy to the king. Only by freeing himself of these troublesome parishioners could Ribera focus his energies on the Colegio de Corpus Christi, then taking shape as the centerpiece of his reform project among Old Christians.

FROM BITTERNESS TO RESIGNATION

In the months after Philip's order to suspend the edict of expulsion in 1582, Ribera wrote a long and embittered letter to the king. This paper presents the anger and despair of a man who had seen his hopes for a final solution to the morisco problem dashed. In this document Ribera attempted to discredit several of the people who were then attempting to convince the king to grant the moriscos a new edict of grace. He urged Philip not to pay heed to the petition of one Maldonado, for example, "because Maldonado knows so little about these people, and in the few months he has been in Valencia he has learned only what a few interested parties [that is, the nobles] tell him."[7] Along the same lines, Ribera insisted that "we know the clergyman that the viceroy wants to send, and the solution that he proposes in this matter. His plan will not improve the situation, since he has little experience in these matters, on account of the little time he has resided in this realm."[8] Ribera went so far as to issue a blanket denunciation of the practice of sending commissioners to Valencia to address the morisco question: "In this kingdom of Valencia it is well known that to send people deputized solely for the conversion of the moriscos is what least promotes this conversion."[9] Apart from the fact that their methods were neither useful nor viable, according to Ribera, "suffice it to say that the commissioners did everything they could to perpetuate the heresies of the moriscos. . . . Those who seek to remedy this situation must be people who will not be corrupted with the large bribes that the moriscos customarily offer, nor fall for lies and false promises."[10] With this exceedingly bleak vision of the Christian officials who viewed the morisco question in a different light, Ribera set an important precedent: in the latter part of his tenure, he consistently sought to discredit those who disagreed with him as pious and misguided at best or corrupt and implicated at worst.

For all of these criticisms of the evangelical efforts of others, in this brief Ribera did not offer much by way of alternative strategies. He claimed that the Inquisition had already tried leniency, as had the secular clergy, in response to which "not a one of the moriscos confesses, and of the sacraments they receive only baptism and marriage, and these by force, and yet we do not punish them. The inquisitors and the bishops order them not to perform Moorish ceremonies, and although they have ample warning and instruction, such is their obstinacy that they would rather burn than abandon their rites."[11] Ribera further argued that those optimists who reported the true conversion of individual moriscos "see things as they would like them to be, rather than as they are," given that long experience had shown that the moriscos told the truth only under torture. Just beneath the surface of this document lay the accusation that by listening to outside advisers rather than to his Council of State, Philip II had grossly misread the situation and failed to seize the opportunity to solve the morisco problem in the only possible manner.

Ribera drew upon his recent preaching tour through the sierras south of Játiva, in which he once again emphasized that man must do his part to take advantage of divine grace, to prove his point. In one crucial passage, moreover, he thought better of something he had written, crossing out one sentence and replacing it with another: "Since leaving Valencia on May 2d, I have visited many places that are close to morisco areas, and they tell me that since [crossed out: the news about the order of expulsion reached Valencia, they are more insolent than ever, and it shows clearly in their activities.] the storms that occurred in their affairs, they are more insolent than ever and freer in their activities."[12] Ribera wrote many petitions to the king in the decades after 1582, but details such as this remind the reader that these should not be taken as transparent windows into his "true" thoughts, as opposed to his increasingly insincere efforts at instruction. Ribera crafted his correspondence with Philip II and Philip III deliberately, with great sensitivity to the exigencies of the moment. These petitions do provide us with a wealth of information relative to the evolution of Ribera's thought, but they must be read within the context of his unfolding relationship with the monarch—the one man who could issue the order that would release Ribera from his obligations to the moriscos.

Although Ribera edited out the most candid statement blaming Philip II for the current state of affairs, he took no pains to hide his opinion that expulsion remained a necessary and appropriate course of action. Ribera concluded this petition by citing a prophecy that recounted the uprising in Granada and predicted a similar revolt in Valencia, this time with the aid of the Turks.[13] In this sharply worded communication, Ribera offered no hope whatsoever for the conversion of the moriscos and planted the idea that the inevitable revolt of the Valencian moriscos would be directly attributable to Philip II's failure to act decisively when the moment presented itself in 1582. Unlike five years earlier, when Ribera had explored the possibility of leaving Valencia altogether, in this instance the archbishop took up the interests of the diocese as his own and petitioned the king for a political solution to its ongoing rift. This letter failed to sway the king, whose frame of reference extended beyond the kingdom of Valencia. The nobility, the clergy, royal councilors, and the moriscos themselves all entreated Philip II to follow courses of action ranging from leniency to expulsion. Rather than capitulating entirely to any one of these groups, Philip ordered them all to work together toward the instruction of the New Christians. More than just a Machiavellian power play, this decision reflected the king's deep-seated religiosity as well as his desire to stabilize the situation from within.

Unsatisfied therefore with the archbishop's initial response, Philip II invited Ribera to offer his opinion once again, asking him to speak more directly to the question of instruction.[14] In this second letter of 1582–83, probably written shortly after the preceding one, Ribera began to grapple with consequences of the continued presence of moriscos in his diocese. He opened this missive with a reluctant recognition of Philip's course of action earlier in 1582 but did not hesitate to repeat his point of view: "I gave Your Majesty several petitions in that year [1582], in which I spoke specifically of these matters, and although I desired and campaigned that these be acted upon, the many pressing concerns that God has allowed to be presented to Your Majesty have prevented it."[15] In the first pages of this letter Ribera reiterated the gravity of the current situation, emphasizing the danger to the state, the greed of the noble lords, and the apostasy of the moriscos. To administer the sacraments to the moriscos, Ribera argued, "scorns God's law, word, and justice, like scattering precious seeds among rocks, or giving sacred objects to dogs, or casting pearls before swine."[16] He added that baptizing morisco children did not prevent their parents from dogmatizing them in Islam immediately thereafter, and he even declared that over time the Muslims could overrun the Christians in Valencia: "They seize the best land in Spain, and within a few days they multiply in number and wealth. In their dealings with Christians they find a few they can pervert, principally by marrying our women."[17]

This statement overestimated both the quality of the land worked by the moriscos and their rate of reproduction. Apart from a few areas on the coast and around Játiva, the moriscos were relegated to dry-farming in the sierras of the interior. And while the morisco population did grow steadily after 1580 in contrast to the stagnation among Old Christians, the relatively high percentage of married moriscas (the vast majority of them wedded to moriscos) was partially offset by a higher infant mortality rate. Nonetheless, Ribera's warning foreshadowed an important argument that would later be used in defense of expulsion.[18] Alongside the possibility of a sudden morisco uprising, Ribera posited the idea of a much more insidious assault from within, centered on the most vulnerable members of Christian society.

In this petition Ribera also made a few halting efforts at proposing alternatives other than expulsion or persecution through fines. The extreme nature of some of these options and the terse manner in which he presented them suggest that he did not necessarily propose them in earnest. First, he stated that the moriscos could be declared heretics and rebels against God and king and put to death. "This option has the drawback that it would seem a novelty [*novedad*] to kill so many people, and the Turks would do the same to those of our people who live among them." By alluding to the thousands of Spanish soldiers, merchants, and captives in North Africa, the archbishop subtly reinforced the concept of the moriscos as an analogous population of Muslims resident in Spain. Next, Ribera suggested sending them to a deserted island "with soldiers and ministers of the Gospel," knowing full well that the endless war against the Dutch rebels consumed all of Philip II's available troops. Ribera similarly proposed that the moriscos be left to live under their own law in order to expose the ludicrousness of this idea. "Some learned people think that before they were compelled to be Christians they were our friends, and that those who want to be Christians could be taken out from among them and taught. Some even believe that leaving them free will lead some of them to our holy Catholic faith, which they presently hate so much because it is forced upon them."[19]

Couched among these three options, so brutal, impracticable, or lenient as to be unthinkable, Ribera suggested simply letting the moriscos go, "as was done with the Jews, though it is more necessary that the moriscos leave."[20] Conceding that the king had declined to follow this advice, Ribera begrudgingly acknowledged the middle ground in his final proposal. "In the event that none of these options appears suitable, we will have to proceed with the present plan."[21] Ultimately, this is exactly what Philip II ordered: a new effort at instruction.

In 1585 Philip II journeyed to eastern Spain to attend the Aragonese Cortes (an Estates General including Valencia, Catalonia, and Aragon) and to preside over the wedding of his daughter Catalina and the Duke of Savoy. According to Hendrik

Cock, a Flemish archer in the king's retinue, the itinerary included a stop in lands belonging to the Duke of Segorbe near Vall de Uxó, the site of a protest against the bishop of Tortosa in 1568. On that occasion, the moriscos refused to receive the bishop when he arrived and stated through messengers that "their baptism by force had been wrong, and thus they were not Christians. The privileges granted to them by Charles V had been broken, and they wanted to appeal to Philip II and, if necessary, His Holiness."[22] More than fifteen years later, the situation among the moriscos living in Vall de Uxó had not changed appreciably. As Cock reported, these moriscos "still maintain their laws and customs, with the nobles' consent. Sometimes they demonstrate their hatred of the Christians, sending signals to the Moors and their spies to join them and rob Christian towns."[23] The continued apostasy of the moriscos of Vall de Uxó evidently did little to dissuade Philip II from his policy of conversion. In January 1586, after attending the Cortes in Monzón, Philip II took up lodgings in the Hieronymite monastery of San Miguel de los Reyes, just outside the city walls of Valencia. On the following Sunday, before the royal entrance into the city, Ribera traveled out to the monastery to greet the king in person.[24] No record survives of their conversation on that occasion, but their correspondence in the following two years made their divergent positions clear.

The king's decision to convene panels of experts in Madrid and Valencia in 1587 gave Ribera the opportunity to expound upon the difficulties preventing conversion and Philip II the chance to reiterate his position. In three letters to the king Ribera offered various proposals, ranging from instruction to a harsh program of fines, while asserting that all were doomed to fail: "According to all the people who have dealt with the moriscos, they are so obstinate in their errors that no human industry would suffice to reduce them, and thus we must content ourselves with having done what we could under the rules of Christian prudence."[25] The archbishop maintained that nothing short of a radical reorganization of Valencian society could bring about the assimilation of the moriscos—a reorganization that fell well beyond his powers. He insisted that without the cooperation of the moriscos and their seigneurs, coerced or otherwise, he could never accomplish even the limited goal of eliminating morisco ceremonies. Beneath his complaints and proposals lurked the idea that the moriscos could never be truly assimilated and that Philip II had erred in choosing not to expel them in 1582. The king, consumed as he was with the revolt in the Netherlands and preparations for the Spanish armada against England, had no intention of diverting resources to the morisco question. Guided perhaps by the same belief in divine providence that characterized his attempt to overthrow Queen Elizabeth, Philip held fast to the idea that with time the moriscos would be reduced to Christianity. Rather than abandon the effort altogether, however, Ribera chose to push for the expulsion of the moriscos in a more veiled but aggressive manner.

SUBVERSION FROM WITHIN: RIBERA'S FINAL CAMPAIGN

Through the 1590s, Ribera pursued a series of initiatives designed to prove that he had used every means at his disposal to fulfill his pastoral obligation to instruct the moriscos. He believed that only an all-out effort would achieve this goal with the reputation of the Church intact, even as it failed to bring about conversion. As he wrote to Philip II in 1587, "I have always insisted that it does less damage to leave the moriscos alone than to make a half-hearted effort at their improvement. If their expectations for this reformation, and the fear it inspires in them, are not satisfied with solid, thorough execution, it will discredit the ministers and their undertaking."[26] In keeping with this objective, Ribera expanded his financial contributions to the morisco parishes, attempted to increase the pool of available priests, and distributed circulars to the clergy in morisco areas. His subsequent activities encompassed elements that appeared "assimilationist" at first blush but took on a different hue when viewed in context. Ironically, these programs enjoyed more success than previous efforts to catechize the moriscos, and the gains that were made ultimately proved problematic for the man who had engineered the entire project. For Ribera had undertaken these measures not to convert the moriscos but rather to demonstrate to the king—and more important, to his son Philip, the heir apparent—the futility of all evangelical methods. The *Catechism for the Instruction of Newly Converted Moors*, published in 1599, captured the cynical and subversive undercurrent that characterized Ribera's morisco policy of the 1590s.

In the years after 1587, the archbishop dedicated himself to the task of distributing the funds from his own contribution among the more needy morisco parishes. Ribera consistently met or exceeded his regular annual commitment, allocating monies to sixty or seventy parishes each year, probably according to the presence or absence of priests in morisco areas (table 1).[27] In addition, he expanded the scope of the separate account founded in 1578 for extraordinary payments to artisans refurbishing the parish churches, itinerant preachers, and diocesan officials. Within ten years, Ribera claimed to have overseen the construction (at low cost, and by the moriscos themselves) of nineteen churches in New Christian areas.[28] Beginning in 1581, Ribera also used this account to issue supplementary payments to priests in morisco parishes, expanding his financial support network to include many areas that had undoubtedly been unmanned in the decades before 1580 (table 2).[29]

TABLE 1

Regular Archiepiscopal Contributions
to the Morisco Parishes

Year	Regular Contribution	Year	Regular Contribution
1587	2,050 L	1600	1,994 L
1590	1,977 L	1601	2,160 L
1591	1,838 L	1602	2,351 L
1592	2,049 L	1603	2,159 L
1593	2,076 L	1604	2,070 L
1594	1,828 L	1605	2,124 L
1595	2,022 L	1606	2,146 L
1596	1,982 L	1607	2,054 L
1597	2,394 L	1608	2,050 L
1598	1,924 L	1609	1,025 L
1599	2,011 L		

Source: CCC, Libros mayores, 1587–88, 1592–1600, 1601–9; CCC, 1, 7, 8,
Resúmenes de pagas.
   Note: The *libros mayores* record the semiannual payments into the fund,
and the *resúmenes de pagas* record disbursements to morisco parishes. The
resúmenes de pagas record only one of the semiannual disbursements for 1591,
1593, 1594, and 1607; the figures for these years are estimates based on deposits
into the fund and the surviving record of disbursements.

TABLE 2

Expanded Archiepiscopal Contributions
to Morisco Parishes

Parish	Annual Contribution	Years
Albalat and Segart	30 L/37 L	1590/1594–98
Alcocer	37 L	1597–98
Alcudia de Canallo	47 L	1594–98
Callosa	20 L	1590–1600
Catamarut and Almodayna	30 L	1595–1601
Ceniza	16 L	1592, 1594
Benifairo	34 L	1588–97
Benimamet	29 L	1592–97
Benrepos and Miramoel	15 L/50 L	1582–97/1598–1601
Estivella and Beselga	30 L/50 L	1590–97/1598–1602
Guadalest (2 priests)	50 L each	1589–98
Llosa and Sarrio	40 L	1585–98
Marines and Atova	60 L	1594–96
Montanejos	100 L	1593–97
Olocau	32 L	1596–1601
Ondara	24 L	1585–98
Orba and Benidoleche	40 L	1594–1602
Potries orta de Oliva	20 L	?
Rafo	128 L	1592–99
Sirat	100 L	1581–94
Toga	20 L	1585–98
Vall de Ebo	40 L	1593–99
Zotes	26 L	1592–93

Source: CCC, Quenta aparte, fol. 1, 6–32; CCC, "Pensión apostólica," 1581–95. CCC,
1, 7, 8, Resúmenes de pagas.

TABLE 3
Loans Issued from the Separate Morisco Account

Debtor	Pension	Total	Payments and Transfer
Alcoy	300 L	6,000 L	1600–1606; "colegio de niñas"
Algemesi	150 L	3,000 L	1599–1604; "colegio del rey"
Alicante	100 L	2,000 L	1600–1604; "colegio del rey"
Almoradi de Orihuela	100 L	2,000 L	1599–1604; "colegio del rey"
Bocayrent	100 L	2,000 L	1598–1604; "colegio del rey"
Carcaxent	50 L	1,000 L	1599–1604; "colegio del rey"
Carcaxent	210 L	4,200 L	1599–1604; "colegio del rey"
Castellon de Játiva	300 L	6,000 L	1598–1604; "colegio del rey"
Cathedral of Valencia	350 L	7,000 L	1601–1606; "colegio de niñas"
Cullera	50 L	1,000 L	1599–1605; "colegio de niñas"
Gandía	623 L 17 S	12,477 L	1601–1606; "colegio de niñas"
Ontinent	200 L	4,000 L	1600–1604; "colegio del rey"
Ontinent	300 L	6,000 L	1600–1604; "colegio del rey"
Ontinent	300 L	6,000 L	1600–1604; "colegio del rey"
Orihuela ciudad	600 L	12,000 L	1599–1604; "colegio del rey"
Vilajoyosa	50 L	1,000 L	1600–1604; "colegio del rey"
Játiva	650 L	13,000 L	1600–1604; "colegio del rey"
Játiva	100 L	2,000 L	1601–1606; "colegio de niñas"

Source: CCC, Quenta aparte, fols. 65–69, 87–97; CCC, "Cargo," 1599–1606, CCC, I, R.

Because the account gathered these new parochial commitments slowly over time, its overall disbursements fell far short of Ribera's annual deposits, and the running balance of the separate account mounted precipitously. Not wishing to assume the burden of endowing the parishes by himself, Ribera chose instead to issue three sizable loans to the city of Valencia.[30] By 1596 the account held an incredible 84,780 L (libras), more than the entire annual income of the diocese of Valencia.[31] Encouraged by Philip II, Ribera paid out 90,677 L in loans between 1597 and 1602 "to cities, towns, and royal universities of the kingdom at 5 percent interest, because at that price you will find the best investments."[32] Each of the debtors completed its interest payments faithfully up until 1604–6, when Ribera transferred the revenues from these loans to the schools for morisco children (table 3).[33]

In this same period of time in the years after 1599, Ribera finally succeeded in collecting some of the monies owed by the Valencian towns and institutions that reaped the benefits of the moriscos' labor. In 1596 Philip II appointed Sebastián de Covarrubias, a cathedral canon from Cuenca who also served as royal chaplain, "to collect the first payments from those who are obliged to contribute to the endowment of the parishes of this archdiocese, as you requested."[34] The king took pains to assure Ribera that unlike the commissioners sent from Madrid before 1570, Covarrubias would not arrive in Valencia with a broad mandate to promote the instruction of the moriscos.[35] Rather, Covarrubias assembled a register of morisco parishes and announced a new tax to be assessed among those drawing their rents, making especial note of those former annexes whose rents continued to be paid to the mother church.[36] Over the next five years, Ribera's accountant collected payments from a number of nobles and institutions, including the Marquis of Guadalest, seigneur of Guadalest; the Duke of Cardona, seigneur of Benaguacil; the Count of Aranda, seigneur of Beniopa; the convent of Portaceli; the Colegio de San Sebastián in Gandía; and the parish of San Nicolás.[37] Although these collections were inconsistent, the new tax did represent, at long last, the forced participation of a broader cross section of Valencian society in the funding of the morisco parishes.

These financial records illustrate two important points with regard to Ribera's morisco policy. First, despite his misgivings concerning the likelihood of conversion, Ribera continued to fulfill and expand his financial commitment to the morisco parishes, even amid the economic crisis of the 1590s.[38] In addition, Ribera increased these funds through the interest collected on loans he made to the people and institutions of Valencia. His entrepreneurial use of the morisco accounts defies the modern stereotype of the Catholic Church as traditionally hostile to capitalism and the profit motive. Second, as a result of the new tax and the annuities, Ribera received a large amount of disposable income to fund his morisco projects. The two principal projects to benefit from these resources were the drive to find priests for the morisco parishes and the catechetical campaign of 1599.

COMBATING ABSENTEEISM IN THE MORISCO PARISHES

Following the panels convened in 1587, Ribera stepped up his continuing efforts to provide all of the morisco parishes with qualified resident priests in Valencia and its suffragan dioceses.[39] Although Ribera had more money at his disposal, he found that money alone could not redress the lack of available priests for morisco areas (especially in the parishes created in 1573–74), and so he solicited Philip II's help. On 2 February 1588, Philip wrote to his ambassador in Rome, the Count of Olivares, ordering him to ask Pope Gregory XIII for two briefs, "one allowing the archbishop and prelates to name foreigners to the New Christian parishes if there are not enough native clerics, and the other allowing them to name friars or members of the Society of Jesus, with the stipulation that despite their vows of confinement and poverty, they can live outside their monasteries and collect the salary of one hundred libras."[40] On the whole, Philip II encouraged Ribera to employ native clerics whenever possible, but despite these reservations he did instruct the superiors of the mendicant orders and the Jesuits to supply the diocese with priests.[41]

Bolstered by the king's support, Ribera employed several dozen friars in morisco areas, including Dominicans, Franciscans, Mercedarians, Trinitarians, and Alcantarines.[42] The regular clergy in morisco areas demonstrated a relatively high rate of turnover, rotating after one or two years at the most. In a few cases, a single monastery provided a series of friars to a given parish over several years, and some individual friars moved around among morisco areas.[43] Ribera played a greater role in the assignment of the secular clergy to morisco parishes, and in this case the archbishop orchestrated the similarly high rate of turnover. The period of service for secular priests ranged from a few months to twelve years, with an average tenure of only two or three years.[44] According to the chronicler Damián Fonseca, Ribera rotated the clergy among the morisco parishes by design. "This good prelate thanked the priests profusely for the work they did in instructing the moriscos, rewarding those who distinguished themselves. In order to inspire them to undertake this task with more industry, he would move them after two, three, or more years to more lucrative Old Christian parishes, relieving them, in keeping with the quality of their persons, of the burdens characteristic of the instruction of the moriscos. He provided very few priests with Old Christian churches in the first instance, obligating them to earn this by passing first through a novitiate in the morisco parishes."[45]

In order to provide the morisco parishes with secular clergy at all, Ribera found himself obliged to send the youngest and least experienced members of the church, on the understanding that if they did well they would be promoted to a more rewarding environment, in both spiritual and financial terms. One logical consequence of this decision, however, was that the priests in morisco areas tended to be either inexperienced or unworthy of promotion.

Aware of the challenges associated with ministering to moriscos, Ribera attempted to prepare the secular and regular clergy with a series of published or reissued documents over the course of the 1590s. In 1594, for example, Ribera ordered the publication of Martín Pérez de Ayala's diocesan synod of 1566, as well as the *Instructions e Ordinacions per als Novament Convertits* of Jorge de Austria and Antonio Ramírez de Haro.[46] Ribera may have published this latter document as a complement to his own synod of 1594, which, like those that had come before it, did not address the morisco question directly.[47] Given the tenor of the *Instructions*, which focused on assigning fines for various infractions, he may also have intended for these decrees to compensate for Philip II's refusal to order heavier penalties for Islamicizing.

Ribera also circulated several important documents as part of a new evangelical campaign in 1599, which he organized in consultation with Covarrubias and the bishops of Orihuela and Segorbe, among others. Following the program devised by the panel of experts in Madrid, Ribera and the other bishops prepared for the arrival of ad hoc commissioners appointed to announce a new, papally approved edict of grace.[48] To pave the way for this effort to encourage the moriscos to confess and seek absolution, Ribera circulated two pastoral letters among the clergy and preachers of his diocese, both dated 16 July 1599. In the first, Ribera ordered the priests in morisco parishes to preach to the morisco men every day at five in the morning for thirty to forty-five minutes and to the women and children at one or two in the afternoon. "Take particular notice of those persons in your diocese who command the most respect among the people of their towns: because if such people surrender and submit to obedience of the Gospel, they can bring much benefit and attract the others with their example and admonitions."[49] Apart from these few specific points, Ribera referred his priests to his synod and the other documents he had published.

In his other letter, directed to preachers in morisco areas, Ribera delved into the subject at much greater length. He opened this missive with a statement little in keeping with the perspective presented in his letters to the king: "We hold this task of conversion to be very difficult (as it really and truly is) but not impossible."[50] He directed the priests to stay in a given area for fifteen to twenty days, explaining the Gospels in plain language, "not only the words of the Gospels but also the sense and meaning of the words, in order to make them capable of believing."[51] Citing the moriscos' claim that they lacked instruction, Ribera warned his preachers to prevent "the deception the moriscos can perpetrate" by simply answering yes to everything they are asked. "It is necessary to inform them of the will of His Majesty, so that they will know that we are content not with words but with works," such as taking the sacraments and ceasing to fast during Ramadan.[52]

The archbishop complemented these recommendations on the art of preaching, reminiscent of his own sermons of the 1570s, with advice for maintaining proper relations in morisco communities. On the one hand, he directed them to keep in contact with the nobles and denied the rumor that the seigneurs wanted their vassals to remain Muslim—putting a much better face on this situation in a public letter than he was inclined to do in private correspondence. Interestingly, Ribera also found it necessary to instruct his preachers not to cause rumors by entering houses with women, adding, "I say the same with regard to joining them in any pleasure, such as a dance, a hunting expedition, or anything similar, as these activities are indecent and incompatible with the office of salt, light, and the torch."[53]

Within this generally practical and confident letter, however, Ribera inserted other statements that tended to deflate this emphasis on the real possibility of conversion. "This task is undertaken with supreme difficulty, because we must engage a people to whom we are abhorrent, because of our different descent, because of the perpetual discord between Moors and Christians, and because of the lack of friendship and charity that we demonstrate toward them: thus they have a saying, that we treat them as slaves."[54] Ribera not only portrayed the moriscos as a people separated from the Old Christians by race and culture but also situated the morisco question within the context of Christian-Muslim conflict. Ribera followed this with a passage that cast light upon the spirit in which he made the other recommendations: "In the event that our industry proves to be in vain, on account of the pertinacity and hardness of the listeners, this will lead to the general benefit of Spain: because His Majesty, as the Catholic king, will have to cleanse her of infidels, and we will find ourselves not only unburdened but enriched."[55] In concluding this letter, Ribera referred his preachers to the document that perhaps best exemplifies the ambivalent tenor and the underlying motives of the campaign of 1599: his *Catechism for the Instruction of Newly Converted Moors.*

THE CATECHISM OF 1599

In an increasingly literate age, catechisms formed an important element in the Catholic Reformation effort to bring the basic prayers and doctrines of the Church to the people. Given that the Church did not have a universal catechism, the early modern literature tended to break down along national and linguistic lines: Germans read the catechism of Peter Canisius, Italians that of Robert Bellarmine. Churchmen in the Hispanic world supplemented the available pool of general works with catechisms dedicated to a specific purpose, such as the evangelization of Basque speakers or natives in the New World.[56] The idea of publishing a new catechism directed specifically at clerics serving in morisco areas originated in the morisco councils of 1587. On 2 September of that year, the assembled councilors in Madrid "resolved that two catechisms be made for the teaching of Christian doctrine, one in Spanish and the other in Valencian." They ordered Ribera to consult "the Latin catechism begun by Martín Pérez de Ayala, former archbishop of Valencia, to see if this could be translated and brought to perfection."[57] The council decided against publishing the catechism in Arabic, just as it opposed the use of Arabic among preachers and the creation of a chair of Arabic at the University of Valencia, arguing that most moriscos at least understood Spanish or Valencian.[58]

Ribera did not immediately act upon this suggestion, and in 1595 the council of Madrid raised the issue once more.[59] On 4 November 1595, Philip II wrote to Ribera ordering him to "choose men of letters and great zeal, with experience in this ministry, who can assist you in reading the catechism [of Pérez de Ayala] and adding and deleting items at your discretion."[60] In the next year and a half, Ribera did follow up on this project, and in 1597 he submitted the catechism to the Madrid council, as the king had requested. The councilors delivered the manuscript to the inquisitor Fray Diego Granero, who reported that the catechism consisted of a dialogue in two books, one rejecting the claims of Islam, Judaism, and "the sect of the philosophers" (paganism) and the other devoted to Christian doctrine.[61] On 24 July 1597, the council and the king endorsed the inquisitor's view that "the first book should be distributed not in Spanish but rather in Latin, so that vulgar and idiotic people will not read it."[62] In his final letter to Ribera on the morisco question, dated 13 August 1597, Philip repeated the concern that a book addressing "delicate matters of theology" could cause harm if published en romance, adding, "It is clear the damage that writing books of theology in the vernacular has caused in Germany and elsewhere."[63] Thus at the end of his life, having steadfastly refused to rule over Protestant heretics in the Netherlands, Philip II remained leery of any project that could lead to heterodoxy at home.

In his response to Philip's letter, Ribera acknowledged the need to protect the Spanish reading public from dangerous ideas but defended his decision to write the Catechismo in the vernacular. First, he argued, no reader, "no matter how rude and ignorant," could be unaware of the basic claims of the Church against Jews and heathens, such as the unity of God, the nature of virtue and sin, and the divinity of Christ as the true Messiah promised in the Old Testament.[64] Ribera maintained that his own catechism would not lead to heresy on account of its form as a dialogue: "Although the speakers address these matters with questions and responses, proposing and answering doubts, all this is done in generalities, making it clear that this style was chosen to facilitate teaching and to avoid nuancing the subject." He further noted that the dialogue took place between a "maestro" and a Moorish proselyte "who is neither a philosopher nor an alfaqui but rather a simple herbalist, and thus his questions and the master's replies are appropriate to the speech of such laborers."[65]

Ribera also pointed out that among the twenty-five chapters of the first book, ostensibly devoted to refuting Islam, "the questions or doubts raised by the disciple number less than twenty. From this it is clear that the questions are designed not to provoke arguments or replies but rather to introduce and affirm Catholic doctrine."[66] Claiming that the vague ideas presented in the catechism would represent nothing new to even the most "ignorant" person, he alluded to a diffuse, popular awareness of other faiths: "These questions arise naturally. . . . There is no one who does not know a few generalities about the Jews and the Moors."[67] In his defense of the use of Spanish over Latin, Ribera did not deny that the Church had a responsibility to shelter its less educated parishioners from heretical ideas. Citing once again his own experience among the moriscos, however, he maintained that in the case of the catechism, the inquisitorial censor and the council had overestimated the subtlety of his work and underestimated the existing knowledge of Islam among the people.

Ribera developed a comparative argument in support of publishing the cate-chism in the vernacular. "The supreme councils of His Majesty are accustomed to printing doctrinal dialogues with questions much more subtle and scholastic—be-yond compare—than those contained in this catechism."[68] He cited as evidence *Symbol of the Faith* by Luis de Granada and its discussion of rabbinic prophecies and interpretations of the Old Testament, in particular—neglecting to mention that Granada had a few brushes with the Inquisition himself. Ribera also referred to the *Names of Christ* of Luis de León and *Dialogues of the Truth* of Pedro de Medina as examples of "highly subtle arguments against heretics, heathens, and Jews" written for an elite audience but in Spanish.[69] He noted with approval the placement of Bernardino Pérez de Chinchón's *Antialcorán* on the index of banned books in 1583 but pointed out that the inquisitor's objection arose from the fact that the author had not obtained a license rather than from the subject matter itself. "Their intention was not to close the door on this kind of book but to exclude those that lacked the necessary accreditation, as can be clearly seen by the licenses granted since this pro-hibition."[70] In the end, Ribera convinced the censors that the catechism could be safely published in the vernacular, and in 1599 the Valencian printer Pedro Patricio Mey printed Ribera's *Catechismo para Instruccion de los Nuevamente Convertidos de Moros*, with both halves in Spanish.

The first paragraph of the *Catechismo* reveals the elements by which Ribera un-dermined his own stated project within this work:

> *Book I. Dialogue I. In which the setting of the Catechism is established, being a rea-soned discussion between a Christian cleric, skilled in the Arabic language, and a Moor of Berbery.*
>
> *Disciple.* God save you, my father.
>
> *Master.* And also you, brother. Where are you from? You seem foreign in your man-ner of speaking.
>
> *Disciple.* I am, although I have been on the coast of Andalusia, and the kingdom of Granada, for some time, and I have done business with a safe-conduct in Málaga and Gibraltar.
>
> *Master.* You must be from abroad.
>
> *Disciple.* Yes, I am from Berbery, from a place on the cape of Tetuán, twenty leagues from the African coast.
>
> *Master.* Then why have you entered this realm?
>
> *Disciple.* Mainly the desire to be a Christian.[71]

In several pivotal respects, the premise of the catechism differed from the situation encountered by priests in morisco areas. The priest, for example, having spent more than five years in Africa, speaks both Granadan Arabic and "even Ceneti, which is more barbarous and obscure."[72] While a few Old Christians did speak the morisco language, usually as a result of commercial contact with moriscos, Ribera himself repeatedly opposed the foundation of chairs of Arabic in Spanish universities.[73] Moreover, even though Ribera believed that the moriscos went out of their way to avoid learning Romance languages, so as to impede instruction, he also opposed the enrollment of New Christians in the Colegio de Corpus Christi. In a 1587 letter to Philip II, the archbishop expressed his fear of educated moriscos "because of the great damage that would result if they connived against us. Those who have the necessary qualities, the first thing they do is forget our language entirely and flee."[74] Thus the linguistic harmony between teacher and disciple in the catechism of 1599 represented an ideal that Ribera had actively opposed in his policies.

Finally, and most important, since the questioner in this dialogue is not a morisco, he sidesteps the crucial first phase in the process of instruction. In his third letter to the king in 1587, Ribera insisted that the problem "does not lie in the teachers, nor in determining what to teach, nor what to prohibit, because all of this is well known. . . . The difficulty lies in how to get the moriscos to want to be instructed."[75] This unbaptized Moor from North Africa could be classified as a neophyte and thus raised none of the thornier issues of apostasy and obstinacy that plagued the morisco question in practice.

The catechism of 1599 echoed several key points of contention that arose between Christian and Muslim theologians in polemical works dating back to the medieval period. In the first half of the *Catechismo*, Ribera presented Islam as an illogical and carnal religion, founded upon hypocrisy and deception rather than divine revelation.[76] Within the dialogue, the master makes multiple references to the Quran, the Sunna, and other Muslim sources to depict Muhammad as a "vicious, bloody, lying, ignorant, carnal man."[77] "If you read all of Muhammad's life, you will see a pure example of a brutal man, a total beast: it is a disgrace to think that the spirit of prophecy could dwell in such an obscene and carnal body."[78] According to the master, the illiteracy of Muhammad and the inconsistency of his followers resulted in a corpus of Muslim scripture riddled with errors in logic and internal inconsistencies.[79] Among these, the master cites two passages from the Quran, one arguing that those who do not receive the law of Muhammad will suffer grave torments and the other maintaining that "all who live righteously, whether Jews, Christians, or otherwise . . . will undoubtedly be saved."[80] In sum, the catechism argued that Muhammad's sinful nature condemned his religion to carnality and error and that "if the Quran were to be translated into the vernacular [that is, Spanish], so that all could see the nonsense within it, the very leaders of this bestial doctrine would be ashamed of it."[81]

The disciple in these dialogues, for the most part, raises leading questions ("What is the ultimate purpose of man?") and appears completely satisfied with the master's responses. On a few occasions, however, he raises objections drawn from his independent knowledge of Muslim and Christian scriptures, prompting a more detailed answer from the priest. These passages, presumably the ones that provoked the unease of the inquisitorial censor, may well have been culled from the experiences of Pérez de Ayala and Ribera among the moriscos. At one point, for example, the disciple alludes to the fact that some Old Testament figures took more than one wife; the master responds with a contextual argument, maintaining that some people in ancient times lived under the "law of nature," for biological rather than carnal reasons, and with a divine dispensation no longer in effect.[82] In their discussion of *taqiyya*, or dissimulation, the disciple presents the possibility that some moriscos who are constant at heart yet feign another religion in public could be saved, because God "is satisfied by the heart alone." This inspires a long tirade by the master against this practice, based on the counterargument that man cannot be saved by walking with God in one way and with the devil in another.[83]

One final example of an exchange in which the disciple challenges the master concerned the nature of heaven. The master depicts the Islamic heaven, with its promises of blue-eyed virgins and gardens of milk and honey, as "more a paradise of beasts than of men" and insists that the pleasures of the true heaven are not of this world. The disciple poses the question, "Could it be that Muhammad expressed these spiritual pleasures in physical terms?" The master's response to this query succinctly encapsulated the subversive undercurrent that characterized both the *Catechismo* and the general effort at instruction in the 1590s. "Muhammad's carnal words do not admit mystical senses. There have been some impiously pious men [that is, well-meaning Christians] who have tried to reconcile the Gospel with the Quran, by which they have shown that they did not read Muhammad well."[84] This passage was possibly an oblique reference to the *plomos* of Granada, leaden plaques "discovered" in 1588 that purported to establish a Christian heritage for the city that predated the Muslim conquest of the eighth century. Probably the work of two assimilated moriscos, the relics and documents described an Arab convert to Christianity, suggesting a syncretic space between Christianity and Islam.

The catechism of 1599, by contrast, reflected a fundamental disdain for Islam that impeded any willingness to engage the moriscos in a truly reciprocal dialogue. Ribera's correspondence clearly established that the catechism avoided contentious exchanges by design, illustrating the divergence between his morisco policy and his reforms among Old Christians in the latter decades of his tenure. In the 1570s Ribera struggled to reach both populations, eventually recognizing that his Tridentine methods and episcopal authority alone would not suffice. By the 1590s, through his patronage of local holy figures and his construction of the Colegio de Corpus Christi, he had established important connections to the Old Christian laity of Valencia. Ribera did not, however, engage in the same process of negotiation with his New Christian parishioners. He recognized the difficulties involved with the instruction of the moriscos, including their refusal to learn and the problem of language. With the catechism of 1599, Ribera doomed his own efforts to failure by choosing not to address the spinier issues at the crux of the matter.

In June 1590 Ribera sent a report to Philip II in which he discussed his differing aspirations for the Old and New Christians of Valencia.[85] The archbishop wrote in response to a petition from the cathedral canons, who had asked Philip II to divert funds from the archdiocese to alleviate their poverty. Ribera addressed each of the chapter's demands in turn, illuminating his own priorities in the process. First, he rejected outright the proposal to draw funds directly from his main archiepiscopal revenues, pointing out that these were in jeopardy: "In the event that the moriscos of the kingdom are thrown out, or if they leave as may be expected, and held for certain, it would be impossible to sustain the archdiocese or even pay the cathedral." Ribera also objected to drawing funds from the morisco parishes, noting that "this would lead to the parishes being governed by unworthy and insufficient people, since men of letters and prudence would not want to take on such an arduous ministry if they did not receive enough sustenance to live comfortably and take care of their relatives." Finally, Ribera turned to the cathedral's third proposal, that their capitular income be supplemented from Ribera's morisco account. This idea "presents fewer obstacles, since the instruction of the moriscos has been postponed so much."

The archbishop reminded Philip II that despite his many requests, the king had still not implemented Pope Gregory XIII's brief ordering Valencia's seigneurs to contribute their share of revenues from morisco lands. Implementing this papal brief "would result in (if not any benefit for the moriscos) at least the unburdening of the Royal conscience and satisfaction for the prelates who are in charge of these people but without the powers or means to instruct them. Given that for their sins, or perhaps for ours, their instruction is not carried out, Your Majesty could take this subvention from the morisco account." Ribera had consistently favored his own household and seminary over the cathedral that resisted his reforms, however, and this apparently generous suggestion makes sense only in light of the following qualifier: to alter the purpose of the morisco fund, Philip II would have to petition the pope to override the previous brief, an unlikely event given the Holy See's consistent support of instruction. Thus rather than endorsing the canons' petition, Ribera used the opportunity to reiterate his disagreements with the king. A decade after Philip II clarified that he had no intention of expelling the moriscos, Ribera wearily argued that the king was in the same boat as other officials entrusted with the moriscos, dutifully carrying out their obligations with no hope of success and trying to limit the damage to Old Christians until the inevitable divide.

Ribera's divergent assessments of his Old Christian and morisco parishioners intersected once again in the following year, in a liturgical rather than financial matter. In 1591 he wrote to the inquisitor general Gaspar de Quiroga petitioning him "to order that on Sundays and festivals the moriscos penanced by the Holy Office not be sent to the cathedral to hear the sermon and attend Mass, because their numbers are so great and they disturb the divine offices." The archbishop offered to provide a priest at his own cost, so the moriscos could hear Mass elsewhere, at "the church of some confraternity."[86] This brief letter captures concisely the changes in Ribera's approach to the morisco question in the years since 1582. Ribera continued to fulfill his outward obligation to pursue the conversion of the moriscos, but by the 1590s he regarded them as a threat to his ongoing efforts to foster the religiosity of his Old Christian parishioners. By the same token, the subversive elements within his circular letters and his catechism cast his efforts to endow the morisco parishes in a new and unfavorable light. Taking the long view, Ribera pursued projects designed to fail, in the dim hope that the king would reconsider the possibility of expulsion and in the greater hope that the king's son and heir apparent would be drawn to see the obstinacy of the moriscos and the pointlessness of continued efforts at conversion.

CHAPTER SIX

Justifying the Expulsion

Ribera and Philip III

In the decade after the accession of Philip III (r. 1598–1621), a host of clerics and laymen renewed the debate over the morisco question. The famous *arbitrista* Martín González de Cellorigo, a lawyer in the employ of the Inquisition and the chancellery of Valladolid, criticized the prospect of expulsion as contrary to "the mercy that Your Majesty demonstrates toward all." He attributed the continued apostasy of the New Christians to the imperfect implementation of the projects drafted by Charles V.[1] Feliciano de Figueroa, Ribera's former secretary who became bishop of Segorbe, addressed "the difference of opinions that exists among prelates in this instruction" and placed himself firmly on the side of continued attempts at conversion and assimilation.[2] In 1606 the humanist Pedro de Valencia based his argument against expulsion on the inherent human dignity of the moriscos, calling for the dispersion and *permixtión* of the moriscos through intermarriage with Old Christians.[3] On the other side of the equation, the Dominican theologian Jaime Bleda (d. 1624) devoted every last ounce of his energy toward promoting the expulsion of the moriscos. Bleda had served as priest to the morisco parish of Corbera in 1585, an experience that evidently awakened him to the moriscos' "contempt and profanation" of the Eucharist.[4] Between 1591 and 1608, Bleda traveled to Rome to make the case for expulsion before three popes, and in 1604 he personally presented Philip III with the manuscript of his *Defensio Fidei*, a juridical tract arguing for the apostasy of the moriscos and the legitimacy of expulsion.[5]

In a grey area between these positions lay the morisco seigneurs, who rehashed their traditional pleas for catechism by the gentlest possible methods in the Valencian Cortes of 1604. Unlike Pedro de Valencia and other proponents of assimilation, however, the nobles' main objectives were to delay any form of outside interference and to perpetuate the de facto coexistence of their largely Muslim vassals. The policy debate among advisers and the seigneurial response reflected the spectrum of opinion concerning the nature of the moriscos and the possibilities of pluralist Spain.

Ribera contributed to the expulsion of the moriscos as an advocate, an adviser, and an apologist. In the years between 1598 and his death, he wrote many detailed letters to the Court, and in December 1608 he directed a final panel of theologians convened in Valencia as an advisory body to the king. The archbishop developed a series of arguments, economic, religious, historical, and racial, to depict the moriscos as a diaspora community of the dreaded Moors living in the heart of Spain. This vision stands in contrast to the multifaceted image of the moriscos arising from the inquisitorial records, criminal trials, and viceregal correspondence from the latter decades of Ribera's tenure. Between a morisco minority who chose assimilation and the roving bandits who preyed upon Old and New Christians alike, a solid majority of moriscos struggled to preserve their Islamic way of life despite an increasingly hostile relationship with the Inquisition.

This range of religious experience was swept aside in the collective vision of the moriscos that Ribera presented to Philip III, based as it was on the dual pillars of heresy and treason. The archbishop's position, which arose from his desire to pursue the interests of his diocese, ultimately coincided with the evolving domestic and foreign policy of the king, leading to a resolution of the disagreement that divided Ribera and Philip II. When Philip III finally ordered the expulsion of the moriscos in September 1609, Ribera offered his complete cooperation, advising the king on difficult issues such as the fate of the morisco children. In his final year and a half of life, Ribera dedicated himself to the process of justifying and celebrating the expulsion, so as to rally Old Christians beset with fears for their economic well-being. Ribera's staunch support of the expulsion of the moriscos has led to his classification as an apostle of the Counter-Reformation, using this term to connote intransigence and intolerance. Yet an examination of the context and evolution of Ribera's ideas reveals that his advocacy represented more than just a straightforward desire for a political solution to the morisco problem.

ADVOCATING THE EXPULSION: 1602–1609

In the years after 1598, Ribera and the new king entered an uncertain period in which they sounded out each other's position on the morisco question. In this area, Philip III initially continued the existing projects of his father, culminating in the

evangelical campaign of 1599.[6] The king's powerful favorite, the Duke of Lerma, derived a considerable portion of his rents from morisco lands in Denia and thus had
economic motives for maintaining the New Christian population.[7] Philip III also
moved toward a more aggressive Mediterranean policy than his father had pursued
in the period after 1580. Whereas Philip II had directed his attention primarily to the
north, allocating limited resources to the fight against Berbery corsairs, Philip III sent
new emissaries to the Ottoman Empire and launched an assault on Algiers in 1600.[8]
Although this mission failed, it nonetheless suggested a renewed interest in the
Christian-Muslim axis, with undetermined implications for morisco Spain. Relations between Ribera and Philip III remained cordial—the archbishop in fact offi-
ciated at the 1599 wedding of Philip and Margarita of Austria—but given these early
indications of the king and his favorite's position, Ribera concerned himself with the
mission to the morisco parishes.[9]

In December 1601, despite his uncertainty over the royal stance on the matter,
Ribera seized the initiative and took up the cause of expulsion once again. In an evidently unsolicited petition to Philip III, Ribera insisted upon the apostasy of the
moriscos and hinted at the sinister implications of their obstinacy. "We know from
moral evidence that all of them are moros who live in the sect of Muhammad, maintaining and observing (to the extent possible) the ceremonies of the Quran and disrespecting the holy laws of the Catholic Church: so much that properly speaking,
we should call them not moriscos but moros." As an example of this "moral evidence," Ribera cited the concerted resistance of the moriscos to the most recent edict
of grace, despite the best efforts of prelates, priests, and preachers. He further argued
that the Spanish armada of 1588 and the attack on Algiers had failed because of the
presence of heretics within Spain, and he urged Philip III to begin remedying matters at home. The archbishop even raised the specter of simultaneous attacks by the
English, the French, and the Turks, citing the English raid on Cádiz (1596) and Ottoman aid to the moriscos to illustrate that "if Your Majesty does not order a resolution in this matter, taking advantage of these inspirations, I will see in my days the
loss of Spain."[10]

In this manner Ribera conflated the menace of Protestants abroad with the threat
of moriscos within Spain, appealing to the concept of godly monarchy to call for decisive action. If this were not enough to make his point, Ribera concluded with a
somewhat liberal translation of an Old Testament passage: "Never trust your enemy. . . . Do not put him next to you, nor elevate him to a place of honor, because
he will certainly steal what is yours and take your seat of honor, and at last you will
realize the truth of my words, and torment yourself to no avail, for not having taken
my counsel" (Sirach 12:10–12).[11]

Ribera's letter produced an unusually strong reaction in Madrid. The royal confessor wrote to Ribera that "in my time here I have never seen a paper more full of spirit and edifying reasons than this one, nor one that has caused more wonder and shock in the king and the Duke," both of whom also responded personally to encourage this line of reasoning.[12] Their enthusiastic responses, however, masked an emerging division among Philip III and his principal advisers. In January 1602 the royal council split over the proposed expulsion of the Valencian moriscos, regarded as the least assimilated and most dangerous population of New Christians. The Duke of Lerma opposed the idea, whereas the king appeared to be swayed by the councilors who argued that he should complete the task his father had left unfinished in 1582.[13] It is possible that Ribera's letter received such a warm welcome from both men because each hoped to demonstrate that the archbishop gave credence to his point of view.

In 1602 Lerma convinced Philip III to hold off on expulsion, but the succeeding years demonstrated that this decision was a strategic move rather than an endorsement of assimilation. On the contrary, Ribera's pessimistic views coincided with a general shift in Philip III's priorities in the early years of his reign. Unlike his father, who devoted vast sums of money to religious wars in Flanders, England, and France, Philip III demonstrated a greater willingness to pursue foreign policy goals through diplomacy. Following the Treaty of Vervins with the French (1598), the king and his minister secured truces with the English (1604) and the Dutch (1609), not out of a simple desire for peace but rather to provide Spain with the opportunity to regroup.[14] Ultimately, the expulsion of the moriscos unfolded within the context of this reorientation of foreign policy away from wars with Christian adversaries and toward the Mediterranean axis, creating the need to assert "the anti-Islamic credentials of Philip III."[15] The king's response to Ribera in 1601 suggests that in contrast to his father, who never seriously considered expelling the moriscos, Philip III never thought to retain them indefinitely.

Encouraged by the king and his favorite Lerma, Ribera responded at the end of January 1602 with a twenty-eight-page letter detailing his vision of the moriscos and his policy recommendations. The arguments in this extensive memorandum fall into three categories, addressing the economic dimension of the morisco question, the issue of apostasy, and the violent character of the traitorous moriscos. This letter reprised ideas that Ribera had raised under Philip II, but in contrast to the 1580s, when his protests were ignored, the archbishop now had reason to hope that the king might follow his advice. This hope led him to develop his arguments more completely and to think carefully about the proper course of action. Ribera's ideas ultimately served as the theological justification for expulsion: when Philip III decided to order the removal of the Spanish moriscos in 1609, he benefited from the fact that the views of his most senior prelate dovetailed perfectly with his own desire for stability and a symbolic victory.

But Ribera's depiction of the moriscos as "pertinacious heretics and traitors to the Crown" offered a moral clarity that did not always correspond to the more multifaceted image of Christian-morisco relations that arises from the financial records, inquisitorial trials, and court cases of the era. The surviving evidence reveals that the archbishop's vision reflected a fundamental misinterpretation of both morisco religion and the role of violence in early modern Valencia. And while Ribera was largely correct that his evangelical campaign had failed to effect the expected conversions, his efforts to attribute this state of affairs to the moriscos alone neglected the activity of an Inquisition determined to profit from this apostasy and a Church reluctant to acknowledge shades of grey in the New Christians' religiosity. The disparity between Ribera's stark views and the contrasting evidence from other quarters would emerge in the debates that prefigured the final decree. Ribera sought expulsion in order to protect the Old Christians whom he by then considered to be his true flock, but opposing voices continued to insist that the moriscos belonged among the faithful.

"THE SPONGE OF ALL THE WEALTH OF SPAIN"

In his petition of 1602, Ribera attempted to counter one of the principal objections to expulsion among the nobility, who noted the potential for economic ruin on account of the loss of morisco labor. Ribera argued that moriscos, rather than enhancing the wealth of Spain, in fact represented a drain on national resources. The New Christians chose professions such as shopkeeper, peddler, muleteer, and saddler so that they could hoard money even in times of need. "The moriscos have become the sponge of all the wealth of Spain, and without a doubt there is a great quantity of gold and silver in their power." Ribera did not portray the moriscos as thrifty or industrious but contended rather that they had undercut the wages of the Old Christians. "They work for less than the Old Christians who buy or rent land, because the moriscos are so frugal and avaricious that they neither eat, nor drink, nor buy clothes." As a result, the Old Christians leave their lands and lose their houses, whereas the moriscos grow rich, as evidenced by the gifts they give their seigneurs above and beyond their high rents. "Fortunately, I have no children; why must my enemies control my land, and live in my cities?"[16]

This assessment of the moriscos, which suggested that expulsion was necessary to reverse the present trend, put Ribera at odds with the seigneurs who relied upon them. In his recommendations, however, the archbishop suggested that the wealth

of the moriscos—and of the New Christian elite, in particular—could be used to offset the losses of expulsion. He raised the possibility that Philip III could retain some
of the moriscos as slaves "to man the galleys, or to send to the mines of the Indies,
without any scruple; this would also be of no small profit."[17] Ribera thought better
of one paragraph, crossing out the statement that confiscating the considerable
wealth of the moriscos would keep this money from aiding the Turks and help the
king defeat his enemies.[18] Although the king was the principal audience for this petition, Ribera sensed that the holdings of the moriscos would give rise to competing
claims and that he and Philip III would need to convince the nobles and the Valencian people that expulsion would not bring economic disaster.

Ribera's assessment of the moriscos' role in the economy echoed an old Spanish
adage, "Where there are moros, there's gold." His views also corresponded to common stereotypes of the time, as suggested by the morisco Ricote in Don Quijote, who
returns to Spain after the expulsion and tries to enlist Sancho Panza's aid in digging
up his buried hoard. But while the record bears out Ribera's contention that the
moriscos generated wealth in Valencia, in other respects the archbishop's arguments
reflected his own particular conception of the moriscos. The tax records of the period illustrate that morisco tenants did usually yield higher rents than their Old
Christian counterparts, despite the disadvantage of working less desirable lands.[19]
The mercantile morisco elite in areas such as Segorbe and Gandía, moreover, dis-
posed of considerable resources, as is made clear by their standing in their communities and their ability to pay extraordinary subsidies and seigneurial dues. Rather
than necessarily burying their wealth in the ground, however, moriscos strove to
increase their holdings and their productivity, investing in improvements such as
irrigation systems and bridges.[20] These efforts could lead to tensions with their
seigneurs, as when a group of moriscos in Segorbe sued to establish themselves as
baptized landholders, no longer subject to the taxes on Muslims that had persisted
since the Reconquest.[21]

In many cases, however, the moriscos involved in court disputes acted on behalf
of their seigneurs. Conflicts of this nature often arose in disputed areas of noble jurisdiction, such as vineyards or uncultivated areas used for grazing livestock. A group
of moriscos from the neighboring town of Cárcer were sued by the seigneur of Al-
cántara after they chased his officials away from the irrigation channel at Benexides
with "a thousand excesses and vituperations" (strong words and threats). In their de-
nial, the moriscos stated only that the channel drew from the river Cárcer and thus
fell inside the lands of their seigneur.[22] Their economic activities could bring
moriscos into competition with Old Christians, but lawsuits over such matters did
not always break along religious lines. Ribera's contention that the moriscos threat-

ened to drive the Old Christians from the cities, moreover, was patently false: the Moorish quarters (morerías) of Valencia, Játiva, and the largest towns in the kingdom dwindled or died out entirely in the sixteenth century as moriscos emigrated to rural areas.[23]

The 1602 petition also neglected the role of the Church and the Inquisition in shaping the economy of morisco Valencia. The moriscos built churches and subsidized the Inquisition; that their seigneurs did not always remit a part of their rents for instruction spoke to a separate issue. In suggesting that morisco goods be confiscated, Ribera overlooked the fact that the Inquisition already had a version of such a program in place. In the years after 1590, the hostile relationship between the moriscos and the Inquisition took on an added dimension. In this period the Holy Office redoubled its fears of an Ottoman fifth column, claiming that more than ever the moriscos were selling their goods and sailing to Algiers, organizing the coming rebellion through mysterious letters in Arabic.[24]

The connections between the moriscos and the Maghreb were more than a paranoid fantasy: Ali Izquierdo of Algiers wrote to the Inquisition in 1590 requesting the release of his cousin's husband and promising favorable treatment of Christian captives in his possession.[25] Paradoxically, the Inquisition was at this moment beginning to expand its participation in the Mediterranean slave trade by commuting the sentences of wealthier moriscos in exchange for substitute slaves and cash payments. Moriscos had long petitioned the tribunal to excuse them from galley service on account of old age, youth, injuries, and illnesses.[26] But in 1590 Gerónimo Ferrer Faraig upped the ante by offering a slave and twenty-two hundred ducats for his release. The inquisitors hesitated: "It appears to us a grave matter, to open the door to this and to let it be known that whoever has wealth can be freed from the penalty he deserves, especially in the matter of heresy."[27] Ribera himself had raised similar concerns years earlier, when he petitioned the Inquisition "on behalf of the nobles of this kingdom" to commute a morisco's sentence so that he could ransom Christian captives in Algiers.[28] The intervention of the powerful Duke of Gandía ultimately persuaded the Inquisition to accept Faraig's offer, and in the ensuing years the tribunal collected information on the net worth of their morisco defendants as a matter of routine.

In the last decade of the sixteenth century and the early years of the seventeenth, the inquisitorial scribe periodically compiled lists of convicted moriscos and their offers, which ranged from several hundred to several thousand ducats and often included slaves. These offers provided the starting point for a process of negotiation, and the inquisitors gradually defined the terms of this procedure, mirroring the process by which friars bargained for Christian captives in North Africa. As a nod to their spiritual obligations, the tribunal accepted only non-Christian slaves, so as to avoid placing their own at risk of capture by Muslims. The inquisitors adjusted the required amount according to the severity of the crime, the morisco's ability to pay, and in some cases the partial completion of a prior sentence, in the event that the morisco had managed to survive at sea and rally his family to organize the petition.[29] In 1604, in a scene that prefigured one episode in *Don Quijote*, a group of moriscos condemned to the galleys managed to break their chains and flee to Alicante, where they were captured again. Considering the case of one escapee, the Inquisition decided to commute his galley sentence for four hundred Valencian libras because he was sixty years old and did not appear to be one of the ringleaders.[30] This practice of bargaining evolved into a brisk business, and in internal memorandums the inquisitors openly cited their need for new jail cells as a factor in their decisions to accept payments from moriscos.

As rumors began to swirl that Philip III would expel the moriscos from Spain, the Inquisition quickened its pace. Just a few months before the decree, the tribunal collected more than sixteen hundred Valencian libras from moriscos accused of running a worship center in Segorbe.[31] The increasingly blatant negotiations over galley sentences after 1590 bolstered the mutual resentment between the Inquisition and the moriscos and established that the financial aspects of this relationship overrode any concomitant spiritual dimension. Circumscribed by a concordia they did not believe in and confronted by a hostile morisco population that responded to duplicity with duplicity, the Inquisition set aside its initial reservations and chose to profit from this apostasy, for as long as the king saw fit to preserve the unhappy arrangement. Ribera's description of the moriscos as wealthy misers elided this ongoing process by which the Inquisition exploited the New Christians' value within the robust Mediterranean trade in slaves and captives.

"WIZENED TREES, FULL OF KNOTS OF HERESY"

In his correspondence with Philip III, Ribera also responded to critics who argued on theological grounds that no bishop could legitimately condemn baptized members of his own congregation to certain perdition among the Muslims of North Africa. In contrast to proponents of assimilation, Ribera contended that the moriscos had in fact been instructed through "gentle means" (*medios suaves*), to no avail. His arguments on this score elaborated upon his earlier ideas concerning the unwillingness of the moriscos to participate in their own catechesis, as in this 1587 letter to Philip II: "[The moriscos] say they have not been instructed, and it is true that according to all the doctors of the Church, one must know that his opinion is contrary to the faith in order to be a heretic. But it is also true that one must have a prompt desire to obey the Church in order not to be a heretic."[32] In his letter of December 1601, Ribera stated that the moriscos claimed to be good Christians and requested instruction, all the while impeding the process by refusing to cooperate with their rectors and preachers. He similarly doubted the motives of six moriscas who approached him requesting instruction: "Experience has shown that they say they want to be Christians because of a dispute with their fathers or husbands, or for some other worldly reason, with no real intention to convert."[33]

Ribera expanded upon this theme of deception in his letter of January 1602, arguing that even moriscos who observed Catholic rituals through years of confinement forgot everything they had learned upon their release, such was their "perverse resolution to be moros."[34] Evoking the language of the Bible, he characterized the moriscos not as new plants but as "wizened trees, full of knots of heresy." This assertion followed up on his opening statement: "The remedy called for by great evils, both spiritual and physical, is to pull them up by the roots, so they will not cause damage nor send out new shoots that quickly grow into trees."[35] Those who disagreed with him, Ribera added, had never dealt with the moriscos or "had allowed themselves to be persuaded by the opinion of serious (but poorly informed) people, who thought to achieve grace with the moriscos."[36] He derided the idea that the moriscos could be compared to seedlings, as in the parable of the sower, and employed the language of horticulture rather to equate their obdurate heresy with weeds, unwisely allowed to take root and spread over time.

The ecclesiastical and inquisitorial records from Valencia support Ribera's contention that the moriscos persisted in their Islamic fasts, weddings, and other ceremonies, although not necessarily for the reasons he cited. The broad majority of moriscos attempted to weather the storm in the final decades of the morisco century, negotiating with priests, inquisitors, and seigneurs to maintain their traditional religious practices. In 1608 a morisco tailor and convert described a series of mosques in northern Valencia, where alfaquis organized ceremonies, instructed moriscos (and a few renegade Christians) in Islam, and offered legal judgments.[37] In Segorbe, the women hired to clean the home of a local widow corroborated the tailor's depiction of the gatherings held in this improvised mosque: "Many male and female worship leaders from around Valencia gathered at meetings in Segorbe, where certain alfaquis in brocade capes of silk and gold, with a staff in their hands like a bishop, read from the Quran." The community hired six men to guard the building from Christians during holy days and Friday ceremonies, when worshippers gathered to hear the sermon and pray on woven mats of black and white, "painted with five fingers to represent the five commandments of Muhammad."[38] The suggestion that

morisca "alfaquinas" participated in these meetings conformed to the pattern of religious education throughout morisco Valencia, in which both men and women
could preserve Islamic documents and pass on their knowledge of rituals.[39] Although men retained exclusive control of certain rituals such as circumcision, many
women took advantage of the fact that morisco practices usually took place in the
home, teaching prayers and even officiating in ceremonies such as ablutions.[40]

By contrast to the 1570s, when he believed in instruction but lacked the priests to
carry it out, after the 1590s Ribera had many more rectors on the ground but doubted
that they would make a difference. The records of the Inquisition suggest that despite Ribera's cynicism, the presence of priests in morisco areas could bring subtle
changes to morisco religiosity—even without a truly honest dialogue between the
New Christians and the novices and foreigners who typically manned these parishes.
Many moriscos simply resented clerical incursions into their communities on all levels: Jaime Cornejo, upon hearing a sermon about the miracle of the loaves and the
fishes, said that "this was all a lie, and that the preacher was drunk and did not know
what he was talking about."[41] In other cases, however, moriscos refer to regular confession with their priest, the kind of sustained contact that the parochial system had
been designed to provide. The morisca Joana Corza claimed that her sister had
taught her rites such as fasting during Ramadan, a practice she maintained until her
sister died, at which point she began to live as a Christian again. She confessed to
her priest regularly thereafter but did not refer to these ceremonies, in part because
(as she ultimately conceded) she had continued to observe some of them.[42]

Even moriscos with a demonstrated knowledge of Christianity felt the need to
tread carefully. Francisca Sebastián of Teruel, a morisca whose Old Christian grandmother had taught her Catholic prayers, testified that although she took communion and confessed each Easter, she had continued to participate in Islamic customs
such as contributing weekly to "a fund for the expenses of the community [al-
jama]."[43] Moriscos often claimed that they had lived as moros until a confession or
sermon inspired them to live as Christians, but their reluctance to admit to any het-
erodox belief or vestigial Islamic practice for fear of persecution limited their ongoing religious education.[44] Many moriscos described their religious life in terms of
actions rather than unchanging, essential beliefs, reflecting a desire to minimize
their crimes before the Inquisition. But this language also raises the possibility that
taking on the trappings of church attendance and confession in response to people
who influenced their lives could lead to a more deep-seated conversion. Whereas
Ribera interpreted the New Christian's rote confession simply as an act of deception,
these cases imply that moriscos could characterize their syncretic practices as "Christian" or "moro" depending on their audience.

The existential idea that a morisco could "live as a Christian" did not coincide with Ribera's conception of the process of conversion, and he eventually grew to distrust those moriscos who claimed to occupy a grey area between Catholic and Muslim. The archbishop's doubts notwithstanding, a significant minority of Valencian moriscos chose to assimilate into Christian society through intermarriage, participation in Catholic ritual, and commercial and social ties with Old Christians. The capital city had once been a haven for assimilated moriscos such as Ferrando de Gali, whose arrest for bearing arms in 1563 led a host of Old Christians, including Gali's wife, to attest to his participation in Christian rituals and society.[45] In the early 1570s, a more optimistic young archbishop elevated the former Moorish quarter from annex to full-fledged parish, christened after St. Michael.[46] By 1590 the parish had been repopulated by Old Christians, with the exception of three houses of assimilated moriscos, who squabbled with the city over the traditional rents of the morería.[47]

But the capital still hosted two schools for the indoctrination of morisco girls and boys. Ribera continued to fund these schools even as he doubted their effectiveness: "These two colleges have been of no use; rather, those who have come from the school for boys are much worse than the other moriscos."[48] Others took a less dim view of the institutions. In 1582 the rector of the royal college for male moriscos claimed that its graduates included preachers in morisco areas, friars in local religious houses, and four or five students who went on to doctorates at the university and benefices in the cathedral. In 1594 the viceroy reported to Philip II that the morisco Juan Nadal, "who was raised in the royal college, always showing the signs of a good and virtuous Christian, is taking courses of theology to great advantage."[49] Limited resources prevented the colleges from taking on more than a handful of students, but the experiences of these graduates defied Ribera's characterization of the moriscos as uniformly resistant to instruction.[50]

Mounting evidence from outside the capital speaks to the presence of assimilated moriscos around the kingdom. Jeroni Castellano, a morisco from Cárcer, served as the local seigneur's bailiff in the 1590s, taking responsibility for public order and upholding the law.[51] In this capacity, he denounced his fellow New Christians for extramarital affairs and turned over a group of men (including his own brother) to the Inquisition because they had been circumcised in the morisco manner. Castellano then vanished into the night, evidently murdered because the moriscos resented seeing "a New Christian who dealt with Old Christians on such familiar terms."[52]

Castellano's decision to improve his standing in society through assimilation and service to Old Christians drew the anger of those who chose a different path, but recent research on the moriscos of Valencia concludes that he was far from alone in making this choice. In Alcalá de Xivert, a northern coast town in the diocese of

Segorbe, the moriscos as a group insisted that "they are not like the other new converts of this kingdom," a contention supported by their adoption of Christian dress, ceramics, and language as well as their intermarriage with Old Christians.[53] The tenants of the Cistercian monastery of Valldigna, near Gandía, retained their language and some morisco customs but came to resemble their Old Christian neighbors in many other ways. Under Ribera's evangelical campaign, their practice of Islam dwindled, and Old Christians and New evolved toward similar eating habits, farming techniques, and views on honor and justice.[54] In areas such as these, a common material culture and shared social practices emerged from prolonged contact between moriscos and Old Christians. Paradoxically, Ribera's own programs hastened the process that challenged his own assessment of the moriscos as jaded heretics.

"OUR GREATEST ENEMIES, BEYOND COMPARE"

Ribera's petition of 1602 buttressed his arguments for the apostasy of the moriscos with a discussion of their violent nature and potential for rebellion. The rampant feuds and crime in early modern Valencia led one traveler to wonder whether the climate provoked brigands to spring from the ground.[55] Addressing this perennial concern, Ribera ascribed the blame for Valencia's lawlessness to the moriscos: "Every day they grow more daring, more haughty, and more shameless in declaring themselves moros. And notwithstanding the great diligence and solicitude of the viceroy in this kingdom, every day there are crimes and murders, and the Old Christians who live near morisco areas do not dare to leave their towns at night."[56] Like other commentators of the era, the archbishop also drew the connection between highway banditry and collusion with the Ottoman Turks; the violence within Spain's borders, he argued, only prefigured the actions the moriscos would take during the anticipated invasion.[57]

During his long tenure in Valencia, Ribera had witnessed firsthand the public spectacle of criminal justice on many occasions in the main plaza, where defendants were flogged or hanged, with their bodies left on the gallows for several days as an example to all. From 1602 to 1604, the archbishop served as viceroy of Valencia as well, earning a reputation for his harsh stance on crime.[58] Cases involving New Christians often fueled the popular perception of the moriscos as allies of foreign Muslims. In 1587, for example, the bailiff of Bernia heard a rumor that the famous morisco bandit and fugitive from justice Joan Arbi had returned from Algiers to visit his brother in Senija (south of Denia). Given Arbi's reputation for violence, the bailiff feared that he would foment a conspiracy among the Valencian moriscos. The two agents sent to capture Arbi found him gambling in the town; after approaching casually, they tackled him and cried out, "Aid to the king!"[59] On the face of it, such an example seems to confirm Ribera's view of the moriscos: conspirators from abroad traveled among the New Christians to stir up rebellion, and only the activity of vigilant Old Christians had (thus far) prevented an uprising. Viewed in more detail, however, these cases demonstrate that violence did not always break evenly along confessional lines: the moriscos of Senija assisted in the arrest of Arbi.

In the first place, to characterize all morisco violence as treason against the Catholic monarchy underestimated the importance of the Old Christian seigneurs.[60] Rather than emerging spontaneously as tempers flared, attacks in the countryside could form part of a more deliberate strategy by which nobles sought to extend their domain and moriscos to augment their profits.[61] A morisco farmer working for the master of Montesa came upon two moriscos grazing their sheep in his fields near Montroy, a town inland of Gandía, leading him to threaten the sheep with his staff. When the ensuing argument escalated into a fight, one of the shepherds fired his shotgun at the farmer, fatally wounding him and setting off a legal dispute among their seigneurs.[62] In Sans, a pair of moriscos murdered the Old Christian guardian of the local monastery's water supply after he caught them stealing from it; the abbot later protested that the Sans judge let the moriscos off with a fine because he himself had ordered the theft to irrigate his rice fields.[63] These cases represented not acts of religious violence between Christians and Muslims but rather an extension of a broader phenomenon. Old Christian seigneurs vied for supremacy through their tenants, in courtrooms, in pastures, and on highways, and these conflicts could lead to bloodshed.

Furthermore, the loyalty among clans of wealthy morisco families and their servants led to periodic attacks on account of feuds, a facet of Muslim society that dated to the Berber and Arab settlement of the region. In the sixteenth century, illustrious moriscos still traced their lineage to the period of Muslim rule, and within their agnatic clans, family ties and loyalty bound the rich and the poor. Although disputes arose over economic matters, the culture of honor among moriscos was not limited to the elite.[64] The rice farmer Abrahim Turra of Benisano, a small town near Benaguacil, bore such "rancor and ill will" toward a local morisco that when Turra came upon his adversary on a road, perhaps by design, he shot him in the gut with an arquebus and then stabbed him to death where he fell.[65] In 1593 alcohol provided the opportunity for an old feud to flare into violence, as a drunken night of revelry turned bloody. Stumbling out of a tavern in Beniflá (near Gandía), a morisco took his revenge on Joseph Llopo, who had spent the evening insulting him. Llopo initially "laughed" when asked if he was wounded, but the tiny puncture in his throat soon proved fatal.[66] The morisco culture of honor—which had its counterpart among Old Christians—often led to violence in cases such as these, but clashes between rival clans did not conform to Ribera's depiction of rebellious morisco aggressors and Old Christian victims.

Even cases involving marauding morisco bandits, viewed in detail, defy the conception of a brewing war between two distinct nations. Some of the criminals denounced as "bandits" in their trials were little more than delinquents from nearby towns who attempted to compensate for their lack of legitimate income through illegal means. In 1590 a group of Old Christian shepherds near the Aragonese border encountered a "tall, polite, brown-skinned man with a black beard" who asked about buying livestock but did not purchase any. Days later he returned with four armed men and attacked the shepherds, shouting, "Death to the dogs!" and binding them. The assailants kept the shepherds under guard as they slaughtered and roasted three sheep in the morisco manner, leaving the severed heads in open defiance of the official prohibition against this practice.[67] As news of the attack spread, witnesses identified the criminals as a group of local moriscos known for drinking, gaming, and strumming the guitar.[68]

Roving bandits from farther afield constituted a legitimate menace to Old Christians and moriscos alike. In some instances these bandits received support from local communities, through family ties or through coercion, but the incursions of brigands also bred resentment among other moriscos, leading to divisions and possible collaboration with the Old Christian bailiffs. The most infamous bandit of the age, Miquel Abiaix, set off an extended manhunt after his band murdered two Old Christian tinkerers on the road to Otonel in western Valencia. The viceroy's men never found Abiaix, but they did prosecute dozens of moriscos in Chiva for healing him, providing him with food and clean clothes, and "publicly cursing those who are called to arms against Abiaix."[69] The moriscos of Catadau refused to help officials search for the notorious bandit Vicent Negret in 1605, fearing retribution from his allies in town.[70] In 1608, by contrast, a local morisco official from Petrer who stumbled upon a group of well-known bandits enjoying a night of wine and song turned them in, perhaps in the hope of restitution or a reward.[71] In all of these cases, the aggrieved witnesses who testified against the criminals included moriscos who resented the violence perpetrated in their communities and looked to Old Christian officials for justice.

In the apt words of a recent social history, "The growing climate of mistrust in Spain provided a licence for official and unofficial violence against the *Moriscos* and ushered in new forms of social negotiations, uneven and one-sided as they were, between the Christian majority and a persecuted religious minority."[72] In many cases, morisco violence against Old Christians in Valencia arose from frustration with their second-class status and the increasing prohibitions on their way of life. These attacks could take on religious and racial overtones, as with the bandits who cursed the Old Christian shepherds as "dogs" and ritually slaughtered their sheep. In other instances, however, acts of violence did not follow the divide between these two nations so closely. Moriscos acting on behalf of shadowy patrons conducted their struggles over vineyards and pastures through violent means. Perceived slights and standing grudges among morisco clans led to battles in town squares and royal highways: as in the Mudejar period, "violence begot violence because social norms demanded that vengeance be exacted if honor was to be maintained."[73] Petty thieves and dreaded bandits preyed upon Old Christians and moriscos alike, sparking conflicts among those who abetted them and those who collaborated with the Valencian officials to bring them to justice.[74] Alarmist reports of morisco uprisings such as Ribera's sparked fear among Old Christians, masking a culture of violence that joined all Valencians.

Ribera's practical recommendations to Philip III followed from his evaluation of the moriscos' essential nature. In historical terms, Ribera extricated the morisco question from the context of the conversion of the infidel and repositioned it within the legend of the Reconquest. Citing the precedent of the expulsion of the Jews, he noted that Ferdinand and Isabella took this step in 1492 "primarily because of the money the Jews earned and kept" rather than on account of any military threat.[75] In this respect, the evidence against the moriscos far outweighed the complaint of the Catholic kings against the Jews: "The Jews were not heretics, nor did they have kings of their sect who could come to their rescue, nor were they naturally bellicose, nor our enemies."[76] By associating the moriscos with Muslims past and present, Ribera reinforced their distinctiveness as a separate *raza* (race). Borrowing from the language of theology, Ribera argued that the various morisco communities of Spain differed only in their "accidents," or outward appearances. Rather than viewing the moriscos of Castile as assimilated, Ribera argued that their use of the Spanish language and mode of dress would allow them to "blend in with our armies and serve as spies for our enemies" in the event of war.[77]

Thus in his definition of race, cultural attributes such as diet and customs served as indicators of racial identity but could be deceptive as well. Beneath the appearance and practices of the moriscos lay a shared nature, passed from parent to child despite all attempts to break this cycle of living memory through instruction.[78] Ribera did not detect a similarly radical separation between Catholics and Protestants: though he commended the prosecution of French Huguenots in Valencia and opposed Philip III's treaty with the English in 1604, he nonetheless expressed hope that

Protestant Europe could be returned to the fold.[79] Unlike Pedro de Valencia, however, who argued for the shared humanity of the moriscos, Ribera saw them as a corrupting force, a threat to the Christian community.

Ribera used these historical and racial arguments to support his advocacy of expulsion. Anticipating the objection that heretics must be formally condemned in court, he countered that the apostasy of the moriscos—the fact that they had been exposed to the Word and had consciously rejected it—more than justified expulsion and confiscation of goods without recourse to a trial. "Nor can it be argued that it is unjust to condemn the moriscos without hearing them, because their notoriety and the legal evidence make up for this defect and would make up for it even if the punishment were execution."[80] The racial unity of all moriscos, in Ribera's view, underpinned their collective guilt as heretics and traitors. Ribera characterized expulsion as Philip III's divine calling, comparable to "the liberation of His people for Moses . . . and the victory over the Philistines for David."[81]

Alongside this Biblical reference to the unfolding of God's will, the archbishop also established a continuity with the Reconquest, calling expulsion a deed worthy of a great king, "of the same esteem as would be to conquer and win Spain anew."[82] Fearing that Philip III might expel the moriscos of Valencia and retain the rest, in January 1602 Ribera urged the king to begin the process in Castile. This petition did not arise from any vacillation on Ribera's part with respect to expulsion: as he underlined in the memorandum, "the only remedy is to expel the moriscos from Spain, and there is no hope of success through any other option."[83] On the contrary, Ribera wanted to avoid a scenario in which Philip III began with the less assimilated moriscos of Valencia and then relented, allowing the New Christians of Castile to remain. Such a series of events, in addition to contradicting Ribera's vision of the expulsion as a new Reconquest, would also bring economic hardship and danger to his adopted home without removing the possibility that moriscos could subsequently immigrate from other parts of Spain. The archbishop's insistence on total expulsion arose from his dedication to the interests of his flock, defined as the Old Christians of Valencia.

ADVISING THE KING: RIBERA AND THE EXPULSION
OF THE MORISCOS

Unlike his father, Philip III eventually did act upon Ribera's advice in the matter of the moriscos, although a few years passed before the opportune moment arose. In 1608, when the king ordered a committee of theologians in Valencia to discuss the morisco question, Ribera interpreted this act as a prelude to expulsion.[84] Whereas the archbishop directed the committee's deliberations toward a theological defense of expulsion, the Franciscan friar Antonio Sobrino raised a problematic discussion of the ethical obligations of prelates. Most of the committee members, in keeping with Ribera, agreed that to baptize morisco children and return them to their parents "would be to commit sacrilege" in light of their continued obstinacy.[85] By the same token, the committee argued against compelling the moriscos to receive the sacraments, stating that "those who would compel them commit a mortal sin."[86] Finally, the committee decided that because the heresy of the moriscos was based on hatred of Christianity rather than "a poor understanding of sacred scripture," it would be better not to let them voice their doubts, "because it is indecent to place our holy religion in dispute with such obstinate and stupid people."[87] These statements illustrated Ribera's belief that no amount of instruction would suffice to convert these heretics, whose apostasy more than justified their exclusion from the fold.

The committee departed from Ribera's goals when Sobrino, a friar who defied Ribera's characterization of his opponents as pious but misguided, zeroed in on the historical and theological weaknesses of Ribera's defense of expulsion.[88] On the subject of apostasy, Sobrino insisted that the moriscos had never been formally condemned as heretics, nor were they treated as such in Valencian society. The appearance of heresy among the moriscos, "no matter how great, cannot prove their notoriety, at least not in matters of canon and civil law."[89] Following this logic, Sobrino insisted that the Church had a responsibility to administer the sacraments to the moriscos and to educate them through an open and sincere dialogue. In order that the participation of the moriscos "not be superficial, feigned, and compelled, as it has been before now, but rather from the very heart, they must know that they can safely communicate all the doubts and sorrows of their conscience with the ministers sent for their instruction."[90]

Sobrino's ideas drew upon those of Pope Paul V, whose brief of 1606 called for the improvement of the morisco churches and schools and reasserted the parallels between the moriscos and neophytes abroad: "If preachers of the Evangel can achieve so much in foreign realms, despite the opposition of infidel kings, can we not hope for more within the doors of our own house, with the favor of our own king?"[91] Like Paul V, Sobrino evoked the example of the disciples, who worked in vain all through the night, only to catch so many fish in the morning that they could not pull in the nets. To Ribera's dismay, even the members of the committee who disagreed with Sobrino concerning the apostasy of the moriscos chose to side with the friar in his opposition to expulsion.

Ribera may have lost the battle, but he won the war. By the time the committee submitted its recommendations in March 1609, the king had long since decided on the matter. In January 1608, the members of the Council of State—including several who had opposed expulsion just months before—determined to expel the moriscos from Spain.[92] In all probability, the influence of the Duke of Lerma constituted the decisive factor behind this change of opinion. The perceived apostasy of the moriscos figured in discussions at the highest levels of government, and the expulsion gave Philip III's apologists an opportunity to offset any questions about his commitment to orthodoxy raised by the simultaneous Twelve Years' Truce with the "heretical" Dutch.[93] The arguments of Ribera assisted Lerma and Philip III in addressing the theological difficulties associated with expelling thousands of baptized Christians, especially since Pope Paul V never bestowed his blessing upon the enterprise.[94] But ultimately, from the royal perspective, the expulsion of the moriscos represented one aspect of a larger political effort to secure stability at home, made possible by the peace treaties in Western Europe.[95] Lerma may have been reacting to the discovery of a conspiracy between the moriscos and the French; the more likely possibility is that for pragmatic reasons, he concluded that the benefits of religious and cultural unity outweighed the economic consequences of expulsion.[96] Following the political treatises of Giovanni Botero and Justus Lipsius, Philip III and Lerma removed a population that had refused to conform to their vision of loyal, civilized subjects.[97]

The Council of State also decided to expel the moriscos from Spain by region, beginning with Valencia. Because most of Valencia's moriscos lived either in isolated settlements or near the coast, the king took steps to forestall the possibility of an uprising in the sierra or in conjunction with North African Muslims. On 4 August 1609, Philip III sent Agustín Mejía, the newly selected *maestre de campo general* with experience in the war in Flanders, to Valencia under the pretense that he had been sent to examine the realm's fortifications.[98] Mejía informed Ribera and the viceroy Caracena of the imminent order of expulsion, to their approval. Ever since his appointment in 1606, Caracena had responded to the conflicted situation by focusing on morisco bandits, and he once sent his own secret commissioner on a tour of the realm to catalogue morisco weapons and arrest offenders.[99] The archbishop, for his part, reiterated his objection to the decision to begin with Valencia; as in 1602, however, he never wavered in his support of expulsion in itself.

Ribera's objection represented neither an eleventh-hour crisis of conscience, in which he agonized over whether he could bring himself to sacrifice his pastoral obligations to the moriscos in the name of political expediency, nor a simple act of economic self-interest.[100] On the contrary, anticipating possible litigation or even bloodshed, he petitioned the king to ascertain the viability of the measure and work out the logistics in another region before proceeding to Valencia. As he had earlier, Ribera also feared that Philip III would subject Valencia to the rigors of expulsion and then fail to implement the decree in Castile, where the partially assimilated moriscos presented less of a numerical threat.[101] In a letter to Lerma, Ribera reaffirmed his loyalty to his diocese: "What is done in Valencia will be of no importance, if the same is not carried out in all of Spain."[102]

Undeterred, Philip III carried out his plan to commence the expulsion in Valencia. On 22 September 1609, Caracena published the royal decree that "all the moriscos be removed from this kingdom and sent to Berbery."[103] In this order Philip III made explicit reference to "the efforts that have been made to instruct the moriscos in our holy faith and the little gain that has been achieved."[104] Citing the moriscos' obstinacy and their "wicked intention" to bring "harm and confusion to our realms," the king simultaneously established the importance of Ribera's ideas to his own logic and exonerated the archbishop of responsibility for the moriscos' apostasy.[105] The decree ordered the moriscos to remain in their villages until summoned by a royal agent, at which point they would be given three days to collect whatever movable goods they could carry and proceed to one of five points of embarkation along the Mediterranean coast. As a concession to the nobility, Philip III ordered that all of the moriscos' fixed goods revert to their lords and prescribed the death penalty for any New Christian attempting to remove or destroy such property. The decree also stipulated lesser punishments for Old Christians who either "dared to maltreat the moriscos" or harbored moriscos within their homes.[106] After the symbolic announcement of this decree in the city of Valencia, the royal commissioners began to direct morisco communities to the designated ports.

The expulsion of the moriscos, though not entirely bloodless, did not fulfill some of the more alarmist predictions of open warfare that circulated in Valencia and at Court.[107] Mejía and Caracena commanded an international force of four thousand seasoned veterans in addition to the Valencian militia.[108] These troops directed the moriscos to fifty galleys stationed at Valencia, Vinaròs, Alicante, Denia, and Moncofa. In a few areas, such as the Sierra de Laguar and Muela de Cortes, bands of moriscos took up defensive positions high in the sierra and had to be broken and removed by brute force. The vast majority of the moriscos, however, left the peninsula peaceably. Between September 1609 and January 1610, royal officials recorded the departure of more than one hundred eleven thousand Valencian moriscos, and by 1614, three hundred thousand moriscos had been expelled from all of Spain.[109] The responses of the moriscos to expulsion mirrored their responses to the conflicted situation before 1609: the majority, now resigned to the end of their time in Spain, was bookended by those few who took up arms against the Christians and those few who attempted to prove their assimilation into Valencian society.

The moriscos who claimed to be genuine converts to Christianity presented Ribera with a genuine challenge. In the decree of September 1609, Philip III accounted for this possibility in two clauses, exempting "those moriscos who have lived among Christians for two years, without attending the gatherings of the aljamas," and "those who receive the Holy Sacrament with the permission of their local parish priests." Ribera, for his part, consistently denied that this exception applied to the moriscos of Valencia. On the eve of expulsion, the archbishop wrote in a desultory manner, "Those moriscos who are known to live among Christians or receive the Holy Sacrament by order of their priest need not be exiled. In this archdiocese not one man falls under this category, nor any woman other than those kept in this city; and the bishops of Tortosa, Segorbe, and Orihuela said the same was true of their bishoprics."[110] Following this reasoning, Ribera continued to exhort the Duke of Lerma and the Council of State to strive for total expulsion, citing the many drawbacks that would result from "leaving any trace of the moriscos in this realm."[111]

In several cases, Ribera's cynicism with respect to the sincerity of the moriscos' alleged conversions to Christianity may have been well merited. In January 1610 the Valencian Inquisition reported that a dozen moriscos had appeared before them to make "spontaneous confessions" attesting to their Christian faith; the thousand elderly moriscos who "wanted to die in the holy faith" may have wanted to avoid the rigors of the journey even more.[112] Along the same lines, in May 1610 Ribera objected to a proposal by Caracena "that seven hundred moriscos be retained to teach the Old Christians to cultivate the crops of the realm," such as sugar, rice, silk, and olives.[113] Despite Caracena's added claim that these moriscos "were all very good Christians," Philip III sided with Ribera, reprimanding the viceroy for retaining so many moriscos and ordering their expulsion.[114]

In other cases, contrary to Ribera's views, the moriscos seeking exemptions most likely emerged from the existing group of converts in the archdiocese. In June 1610, the viceroy Caracena reported the retention of eighty or one hundred "good and Catholic Christians, who remain with the permission of their prelates."[115] On 25 August 1610, the bishop Andrés Balaguer of Orihuela noted the presence in his diocese of forty-seven "moriscos who have a license from their bishop to remain, having made demonstrations of their Christianity before the expulsion," as well as a dozen children and widows of Old Christian men.[116] An outpouring of recent research has demonstrated that the "assimilating morisco" lived on in various communities throughout the peninsula, particularly in Castile.[117] In August 1610, Philip III solicited Ribera's opinion concerning the remaining moriscos in Valencia, prompting a sardonic response in which Ribera clarified that he had not approved these exceptions. In addition, the archbishop faulted the Marquis and Marquise of Caracena for their credulity and their failure to carry out the king's orders: "The viceroy and his wife are great Christians, and the viceroy deserves the position that Your Majesty has given him. They have concluded that it is Christian piety to dissimulate and to admit opinions of poorly informed, financially implicated people who want to appease them. In this way the viceroy and his wife have complicated a process [expulsion] that was simple at the beginning."[118] Thus Ribera impugned the motives of those who advocated the retention of the moriscos, suggesting that they acted on behalf of the Valencian nobility.

Reviving some of his previous arguments, the archbishop also pointed out the potential dangers of allowing adult moriscos to remain. "Among those who were distributed among Old Christians, some have fled to join the moriscos in the sierra," rebels who had hidden themselves in rugged terrain.[119] These fugitives contributed to "the deaths of many Old Christians, the impossibility of settling outlying areas, robberies, sacrileges in the churches, and many other evils." Ribera urged the king to expel all the moriscos, "because if this step is not taken Your Majesty will spend much with little gain, and every day the morisco population will grow larger and the dangers greater."[120]

Ribera brought this same philosophy to the discussion of the fate of morisco children, a debate that began before the expulsion. Ribera's theological justification of expulsion did not hold for those who had not yet reached the age of reason and thus could not be accused of having consciously rejected Christianity. For this reason, on 27 August 1609, Ribera assured the king that he could retain those children under the age of ten or eleven, "even if their parents ask for them: because the parents are apostates, they should be separated from the children so that these will not fall into the same errors."[121] Ribera advised Philip III to order the distribution of the children among "Old Christians, officials, and citizens, obliging the children to serve them until the age of twenty-five or thirty years in exchange for food and clothing."[122] Both the Council of State and Antonio Sobrino endorsed the idea of dispersion, and in a follow-up letter Ribera suggested that the rents of the morisco schools in Valencia could be dedicated to the support of the children left behind.[123]

As the preparations for expulsion progressed, however, the logistical problems of retaining such a large segment of the morisco population prompted Ribera to alter his views.[124] In this same period of time, Jaime Bleda and the reassembled panel of Valencian theologians dropped the age of children to be exempted from ten years to four and argued that the king should retain only as many children as could be taken in by Old Christians.[125] Ribera ultimately adopted this view: "At first blush, the piety of keeping the children among us led me to choose this as the surest path. But after reconsidering, and losing many hours of sleep, it seems to me that what may appear

to be piety for the moriscos is cruelty for our own people, to whom we have a pri-
mary obligation."[126] In the debates leading up to the expulsion, the falling age of the
children to be kept behind served as an indicator of the political pressures bearing
down upon the officials involved in the process, out of fear that excepting too many
children might tempt the Valencian nobility to rebuild their labor force as it had existed before.[127] Philip III adopted the committee's advice, and in the decree of expulsion he ordered the retention of morisco "boys and girls under the age of four,"
with the consent of their parents.[128]

In the year following the decree of September 1609, Ribera took an increasingly
severe stance with regard to the fate of the morisco children. On the one hand, the
schools for morisco boys and girls retained a number of children who had already
been separated from their parents. In addition, many noble families flaunted the decree and retained morisco children without the parents' consent; these "kidnap-
pings" accounted for many of the three thousand children who remained in Valencia in 1610.[129] In his last year of life, Ribera dedicated himself to ensuring that these
children did not perpetuate the morisco population for another generation. In February 1610, the archbishop petitioned the king to place all the children from the
morisco schools in private homes so that they could learn a trade—allowing Ribera
to divert the colleges' rents to his prized foundation, the Colegio de Corpus
Christi.[130] When Philip III rejected this plan and ordered Ribera to maintain the
schools, the archbishop responded by asking the king to stipulate specific age limits
for the children in the colleges and the circumstances under which they could
leave.[131] In the summer of 1610, citing the morisco practice of "substituting people,
and baptizing the same child three or four times, so the others would remain unbaptized," Ribera ordered his clergy to rebaptize all morisco children to prevent this
uncertainty from surviving the morisco era.[132] As this correspondence demonstrates,
Ribera had virtually no faith in the morisco schools, even after the expulsion of the
parents, and rather sought to rid himself of the financial burden of the children—to
the benefit of his legacy as a reformer among the Old Christians of the diocese.

Despite the approval of Philip III, the Valencian nobility effectively prevented
both the dispersion and the rebaptism of the morisco children.[133] Thus on 9 November 1610, two months before his death at the age of seventy-nine, Ribera tried yet
another tack. Acknowledging that keeping the children in Valencia would avoid "the
nightmare of sending them to Castile," he suggested that Philip III could "order that
they be sold into slavery at moderate prices."[134] Such a practice would benefit the
masters financially and the children both spiritually and materially: "To ensure that
the children are not burned by the Inquisition, the masters will take steps to guarantee that they know and observe our holy faith. And to ensure that the children are

not hanged, the masters will correct them, whip them, and shackle them, to punish them, as well as love them and teach them useful skills."[135] Such extreme measures were necessary, in Ribera's view, because "if these children remain free, within a few years many of them will be highway robbers and prostitutes."[136]

Finally, this plan would also profit the realm as a whole "because in this way the men and women will not marry, and the propagation of this evil breed in these realms will cease."[137] In this letter, his final written word on the subject, Ribera encapsulated his vision of the moriscos as a race apart, embodying a heresy passed down through the generations: "Morally speaking, all the hope that can be had, that these children will forget the sect of Muhammad, consists in them being separated one from another, and in there being no one to remind them that their parents are Moors. Thus it would do great damage if those older than the age I have specified were to remain."[138] Even faced with the bare remnants of the morisco population—three thousand young children, converts, and elderly moriscos too feeble to relocate—Ribera issued virtually none of the pardons that authorized some moriscos to remain in other regions of Spain. He had long since abandoned any conception of the moriscos as truly diverse or assimilable, and he clung to his vision of their collective heresy despite evidence to the contrary.

RIBERA AS APOLOGIST

The expulsion decree in 1609 effectively ended the debate that preceded its publication, as evangelists such as Sobrino largely fell silent. Former moriscos both lamented the loss of Al-Andalus and criticized the Christian "sultan" who had exiled them: in *The Supporter of Religion against the Infidels*, the Muslim writer Al-Hajari (d. after 1640) recounted "the oppression and injustice of the Christians" in Spain and noted that "during their exodus, it befell to many of the Andalusian Muslims [moriscos] that the Christians robbed them at sea."[139]

Spanish artists and writers did not question the will of the king in such a direct manner, but they did use the ambiguity of their media to capture the tragedy of the expulsion. The second installment of Miguel de Cervantes' *Don Quijote* (1615) featured the noble morisco Ricote, "more Christian than Moor," who demonstrated his loyalty to Philip III by complying with the decree even though his Old Christian townsmen implored him to stay. A series of paintings commissioned by Philip III to celebrate the expulsion included images of rebel moriscos throwing themselves off the cliffs of Muela de Cortes as the Christian forces advanced, illustrating the well-ordered strength of the Spanish military and the potential for treason among the moriscos. Also depicted are tearful farewells between moriscas and their noble mistresses, and moriscos and Old Christians teaching one another dances on the beach, underlining the bonds that could unite Old Christians and New. A painting of the port of Valencia included an image of a departing morisco father on his knees, speaking his final words to his daughter, now dressed as a Christian in anticipation of her future life under her new guardians.[140]

Defenders of the expulsion in Spain, who did not need to tread so carefully, made a public and seamless transition from advocates to apologists. On 27 September 1609, five days after the promulgation of the *bandos de expulsión*, Ribera delivered a famous sermon in the cathedral of Valencia city. Taking as his text the bitter words of Paul in Galatians 5:12, which he rendered as "Expel those who perturb you," Ribera revisited the major themes of his defense of expulsion.[141] He argued that a succession of kings, from James I to Ferdinand, Charles V, and Philip II, had all desired the expulsion of the moriscos, but that the hope of conversion and the various demands upon the state had prevented them from following through. In the same vein, Ribera praised Philip III for his "piety and gentleness," which led him to attempt all possible means of converting the moriscos through instruction. Only when the obstinacy of the moriscos thwarted these efforts, he continued, did Philip III demonstrate his great prudence and zeal in expelling the moriscos, thereby accomplishing a feat that had eluded his illustrious predecessors: "Does it not seem that this is the greatest event we have seen in our time or read about in past ages?"[142] In this panegyric for expulsion, Ribera also sought to alleviate the Valencians' fears for their economic security. The archbishop simultaneously praised the virtues of forbearance and patience in the face of hardship and attempted to argue that the economic losses would not be excessive.[143] This lengthy sermon represented Ribera's transition from advocate to apologist, as he attempted to rally the people of Valencia behind a measure destined to alter the fundamental structures of Valencian society.

This sermon has justifiably been characterized as propaganda for the expulsion at a time when the king and his officials most needed the support of the Valencian people. Within weeks of its delivery, Ribera printed and distributed a hundred "anonymous" copies of the sermon.[144] Not surprisingly, Ribera's words—and his enthusiasm for expulsion in general—were well received in Madrid. In December 1609, the Duke of Lerma praised Ribera's sermon in a lengthy autograph addendum to a letter about the progress of the expulsion: "Such a sermon you preached in your church! The king and queen were impressed with your doctrine and great prudence. You understood how necessary it was to speak to the realm about the expulsion, helping the enterprise in terms designed for our edification, and for the general public. As you did not back down from the task, anyone who reads the sermon will take up the cause."[145] In the year after the expulsion decree, Philip III also wrote Ribera repeatedly to praise the archbishop and to commend him for his collaboration: "I understand you have excommunicated people who had moriscos hidden and refused to show them; I thank you for your zeal in this matter."[146]

Given this level of cooperation between the miter and the Crown, it might be tempting to conclude that Philip III, Lerma, and Ribera all advocated expulsion for the same reasons. As I have argued, however, from the royal perspective the decision to expel the moriscos emerged in the years before the fact, from shifting priorities in their foreign and domestic policy. In Ribera's case, the expulsion represented both the culmination and the vindication of his evolving morisco policy, developed over forty-two years in the diocese. Abandoning his initial optimism with regard to the true conversion of the moriscos forced Ribera to abandon the providential context in which he had viewed the morisco question.

The history of the conversion of the infidel recounted the unfolding will of God and thus could not encompass a history of obstinacy in the presence of the Word. In shifting to the political context of the Reconquest and recasting the moriscos as Moors rather than neophytes, Ribera also directed his focus from the universal to the particular. By 1609, the lines of Ribera's world were much more sharply drawn, and the reforming possibilities of the Valencian Church much more locally based. Ribera used the pulpit as a platform to celebrate the exile of a people who had long threatened to disrupt the Christian community he had dedicated his life to creating in Valencia. Although he no longer believed that individual moriscos could escape the cycle of living memory by which Islam was perpetuated, he joyfully expressed his hope that the Old Christians would be able to do so. Ribera called upon all of Valencia, beginning with himself and the nobility, to confess and cleanse themselves of their dealings with their former neighbors, with whom they had shared the land for nine centuries. "Forget, I implore you, the language of these wicked people, if there is anyone who knows it."[147]

The Ideal Bishop and the End of Spanish Islam

On 6 January 1611, Juan de Ribera passed away within the walls of his principal contribution to the city of Valencia, the Colegio de Corpus Christi. The drive to procure his beatification and canonization began at this moment, precisely when Ribera turned his legacy over to his followers. The success or failure of the many campaigns for the canonization of early modern Spaniards depended upon the influence and efficiency of the supporters who took up the cause as much as upon the actions of the putative saint in life. Ribera himself, for example, had assisted in the massive effort to collect information concerning the life and miracles of the Jesuit founder, Ignatius of Loyola.[1] Along the same lines, Ribera's supporters at the Colegio de Corpus Christi mounted a campaign to gather testimony to his life, with an eye toward the two miracles necessary for beatification. The new rector of the Colegio sent out a series of surveys to be administered to the people by the priests of the diocese, including questions such as, "Do they know that God bestowed great gifts upon his servant [Ribera] from an early age, preparing him with many blessings, skills, and natural and supernatural graces, and protecting him from the traps with which the enemy tried to impede him from the services which he was to give to God?"[2] The leading nature of the survey questions prefigured the manner in which this information would be used by Ribera's apologists, to create an image of the archbishop worthy of sainthood.

One of the most important elements in the process of canonization in early modern Spain, along with local devotions, consisted of the hagiographical vida. This written life, codified and widely available, served as the linchpin of many successful campaigns for canonization. Almost immediately after his death, Ribera's confessor and confidant of forty years, the Jesuit Francisco Escrivá (d. 1617), began assembling a biography of the archbishop.[3] This rapid turnaround, along with the absence of any debate on the issue, strongly suggests that Ribera had chosen Escrivá to render his life in prose. Already in January 1611, Escrivá wrote to Diego Clavero in Madrid, seeking assistance in soliciting the necessary licenses from General Claudius Acquaviva.[4] The following year, Escrivá circulated his growing manuscript to readers including Jerónimo Vilanova, the rector of the Jesuit College of San Pablo, and Bartolomé Pérez, the regional administrator (*provincial*) of the Jesuits in Spain. A few of his critics raised concerns, but all of these focused on the form of the work rather than any question surrounding its orthodoxy. Pérez, for example, argued that Escrivá should eliminate some of the lengthy examples of morals, such as humility and temperance, in favor of a more detailed chronological narrative of events. Clavero, upon hearing of this criticism, wrote to Escrivá encouraging him to stick to his guns: "Rewrite some of the moral exempla, but not so much that the history becomes naked. In all honesty I like the morals, and even if Father Bartolomé Pérez and the other learned ones do not need them, most of us are not so learned."[5] In Clavero's mind, the facts of Ribera's life interested the elite few, whereas his timeless virtues should be an example to everyone.

In this biography, published in 1612, Escrivá sought to address the two potential impediments to Ribera's beatification: the fact that he never held a provincial council, as mandated by the Council of Trent, and his role in the expulsion of the moriscos. On the one hand, Escrivá provided countless examples of the many other ways in which the archbishop had implemented the decrees of Trent, such as his charitable donations, his tireless preaching, and his seven diocesan synods. He celebrated Ribera's foundation of the Colegio de Corpus Christi in particular, calling it "second only to the Escorial in grandeur, richness, and beauty."[6] He further noted, perhaps in response to those who accused the archbishop of profligacy, that Ribera had selected the chaplains, musicians, and other attendants from among the poor. The archbishop built the ornate chapel with its paintings and sepulchers "such that the Eucharist might be venerated, honored, and exalted as much as possible by the faithful, in an age when the Host was so disrespected, humbled, and outraged by heretics."[7] In Escrivá's formulation, the Colegio stood as a testament to Ribera's activities as a reforming bishop and a symbol of his redemption of the kingdom after the blasphemies of the moriscos.

In the latter half of the work, Escrivá addressed the ongoing controversy over the expulsion of the moriscos. Philip III had not secured papal support before the expulsion, and Ribera's supporters feared that Pope Paul V would impede the beatification of the archbishop over this issue.[8] In his hagiography, Escrivá drew from the tradition of the lives of the saints to depict Ribera as an ideal Tridentine bishop confronted with an insurmountable challenge in the form of the moriscos. Reverting to the first person, Escrivá related a scene in which he and Ribera went out among the moriscos to preach for more than a month, carefully explaining the rudiments of Christian doctrine. "This would have had no more of an effect on the moriscos if they had been stones."[9] He also reprinted several of Ribera's writings in defense of expulsion, including a memorandum of 1602 and the sermon of 27 August 1609. In this way, Escrivá attempted to answer the criticisms of the pope and others who had maintained their faith in the possibility of converting the moriscos. The vida of Escrivá depicted the expulsion not as the bitter culmination of a failed campaign of instruction but rather as the triumphant victory of Ribera and Christendom over the heretical Moors.[10]

Escrivá's apologetic vision exerted a profound influence upon subsequent biographies of Ribera, all of which coincided with the key dates in the process of beatification and canonization. In 1798 Juan Ximénez published his *Vida del Beato Juan de Ribera*, a biography written to promote and celebrate the archbishop's beatification by Pius VI in 1796. In 1901 the conservative scholar Pascual Boronat y Barrachina published his monumental *Los Moriscos Españoles y Su Expulsión*, followed by *El Beato Juan de Ribera y el Colegio de Corpus Christi* (1904), both attempts to vindicate the racial and spiritual views of Ribera in light of Boronat's nineteenth-century vision of Spanish history as a march toward political and religious unity. In 1960, the year of Ribera's canonization by Pope John XXIII, Ramón Robres provided the culmination of this apologetic tradition in his *San Juan de Ribera*, a biography encompassing the advantages and drawbacks of the genre to a remarkable degree. In this well-researched work, Robres collated sources from Valencia, Spain, and abroad to create a unified vision of Ribera from cradle to grave, as a student, reformer, adviser, and theologian. Robres's tendency to identify closely with his subject allowed him to illustrate the important ways in which Ribera and his seminary remained cogent to the people of Valencia under the dictatorship of General Francisco Franco (d. 1975).

In the final analysis, however, their enthusiasm to convey Ribera's eternal virtues led his apologists to rob him of perhaps his most interesting attribute—his dynamism. As I have argued, in the pasquinades of 1570–71 Ribera quickly encountered the limits of his de facto powers as archbishop. In Valencia he discovered a people whose fierce loyalties to their region led them to regard his background and his office with suspicion. Confronted with this resistance, Ribera realized that he would not be able to legislate unilaterally the implementation of the decrees of the Council of Trent. After this rough landing, therefore, Ribera sought to find ways to tap into

the existing, rich veins of religiosity among the Valencian people in order to introduce his vision of reform to the spiritual landscape.

This open philosophy could entail risks, as when he lent his support to the
prophetess and charismatic Catalina Muñoz, ultimately discredited in the eyes of
the people. But female visionaries could also form an important part of his efforts:
in Sor Margarita Agullona he found a figure who mediated between the institutional
Church and the laity of Valencia in ways he could not. Rather than regarding her
personal, interior form of religion as a threat, the archbishop endorsed her spiritual
exercises and protected her through his authority. During Agullona's life and after
her death, Ribera attempted to draw the following she had created to his principal
foundation, the Colegio de Corpus Christi. By contracting local artists to depict the
patron saints of Valencia, by commissioning portraits of Agullona and other Valencian holy figures, and by procuring relics of St. Vincent Ferrer and countless others,
Ribera sought to create a symbolic capital with multiple ties to the local community.

Ribera's ability to promote the adoration of the Host—the centerpiece of his Tridentine program of reform—depended upon his ability to create a relevant context
for his Eucharistic liturgies and sermons. Only by embracing the devotional impulses of the Valencian people was he able to infuse the concept of the body of
Christ, as symbolized in the Colegio of that name, into their multifaceted religiosity. Ribera's Castilian education and his wealth initially distanced him from his diocese, but over his lifetime he took advantage of both to foster common interests with
his flock, through investment in inclusive programs of spiritual growth. In 1568 the
very office of archbishop of Valencia defined him as a foreigner, but he used this position as a platform to redetermine the role of the higher clergy in the Catholic Reformation.

For a constellation of reasons, Ribera did not engage in a similarly fruitful reci-
procity with the New Christian members of his congregation. Separated from the
moriscos by even greater geographical and cultural divides, Ribera did not risk op-
erating within the same intermediate spaces that enabled him to establish points of
contact with the Old Christian laity in the capital. In the first ten years of his episcopate, Ribera invested an unprecedented amount of time and resources into creating a spiritual and economic climate in which he could use the tools at his disposal
to bring the moriscos into the fold. Frustrated by resistance from moriscos and Old
Christian landowners who strove to maintain the medieval status quo, Ribera ultimately determined that the moriscos could form no part of a Christian community.
Abandoning his hopes of conversion, the archbishop embraced the option of expelling them from Spain as inveterate Moors.

These experiences of the 1570s exerted a profound influence upon Ribera's subsequent morisco policy. Once Philip II established that he had no immediate plans to expel the moriscos, Ribera set about proving their apostasy to the king. This strategy both allowed him to fulfill his ostensible pastoral duties and gave him the opportunity to demonstrate that all possible avenues toward conversion had been exhausted. Ribera's willingness to commit his time and resources to this effort, however, was not matched by a willingness to endanger the reputation of the Church by engaging in a truly reciprocal dialogue with the moriscos. In the years after 1587, Ribera took steps designed to ensure that these programs would not lead to the debasing of the Word through open debate, and in the process he forestalled the creation of syncretic spaces in which assimilation could begin. As a result of his fundamental distrust of Islam, Ribera refrained from reaching too far into the culture of the moriscos: "Arabic is of no use in the instruction of Christian faith, and even causes the moriscos to perpetuate their errors, because it gives them new pride in their sect."[11] His fear of ceding sacral status to the Arabic language, and thereby validating morisco culture, underscored the antagonistic character of his later morisco policy.

This sharply drawn vision of the moriscos focused on reports of religious violence and bandits with ties to the Maghreb, disregarding the equally compelling evidence for the continued loyalty of most moriscos and the conversion of a significant few. Between renegade bands of criminals and an assimilated minority, the solid majority of moriscos persisted in their quest to practice their way of life in Spain. Their predicament prefigured the challenges faced by Muslim societies in the modern era of Western expansion, forced to choose among accommodation, survival, and resistance. Wary of priests and inquisitors and resentful of converts, most moriscos adopted practices such as regular confession when necessary but continued the beliefs of their ancestors in private. Fearful of brigands and rival clans, they settled old scores and called upon Old Christian judges when it suited their purposes. The greater part of the moriscos, abetted by their seigneurs, wished to live under their own law and refused to accept that political loyalty must be joined by conformity in religion.

In Ribera's eyes, however, these actions constituted heresy and treason, crimes he extrapolated to the morisco population as a whole. The archbishop's essentialist arguments for the collective guilt of the moriscos offered moral clarity in an age of unresolved ambiguity, and this line of reasoning appealed to Philip III. Ribera's designs came to fruition under Philip III, when he rededicated himself to advocating expulsion despite the consequent economic losses to both the realm and the archdiocese. Having come to see the moriscos as a diaspora of Moors rather than neophytes, Ribera celebrated the literal diaspora of 1609–14 as the removal of a potentially corrupting force from the Christian community.

Both facets of Ribera's tenure as archbishop of Valencia illustrate the localizing aspect of the process of reform in the early modern period. Ribera arrived in Valencia with a vision of reform based upon the prescriptive legislation of the Council of Trent, intended as a universally applicable program for the renewal of the Catholic Church. Over the course of his episcopate, Ribera succeeded—or failed—to implement this vision of reform according to his ability to integrate these ideas within the broad range of devotional practices that characterized the Valencian people. Ribera took an active role in promoting the cult of the Eucharist, the veneration of Agullona and Ferrer, and the expulsion of the moriscos, but these were not changes that he dictated from above; in all of these cases he adapted his goals and views to the situation as he encountered it.

His initial proposal for a new foundation in the city outlined a Tridentine seminary, but the Colegio de Corpus Christi ultimately evolved into a much broader institution embodying the ties that joined the archbishop to his people. For this reason his experiences mitigate against any sharp division between official and popular religion or any conception of early modern history in which the bishop plays a purely antagonistic role with regard to the changes in lay religiosity in this period. As Ribera strove to bring reform to Valencia, his efforts led him to identify closely with the interests of the Old Christians in his diocese, at the expense of his previous, universal visions of reform and conversion. In advocating the expulsion of the moriscos, Ribera did not set aside his spiritual obligations in the name of political expediency; on the contrary, this policy emerged from his desire to promote the welfare of his Old Christian congregation, whom he now identified as his one and only flock.

Two events from shortly after his death hint at Ribera's legacy in Valencia. In 1612 the passing of Father Francisco Simó, a visionary and recipient of miracles, prompted an unexpected display of veneration among the Valencian people. Concerned by doubts over Simó's miracles and excesses among his followers, the new archbishop Isidoro Aliaga waged a campaign to suppress this cult, collaborating with the Inquisition to remove all images of the priest from public view.[12] The contemplative aspect of Simó's thought, in particular, led Aliaga to cut off any attempts to pursue the priest's beatification. This controversy might never have erupted had Ribera lived a few years longer. Undeterred by Simó's visions and impressed by his vows of poverty and chastity, Ribera had once granted the priest a license to hear confessions.[13] Given Ribera's desire to co-opt popular devotions and channel them to his own purposes, it is not difficult to imagine Ribalta's painting of the visions of Father

Simó hanging in a chapel dedicated to the local priest in the Colegio de Corpus Christi.

In 1614, as these events unfolded, an ailing couple in the city of Valencia hired the doctor Miguel Martínez. They turned Martínez in to the Inquisition after he claimed that the true Mass was the zalá; under questioning, the morisco confessed that he had slipped back into Spain during the expulsion, when his ship returned to Játiva on account of poor weather. Martínez further admitted to practicing Islamic ritual, although he said he did so out of sight of his children: "He did not teach them the sect of Muhammad so that they would not fall into danger." He testified that although "he had confessed and taken communion many times, he did not have total belief in the faith of Jesus Christ" and did not know which law was the true one. For this cognitive dissonance, this claim to occupy a space between Christians and moriscos, the Inquisition sent Martínez to the countryside to be cured of his insanity.[14] A more discreet doctor, however, may well have persisted in Valencia to the end of his days.

Viewed from other perspectives, the expulsion of 1609–14 did not constitute the end of Spanish Islam. For a number of aristocratic Muslim families in Al-Andalus, the end had come with the Reconquest of the medieval period; many Granadans who fled the peninsula for the Maghreb dated the end to 1492 or to 1570. The Muslims who worship at the mosque near the present-day University of Valencia, across the dry riverbed from the historic city center, represent a rebirth of Islam in a democratic nation with freedom of religion. But their experiences echo the challenges faced by Muslims across the centuries, and in this broad context the age of Ribera does mark a watershed. The expulsion manifested not only the failure of assimilation but also the failure of coexistence. Ribera's vision of the moriscos as heretics and traitors hastened the end of a nine-hundred-year period in which Christians and Muslims, through warfare, commerce, and negotiation, had found a means of sharing the common ground in Spain.

Notes

ABBREVIATIONS

AA	Archivo del Ayuntamiento
AGS	Archivo General de Simancas
AHN	Archivo Histórico Nacional
ARV	Archivo del Reino de Valencia
BGUV	Biblioteca General de la Universidad de Valencia
BL	British Library
BN	Biblioteca Nacional
CCC	Colegio de Corpus Christi, Archivo del Patriarca
HCL	Henry Charles Lea Collection
IVDJ	Instituto de Valencia de Don Juan
RAH	Real Academia de la Historia

PREFACE

Unless otherwise indicated, all translations are the author's.

1. Council of State, 25 Feb. 1610, AGS, Estado, leg. 228.

2. In his discussion of the crisis that erupted in the Netherlands in the 1560s, Ranke argues that "the protestant movement excited but little sympathy in the Walloon provinces" because "their new bishops, almost all of them men of great practical ability, had been quietly installed. The bishop of Arras was François de Richardot, who had fully imbibed the principle of catholic restoration in the council of Trent, and who was the subject of unceasing panegyric, for the striking combination of solidity and force in his preaching, with exquisite refinement and polish, and for the zeal tempered with knowledge of the world displayed in his life"; Ranke, *History of the Popes*, 189.

3. The death of Francisco Franco in 1975 and the emergence of the *Annales* school hastened the transition among native Spanish historians away from apologetic works and narrowly antiquarian studies, toward applying new historical and anthropological methods to Spanish Catholicism. Economic studies inspired by the *Annales* school include Hermann, *L'eglise d'Espagne*, and Domínguez Ortiz, *Las clases privilegiadas*.

4. Evennett, *Spirit of the Counter-Reformation*, 43. Evennett depicts the "new Spain" of

1450–1550 as very open to northern, Italian, Jewish, and Islamic thought. From this milieu, Loyola created a philosophy that was humanistic if not entirely humanist, modernizing yet orthodox, prescriptive yet flexible.

5. Bossy plays down the distinction between popular and elite religion, basing his conclusion about changes in society at large on changes in church theology, sacraments, charitable works, and architecture. Although Bossy does not focus on Spain, his thought has been influential among Hispanists; Bossy, *Christianity in the West*.

6. Christian, *Local Religion in Sixteenth-Century Spain*, 20.

7. "The Catholic Reformation affirmed the local side of religion and merely tried to correct what it saw as its excesses. The history of Catholicism in practice, both before and after the sixteenth century, is a constant process of new agents and devotions creating a commonality across boundaries of place and nation, and a constant adaptation and cooptation of the general agents and devotions for local purposes"; ibid., 179.

8. In the same vein as Christian, Henry Kamen assesses the dialogue between parishioner and confessor primarily from the point of view of the people. He differs from Christian, however, in arguing that the Counter-Reformation did bring fundamental changes to the religion and the lives of the laity. Rather than seeing Spanish Catholicism as a "perennial event," Kamen argues that the early modern period witnessed a "substantial reshaping of the dimensions of faith"; Kamen, preface to *Phoenix and the Flame*, xi–xiii. Jody Bilinkoff and Sara Nalle focus on the impact of reform upon the Discalced Carmelites and the Cuencan laity, respectively. In the peripheral diocese of Ourense, Allyson Poska finds less evidence of change in lay religiosity; Bilinkoff, *Avila of St. Teresa*; Nalle, *God in La Mancha*; Poska, *Regulating the People*.

9. The best guides to the historiography of the moriscos are Bunes Ibarra, *Los moriscos*; Candau Chacón, *Los moriscos*; and Rafael Benítez's introduction to Lea, *Moriscos of Spain*.

10. Cited in Candau Chacón, *Los moriscos*, 111–12. Mármol Carvajal, a veteran of the Granadan rebellion, compared Philip II's victory over the moriscos to the Reconquest of Granada in 1492: "O what a happy hour for you, worthy city of Granada, when the Catholic Kings Ferdinand and Isabella freed you from subjection to the devil!"; Mármol Carvajal, *Historia del rebelión*, 365.

11. Cited in Candau Chacón, *Los moriscos*, 111. Hurtado de Mendoza criticized the aggressive royal order of 1566 depriving the moriscos of their language, "and with it commerce and communication among them," and their baths, which "had served for both cleanliness and entertainment"; Hurtado de Mendoza, *Guerra de Granada*, 108. This passage is translated in Smith, *Christians and Moors*, 2:165.

12. Miller, "Muslim Minorities."

13. Bleda, *Defensio fidei*. See also Peset and Hernández, "De la justa expulsión." On the paintings of the expulsion, see Villalmanzo Cameno, *La expulsión de los moriscos*. On the morisco Ricote, see Márquez Villanueva, *Personajes y temas del Quijote*; and Márquez Villanueva, *El problema morisco*. Cardaillac, *Moriscos y cristianos*, presents a guide to the *aljamiado* literature of the moriscos.

14. The *arbitrista* Pedro Fernández de Navarrete, writing less than twenty years after the fact, drew a connection between the change in Spain's fortunes and the loss of population re-

sulting from the expulsions of the Jews in 1492 and the moriscos in 1609; Fernández de Navarrete, *Conservación de Monarquías* (1626), cited in Candau Chacón, *Los moriscos*, 51.

15. Florencio Janer decried the "religious intolerance of the Spanish in those times" and blamed the failure of assimilation, in part, on the lack of a coherent morisco policy among Old Christian officials; Janer, *Condición social*, 120. Marcelino Menéndez y Pelayo, by contrast, in his effort to justify the expulsion of the moriscos, criticized Charles V and Philip II for their failure to recognize the inevitability of this measure and carry it out; Menéndez y Pelayo, *Historia*, 4:330–35.

16. Writing of morisco conspiracies to overthrow the Spanish, Boronat stated that "if it were possible to deny their insubmission . . . I would be the first to sing a hymn in praise of this community of martyrs. . . . But critical history shows us that the infidelity of the moriscos toward the Christian religion, and the monarchy established in its name, was a logical consequence of the circumstances their race encountered in Spain"; Boronat y Barrachina, *Los moriscos*, 1:255–56.

17. "If, as Menéndez y Pelayo asserts, the expulsion was but the inevitable outcome of an historical law, that law can only be that retribution follows wrong"; Lea, *Moriscos of Spain*, 397. Like other Anglo-American historians of his time, Lea contrasts the authoritarianism, dogmatism, and intolerance of Spain to the democracy and religious freedom of Protestant nations such as his own. The varied fortunes of the United States and Latin America in the modern era provide further evidence for his criticisms of early modern Spain, the source of backwardness among Hispanic countries. See also Kagan, "Prescott's Paradigm"; and Kagan, *Spain in America*.

18. Braudel, *Mediterranean and the Mediterranean World*, 559.

19. Halperin Donghi, *Un conflicto nacional*.

20. Mercedes García-Arenal has written and edited many works of this nature, including *Islamic Conversions*.

21. See Benítez, *Heroicas decisiones*, and Pérez Boyero, *Moriscos y cristianos*, to cite but two examples. Several recent English-language works have studied the relatively assimilated moriscos of Castile, including Perry, "Moriscas and the Limits of Assimilation," and Tueller, *Good and Faithful Christians*.

22. Recent studies examining this process in other contexts include Harline and Put, *Bishop's Tale*; Patrouch, *Negotiated Settlement*; Carleton, *Bishops and Reform*; and Coleman, *Creating Christian Granada*.

PROLOGUE. THE FORMATION OF A TRIDENTINE BISHOP

1. Ribera's direct forefathers included a maestre de Santiago and the first *almirante mayor* of Castile. The Ribera clan, Galician in origin, featured the first four men to hold the title *adelantado mayor* of Andalusia.

2. González Moreno, *Don Fadrique Enríquez de Ribera*, 7, 10, 17.

3. Ribera, *El viage de la Tierra Santa*, Advertencia al lector.

4. Ibid., 34.

5. González Moreno, *Don Fadrique Enríquez de Ribera*, 57–60.

6. Ribera was supporting Catalina financially by 1568 at the latest, and in 1591 he allocated 59 L, 3 s, 9 (59 libras, 3 sueldos, 9 dineros) "por 21000 maravedís los 12000 a mi señora doña Catalina de Ribera y los 9000 maravedís a mi señora María Enríquez [abadesa] en Santa Yñez que se les da cada un año y son del año 1591"; 3 Dec. 1591, CCC, Libro mayor, 1592–1600, fol. 37.

7. Robres Lluch, *San Juan de Ribera*, 15, 21.

8. Pilar Valero, "Impresión de libros"; Andrés Martín, "Pensamiento teológico." The nine volumes of Ribera's lecture notes survive in the Colegio (CCC, Biblioteca del Fundador).

9. Kagan, *Students and Society*, 185.

10. Robres Lluch, *San Juan de Ribera*, 25–27.

11. Ribera underwent his oral examination before Melchor Cano, Domingo de Soto, and Pedro de Sotomayor; Robres Lluch, *San Juan de Ribera*, 41–42. In the early 1560s, Ribera remained at Salamanca as an instructor in theology, as witnessed by the portrait of him still hanging on the evangel side of the university chapel.

12. Philip II vigorously defended his *patronato real* against all rival claimants, including the papacy; Fernández Terricabras, *Felipe II*, 173, 225.

13. Rawlings, *Church, State and Society*, 53. In 1561 Philip appointed his confessor, Bernardo de Fresneda, to the diocese of Cuenca, reflecting both the king's commitment to reform and the tendency among the episcopate to hold multiple offices; Nalle, *God in La Mancha*, 38.

14. Council of Trent, sess. 22, 17 Sept. 1562, chap. 3, in Tanner, *Decrees*, 2:734.

15. On the residence debate, see Vizuete Mendoza, *La iglesia*, 167–71; and Fernández Terricabras, *Felipe II*, 75–77. Bartolomé Carranza set a precedent for the Spanish position in 1547 by criticizing those bishops who would hire "mercenaries" to tend their sheep; Carranza de Miranda, *Controversia*, 42.

16. Forster, *Counter-Reformation in the Villages*, 42–43.

17. "Parecer del Obispo de Badajoz sobre lo que debia hacerse en cierto concilio Provl. de Santiago de Compostela," 1565, CCC, I, 7, 6, 1.

18. "Limosnas por el obispo de Badajoz a varios párrocos, 1564," CCC, I, 7, 6, 2.

19. Robres Lluch, *San Juan de Ribera*, 98.

20. Marginal note, Badajoz, 25 Dec. 1563, in Ribera, *Sermones*, 1:15.

21. "Alumbróles la claridad de Dios, porque la que venía al mundo había de alumbrar a todos. Dice que *timuerent timore magno*. . . . Teme el hombre porque no caben en su entendimiento los sacramentos de Dios. Dos cosas. La una, que tras el resplandor, viene el temor. De donde se sigue que no es malo. No es tan perfecto como el amor, pero principio"; Ribera, *Sermones*, 1:36.

22. "La oración alumbra el alma. ¡Qué de ceguedades se le quitan al hombre en la oración con la meditación! ¡Qué hacha es del alma!"; sermon preached on St. Elizabeth's Day, Badajoz, 1568, in Ribera, *Sermones*, 1:41.

23. Laredo, *Ascent of Mount Sion*; Osuna, *Third Spiritual Alphabet*.

24. "No ha de hallar remedio el hombre entre la malicia y el bullicio del día. Venga la sosegada noche, y en medio de ese silencio vendrá Dios, no en el torbellino, sino en el silbo delgado. Quien busca a Dios, búsquele en sosiego"; sermon preached in Frejenal, Badajoz, 1565, in Ribera, *Sermones*, 1:43.

25. Laredo, *Ascent of Mount Sion*, 49. This particular phrase, *no pensar nada*, exerted a strong influence in the thought of Teresa of Avila.

26. CCC, I, 7, B. Also see Bataillon, *Erasmo y España*, 523–40.

27. "Por todo esto se colige el particular cuidado, y providencia paternal que ha tenido Dios nuestro señor sobre este miserable pecador. . . . Porque siendo aquellas personas tan estimadas, y aventajadas en opinión, y yo tan niño en edad, y sin noticia alguna de las heregías que corrían, pudieran enseñarme alguna mala doctrina contraria a nuestra sancta fe"; CCC, I, 7, B.

28. "Copia de carta pa su mgd del patriarca arçobispo de Valencia escrive a 13 de mayo de 1608," BN, MS 1492.

29. "El que quiere saber el camino del cielo, pregunta. . . . ¿Qué ve, qué hace al hombre ir por el camino de Dios, sin espantarse que no le haga contradicción la murmuración de los necios y desatinos, y miembros del demonio? Sólo el bueno ve"; Badajoz, third Sunday of Advent 1564, in Ribera, *Sermones*, 1:45. In his 1575 report to Philip II, Alonso de la Fuente accused Ribera of prophesizing the persecution of the *alumbrados;* reprinted in Huerga, *Historia*, 1:355.

30. Barrio, *Los obispos de Castilla y León*, 40. The relatively poor diocese of Ourense in Galicia "served merely as a stepping stone for the careers of numerous Spanish clerics. Some twenty bishops served the diocese between 1550 and 1700"; Poska, *Regulating the People*, 35.

31. Rawlings, *Church, State, and Society*, 66.

32. Elliott, *Spain and Its World*, 17.

33 Barrio, *Los obispos de Castilla y León*, 54. After the death of Archbishop Tomás de Villanueva in 1555, four men held the see of Valencia in the next thirteen years: Francisco de Navarra (1556–63), Acisco Moya de Contreras (1564), Martín Pérez de Ayala (1565–66), and Fernando de Loaces (1567–68).

34. The cooperation between the pope and the king marked a small example of consensus in a year marked by bitter disputes over bullfighting, the papal bull *In Coena Domini*, and the imprisonment of Don Carlos; Pastor, *History of the Popes*, 27–71.

CHAPTER 1. TWO FLOCKS, ONE SHEPHERD

1. Glick, *From Muslim Fortress*, 65, 79, 88. An eleventh-century Muslim chronicle celebrated the city's walls, battlements, meadows, and market gardens, associating these things with Islamic law and the proper functioning of society: "Just as the trees and other things by which men maintain life could not survive without water, your people, Valencia, cannot survive without this book of our law from which have come many good rulings for the city and all the realm concerning how we should act"; "Lament for the loss of Valencia" (1094), in Smith, *Christians and Moors*, 1:111.

2. Constable, *Trade and Traders*, 20. In the early eleventh century, Valencia and Muslim Spain as a whole were thrown into disarray by the growing incursions of Christian warlords from Castile and the north and the fall of the Caliphate of Córdoba, at its height a prosperous and sophisticated Islamic capital.

3. These converts, or *muladíes*, adopted Islam for various reasons, including the desire to avoid the higher taxes imposed upon non-Muslims; Fletcher, *Moorish Spain*, 36–37, 47–49.

4. These Christians apparently had a church building in one of the city's suburbs outside the city walls, and the congregation remained in existence after the Berber general Mazdali reclaimed the city in 1102; Fletcher, *Quest for El Cid*, 166, 182, 186. See also Peñarroja Torrejòn, *Cristianos bajo el Islam*, 87–121.

5. O'Callaghan, *Reconquest and Crusade*, 99–105. Earlier Muslim rulers such as ibn Mardanish (1147–1172), called the "Wolf King," had also contracted alliances with Christians against rival Muslims when it suited their purposes; Reilly, *Medieval Spains*, 131.

6. Burns, *Crusader Kingdom*. These new offices complemented holdovers including the Water Court (which still meets ceremonially every Thursday at noon) and the *mustaçaf*, a judge of weights, measures, and business ethics.

7. Burns, "Múdejars." In many areas the repartition of Mudejar lands led to their destabilization, replacing collective Muslim ownership with privately held individual units; Glick, *From Muslim Fortress*, 134–36.

8. Smith, *Christians and Moors*, 2:51–53.

9. "Muslim and Christian societies then, religious in root and branch, recoiled from one another in mutual contempt"; Burns, "Múdejars," 591–92.

10. The Muslims of Vall de Uxó, for example, retained the right to appoint their own *amin* (an administrator with broad powers, including tax collection) and *qadi* (a principal magistrate) in accordance with Islamic law; Harvey, *Islamic Spain*, 125–27; Burns, *Islam under the Crusaders*, 374–400.

11. In addition to farming, Valencian Mudejars engaged in the production of paper and salt, sheep herding, and commerce with Granada; O'Connor, *Forgotten Community*, 117–18.

12. The Valencian Muslims "do not seem to have participated in the interchange of intellectual life of the Islamic world as a whole, and they produce[d] no writers of any note after the conquest"; Harvey, *Islamic Spain*, 118–19. Robert Burns qualifies this assertion: "Intellectual and creative elements continued to function in Mudejar society, doubtless at diminished levels of intensity that dimmed more and more as the decades wore on"; Burns, *Islam under the Crusaders*, 413.

13. O'Connor, *Forgotten Community*, 55–63. Burns has shown that some former military leaders surrendered their castles in exchange for generous estates, where they continued to pursue an aristocratic existence; Burns, *Islam under the Crusaders*, 320.

14. Miller, "Muslim Minorities," 258.

15. King James the Conqueror himself reportedly said in his final years that he "should expel all the Moors of the Kingdom of Valencia, because they are all traitors, and have often made us understand that whereas we treat them well, they are ever seeking to do us harm"; Harvey, *Islamic Spain*, 134–37.

16. Lull wrote dozens of works on the subject of conversion, including both scholarly treatises and vernacular narratives such as *Blanquerna*, the story of a young man who forgoes marriage for a spiritual vocation to reform Christian behavior and evangelize Muslims and Jews; Abulafia, "Apostolic Imperative."

17. Burns, *Muslims, Christians, and Jews*, 87–95.

18. Fletcher, *Moorish Spain*, 143.

19. Ferror i Mallol, *La frontera*, 134–37; Díaz Borrás, *Los orígenes*, 95.

20. Harvey, *Islamic Spain*, 135.

21. Carrasco, *Historia*, 310–11.

22. O'Connor, *Forgotten Community*, 225–32.

23. Meyerson, *Muslims of Valencia*, 271.

24. The "Athens of the Turia" also witnessed the development of a Valencian literature: Jaime Roig's novel *Libre de les dones, o spill* attests to the subtle tastes of the urban merchant class, whereas Joanot Martorell's chivalric epic *Tirant lo Blanch* reflects the culture of those who aspired to the high nobility.

25. Hamilton, *Money, Prices, and Wages*, 194. As the German traveler Hieronymous Münzer expressed it in 1494, "The principal trade and commerce of all of Spain was in Barcelona fifty years ago. . . . But after the seditions and internecine wars, the merchants took refuge in Valencia, today head of commerce"; Münzer, *Viaje*, 43.

26. Meyerson, *Muslims of Valencia*, 220. On Muslim traders, see Bordes and Sanz, "El protagonismo mudéjar," 275.

27. Meyerson, *Muslims of Valencia*, 2–3.

28. Ibid., 4–5, 272.

29. Haliczer, *Inquisition and Society*, 244.

30. García Cárcel, *Las germanías de Valencia*, 124.

31. Vallés Borràs, *La germanía*, 255–57.

32. In 1524 a commission led by the inquisitor Juan Churruca traveled through the areas of Valencia affected by the germanías, interviewing dozens of witnesses as to the circumstances of the forced baptisms. The manuscript recording these interviews is now housed among the papers of Henry Charles Lea at the University of Pennsylvania. "Dixo que el sábado de manyana hiendo a buscar su hijo que se lo había muerto fallo muchos moros muertos de la puerta de la villa hasta sant anthonio mas de cient y cinquenta"; HCL, MS 20, fol. 132v.

33. "Vido este testigo como los soldados tomavan los moros y los despujavan y robavan y los levavan con gran furia para que se fuessen a babtizar a la yglia"; HCL, MS 20, fol. 137r.

34. "Entonces estava la yglesia plena y vido que les echavan agua bendita empo que no se acuerda si con salpacer o ysopo o como ni las palabras que les dezía ni si les ponía nombres de xpianos"; HCL, MS 20, fol. 135v.

35. "Poco tiempo antes que fuesse la conversión de los moros en la villa de Alzira este testigo hoyó como los Capitanes de la germanía yuan diciendo por la villa que si los moros no se hazían xpianos que los havían a degollar y quitarles lo que tenían"; HCL, MS 20, fol. 21r.

36. According to the council, the rebels "los matassen o robassen sus haziendas, se convertieron a nra. fe cathólica y recibieron el agua del santo bautismo, unos viniendo voluntarios a pedido y otros con alguna premia y caminación de los dichos pueblos, aunque no tal que los escusasse de quedar xpianos"; BL, Egerton MS 1832, fol. 21r.

37. Redondo, *Antonio de Guevara*, 230.

38. "En la dicha conversion o bautismo no entrevino fuerça o violencia precisa o absoluta"; petition from the Madrid junta to Rome, Mar. 1525, BL, Egerton MS 1832, fol. 21r.

39. Sandoval, *Historia*, 2:121. The archbishop of Seville, in a letter to Charles, treated this information as common knowledge: "As you probably know, the inquisitors of Valencia report that in the time of the germanías all the Moors of that region, or almost all of them, became Christians, and their mosques were consecrated. After a while, these Moors returned to their sect and made these churches, so recently reduced to our Christian religion, into temples of

Islam again"; Archbishop of Seville to Charles V, Burgos, 24 Jan. 1524, in Boronat y Barrachina, *Los moriscos*, 1:401.

40. BL, Egerton MS 1832, fol. 21r. In Alzira, many of the newly baptized fled when the viceroy arrived with his troops; when these exiles returned, around Easter of 1523, they induced those converts who had remained to live as moros again; HCL, MS 20, fol. 3v. Don Galcerón de Castellvi, lord of Carlet, evidently said that "these Moorish dogs . . . were baptized by force" and promised a new morisco that he would open the mosque again; HCL, MS 20, fol. 15v.

41. Despite these obstacles, Guevara and his fellow commissioners persisted, and on 5 July 1525, they reported the successful reconversion of twenty-one mosques into Christian churches; letter from Manrique to Guevara and Suñer, 28 July 1525, in Redondo, *Antonio de Guevara*, 241.

42. Benítez, "Carlos V"; Pardo Molero, "Imperio y cruzada."

43. With the help of his ambassador in Rome, the Duke of Sessa, Charles secured a papal bull absolving him of the oath he had sworn in 1518 to refrain from compelling the Levantine Muslims to receive baptism. In this bull, Clement VII pointed to the dangers of allowing Moors to live among Christian converts, arguing that the Muslims "can incline the converts toward superstition and perfidy" (ad aliquem eius superstitionem et perfidiam inclinare possunt); Clement VII, Rome, 15 May 1524, in Boronat y Barrachina, *Los moriscos*, 1:404.

44. "Copia de un asiento de las cosas que se concedieron a los nuevamente convertidos del reino de Valencia"; Monzón, 17 July 1528, Simancas, Cons. de Inquisición, libro 15, fol. 468, reprinted in Boronat y Barrachina, *Los moriscos*, 1:423–27. The compromise also called for the abolition of the special taxes and labor obligations previously demanded of Mudejars, although the king agreed to preserve existing tax structures in the Moorish quarters of Valencia, Játiva, Alzira, and Castellón as an incentive to keep the moriscos from emigrating; edict of 15 Jan. 1526, BL, Egerton MS 1832, fols. 22v–23r. The Inquisition and the Mudejars agreed to the deal on 6 January 1526, but Charles did not announce it publicly until he and the grand inquisitor Manrique visited Valencia in May 1528.

45. "Crimi nefandissim paguells comes del haver conspirat contra la dita cesa Mat"; "Dix que si pero que los moros de benaguazir los deyen que no eren manaments de Sa Mat"; testimony of Cosme de Urrea, ARV, Real Audiencia, procesos criminales, asig. 8, 1526.

46. Poska, *Regulating the People*, 79.

47. León-Portilla, *Broken Spears*, 59.

48. In 1531–32, Pope Clement VIII granted the Inquisition near-total authority over the morisco question, including the power "to order the barons and caballeros of Valencia not to collect more taxes and impositions from the converts than those which they usually had collected from the Old Christians"; Lea, *Moriscos of Spain*, 139. Also see "Relación de lo que ha pasado," in Boronat y Barrachina, *Los moriscos*, 1:411.

49. Halperin Donghi, *Un conflicto nacional*, 154. Also see "Memorial elevado por el Ilustrísimo D. Feliciano de Figueroa, obispo de Segorbe, a S.M.," ca. 1601, in Boronat y Barrachina, *Los moriscos*, 2:433; García Cárcel, *Herejía y sociedad*, 31; Lea, *Moriscos of Spain*, 141–43.

50. Halperin Donghi, *Un conflicto nacional*, 161. Los Angeles was tried by the Inquisition for scandalous behavior and "murmuraciones . . . contra personas de mucha qualidad." As a

result, Ramírez de Haro revoked his license to preach and ordered his reclusion in a Franciscan monastery; inquisitorial trial of Bartolomé de los Angeles, 28 July 1544, in Boronat y Barrachina, *Los moriscos*, 1:485–92.

51. The Duke of Segorbe, for example, deprived his moriscos of their status as familiars, claiming that it infringed upon his jurisdiction over his own vassals.

52. In 1528 the Church rewarded several moriscos for assisting in the war against the rebels and facilitating baptisms. Yet in that same year, the commissioners found it necessary to issue a clarification that the agreement with the Inquisition covered only minor offenses, not "public crimes and morisco ceremonies"; report of 21 July 1528, BL, Egerton MS 1832, fol. 26r; edict of Dec. 1528, BL, Egerton MS 1832, fols. 24v–25r.

53. When the rector of Quart brought in three other priests to assist him in celebrating Mass on the feast of Santa Ana, "after singing the Mass they went out to celebrate the festival and found the holy bread that the moriscos had thrown out the door of the church . . . to vituperate the blessed bread"; 31 July 1544, BL, Egerton MS 1832, fols. 55v–56r.

54. Lea, *Moriscos of Spain*, 99.

55. In 1533 the nobles wrote to Charles, "The craftiness with which the moros were converted to our holy Catholic faith is well known, as is the fact that they have been given little or no instruction since then." Following this logic, the seigneurs protested as illegal the prosecution of the moriscos as heretics and the seizure of goods that properly should have reverted to their lords; BL, Egerton MS 1832, fol. 38r.

56. BL, Egerton MS 1832, fol. 39v; Lea, *Moriscos of Spain*, 100; García Cárcel, *Herejía y sociedad*, 32.

57. Junta of 14 June 1528, BL, Egerton MS 1832, fols. 28r–v.

58. A son of the Holy Roman Emperor Maximilian and an uncle of Charles V, Jorge de Austria remained in Valencia until 1545.

59. Austria and Ramírez de Haro, *Les instructions*. Pérez de Ayala published this document in 1566.

60. "E per que no creguen los dits novament convertits que nostra religio Christiana esta posada en interes"; ibid.

61. Villanueva to Prince Philip, Valencia, 12 Apr. 1547, *Colección de documentos inéditos*, 5:100.

62. Villanueva to Philip, Valencia, 13 Aug. 1552, *Colección de documentos inéditos*, 5:123.

63. In 1554 Villanueva presided over a morisco council that empowered the commissioner Miranda "to compel the moriscos to baptize their children without circumcising them or giving them Moorish names, to confess, to go to Mass, to observe the holidays, and to do all the works of Christians and not other tasks—or at least, to ensure that they do not do these publicly"; "Conclusiones de la junta celebrada en Valencia en 1554," in Benítez, "El arzobispo Villanueva," 120.

64. Valencian provincial council of 1565, in Tejado y Ramiro, *Colección*, 273, 280.

65. "La Inquisición no tuviese con ellos que hacer, salvo en los que con desvergüenza y al descubierto pecasen"; Pérez de Ayala, "Discurso de la vida," 237.

66. García Martínez, *Bandolerismo, piratería y control de moriscos*; Benítez, *Heroicas decisiones*, 190–95.

67. These raids prompted a number of towns, including Denia and Cullera, to build a series of fortifications along the coast; García Martínez, *Bandolerismo, piratería y control de moriscos*. On Charles V, see Alonso Acero, "Cristiandad *versus* Islam."

68. ARV, Real Audiencia, procesos criminales, sig. 38; "Pragmàtica de Carlos V," 84. This distrust of outsiders extended even to a sodomy trial in which the accusation stated that "all moriscos, and particularly the Berbers from abroad, are given to the detestable and infamous crime of sodomy"; ARV, Gobernación, procesos criminales, no. 593.

69. ARV, Real Audiencia, procesos criminales, sig. 38. Two morisco merchants traveling near Sagunto found themselves under arrest because of their poor command of the "Christian language." Former galley slaves from Fez who had been brought north from Seville by their last owner, the merchants secured their release only by producing papers and witnesses attesting to their manumission and their status as good Christians; ARV, Real Audiencia, procesos criminales, sig. 198.

70. In the 1540s Conde signed a peace and truce (*pau i treva*) with his brother-in-law following a dispute over land. After an argument with the brother-in-law's son escalated into an armed struggle, Conde was forced to relocate to Valencia; ARV, Gobernación, procesos criminales, no. 635.

71. ARV, Real Audiencia, procesos criminales, sig. 125.

72. 30 Apr. 1562, ARV, Cartas a los Virreyes, carpeta 5.

73. In 1560 the viceroy complained after the Count of Oliva and the Duke of Gandía seized a former morisco who had fled to North Africa and returned with a group of "moros who went down the coast of the realm, committing atrocities" and capturing Christians. The Duke of Gandía had the morisco quartered on his own authority, with "great prejudice" to the king's jurisdiction; 3 Aug. 1560, ARV, Cartas a los Virreyes, carpeta 4.

74. Hess, *Forgotten Frontier*, 142–43.

75. Under the edict of 8 February 1563, moriscos could not carry or keep "armes algunes offensives, ni defensives, propries, ni de altri: excepto ganiuets, e instruments necessaries pera usos de casa, arts, y officis de cascu"; Canet and Romero, *Crides*, 2:91. The viceroy Villarasa noted the difficulty of collecting these weapons, "which are dispersed in many places," and requested permission to sell the stockpile he had found; 4 Sept. 1565, ARV, Cartas a los Virreyes, carpeta 6.

76. When bailiffs in Alcacer noticed a morisca run into her house at their approach, they ransacked her bed and tore open the walls in a (successful) search for weapons. The officials were in the area investigating a recent attack that had taken place on the royal road; ARV, Real Audiencia, procesos criminales, sigs. 159, 154.

77. ARV, Real Audiencia, procesos criminales, sigs. 149, 190.

78. ARV, Real Audiencia, procesos criminales, sig. 202.

79. Boronat y Barrachina, *Los moriscos*, 1:237; Salvador Esteban, *Felipe II*, 26; Benítez, "La política de Felipe II."

80. The trade in morisco children from Granada, sold as slaves and transported north, presented such a problem that the viceroy brought the matter to the attention of Philip II; 25 Apr. 1569, ARV, Cartas a los Virreyes, carpeta 8. In 1571 a morisco arrested at the inn in Alcocer for transporting a five-year-old Granadan girl tried unsuccessfully to bribe the guards with money he raised by selling his mule; ARV, Real Audiencia, procesos criminales, sig. 263.

81. 16 Jan. 1569, and 20 Feb. 1569, ARV, Cartas a los Virreyes, carpeta 8. "Quienes son entre ellos inquietos, briosos y de más autoridad y opinión, y de quien puede hazer cabeças"; Mar. 1570, ARV, Cartas a los Virreyes, carpeta 117.

82. Salvador Esteban, *Felipe II*, 57.

83. Escolano, *Década primera*, 1:1038.

84. Ruiz, *Spanish Society*, 153–55.

85. "Que muchas noches los Viernes acudían a su casa los moriscos y moriscas adereçadas e conpuestas, e sospechando que les predicava la seta determinaron cierta noche de cogerlos de repente e hallando cerrada la puerta principal entraron por una puerta falsa e hallaron al reo asentado en una silla con un laud en las manos y el un pie descalço que un morisco la tenía un libro abierto delante en el qual leya e cantava"; AHN, Inquisition, lib. 934, fol. 230r.

86. Arias, *Spanish Sacramental Plays*, 17–18, 30.

87. Mérimée, *El arte dramático*, 21–22, 25, 27. In my reconstruction of the Corpus of 1569 I have drawn upon two principal sources: a 1547 entry in the *Llibres d'actes* specifying the order of the processants, reprinted in Sanchis Guarner, *La processó valenciana*, 34, and a financial record from 1571, "Quern de la festa del Corpus del any MDLXXI en LXXII, essent clavari comú lo honorable En Nofre Adell," reprinted in Corbató, *Los misterios*, 153.

88. Corbató, *Los misterios*, 69; Mérimée, *El arte dramático*, 35, 38, 44. These mysteries would eventually be supplanted by the Castilian *autos sacramentales* of Lope de Vega and Calderón de la Barca in the Baroque era.

89. The viceroy observed the proceedings accompanied by the head of the Valencian Audiencia Real, a royal appellate court, and the *baile general*, a "Quaestor: he is charged with the conservation and the collection of the royal patrimony"; Ferrando Badia, *El histórico reino*, 129; Escolano, *Década primera*, 1:1081. The viceroy and his officials watched from the Diputación because the Palacio Real was situated across the river and well off the route of the procession. On Benavente's appointment to Valencia, see Diago, *Apuntamientos*, 2:38.

90. Joan Fuster has argued that the Castilianization of the Valencian nobility was already under way in the 1520s, but the vicereine Germana de la Foix's disdain for the Valencian language certainly accelerated this process; Fuster, *Rebeldes y heterodoxos*, 84.

91. The Plaza of the Market, an irregular space surrounded by the silk exchange (Lonja), the Consulate of the Sea, and a parish church, served the city as a focal point for jousting tournaments, running of the bulls, autos de fe, and hangings: the cityscape of Anthonie van den Wijngaerde in 1563 clearly shows a gallows supported by three posts; Rosselló, *Les vistes valencianes*, 144.

92. Cebriá y Arazil, *Ceremonial*, 22.

93. Sanchis Guarner, *La processó valenciana*, 28.

94. Ferrando Badía, *El histórico reino*, 136. The manner of electing town councillors (*jurados*) went through a great many changes over the course of the fourteenth century as the king intervened in the process; Narbona Vizcaíno, *Valencia*, 40–52.

95. Felipo Orts, "Control monárquico," 343.

96. Escolano, *Década primera*, 1:210. The major noble houses, including those of the marquis of Guadalest, the marquis of Albayda, the count of Buñol, and the viscount of Chelva, would have been well represented both among the town councilors and among the spectators. On the other hand, the five grandees of Valencia—the dukes of Segorbe, Gandía, and Villa-

hermosa, the marquis of Denia, and the master of Montesa—typically resided at the recently established Habsburg court in Madrid.

97. As Valencia faded in importance with the influx of specie from the Americas, the upper classes carried out the classic shift from entrepreneurs to rentiers in a moment of crisis. In 1569, however, the Valencian merchants were poised to benefit from the outbreak of war the year before in France, Flanders, and Andalusia, developments that would lead Philip II away from the Castile-Antwerp axis and toward the Mediterranean trade with Genoa for financial support; Salvador, *La economía valenciana*, 62; Reglà, *La història*, 43, 50–51.

98. Cebriá y Arazil, *Ceremonial*, 31–32; Escolano, *Década primera*, 1:1038.

99. Salavert and Graullera, *Professió*.

100. Catalá de Valeriola, *Autobiografía*, 10–11, 25.

101. Poska, "From Parties to Pieties," 231.

102. Sanchis y Sivera, *Nomenclator geográfico-eclesiástico*, 421.

103. The urban parish of San Miguel y San Dionysio dated to the frenzied times of the germanías. According to Gaspar Escolano, a group of Christian boys acting under the influence of "some divine spirit" took a retable of St. Michael to the mosque in the Moorish quarter, where the unsuspecting Muslims were performing their daily prayers. "They entered the mosque calling out by name, 'Long live St. Michael and the See of Christ': and with the Moors unable to resist, they planted the retable in the mosque"; Escolano, *Década primera*, 1:924–25. The archbishop Martín Pérez de Ayala elevated the church to parish status in the 1560s.

104. Ibid., 1:890.

105. Ibid., 1:1037.

106. Cordero, "Vida"; Ximeno, *Escritores*, 1:183–84.

107. Cordero also composed a Castilian poem describing the events in octaves, and the professor of rhetoric Vicente Blay García wrote a prose account of the fire; Martí Mestre, *El Libre de antiquitats*, 234nn799–801; Carreres Zacarés, *Libre de memories*, 957–59.

108. Llobregat Conesa, *El corpus de Valencia*, Glossari, "Àguiles." The twenty-four bearded men in white tunics, each bearing a thick candle three feet in height, represented the patriarchs gathered to adore the Lamb in Rev. 4:4.

109. Sanchis Guarner, *La processó valenciana*, 87.

110. Ibid., 94.

111. "Tiene este reino tanta frescura y templanza de tierra que todo el año está florida; y así traen manojos de flores por Navidad y Enero como en otras partes por Abril y Mayo"; Medina, *Libro de grandezas*, 196.

112. Münzer, *Viaje*, 47.

113. "Relación de las casas," in Boronat y Barrachina, *Los moriscos*, 1:428–43. This document, evidently begun in 1520, includes modifications spanning the next fifty years. By crossreferencing the señores indicated here with the map of Lapeyre, the prevailing pattern emerges. The coastal morisco communities of Beniopa and Benirredrá, for example, pertained to the Duke of Gandía, whereas the master of Montesa and the king owned northern towns such as Morella and Borriana; Lapeyre, *Géographie*, 285–86. According to Lapeyre's estimates, the morisco households numbered 18,683 in 1565–72; ibid., 30. I have used a multiplier of 4.5.

114. The bishop of Segorbe, Feliciano de Figueroa, counted 460 "lugares" in 1601; in 1610 the Dominican Jaime Bleda argued for a total of 453; "Memorial elevado por el Ilustrísimo D.

Feliciano de Figueroa," in Boronat y Barrachina, *Los moriscos*, 2:431; Bleda, *Defensio fidei*, 583. On morisco farming practices, see Saavedra, "Cambios demográficos," 1:61–63; Ardit, *Els homes i la terra*, 252–311.

115. Meyerson, *Muslims of Valencia*, 50, 227.

116. ARV, Real Audiencia, procesos criminales, sig. 157.

117. Cebriá y Arazil, *Ceremonial*, 30–31.

118. AHN, Inquisition, lib. 937, fols. 18–19; AHN, Inquisition, lib. 934, fols. 228–32; Longás Bartibás, *Vida religiosa*, 59–62.

119. AHN, Inquisition, lib. 934, fols. 4r–v, 445r–v; García-Arenal, *Inquisición y moriscos*, 49–51; Longás Bartibás, *Vida religiosa*, 21–28.

120. AHN, Inquisition, lib. 937, fol. 462.

121. As I have noted, Muslim scholars abroad disagreed as to the legitimacy of Spanish Islam after the Reconquest, but the moriscos' response to their predicament echoed long-standing traditions that acknowledged the role of individual discretion and community opinion in addressing legal and theological dilemmas; Epalza, "Los voz oficial"; Cornell, "Fruit of the Tree of Knowledge," 90–92; Robinson, "Knowledge," 211–13.

122. Longás Bartibás, *Vida religiosa*, 58–59.

123. Translated in Cornell, "Fruit of the Tree of Knowledge," 80.

124. Robinson, "Knowledge," 219–23.

125. AHN, Inquisition, lib. 934, fol. 229r; Longás Bartibás, *Vida religiosa*, 256–63; García-Arenal, *Inquisición y moriscos*, 56–59.

126. Longás Bartibás, *Vida religiosa*, 264–70.

127. Ibid., 214–28, 284–95.

128. AHN, Inquisition, lib. 934, fol. 230v.

129. Trial of Miquel Ciurana, 1564, ARV, Real Audiencia, procesos criminales, sig. 166.

130. Hegyi, *Cinco leyendas*, 11–16.

131. Chejne, *Islam and the West*, 38, 43.

132. Halperin Donghi, *Un conflicto nacional*, 100.

133. "Eça, que es tenido por muy sabio en su ley, tanto allí como en todo el reyno de Valencia, por lo cual acuden a solicitar sus consejos muchos moriscos, a quienes el resuelve dudas y pleitos, y que sabe leer y escribir nuestra lengua castellana, viviendo en todo como un verdadero moro"; inquisitorial trial of Cosme Abenamir, in Boronat y Barrachina, *Los moriscos*, 1:541.

134. Císcar Pallarés, "'Algaravía' y 'algemía,'" 159.

135. Halperin Donghi, *Un conflicto nacional*, 109.

136. ARV, Real Audiencia, procesos criminales, sig. 166.

137. "Escribía unas cartas con letras arábigas coloradas que ponían a los moriscos por nómina sobre el pecho cuando estaban para morir, a fin de que quedaran limpios de sus pecados. . . . El debía tener, a pesar de su oficio de sastre, mucho de alfaqui"; inquisitorial trial of Gaspar Faena, in Boronat y Barrachina, *Los moriscos*, 1:492.

138. AHN, Inquisition, lib. 934, fols. 173v, 385r; Barceló Torres, *Minorías islámicas*, 141.

139. Benítez, "La política de Felipe II," 512–14.

140. Vincent, "La guerre," 267.

CHAPTER 2. THE LIMITS OF EPISCOPAL AUTHORITY

1. "Nos los estudiantes de la famosa utilosa celebre e Ille Universidad de Vala. a vos mosen Joan Ribera borde hijo de la mas sucia y baxa puta de salamanca y del mas sarnoso y pobre estudiante aunque dado falsamente por hijo al exmo. duque de alcalá. Por quanto a venido a nra. noticia que por cunplir con los falsos fictos y engañadores theatinos alborotadores y marañadores de cizañas entre las gentes y pueblos aveys puesto sin causa ni razón alguna al muy magco. y rdo. Rector destas nras. escuelas en prisión. Por tanto con la present os mandamos que oy viernes en todo el día Vos libreys y escarcereys a los gentes con alvaranes puestos por las plaças desta ciudad quien vos soys porque lo sabemos mejor que vos pensays dada en Vala. en nras escuelas diez de agosto de Mdvxx"; broadsheet inserted in the trial of Antonio Pineda, CCC, I, 5, Procesos difamatorios II.

2. The pasquinades of 1570–71 have received serious attention on four occasions: Robres Lluch, *San Juan de Ribera*, 122–71, defends Ribera's position and reprints some of the key documents; Mestre, "Jerarquía católica," examines the connections between the university and the oligarchy; García Martínez, "San Juan de Ribera," expands this argument; and Benítez, "El patriarca Ribera," makes use of the sources in the Archivo Histórico Nacional to follow the events of August 1570 in more detail and analyze the strained relations between Calderón and Ribera.

3. MacKay, *Limits of Royal Authority*; Corteguera, *For the Common Good*.

4. This issue also informed the debates of the Second Vatican Council: "Here and there some anxiety has been felt about the consequences of marking out more clearly the mission and authority of the bishop as one who rules his diocese in the name of Christ and not merely as an official of the pope. In place of a Roman-centralist (supposedly or really) autocratic government, may there not be a danger of "episcopalism" appearing in practice and an autocratic diocesan government?"; Rahner, *Bishops*, 44.

5. Robres Lluch, *San Juan de Ribera*, 98–99; Carreres Zacarés, *Libre de memories*, 890.

6. See especially the twenty-third (15 July 1563) and twenty-fourth (11 Nov. 1563) sessions of the Council of Trent, 1563, in Tanner, *Decrees*, 2:742–74.

7. Bleda, *Quatrocientos milagros*, 557.

8. Hermann, *L'eglise d'Espagne*. Ribera wielded much less influence over his suffragan bishoprics, Orihuela, Tortosa, and Segorbe. At all events these smaller dioceses and their impoverished cathedral chapters generated paltry revenues compared with the metropolitan; Casey, *Kingdom of Valencia*, 225–26.

9. CCC, Procesos, siglos XVI–XVII.

10. In his will, Per Afán bequeathed to Ribera "todo el aderesco e hornamento de mi capilla así de oro e de plata a más de vestimentos y adrescos de altar de toda suerte con el paño de devoción y altar portátil salvo el tela de oro," as well as one thousand ducats and assorted other items; testament of Per Afán de Ribera, CCC, I, 7, 4, 29(2).

11. The episcopal revenues, collected in two annual installments, yielded between 50,000 and 60,000 L. With the addition of loan repayments and various smaller sources of revenue, the total annual income in Valencia mounted to 70,000 or 80,000 L; CCC, Libros mayores,

1579–80, 1587–88, and 1592–1610; "Relación de las casas," in Boronat y Barrachina, *Los moriscos*, 1:428, 432.

12. Around the time of Ribera's appointment, Philip II took steps to bring the boundaries of the archdiocese into line with its political borders, separating Orihuela (founded 1564) in the south from the see in Cartagena and dividing Segorbe (founded 1577) in the north from Albarracín, which pertained to Zaragoza; Fernández Terricabras, *Felipe II*, 228–32.

13. Episcopal edict of 1 June 1569, in Canet and Romero, *Crides*, 2:267–82.

14. CCC, Asientos de criados, 1575–92; cuenta de librería, reprinted in Robres Lluch, *San Juan de Ribera*, 335.

15. In 1587–88, for example, Ribera disbursed more than thirty such dowries of 30 L each. For example, "Dia a Miguel Xpobal Pescador y a Margaritta Pasqual su mujer con apoca recebida por Melchior Tafalla en dicho día treynta libras en los quales la dotto el patriarcha mi señor su 8 de sette 1586"; CCC, Libro mayor, 1587–88.

16. Ribera, *Sermones*.

17. Kamen, *Phoenix and the Flame*, 275–77; Poska, *Regulating the People*, 101–3.

18. The episcopal curia of Cuenca, for which the records survive, "provided a forum for constructive, reforming litigation" in conjunction with Tridentine law; Nalle, *God in La Mancha*, 53.

19. Kamen, *Phoenix and the Flame*, 340–41; Nalle, *God in La Mancha*, 96–97; Poska, *Regulating the People*, 45–50.

20. For a discussion of this subject in other contexts, see Kagan, *Students and Society*; Altman, *Emigrants and Society*.

21. Salvador Esteban, "Felipe II," 44.

22. Vila Moreno, *La lengua valenciana*; Narbona Vizcaíno, *El nou d'octubre*.

23. Mestre, "Jerarquía católica," 9–35.

24. In 1604, to cite but one example, the Valencian Cortes complained that despite the Valencian law of 1564 and an apostolic constitution in 1586 prohibiting the appointment of foreigners, a Mallorcan had been granted a benefice in the cathedral of Segorbe; *Furs de València*, cap. 12, fol. 4r.

25. "El santo officio pierde mucho su autoridad en que el inquisidor este an subordinado y sugeto al arçobispo de aquí"; memorial from the city of Valencia to the Consejo de Inquisición, received in Madrid, 4 Mar. 1600, AHN, Inquisition, lib. 918, fol. 174v. Dr. Honorat Figuerola, a doctor in theology and canon law, also served Ribera as synodal examiner in 1590 and as an official visitor; Ximeno, *Escritores*, 1:238.

26. Quoted in Benítez, "La provisión del virreinato," 204–5.

27. Fuente, *Historia*, 1:228–35, 347–54. The jurados of Valencia exerted more influence over the university than did their counterparts, the *ayuntamientos* (municipal governments) of Castile; Gallego Salvadores, "Provisión de cátedras."

28. Felipo Orts, *La Universidad de Valencia*, 17–19, 67.

29. Ibid., 156–75.

30. Cárcel Ortí, *Historia*, 1:216–17. See also Ribadeneyra, *Vida*.

31. Cárcel Ortí, *Historia*, 1:165; Pedro de Ribadeneira to Francisco Boldó, Madrid, 6 Feb. 1593, in *Monumenta Historica Societatis Iesu*, 60:159–64.

32. Fernández and López, "Los colegios jesuíticos valencianos," 195; Cárcel Ortí, *Historia*, 1:258.

33. Mestre, "Jerarquía católica," 25; Nalle, *God in La Mancha*, 87–89.

34. Felipo Orts, "El rectorado," 81–82.

35. Vives singled out the Spaniards at the Sorbonne as "hombres invictos cuyo valor se ejercita en guardar la ciudadela de la ignorancia"; Bataillon, *Erasmo y España*, 20.

36. *Corrientes espirituales*, 65. The Erasmian Jeroni Conques, processed by the Inquisition in the 1550s, brutally satirized the preaching style of the Valencian theologian Luviela; Bataillon, *Erasmo y España*, 723–32.

37. Haliczer, *Inquisition and Society*, 282–83.

38. This memorial is quoted in Robres Lluch, *San Juan de Ribera*, 134–37.

39. Santos Hernández, *Jesuitas y obispados*, 21. Ricardo García Cárcel has argued that the early 1570s marked the beginning of a "Romanist offensive," leading to a less Hispanic order and greater resistance in Spain under Philip II; García Cárcel, "Las relaciones," 219–32. See also Kamen, *Phoenix and the Flame*, 375.

40. "Los jurados de Valencia, tomando por color favorecer a su Universidad, han querido impedir que no se oiga en algunas casas de religión (donde con más aprovechamiento de la facultad y de la virtud se see teología). . . . Es cosa de lástima que hombres que en su vida supieron qué cosa es leer o oír, rijan esta Universidad"; Ribera to Bernardo Bolea, Valencia, 14 Jan. 1570, quoted in Robres Lluch, *San Juan de Ribera*, 140.

41. González Navarro, *Felipe II*, 35.

42. "Visiteys reformeys y redreceys el dicho studio y colligios y los dichos statutos y ordinationes quitando de aquellos los que os paresciere y anyadiendo los que vieredes convenir"; Philip II to Ribera, Córdoba, 31 Mar. 1570, AA, Cartas reales, vol. h3-5, fol. 184r.

43. Sainz de Zuñiga, *Historia*, 2:574–76.

44. "E los dits molt mag jurats recional e syndich dixeren e respongueren que hagut consell ab los advocates de la dita ciutat, repondran e faran lo que devran conforme a justicia"; AA, Cartas reales, vol. h3-5, fol. 186r.

45. "No som conformes als furs y privilegis desta ciutat y regne ans notablement prejudicials y dañoses a la dita ciutat"; jurados to Philip II, Valencia, 25 May 1570, AA, Lletres misives, G 3, vol. 53, 264v.

46. Jurados to Jerónimo Climent, Valencia, 9 Aug. 1570, AA, Lletres misives, G 3, vol. 53, 272r. The official *actas* (minutes) of this visit do not survive, but the ensuing complaints by the jurados reveal the nature of Ribera's proposed reforms.

47. Under the existing arrangement, the students were prevented from taking outside classes by both their rigorous schedules and the university's official prohibition. In their initial memorial, the Jesuits had requested that the students be freed for two hours each day; Robres Lluch, *San Juan de Ribera*, 135.

48. Even though Ribera did not formally communicate his findings to the town council, they heard a report that he planned to order "fewer *cátedras*, fewer lessons, and that more people be involved in the provision of the faculty chairs" (menys cathedres y menys lliçons y que en lo de provehir de les cathedres ha haja mes persones de les que fins a huy y ha hagut y algunes altres cosas en dany del dit estudi); jurados to Climent, Valencia, 9 Aug. 1570, AA, Lletres misives, G 3, vol. 53, fol. 272r.

49. This is also the conclusion of Mestre, "Jerarquía católica." The minutes did change hands several times after August 1570, and the ensuing events make it clear that these concerns were the source of contention.

50. Thus Ribera aligned himself against the powerful vested interests of the local nobility, by virtue of his reforms and of the company he kept: in a letter to Climent, the jurados noted that Francisco Juan Roca, Don Miguel Vich, and the other canons "have shown themselves to be enemies of this city in the matter of the repayment of the loans of the Church" (los qual per negoci dels quitaments dels censals de la sglesia se ha mostrat enemichs desta ciutat), referring to a previous economic dispute between the cathedral and the city; jurados to Climent, Valencia, 9 Aug. 1570, AA, Lletres misives, G 3, vol. 53, 272r.

51. Jurados to Philip II, Valencia, 7 Aug. 1570, AA, Lletres misives, G 3, vol. 53, fol. 269v.

52. "Estos vellacos de don Miguel Vich y el Dean Roca que nos hazen la guerra en la visita del estudio"; testimony of Figueroa against Monzón, 15 Dec. 1571, CCC, I, 5, Procesos difamatorios II.

53. "Tratándole de borde"; accusation against Antonio Pineda, 16 Jan. 1572, CCC, I, 5, Procesos difamatorios II. The trial records establish that over the course of the pasquinades the students virtually always acted with the knowledge and consent of their professors.

54. "Constóme por ynformación que la total causa de este desasosiego eran quatro clérigos maestros y cathedráticos de esta Universidad, los quales han sido hasta agora los señores de ella, por tener mucha mano con los officiales"; Ribera to Philip II, 18 Aug. 1570, AHN, Inquisition, lib. 912, fol. 365r.

55. Ribera neglected to mention the fact that the jurados had solicited the visitation to begin with and objected rather to the king's choice of visitors; Ribera to Philip II, 18 Aug. 1570, AHN, Inquisition, lib. 912, 365r.

56. On the inquisitors' background, see García Cárcel, Herejía y sociedad, 127. At the time of its inception in 1484, the Valencian Inquisition provoked a united opposition on the part of the local government, culminating in an embassy to the king seeking to curtail the panel's powers. "By the middle of the sixteenth century, the heroic period of charismatic authority was coming to an end and the long career of the Valencia tribunal as a regional bureaucratic institution was just beginning"; Haliczer, Inquisition and Society, 14, 362.

57. "El dicho señor patriarca me dixo que el no daría Informaciones algunas y que los señores Inqores les embiassen a sus casas"; Bellot to Rojas and Calderón, 9 Aug. 1570, AHN, Inquisition, lib. 912, fol. 349r.

58. Ribera to Philip II, 18 Aug. 1570, AHN, Inquisition, lib. 912, fol. 368v.

59. In Valencia as in other parts of Spain, the suspicion of heresy in a sermon usually landed a preacher before the Inquisition, not the bishop; Kamen, Phoenix and the Flame, 361.

60. As late as 1960, Robres neglects to mention Ribera's illegitimacy, opening the book with vague references to "el solar [lineage] de los Ribera"; Robres Lluch, San Juan de Ribera, 3.

61. "Todo el pueblo está alborotado de ver quánto a podido en Vos la malicia y pasión que tenéis contra los valencianos doctos, que ayáis puesto en vuestras cárceles hombres de tanto valor, lustre y buen exemplo, como son el Rdo. maestre Luviela, maestre Menjavila, doctores tan antiguos de theología y maestros desta nuestra Universidad"; CCC, I, 5, Procesos difamatorios II. See also Robres Lluch, San Juan de Ribera, 142–45.

62. "Isaia propheta loquente de Exmo. comiti benaventi in xxviiii cap. inquit: et dabitur liber nescienti litteras, dicetur q. ei, lege: et respondebit, nescio literas. Item in eodem cap. procedens inquit: et dixit dnus., eo q. appropinquat populus iste ore suo, et labiis suis glorificat me, cor autem eius longe est a me, et timuerunt me mandato hominum et doctrinis. . . . Ioannes a Ribera patriar. antio. &c. magistro santander gymnasii valentini rectoriam desideranti. S. D. Adolescentulus sum ego et contemptus, adulationes tuas non sum oblitus & pax tibi"; CCC, I, 5, Procesos difamatorios II.

63. Trial of Monzón, testimony of Canónigo Pedro Hieronimo Gambau, 1 Feb. 1572, CCC, I, 5, Procesos difamatorios II.

64. "Simeon et Levi vasa iniquitatis bellantia et in consilio eorum non veniat anima mea. Maledictio furor eorum quia pertinax et indignatio eorum quia dura." "Caro autem non prodest quicquam quia manifesta sunt opera carnis." "Videns Herodes quod placeret judaeis apposuit apprehendere Petrum"; accusation against José Esteve, 2 Oct. 1571, CCC, I, 5, Procesos difamatorios II.

65. "Dixo el Arçobispo que a él era necessario auctorizar la prisión que havía hecho attento que los dichos maestros eran naturales de aquí, y tenían muchos que los deffendían"; Ribera to Espinosa, Valencia, 18 Aug. 1570, AHN, Inquisition, lib. 912, fol. 370r.

66. At one point in the negotiations, the inquisitors informed Ribera that they had consulted with the professors, who saw no reason why they should spend time in a monastery. Ribera commented somewhat sardonically that "he was very amazed to see the inquisitors asking defendants for their consent to administer justice. This struck him as a new development among tribunals, and particularly in the Holy Office, which usually maintained such secrecy" (estava muy maravillado de que los ynquisidores comunicassen con las partes pidiéndoles consentimiento para lo que era Razón, hazer de Justicia, siendo esta cosa tan nueva que todos los tribunales y particularmente en el sancto Offo. donde tanto secreto se suele guardar); Ribera to Espinosa, Valencia, 18 Aug. 1570, AHN, Inquisition, lib. 912, fol. 370v.

67. "Que así por derecho común, como por el concilio Tridentino tocavan a solos los ordinarios"; Ribera to Espinosa, Valencia, 18 Aug. 1570, AHN, Inquisition, lib. 912, fol. 370v.

68. "Si vuesas mercedes les mandassen en esta occasión libertar sería dar mucho inconveniente para el servicio de su Magt y para la autoridad de la visita y los que tratamos en ella"; Ribera to Rojas and Calderón, Valencia, 14 Aug. 1570, AHN, Inquisition, lib. 912, fol. 361v.

69. Council of Trent, sess. 25, 3–4 Dec. 1563, chap. 2, in Tanner, *Decrees*, 2:785.

70. Through a series of miscommunications, a planned transfer of the professors to the jurisdiction of the Inquisition failed, after Ribera realized that the tribunal had little intention of prosecuting the matter. Rojas and Calderón had in fact been writing to the Council of the Inquisition all along, complaining of Ribera's refusals and defending the two professors; Benavente to Philip II, 18 June 1570, ARV, Cartas a los Virreyes, carpeta 8; Ribera to Espinosa, Valencia, 18 Aug. 1570, AHN, Inquisition, lib. 912, fol. 371r; Ribera to Espinosa, Valencia, 18 Aug. 1570, AHN, Inquisition, lib. 912, fol. 371r; Rojas and Calderón to the Suprema, Valencia 14 Aug. 1570, AHN, Inquisition, lib. 912, fol. 351v. On 17 August 1570, the inquisitors attempted to take the case to trial without the charges (to secure an acquittal), but the *promotor fiscal* (prosecutor) refused; AHN, Inquisition, lib. 912, fol. 356r, 352v–53r.

71. On 18 August Ribera sent out no fewer than eight pieces of correspondence, including

two letters and an attached report to Philip II, two letters and two reports to the grand inquisitor Espinosa, and a letter to Bolea.

72. "Aunque tengo poca quenta con la honrra quando consydero que la tengo de emplear siempre en el pupo., de N Sr de VM deseo antes perder la vida"; Ribera to Philip II, Valencia, 18 Aug. 1570, AHN, Inquisition, lib. 912, fols. 378r–v.

73. "Que por la misericordia de N. Sor. no e hecho cosa por donde perder el crédito tan necessario para el exercicio deste officio en que dios y su M. me an puesto, y que el D. Calderón me le quyra quitar sin otra occasión más de guardar la costumbre que tiene pasando las buenas obras que recibe con mucha ingratitud. . . . Si hasta agora este nego se podía acabar con mandar V. S. Illa., avocarse la causa agora no puede quedar reintegrado ni particular sin que demás de aquello mande V. S. Illa. que el D. Calderón o yo nos vamos de aquí"; Ribera to Espinosa, 18 Aug. 1570, AHN, Inquisition, lib. 912, fols. 376r–77r.

74. "Para las personas públicas importa mas la fama que la vida, y así deseo que primero me la mandase su Md quitar que fuese servido de desacreditarme con esta gente"; Ribera to Bolea, 18 Aug. 1570, RAH, Salazar y Castro, vol. 5, asig. 9/49, doc. 7750.

75. Rojas and Calderón, the jurados, and their representatives residing in the Court also wrote to Espinosa and Philip II, defending the conduct of the professors and challenging Ribera's pretensions; jurados to Climent, Valencia, 18 Aug. 1570, AA, Lletres misives, G 3, vol. 53, 275r; jurados to Espinosa, Valencia, 18 Aug. 1570, AHN, Inquisition, lib. 912, fol. 357r; Calderón and Rojas to Consejo de Inquisición, Valencia, 21 Aug. 1570, AHN, Inquisition, lib. 912, fol. 360r. The response: Espinosa to Rojas and Calderón, Madrid, 26 Aug. 1570, AHN, Inquisition, lib. 356, fol. 189r; Vázquez to Calderón, Madrid, 26 Aug. 1570, AHN, Inquisition, lib. 356, fol. 189v.

76. "Ha manat posar aquells no en millor presó ni en la mateixa que estaven sino en molt pijor en unes cambres damunt la presó comuna y ha manat que ninguls parle yls"; jurados to Climent, Valencia, 29 Aug. 1570, AA, Lletres misives, G 3, vol. 53, 275v.

77. Philip II to Ribera, Madrid, 8 Sept. 1570 and 24 Sept. 1570, CCC, I, 7, 3; Espinosa to Ribera, Madrid, 26 Aug. 1570, AHN, Inquisition, lib. 356, fol. 188v.

78. "De tres coses estava sentit lo dir Rvmo archebisbe, la una perquè molts cavallers y altres persones axi principals com de altra sort eren anats a visitar als reverents mestre Luviela y mestre Mijavila los dies que permanament dels Inquisidors eren estats arrestats en ses cases y la altra perquè don Luys Ferrer y lo senyor de betera havien aguardat que lo dit mestre Mijavila pogues exir de sa casa pera que digues la misa nupcial a la filla del dit don Luys y al dit senyor de betera, segons la digue en aquells dies que per manament dels dits Inquisidors pogueren exir de casa y l altra perquè diu que lo senyor de bunyol y sa muller habien parlat del dit archebisbe"; AA, Lletres misives, G 3, vol. 53, fols. 277r–v.

79. "Si no fuesen dos o tres personas de la sala, y seys de los de la Universidad tan protervas en defender sus intereses, se avría recibido con mucho aplauso la visita, pero estas con la prudencia que suelen tener los hijos deste siglo harán mas demostración que muchos de los que la desean"; Ribera to Bolea, Seville, 28 Sept. 1570, RAH, Salazar y Castro, vol. 5, 9/49, doc. 7751.

80. See, for example, Benítez, "El patriarca Ribera," 348. Benítez notes briefly (341) that the resistance to Ribera stemmed from issues other than the pasquinade. Robres addresses the

wider significance but in an apologetic context, viewing the pasquinades as one tribulation in the life of "el santo"; Robres Lluch, *San Juan de Ribera*, 169–70.

81. CCC, I, 5, Procesos difamatorios I and II. "Todo en Razón de la dha Visita," Ribera to Espinosa, 18 Aug. 1570, AHN, Inquisition, lib. 912, fol. 370r.

82. "Aunque deve aver xxv días que se les entregaron las constituciones: no an hablado palabra, ni yo se la he dicho, pareciéndome que cumple así al negocio"; Ribera to Bolea, 23 Oct. 1570, RAH, Salazar y Castro, vol. 5, 9/49, doc. 7752.

83. "Y demás que esto será proceder en ynfinito, no será necesso. Pues haviendo (como es razón) de embiarse a VS serán de poca ymportancia las razones que dixeren de palabra"; Ribera to Bolea, 23 Oct. 1570, RAH, Salazar y Castro, vol. 5, 9/49, doc. 7752.

84. On 3 November 1570, the jurados complained to Climent that "encara que tostemps havem entes y tengut per cert que tot lo que aplicavem als rector y mestres theolechs era ayre"; AA, Lletres misives, G 3, vol. 53, fol. 283v. An unnamed ally at Court forwarded their criticisms of Ribera to the king on the same day; ARV, Cartas a los Virreyes, carpeta 71.

85. "Y la darrera vegada que havem parlat al dit archebisbe lo havem trobat amb tanta pasio en dit negoci que parlant ab aquell james lo nomena sino mi negoci y mis testigos y tracta de dits mestres ab paraules que offenen les orelles de que coneix y sab que son que cert ni resta molt maravellats"; jurados to Climent, Valencia, 16 Dec. 1570, AA, Lletres misives, G 3, vol. 53, fol. 288r.

86. Ribera to Philip II, 17 Feb. 1571, ARV, Cartas a los Virreyes, carpeta 71.

87. In his letter to Bolea, Ribera referred to "la determinación que tengo de salir a visitar los lugares de xpianos viejos de este obispo. por la grande necessidad que ay de ello," and he subsequently spent the period between February and May in Játiva; Ribera to Bolea, 23 Oct. 1570, RAH, Salazar y Castro, vol. 5, 9/49, doc. 7752; Ribera, *Sermones*, 2:15–17, 3:95.

88. "Anaren les dits doctors a la ciutat de xàtiva y li besa reales mans y feren totoes les submissions y umiliacions que devren"; jurados to Philip II, Valencia, 28 Apr. 1571, AA, Lletres misives, G 3, vol. 54.

89. "A se puesto hombres en ávyto de mugeres de noche a las ventanas de los aposentos de sus criados y andan otros por la calle diziendo reyio buena mugeres en casa el patriarca para que lo oygan los vezinos"; Ribera to Fadrique Enríquez de Ribera, Marquis of Villanueva, AHN, Inquisition, lib. 912, fol. 533r.

90. "Dieren una carta de noche para él diziendo ciertas cosas de que le avisava y otogavanle que para que sentendiese que la avía rpdo. pusiese un lienço en la ventana de su studio de seis a siete, con anymo que los que lo vyesen entendesen que eran señas que el ayía"; AHN, Inquisition, lib. 912, fol. 533r.

91. "Estas son la gente mas levantada y que algo paresce en la república que enseñados en la cátedra de sátanas y graduados en la escuela de la soberuia y enbidia con los antiguos grados de la malicia"; "Diligencias que en este officio se hazen," fol. 3r, CCC, I, 5, Procesos difamatorios II.

92. "En casa de nadie ni vra. Sa. consienta que nadie enbíe presentes fuera de la limosna que ve en las acechadores del demonio ir los presentes a casas de los vezinos y a donde ay mugeres aunque buenas y principales . . . y que esa casa sea castillo puesta en medio de turquía"; "Diligencias que en este officio se hazen," fol. 3v, CCC, I, 5, Procesos difamatorios II.

93. "Dizen que ni osa vra. señoria hablar contra 3 o 4 personas de esta diócesis porque so-los ellos son en su favor, y todos los demás están con las saetas enerboladas todo esta corato y perdido"; "Diligencias que en este officio se hazen," fol. 4r, CCC, I, 5, Procesos difamatorios II.

94. "Escándalo de toda la cleresía y esto es verdad público y . . . y lo dizan quantos cléri-gos son . . . valencia y te . . . ciertos escrivanos en vra carta desvergonçados i también públicos amancebadas remedialdo primero y no descubrays vra. malicia, contra los theólogos que tanto provecho y honrra han hecho a esa ciudad"; CCC, I, 5, Procesos difamatorios II. The original of this broadsheet is stuck to another, and both are full of holes.

95. Real Audiencia to Philip II, 20 Jan. 1571, ARV, Cartas a los Virreyes, carpeta 71.

96. "A nos dizen los que a la corte han llegado que no tratays sino con vellacos traydores hypócritas indios comuneros y males hombres germineros del qual te da esa ciudad está es-candalizada y muy alborotada"; CCC, I, 5, Procesos difamatorios II.

97. "Farsa. . . . la tragedia de los amores del Illmo. Sor. Patriarcha. es obra muy exemplar y consolatoria a los concubinarios. Acudan temprano que en el discurso conocerán quién es la dama y los demás representantes que en dichos amores intervienen"; CCC, I, 5, Procesos difamatorios II.

98. Salavert and Graullera, *Professió*, 173–74, 216.

99. Accusation against Gil Polo, 29 Oct. 1571, CCC, I, 5, Procesos difamatorios II.

100. "Psalm xxiiii. Delicta iuventutis mee, et ignorantias meas ne memineris. Respice in-imicos meos, quoniam multiplicati sunt, et odio iniquo oderunt me. xxv. Ego autem in inno-centia mea ingressus sum: redime me et miserere mei. lxviii. Et ne avertas faciem tuam a puero tuo: quoniam tribulor. lxxx. Vir insipiens non . . . et stultus non int . . . haec"; CCC, I, 5, Pro-cesos difamatorios II. In the Revised Standard Version, Psalms 25:7, 25:19, 26:11, 69:17, and 92:6.

101. On the subject of the ideal bishop, see Tellechea, *El obispo ideal*.

102. Ribera acted through his uncle the Marquis of Villanueva, who forwarded a summary of the letter to Espinosa; Ribera to Espinosa, 3 Sept. 1571, AHN, Inquisition, lib. 912, fol. 531; Ribera to Espinosa, Valencia, 18 Aug. 1570, AHN, Inquisition, lib. 912, fols. 372r–v; AHN, In-quisition, lib. 912, fols. 533r–34r.

103. "De los primeros que tocavan a su persona en dezille que no era hijo de su padre y otras cosas no se le dió nada pero los de aora por tocar a la honra de dios y ser defensa suya, está obligado a no dissimulallo"; AHN, Inquisition, lib. 912, fol. 533r.

104. "An puesto aora papeles en las casas mas públicas diziendo, que rueguen a dios le saquen de un adulteryo en questa, y junto conesto an considerado la persona a quien mas facil-mente podrían ynquietar, y mover a que hiziese algun disparate"; AHN, Inquisition, lib. 912, fol. 533r.

105. "Suplicándole que se entienda que su md. se aquerda de jaborcerle cen el. Pro-supuesto que será de nyngun efetto todo quanto se hiziere por los mynistros reales, porque to-dos tienen sus trabajones y enemistad con los castellans y quando esto no se hiziere, lo dejará todo"; AHN, Inquisition, lib. 912, fol. 533v.

106. Espinosa to Rojas and Calderón, 29 Aug. 1571, AHN, Inquisition, lib. 325, fols. 282v–83r. "Con la auctoridad y mano del sto offo se puede procurar la emienda y casstigo de los que se hallaren culpados"; Espinosa to Rojas and Calderón, 7 Sept. 1571, AHN, Inquisition, lib. 356, fol. 225r.

107. "Y el nego se ha representado por tan grave, que toca tan en lo vicio de la auctoridad y estimación de la yglesia"; AHN, Inquisition, lib. 356, fol. 225r. Espinosa identified Ribera as an *inquisidor ordinario*.

108. The edict is copied in "Diligencias que en este officio se hazen," fol. 22r, CCC, I, 5, Procesos difamatorios II.

109. Ribera to Espinosa, Seville, 10 Oct. 1571, AHN, Inquisition, lib. 912, fol. 527r.

110. "Porque se mostrava mas delantero que otros en lo de la universidad con los teatinos"; testimony of Gregorio Ibañez, beneficiado, in defense of Monzón, 31 Jan. 1572, CCC, I, 5, Procesos difamatorios II.

111. "Y como el dicho Monçón no lo quisiesse hazer dende ali le quito la habla y a este declarante ha dicho palabras que claramente mostrava quererle mal y amenazándole que era un loco y que no se quería dexar regir y que podría ser que le pesasse"; testimony of Pedro Jerónimo Gambau, 1 Feb. 1572, CCC, I, 5, Procesos difamatorios II.

112. "Ellos haría saber por las plaças y por la corte y por Roma y por el mundo las vellaquerías de don Miguel Vigne y del Dean Roca micer Roig y otros"; testimony of Juan Bautista Caro, 28 Sept. 1571, CCC, I, 5, Procesos difamatorios II. Caro was a former ally of Monzón, and when he refused, the rector accused him of wanting to ingratiate himself with the archbishop; testimony of Gregorio Ibañez, 31 Jan. 1572, CCC, I, 5, Procesos difamatorios II.

113. "Hizo un cartel en romance en el qual en nombre de los estudiantes pedían al sr. patriarcha que sacase de las carceles a los maestros que estavan presos, por los daños que en la universidad se seguian y que en el dicho cartel dixo y llamó de borde al arcobpo. y que no tomase consejo del cano. Bich ni del Dean Roca ni de Sanctander"; testimony of Serra against Pineda, 23 Jan. 1572, CCC, I, 5, Procesos difamatorios II.

114. "Todos los discípulos son muy apassionados contra el patriarcha, y tengo para mi que estos los harían y pondrán y que pretendiendo en zer plazer a los dichos mros y ganar con ellos gracia." Figueroa suspected that Monzón knew who had put up the pasquinades "because I spoke with him afterwards and he laughed about it, seeming content to play games with his words. In his bearing and demeanor he is satirical man, and inclined to such actions" (porque estando preso por el patriarcha mi sor. y aviéndose puesto algunos pasquines yo tintava con el y se reya dello y mostrava olgarse con artificio de palabras y porque en su condición y manera de tratar me parece que es hombre satírico e inclinado a semejantes cosas); testimony of Figueroa against Monzón, 15 Dec. 1571, CCC, I, 5, Procesos difamatorios II.

115. "Yy con ellos seis o siete caballeros moços a quyen confesavan y algunos clérigos los mas disfamados de allo a quyen a reprehendido o castigado"; AHN, Inquisition, lib. 912, fol. 533v.

116. "Que estuvo preso por el arçobispo más de un año sobre mugeres"; testimony of Philipe Joan Alonso against Pineda, 3 Oct. 1571, CCC, I, 5, Procesos difamatorios II.

117. "Dixo que a mucha parte de toda la ciudad acabsa de la rebuelta y prisión de los theólogos a oydo murmurar que no sentían bien de su trato y govierno y que tenía psion y mala voluntad a los theólogos," with reference to Carroz; testimony of Juan Blay Navarro, 6 Oct. 1571, CCC, I, 5, Procesos difamatorios I.

118. Rojas and Calderón to the Consejo de Inquisición, 11 Mar. 1572, 18 July 1572, and 12 Aug. 1572, AHN, Inquisition, lib. 912, fols. 644r, 639r, 643r.

119. The names of Carroz, Juan Blay Navarro, and others are crossed out each time they appear in the surviving documentation; Valencian tribunal to the Council, 9 Jan. 1576, AHN, Inquisition, lib. 914, fol. 7r.

120. Antonio Pineda, for example, was sentenced to public humiliation, perpetual exile, and ten years in the galleys; 6 Feb. 1572, CCC, I, 5, Procesos difamatorios I. Three of the defendants, including Pineda, were turned over to the ecclesiastical court, but no record survives of the decisions of this tribunal.

121. At one point, for example, the Carroz family demanded the names of the witnesses against the sacristan. Rojas and Calderón urged Espinosa to reject the Carrozes' request because "the greater part of the city is indignantly opposed to the archbishop, and this would ruin him" (la mayor parte de la ciudad esta indignada contra el arçobispo y . . . viendo las cosas que algunos testigos dezen de sospechas de su persona sera arruinalla del todo). Calderón and Rojas added ominously, "Los Carroçes son cavalleros principales muchos y muy aparentados y contra el sacristán han testificado de su yglesia beneficiados y dicho cosas notables que entendido quien es el auctor de fuerça ha de ser perseguido y otros que son testigos de menos qualidad estan a peligro de ser muertos que se sabe aquí hazer con facilidad"; Calderón and Rojas to Espinosa, 12 Dec. 1571, AHN, Inquisition, lib. 912, fol. 523r.

122. "Algunes liçons en lo Collegi dels enegusites y en alguns monestirs de la pnt ciutat lo que es prohibit per una de dites constitucions del dit studi general, la qual prohibix que ningun studiant puixa hoir fora del dit studi sols pena de no ser admès a alguns beneficis, ni a perndre graus alguns e pla dita universitat . . . restant la dita constitució en sa força y valor de manera que no puga ser treta en consequencia la pnt provisió y abilitació"; 10 May 1586, AA, Manuals de Consells, 110 A, fol. 544r.

123. Robres Lluch, San Juan de Ribera, 187.

124. In a famous article, Sebastián García Martínez offers a devastating critique of the idea that Ribera was responsible for the eradication of Erasmian thought in Valencia by demonstrating that the more vital "first wave" of Erasmianism had already passed by 1569; García Martínez, "El patriarca Ribera." Yet the writings of Juan Bautista Pérez and others indicate that humanist activity had not been limited exclusively to editions of classical texts such as those of Pedro Juan Nuñez and Juan Martín Cordero; Ehlers, "Plomos de Granada."

125. "Anyone who dared speak of reform, or even insinuate that it was appropriate, was ipso facto declared a madman and an outlaw. He was cast off on a tangent from the circle of normal Spanish society, regardless of who he might be, and condemned to a marginal existence, as if reform were leprosy. . . . Those of us who advocated change and proposed to revise antiquated forms were called again and again 'enemies of the University'"; Ortega y Gasset, Mission of the University, 3–6.

126. This ceremony had been delayed for almost a month owing to a dispute over matters of precedence between the town council and the Duke of Nájera, who had been appointed viceroy just over a year earlier. In this case, Ribera acted as a mediator in the controversy; Carreres Zacarés, Libre de memories, 920–34.

127. Martí Mestre, El Libre de antiquitats, 222.

128. In addition, Monzón was succeeded as rector of the university by Juan Blay Navarro in 1573; Robres Lluch, San Juan de Ribera, 169.

129. "An hecho elección para estos effectos de la persona del maestro Pedro Monçon cathedrático de theología en esta universidad persona de muchas letras y virtud"; Ribera to Philip II, 17 Dec. 1578, ARV, Cartas a los Virreyes, carpeta 75.

130. Jurados to Philip II, Valencia, 24 Oct. 1583, ARV, Cartas a los Virreyes, carpeta 81.

131. Referring to the *pavordías*, a set of benefices that led to great controversy in the 1580s, "Y ansi han dado quatro a theólogos y an hecho buena eleción, porque aunque algunos de ellos son de poco provecho para los estudiantes, por los muchos años que an servido en la universidad merecen esta gratificación"; Ribera to Philip II, 31 Aug. 1588, ARV, Cartas a los Virreyes, carpeta 86.

132. On Ribera's dispute with the viceroy Iñigo Lopez de Mendoza, marquis of Mondéjar, which also led to the excommunication of the Audiencia Real, see Astraín, *Historia*, 48–56. The archbishop's disagreement with the Valencian Inquisition led to a period of absenteeism at autos de fe on his part and a bit of investigation into the history of precedence on theirs; Consejo de Inquisición to Valencian tribunal, 18 Apr. 1573, AHN, Inquisition, lib. 326, fols. 102r–v. On Ribera and the Cortes, see "Razonamiento que el patriarcha arçobispo de Valencia Don Juan de Rivera hiço a la Magd de Felipe segundo en las Cortes de Monçon el año de 1585 sobre la precedencia del Reyno de Valencia al Principado de Cataluña, y la respuesta de su Magd. 1585," CCC, Colección Gregorio Mayans, vol. 585, doc. 5.

133. Duke of Nájera to Philip II, Valencia, 9 Nov. 1579, ARV, Cartas a los Virreyes, carpeta 13.

CHAPTER 3. REFORM BY OTHER MEANS

1. Notarial document ratified by Jaime Cristóbal Ferrer, Valencia, 24 Oct. 1591, reprinted in *Carta de la M. Ill. ciudad de Valencia al Ssmo. Pio Sexto* (Valencia: Benito Monfort, 1797), 30–36, CCC, Varios de S. Juan de Ribera, vol. 2.

2. Herzog, "Private Organizations."

3. A graduate of Salamanca in scholastic theology, Ribera nonetheless infused humanist elements into his projects. In this sense, his reforms corroborate Lu Ann Homza's contention that early modern Spaniards could adopt either scholastic or humanist perspectives according to their purposes; Homza, *Religious Authority*.

4. In 1583, for example, Ribera ordered a general procession dedicated to St. Vincent the martyr in the hopes of bringing rain; Martí Mestre, *El Libre de antiquitats*, 231. In 1586 he capitalized on his position as head of the cathedral to gain access to Philip II; Martí Mestre, *El Libre de antiquitats*, 240–42; Carreres Zacarés, *Libre de memories*, 980–83; Cock, *Relacion del viaje*, 250–51.

5. This is a succinct description of a complicated situation. The dignidades included pavordías, holdovers from a largely superseded system of funding who nonetheless received some of the ceremonial courtesies of canons and dignidades; Cipres de Pobar, *Origen y progresso*.

6. In the fifteenth and early sixteenth centuries, the canons effectively ran the Valencian church during a century-long period in which various members of the Borgia family held the see (and collected its episcopal rents) without ever actually setting foot in the diocese.

7. Martí Mestre, *El Libre de antiquitats*, 208, 210; Carreres Zacarés, *Libre de memories*, 1003.

8. Cipres de Pobar, *Origen y progresso*, 65–66; letter from an anonymous Valencian chap-

lain to Philip II, 4 Oct. 1586, ARV, Cartas a los Virreyes, carpeta 84; Ribera to Philip II, Gandía, 24 Apr. 1587, ARV, Cartas a los Virreyes, carpeta 85.

9. Fernández Terricabras, *Felipe II*, 300.

10. *Epitome sive compendium constitutionum.* "Dubitante de solatio quattuor mensium, quod Canonici residentes quolibet anno percipere soliti erant, proptere a quod Tridentina Synodus, ubiuis Ecclesiarum solatium Canonicorum ad tres dumtaxat menses reduxit"; ibid., 36.

11. "Riñiendo, o bozeando, moviendo algun escándalo"; Ribera, *Synodus diocesana valentiae, 1578*, 61–68. These synodal decrees applied equally to all of the churches in the diocese, but unlike his orders regarding the poverty of the rural clergy, Ribera's statements concerning the *vicarios de coro* (choirmasters) held much more relevance for larger churches such as the cathedral.

12. The inquisitors Pedro de Zárate and Juan de Llano de Valdés to the Consejo de Inquisición, Valencia, 3 Aug. 1584, AHN, Inquisition, lib. 915, fol. 607r. "Capitulos acordados para remedio de los retraidos que se recogen en la santa iglesia de Valencia entre la magestad del rei don Felipe tercero, nuestro señor, arzobispo i cabildo de dicha Iglesia"; CCC, Colección Gregorio Mayans, vol. 633, 1–5. Sadly, the ecclesiastical court records that have allowed historians to study clerical reform in other contexts—most notably, the research synthesized in Hsia, *Social Discipline*—do not exist for Valencia.

13. Rawlings, *Church, State and Society*, 57. The cathedral chapter in Cuenca also replicated this common pattern of resistance to reform; Nalle, *God in La Mancha*, 74–80.

14. At this point the archbishop lowered Tudela's regular annual salary from 120 L to 60 L, though Tudela would still have received a raise overall; CCC, Asientos de criados, 1575–1592, fol. 25. On Miguel de Espinosa, see Guitarte Izquierdo, *Obispos auxiliares*, 49.

15. Martí Mestre, *El Libre de antiquitats*, 257n840.

16. Ribera performed the consecration on a special dais constructed for the occasion; the ceremony went on for so long that the archbishop decided to forgo the sermon; Martí Mestre, *El Libre de antiquitats*, 248.

17. The first canon appointed after Ribera's arrival, for example, was Don Federico de Borja (canon 1573; d. 1605), who had succeeded Don Gaspar Jofré de Borja as *ardiaca major* in 1556; Martí Mestre, *El Libre de antiquitats*, 222.

18. "Y aunque a muchos días que yo deseaba hazer esta obra: las obligaciones y cargos desta dignidad no avían dado lugar para ello, e agora que VMagd la tiene por útil, estoy muy cierto que la mandará favorescer hasta lo último con su christianíssimo zelo"; Ribera to Philip II, Valencia, 31 Oct. 1581, ARV, Cartas a los Virreyes, carpeta 78.

19. Vizuete Mendoza, *La iglesia*, 171, 190–91; Rawlings, *Church, State and Society*, 71–72.

20. Ribera, untitled document notarized by Francisco Jerónimo Metaller, Valencia, 14 Mar. 1583, CCC, I, 7, A.

21. "Borromean Milan aside, this Tridentine provision [to establish diocesan seminaries] was by and large a failure"; Hsia, *Catholic Renewal*, 116. On the correspondence, see Robres Lluch, "San Carlos Borromeo."

22. Sermon delivered in Alcoy, 6 June 1577, Ribera, *Sermones*, 4:49.

23. Nalle, *God in La Mancha*, 29. On the importance of the Eucharist, see Muir, *Ritual*, esp. 160 and 205.

24. García Cárcel, "Notas," 146.

25. Ribera's efforts did not go unnoticed among the wider community in Valencia. In 1589, the jurados wrote to Philip II complaining about the construction of the Jesuit *casa profesa* in 1579 and of the ongoing work on the Colegio; CCC, Colección Gregorio Mayans, vol. 677.

26. "Axi per al seminari que fa lo Patriarca com pera la casa profesa dels pares de la companyia y altres religions"; jurados to Philip II, Valencia, 7 Sept. 1589, ARV, Cartas a los Virreyes, carpeta 88.

27. Contract between Espinosa and Matarana, 14 June 1600, CCC, I, 6, 2, 1. See also Benito Domenech, *Pinturas*, 65–72; Mulcahy, *Decoration*.

28. According to Jonathan Brown, by 1597, when Matarana "started to cover the walls with frescoes, his style was about to pass from fashion"; Brown, *Painting in Spain*, 95.

29. Nalle, *God in La Mancha*, 148–51.

30. Contracts with Sariñena, 1585, 1592, reprinted in Boronat y Barrachina, *Juan de Ribera*, 336; Benito Domenech, *Pinturas*, 145–56.

31. "Memorial echo en 20 de Ebrero 1604 de las joyas y otros gastos echos en la prossesión del Sanctíssimo Sacramento"; CCC, I, 6, 2, 13.

32. Document notarized by Jaime Cristóbal Ferrer, 29 Jan. 1604, CCC, I, 6, 2, 13.

33. Castañeda y Alcover, *Coses evengudes*, 67. Ribera spent more than 200 L on candles alone; "Quenta de la sera," 13 Mar. 1604, CCC, I, 6, 2, 13.

34. Pradas, *Libro de memorias*, fols. 18–20, BGUV, MS 529.

35. "Avia molts fanchs y un quart ans ques accabas plouisnaua molt y axi es donaren mew presa y accabaren desconcertadament"; Castañeda y Alcover, *Coses evengudes*, 67.

36. "Memorial echo en 20 de Ebrero 1604 de las joyas," CCC, I, 6, 2, 13.

37. By virtue of a papal brief issued by Clement VIII in 1598, Ribera enjoyed even wider powers over his seminary than those stipulated in the Council of Trent; brief dated 16 Mar. 1598, reprinted in Ribera, *Constituciones del Colegio*, xv.

38. Ribera, *Constituciones del Colegio*, 17–19.

39. Ibid., chap. 16. By this latter stage of his episcopate, Ribera had adopted a much more cynical, pragmatic stance with respect to the moriscos in his diocese.

40. Ibid., 41–43, 77–78; Nalle, *God in La Mancha*, 92.

41. Ribera, *Constituciones de la Capilla*, 8–9.

42. Ibid., 4, 7.

43. Ibid., 9. On more than one occasion, Ribera's quest for solemnity led him into conflict with his neighbors. In 1604–5 he paid the Estudio General to remove its principal doors from the plaza shared with the Colegio and reinstall them on the other side of the complex, so that the students would not disrupt the Colegio as they moved between classes. The archbishop also engaged in an ongoing dispute with a nearby bakery, which evidently produced enough smoke to hinder the celebration of the Mass when the ovens were fired; Castañeda y Alcover, *Coses evengudes*, 71; CCC, I, 7, A.

44. Ribera, *Constituciones de la Capilla*, 129.

45. Ibid., 124.

46. Soergel, *Wondrous in His Saints*, 80.

47. Ximeno, *Escritores*, 1:177; Poska, *Regulating the People*, 127–57.

48. Carreres Zacarés, *Libre de memories*, 945.

49. Ibid., 946.

50. "Cosa james vista que pujans a sermonar un tan gran princep y perlat lo gran concurs de gent no li donas lloch"; ibid.

51. Castañeda y Alcover, *Coses evengudes*, 11; Antist, *Verdedera relacion*; Antist, *Adiciones*.

52. Ribera eventually installed this painting in the Colegio; Benito Domenech, *Pinturas*, 319–20.

53. 30 Aug. 1608, Martí Mestre, *El* Libre de antiquitats, 268. Bertrán was subsequently canonized in 1671.

54. This work has erroneously been attributed to Ribalta; Benito Domenech, *Pinturas*, 326.

55. Huerga, *Historia*, 1:112, 125, 578; Valencian tribunal to the Council of Inquisition, Valencia, 19 Aug. 1575, AHN, Inquisition, lib. 913, fol. 515r. "En algunos destos lugares hallé gran multitud de Beatas de las que hazen estos alumbrados y teatinos, y todas confessas, en cuyas casas domatizan de noche y de día, y hazen sus conventiculos, poxan y duermen en las mismas casas, y estas doctrinas ocultas y de rincones siempre tienen malos fines. . . . Favoréscense para esto, según me dizen, de los Arçobispos de Sevilla [Cristóbal de Rojas] y Valencia que son las amas que han criado estos alumbrados de Estremadura, siendo obispos en Badajoz"; letter from Juan de Fresneda to Philip II, 5 June 1575, IVDJ, envío 89, doc. 393.

56. Ehlers, "La esclava y el patriarca."

57. Jodi Bilinkoff has drawn a parallel between the beata and the courtier, noting that both needed the ability to navigate the subtle world of the court; Bilinkoff, "Saint for a City," 325, 330.

58. Sanchis, *Sor Margarita Agullona*, 20–22, 156, 179, 188.

59. Notarial document dated 11 Dec. 1600, CCC, I, 7, 6, 73.

60. "Y casi las más veces vienen juntas estas dos saetas del conocimiento del Altísimo y del proprio: y cuanto más encendidas vienen, más claro es este conocimiento, y da la una saeta con la otra, hasta que se enciende tanto el fuego, que sólo el que tiene experiencia lo puede crecer, pero no entender ni hablar, por más que por señas descubra el abismo de maravillas nunca entendidas, que agotan el entendimiento, la voluntad se abrasa, el corazón a las veces se ensancha, tanto que parece verdaderamente tener todo lo criado dentro de sí"; Agullona lo Ribera, quoted in Sanchis, *Sor Margarita Agullona*, 213.

61. Teresa of Avila, *Interior Castle*, 36.

62. Sanchis, *Sor Margarita Agullona*, 209, 218–19, 237–41.

63. Ibid., 160.

64. "Item fray Jayme Sánchez y fray Simón le metían a la dicha Beata las manos por los pechos quando fingía que estava elevada"; Pons Fuster, *Místicos, beatas y alumbrados*, 34–35.

65. Sanchis, *Sor Margarita Agullona*, 64.

66. Lehfeldt, "Discipline, Vocation, and Patronage."

67. Ribera, "Al lector," 17.

68. "Foren padrins don Pedro Andres, prevere, comanador de sent Anthoni, y sor Margarita Agullo, beata profesa de la tercera regla de sent Françes"; Catalá de Valeriola, *Autobiografía*, 49.

69. Castañeda y Alcover, *Coses evengudes*, 50.

70. "Y en particular nombraba entre dientes algunas necesidades públicas"; Ribera, "Al lector," 11–14.

71. Christian, *Apparitions.*

72. Ribera, "Al lector," 9.

73. Sanchis, *Sor Margarita Agullona*, 160.

74. Ribera's promotion of the veneration of Agullona thus differed dramatically from the agenda of Teresa of Avila's followers, who played down the more controversial aspects of her life; see Ahlgren, *Teresa of Avila.*

75. In the same year the archbishop also commissioned a copy by Sariñena, "for the Colegio"; Benito Domenech, *Pinturas*, 302, 323.

76. "Lo pintor Sarinyena la retrata tenia una garlanda de flors al cap y les mans posada una bore el altra y una creu entre les mans y los pits"; Castañeda y Alcover, *Coses evengudes*, 50. Benito argues that it was actually Ribalta who made the first painting on the basis of his viewing of Agullona's body during 9–13 December 1600; Benito Domenech, *Pinturas*, 301–302.

77. Ribera, "Al lector," 19.

78. See Strasser, "Bones of Contention."

79. Prades, *Historia*, 7, 15.

80. Falomir, *La pintura*, 87–88.

81. Council of Trent, sess. 25, 3–4 Dec. 1563, in Tanner, *Decrees*, 2:775.

82. Bouza Alvarez, *Religiosidad contrarreformista*, 475.

83. "El negocio de las reliquias a ydo bien hasta agora, Bendito sea Dios. Tuve determinado de acavar la qualificación por el mes de septiembre, o octubre"; Pedro de Castro to Ribera, Granada, July 1598, CCC, I, 7, 4, 17(5). Juan Bautista Pérez, bishop of Segorbe, antiquarian, numismatist, and correspondent of Antonio Agustín, wrote a scathing condemnation of the *plomos de Granada* in 1595 entitled "Parecer sobre las Planchas de plomo que se han hallado en Granada" (BGUV). See also Ehlers, *"Plomos de Granada."*

84. Ribera to the clerics of Valencia, 16 Nov. 1600, CCC, I, 8, 2, 7.

85. Aguila to the jurados, Madrid, 1 Apr. 1600, AA, Manuals de Consells 126 A, fols. 610r–v.

86. Castañeda y Alcover, *Coses evengudes*, 42; Vidal y Micò, *Historia*, 393; 24 Apr. 1600, AA, Manuals de Consells, 126 A, fols. 641r–v.

87. Philip III to Ribera, 29 June 1600, CCC, I, 7, 3.

88. Castañeda y Alcover, *Coses evengudes*, 48.

89. Ibid., 48–49.

90. Ribera purchased many relics from Cardona, who also supplied Philip II; CCC, I, 4, 5.

91. Cardinal Pierre de Gondi to the cathedral of Vannes, Paris, 16 Aug. 1601, CCC, I, 8, 2, 13.

92. Henri Gondi to Ribera, 26 Sept. 1601, CCC, I, 8, 2, 13. See also Bergin, *French Episcopate*, 632.

93. Canons of Vannes to Cardinal Gondi, Vennes, 22 Sept. 1601, CCC, I, 8, 2, 13.

94. Diago, *Apuntamientos*, 2:40.

95. Escolano, *Década primera*, 1:1076.

96. "Information de testigos recebidos por mandamiento y procision del Illmo y Rmo don Joan de Ribera," CCC, I, 8, 2, 14.

97. *Las insignes reliquias.*

98. Autograph letter from Lerma to Ribera, Naples, 11 May 1606, CCC, I, 8, 2, 18.

99. Vidal y Micò, *Historia*, 399.

100. Bouza Alvarez, *Religiosidad contrarreformista*, 45–56.

101. "Acte del entrego del cos del Glorios martyr St. Mauro per al Collegi de Corpus Christi," 18 Nov. 1599, CCC, I, 8, 2, 2.

102. "1599. Gastos hechos en Roma por el dotor Luis de Cordoba en hallar y procurar el cuerpo del glorioso St. Mauro," CCC, I, 7, 6, 12(2).

103. Guevara to Ribera, Martorel (Catalonia), 6 Nov. 1599, CCC, I, 8, 2, 1.

104. Castañeda y Alcover, *Coses evengudes*, 38–39; "Acte del entrego," CCC, I, 8, 2, 2.

105. "Testimonio de cuerpo de S. Mauro. Memoria de la entrada en Vala. del cuerpo del glorioso san Mauro," CCC, I, 8, 2, 3.

106. Castañeda y Alcover, *Coses evengudes*, 41.

107. Ribera to the clergy of Valencia, 16 Nov. 1600, CCC, I, 8, 2, 7.

108. *Historia beati Mauri martiris*, Lecciones del brevario (Valencia: Felipe Mey, 1609), CCC, I, 8, 2, 9.

109. "Noticias relativas al cuerpo de San Mauro," 1796, CCC, I, 8, 2, 10(2).

110. "Que según vemos agora adornada de lugares sagrados, y habitada de tan grande número de Ecclesiásticos; y en el pueblo generalmente una propensión natural a cosas de deuoción con summa sineza en el culto divino, toda la ciudad por junto parece una Iglesia o Monasterio de Religion"; Escolano, *Decada primera*, 1:869–70.

111. CCC, Asientos de criados, 1575–1592, fols. 15–17. Joan Porcar noted Avalos's conse cration on 18 Oct. 1598; Castañeda y Alcover, *Coses evengudes*, 11.

112. CCC, Asientos de criados, 1575–1592, fols. 33, 165; CCC, Asientos de criados, 1592–97, fol. 7; Martí Mestre, *El Libre de antiquitats*, 265; Guitarte Izquierdo, *Obispos auxiliares*, 49–54.

113. O'Malley, *First Jesuits*; Bilinkoff, *Avila of Saint Teresa.*

CHAPTER 4. FROM MORISCOS TO MOROS

1. AHN, Inquisición, lib. 936, fol. 358v.

2. Rawlings, *Church, State and Society*, 77.

3. Robres Lluch, *San Juan de Ribera*, 322; see also Cárcel Ortí and Trenchs Odena, "Una visita pastoral"; Cárcel Ortí, *Las visitas pastorales*, 76.

4. Royo Martínez, *Las visitas pastorales*; Poska, *Regulating the People*, 160.

5. Robres Lluch, *San Juan de Ribera*, 96. In 1613 the chronicler Marco de Guadalajara reported, with a hint of teleology, that "con mucha repugnancia admitió don Juan de Ribera . . . el Arçobispado de Valencia, por el escrúpulo que tenía, de encargarse de tantos Apóstatas Moriscos"; Guadalajara, *Memorable expulsion*, 59–60. Shortly after his arrival in Valencia, Ribera evidently wrote to his friend Navarro in despair. In his response, Navarro commiserated, "Lamentable cosa cierto me parece lo que vra. Sa. Sanma. llora y casi imposible el buen remedio de tanto mal que *mitit in scyllam dun charibdim vitat*"; Navarro to Ribera, Rome, 15? Sept. 1570, CCC, I, 7, 8, Moriscos I, 1.

6. Pike, *Aristocrats and Traders*, 154–70.

7. Thomas Aquinas, *Summa theologica*, I–II, q. 109, a. 6, quoted in Bouillard, *Conversion et grace*, 173–74.

8. Aubin, *Le problème de la "conversion,"* 30–31.

9. Arroyas Serrano and Gil Vicent, *Revuelta y represión*, 9–10.

10. *Colección de documentos inéditos*, 90:357.

11. *Calendar of State Papers*, 9:283.

12. After negotiations with the Valencian nobility broke down over the issue of illegal seizures of morisco goods, the Supreme Council of the Inquisition ordered the Valencian Inquisition to deal directly with the morisco leaders; Benítez, "Duras negociaciones," 114–15; Haliczer, *Inquisition and Society*, 263; Danvila, *Conferencias*, 182.

13. Danvila, *Conferencias*, 187.

14. Benítez has argued that this concordia tended to strengthen the position of the noble lords relative to their morisco vassals, consolidating their control of the *dominio útil* of morisco goods; Benítez, *Heroicas decisiones*, 263.

15. "Y que se presume han delinquido por ignorancia, y falta de enseñamiento, más que por malicia. Y que sería usar de mucho rigor, so las penas del derecho se oviessen de executar en los que han delinquido: y sería occasión de mucho daño en las personas y bienes de sus súbditos de esse Reyno y districto"; BL, Egerton MS 1510, fol. 260.

16. AHN, Inquisition, lib. 912, fols. 35, 72–73.

17. "Muestrase tanbién el ánimo de los que lo dieron, en que buscaron persona que no los conociese ni uviese tratado, per que así viniese boçal al negocio, y ellos le pudiessen engañar puedo yo hablar en esto con experiencia por lo que hizieron conmigo poco tiempo después de aver venido a este reyno, y salieron con lo que pretendían, porque me engañaron y los crey y screví a su Magd en su pretensión"; undated memorial from Ribera to Philip II (1582), CCC, I, 7, 8, Moriscos I, 28, fol. 1.

18. Concilio provincial de Valencia, año 1565, in Tejada y Ramiro, *Colección de canones*, 261–313. See also Pérez de Ayala, *Sínodo*. Philip II demonstrated a great deal of confidence in Pérez de Ayala's proposed reforms and wrote Ribera on several occasions encouraging him to follow through on these projects; ARV, Real 253, fols. 118, 138, 152.

19. Rojas to the Council of the Inquisition, Valencia, 31 July 1573, BL, Egerton MS 1510, fol. 206. The initial committee included the inquisitor Juan de Rojas, the viceroy Mondéjar, Bishop Gregorio Gallo of Orihuela, and Bishop Martín de Córdoba of Tortosa. It ended in a deadlock because in contrast to the other members, Ribera took the more controversial stance that the salaries should be paid from the parishes' firstfruits before turning to the tithes, an annual tax levied upon goods such as crops, animals, cheese, wool, and wax; BL, Egerton MS 1510, fol. 206v.

20. The new committee included Roca, the dean of the cathedral; Vich, a cathedral canon; Juan Paulo Porta and Juan Baptista Caro, official visitors to the moriscos; and Gabriel Trobado, the diocesan treasurer. The council noted that where adding a new parish proved impossible, the parishes should at least build a second church in the annex, with the priest giving mass twice on Sundays and holidays, once for each congregation; BL, Egerton MS 1510, fols. 213v–14.

21. Ramírez de Haro, in an effort to endow Valencia's 190 morisco parishes with 30 L per

year, had established an annual diocesan contribution of 2,050 L to subsidize parishes whose rents fell short of this sum.

22. Ribera expressly stated that he would not call upon the king's share of the tithes, even in areas where this "royal third" had come to be controlled by the seigneurs; BL, Egerton MS 1510, fol. 214v. The council of 1574 also addressed the possibility that in some parishes, all of these sources might not total 100 libras. "When neither the firstfruits nor the tithes collected within the new parish amount to 100 L per year, so long as the required quantity is not great, the archbishopric will assume all of these costs even though it is not obligated to do so, because this is what the archbishop wants. To this end he will donate an additional 3,299 L 9 s 8 beyond the 2000 ducats he paid before under the old system." "Sino que faltava gran quantidad toda esta se cargava a la mensa Arzobispal aunque no estava obligada a ello, porque el Arzobispo lo quiso así"; BL, Egerton MS 1510, fol. 215v.

23. "Memoria de la contribucion de la mensa episcopal y dignitat prepositures parrochials antidis privades persones rendit mesquitar en antica et nova dotacione quid facta fuyt parrochialibus opidor hors que nuxer ad fidem sunt conversi archiepto. Valens"; CCC, I, 7, 8, Resúmenes de pagas. A note on the back regarding a payment to the "colegio de nuevos convertidos" (school for moriscos) suggests a date around 20 December 1577.

24. The archdiocese raised its contribution from 2,050 L to 3,299 L, 9 s, 8, and the total assessment rose from 3,723 L, 7 s, 8 under the old system to 8,130 L, 19 s, 7 under the new. The assessment of the archdeaconate of Játiva rose from 87 L, 3 s, 11 to 246 L; the archdeaconate of Sagunto, from 15 L to 100 L; and the abbey and convent of Valldigna, from 150 L to 265 L. Among the canons, deacons, and monasteries, Ribera also included a few noble seigneurs, such as Don Vilariz Carroz, seigneur of Sirat, who was reassessed at 100 L per year after having contributed nothing at all; "Memoria de la contribucio," CCC, I, 7, 8, Resúmenes de pagas; "Relación de las casas," in Boronat y Barrachina, *Los moriscos*, 1:433.

25. Ribera disbursed supplemental payments averaging 20 L to approximately sixty priests in morisco parishes. He also devoted 718 L of the regular contribution annually to Pablo Joan Porta, maestro of the school for morisco children founded under Charles V.

26. After a series of extraordinary start-up donations from the archdiocese totaling more than 14,000 L, Ribera regularized his annual contribution at 3,780 L. "Pensión apostolica de los 3600 L reservados sobre la mensa Arzobispal de Valencia para la conversión de los nuevos convertidos del Arzobispado," CCC, I, 7, 8, Resúmenes de pagas. Ribera's accountant, Saubat de Ureta, recorded the deposits into the account in a folder marked "Cargo," in CCC, I, R. The running totals for both type of transaction appear in the libros mayores of the archdiocese, but without the same level of detail.

27. On 23 August 1580, Ureta donated 40 L to the jurados of Mirarrosa to defray the costs of building a church; "Cargo," fols. 1–3, CCC, I, R.

28. Rector Vizcarra to Philip II, 23 Feb. 1575, ARV, Cartas a los Virreyes, carpeta 73; Rector Porta to Philip II, 3 Jan. 1582, ARV, Cartas a los Virreyes, carpeta 79. On schools for Old Christian children, see Nalle, *God in La Mancha*, 111–14.

29. Poska, *Regulating the People*, 11.

30. Episcopal edict of 1 June 1569, in Canet and Romero, *Crides*, 2:267–82; Ribera, *Synodus diocesana valentiae*, 1578, 22–27, 34–35. Ribera did address the moriscos specifically in

separate pastoral letters, but the synod itself singles them out only at the very end, in a list enumerating the amount that each of the towns in the diocese should be assessed to cover the visitors' per diem costs. Ribera ordered that those morisco parishes "with firstfruits" pay for two days, whereas those without were to pay for just one, the minimum amount demanded of any parish.

31. Council of Trent, sess. 5, 17 June 1546, 2d decree, point 9, in Tanner, *Decrees*, 2:669.

32. McGinness, *Right Thinking*, 3. For a contrasting view of the history of preaching in this era, see Taylor, *Soldiers of Christ*.

33. O'Malley, *Praise and Blame*, 3:238–40.

34. Martí, *La preceptiva retórica*, 95–100.

35. O'Malley, "Saint Charles Borromeo."

36. Harline and Put, *Bishop's Tale*.

37. Cárcel Ortí, "El inventario."

38. Antist, *La vida y historia*; Bueno Tárrega, *Sant Vicent Ferrer*.

39. William Klingshirn, for example, in his study of Arles in late antiquity, emphasizes the necessity of the participation and the consent of the people in the long, slow, reversible process of Christianization and depaganization. Even in a nominally Christian region, traditional Gallo-Roman communal rituals could persist without evident tension where Christianity failed to offer viable alternatives, and to the extent that the laity did adopt Christianity, they adapted official doctrine to suit their communal needs; Klingshern, *Caesarius of Arles*. Anthropologists studying non-Western peoples have challenged the Weberian association of the spread of world religions with rationalization, both by defending the rationality of traditional religions on their own terms and by illustrating the range of contingent factors facilitating conversion: the often-simultaneous change in political regime, the prospect of economic advancement in the newly formulated society, and the individualistic appeal of Christianity at a time of relativization of traditional ways; Hefner, introduction to *Conversion to Christianity*.

40. Castillo Mattasoglio, *Libres para creer*, 79–83.

41. "Cargo," fol. 1, CCC, I, R.

42. Ehlers, "Archbishop Juan de Ribera."

43. Ramón Robres's editions of Ribera's sermons are based upon Ribera's own autograph notes, which he never revised for publication. In the vast majority of cases, Ribera indicates the date and place in which the sermons were delivered; Ribera, *Sermones*.

44. More than a few Old Christians in mixed areas attained at least a basic knowledge of the morisco language; Císcar Pallarés, "'Algaravía' y 'algemía,'" 145–47.

45. "Comienza hoy la Cuaresma. Pero digamos qué intención tuvo la Santa Iglesia para instituir la Cuaresma"; Játiva, 28 Feb. 1571, Ribera, *Sermones*, 2:15.

46. Játiva, 9 Mar. 1571, Ribera, *Sermones*, 2:80; Benigánim, 6 May 1571, Ribera, *Sermones*, 3:95.

47. María la Herrera, auto de fe of 10 Sept. 1581, AHN, Inquisition, lib. 934, fols. 107–8. The jurisdiction of the Valencian Inquisition corresponded roughly to the kingdom and diocese of Valencia, although the tribunal included a few Aragonese towns in the north (such as Gea) and excluded parts of Orihuela in the south; see Labarta, *La onomástica*, 17. The moriscos processed by the Valencian Inquisition and penanced in autos de fe nonetheless influenced Ribera's views on the morisco question in his diocese.

48. Miguel Vayo Madonet, auto de fe of 10 Sept. 1581, AHN, Inquisition, lib. 936, fols. 301–2.

49. Arroyas Serrano and Gil Vicent, *Revuelta y represión*, 9–10; Ramírez Martínez, *Los moriscos*, 111–12.

50. Monter, *Frontiers of Heresy*, 193–95.

51. The town of Gea, a "lugar de cerca de 400 casas," which did not participate in the concordia on account of the subsidy, illustrates a common reponse to edicts of grace; Sotomayor to the Inquisition of Valencia, 3 Mar. 1563, BL, Egerton MS 1833, fol. 18. On the Count of Fuentes, see Inquisition of Valencia to Council of Inquisition, 4 Nov. 1566, AHN, Inquisition, lib. 936, fol. 25; relación of auto de fe, 7 June 1568, AHN, Inquisition, lib. 936, fols. 38–39; appeal from Conde de Fuentes, 1566, BL, Egerton MS 1833, fol. 35.

52. Inquisition of Aragon to Council of Inquisition, Aljaferia, 7 Dec. 1573, BL, Egerton MS 1833, fol. 105. Haedo complained to the Count of Fuentes, "Representándole muchos insultos que los moriscos de Xea sus vassallos habían cometido y de cada día cometían en ministros del sto officio y otras personas que sospechaban habían testificado conta ellos en la inqon"; ibid.

53. "El no averla acceptado quando en aquella villa stubo el inquisidor Haedo no fue por menosprecio sino po no aver entendido lo que era, lo qual luego que entendieron la pidieron, y piden agora con todo amor y humildad"; moriscos of Gea, received in Madrid, 19 Aug. 1574, BL, Egerton MS 1833, fol. 112.

54. Haedo to Council of Inquisition, Gea, 4 Sept. 1573, BL, Egerton MS 1833, fol. 99; Inquisition of Valencia, 19 Feb. 1574, BL, Egerton MS 1833, fol. 111. "Donde e procurado saber los tratos y designos de los xpianos nuevos della, son tan secretos y recatados"; Rojas to Council of Inquisition, Gea 6 Apr. 1575, BL, Egerton MS 1833, fol. 117. The Marquis of Denia engaged the Inquisition in a similar discussion over his moriscos' supposed lack of instruction; AHN, Inquisition, lib. 327, fols. 378v–379r.

55. "Dixo e confesó que sus compañeros de cárcel le avían dicho que si confesava hera perdido"; Jaime Ciscar of Barriol, arrested 11 Feb. 1579, AHN, Inquisition, lib. 934, fol. 157.

56. Auto de fe, 18 Aug. 1577, AHN, Inquisition, lib. 936, fols. 149r–v.

57. Francisca la Portuguesa, auto de fe, 23 Mar. 1586, AHN, Inquisition, lib. 934, fol. 336.

58. Auto de fe, 18 Aug. 1577, AHN, Inquisition, lib. 936, fol. 151.

59. Auto de fe, 23 Mar. 1586, AHN, Inquisition, lib. 934, fols. 276–77. Along the same lines, Jerónimo Cosco of Borriol confessed in 1579 that he had exaggerated his testimony for fear of torture; AHN, Inquisition, lib. 934, fol. 163.

60. AHN, Inquisition, lib. 327, fols. 378v–79r.

61. Gregory XIII confirmed the agreements in a brief dated 16 June 1576; CCC, I, 7, 8, Moriscos I, 46; Boronat y Barrachina, *Los moriscos*, 1:286.

62. "Mandato expedido . . . acerca de la nueva dotació de las retorias de moros"; CCC, I, 7, 8, Moriscos I, 47. On 23 April 1578, Ribera disbursed 73 L, 4 s to Raphael Juan Tasalla for the mandates; "Pensión apostólica," fol. 1, CCC, I, 7, 8, Resúmenes de pagas.

63. "Proceso del pleito entre el Ilmo. y Rvdmo. Sr. D. Juan de Ribera, Arzobispo de Valencia, contra el discreto Pedro Sancho, notario, sobre arrendamiento de diezmos," 6 Oct. 1581, CCC, Inventario de procesos; "Proceso del pleito entre el Ilmo. y Rvdmo. Sr. D. Juan de Ribera Arzobispo de valencia, contra el ilustre y rvdo. abad y convento de Na. Sa. de Valldigna," 11 May 1582, CCC, Inventario de procesos; "Proceso del Ilmo. Sr. Patriarca de Valencia contra Gabriel Trobador," 19 Dec. 1583, CCC, Inventario de procesos.

64. 14 Oct. 1581, 50 L "a Micer Thomas Cerdán por el trabajo de advogar en las causas de las olim Mezquita con libranza del Patriarca"; "Pensión apostólica," fol. 4, CCC, I, 7, 8, Resúmenes de pagas.

65. "Escusado, cierto subsidio, impuesto en las rentas ecclesiásticas, por concessión de su Santidad, al Rey nuestro señor: en que exime y escusa un dezmero de cada pila, para ayuda a los gastos de la guerra contra infieles"; Covarrubias, *Tesoro*, 85. The archbishop and the cathedral lost on appeal and dutifully restored the revenues to the original collectors; letter from Gregori Ibanyez to Señor Meseller, 23 Sept. 1581, CCC, I, 7, 8, Resúmenes de pagas.

66. Robres calculates 195 annexes out of 421 morisco communities; Robres Lluch, "Catálogo."

67. Moriscos were generally reticent before the Inquisition, but there is little reason to believe that they would withhold such knowledge if they had it, as evidenced by their occasional unsuccessful attempts ("he knew no prayers, apart from a few poorly stated words from the Our Father and the Ave Maria") and the openness of those few who did know their prayers; trial of Miguel Sanzer de la Torre, AHN, Inquisition, lib. 934, fol. 476; Nalle, *God in La Mancha*, 128–29.

68. "Y que de hedad de veynte y cinco a veinte y seis anos enpezó a tener por buena la ley de los moros y le a durado gasta cierto tiempo que declaró porque oyó un cartel en la yglesia de parcent y el es de entonces determinó de hazer vida de xpiano"; AHN, Inquisition, lib. 934, fols. 345r–50r.

69. Auto de fe, 10 Sept. 1581, AHN, Inquisition, lib. 936, fol. 300v.

70. On this subject, see Dopico Black, *Perfect Wives, Other Women*, 8, 42.

71. AHN, Inquisition, lib. 934, fols. 18r–v, 123r, 408r.

72. "Confesó que luego que nació el mochacho la madrina le havía dicho que havía nacido de aquella manera, y havía ido a llamar al rector para que lo biese y no lo havía hallado"; relación of the auto de fe of 29 Sept. 1579, AHN, Inquisition, lib. 936, fol. 232v.

73. "Como tienen minado el pueblo para esconderse quando los van a prender y librar se de la justicia"; testimony of Mosen Miguel Nuñez, rector of Gea, 17 June 1573, BL, Egerton MS 1833, fols. 72–75.

74. "Y que tiene por tales a los moriscos que si los susodichos fuesen buenos xpianos que no se fiarían dellos ni les ayudarían como lo hacen"; BL, Egerton MS 1833, fol. 74.

75. BL, Egerton MS 1833, fols. 85–88.

76. "Tienen en el término desta villa a media legua della una casa que llaman la ravita en la qual tienen un pozo lleno de agua a la qual van una vez al año que tienen día señalado y el que quiere yr mas veces la por su devoción y allí rezan las oraciones de moros . . . en la dicha ravita están por los maderos scripto en arávigo y no otras ymagenes"; BL, Egerton MS 1833, fols. 89r–v.

77. AHN, Inquisition, lib. 936, fols. 69r–v.

78. "Por haver desenterrado una morisca que estava enterrada a la xpiana y buelta a enterrar a la morisca"; trial of Miguel Muça de Chiva, 1571, AHN, Inquisition, lib. 936, fol. 59v; auto de fe of 14 Aug. 1575, AHN, Inquisition, lib. 934, fol. 68r.

79. "Y haver jugado con opprobrio a un juego que dezían adorote señor sanct salvador, estando uno sentado viniendo otro de rodillas y con un paño mojado dava al que estava sentado en el rostro diziendo adorote señor sanct salvador"; AHN, Inquisition, lib. 936, fol. 70r.

80. The conversos of Guadalupe faced similar scrutiny of their dietary practices; Starr-LeBeau, *Shadow of the Virgin*, 66–71.

81. AHN, Inquisition, lib. 934, fols. 12r–13v.

82. AHN, Inquisition, lib. 934, fols. 107r–10r.

83. AHN, Inquisition, lib. 914, fols. 596r–600v.

84. AHN, Inquisition, lib. 934, fol. 129r.

85. AHN, Inquisition, lib. 936, fols. 299r–300v.

86. AHN, Inquisition, lib. 936, fols. 390r–v.

87. Noble estate to Philip II, 4 Feb. 1579, ARV, Cartas a los Virreyes, carpeta 76.

88. Inquisition of Valencia to the Council of Inquisition, Valencia, 6 Feb. 1579 and 19 Mar. 1579, AHN, Inquisition, lib. 914, fols. 593r–v, 621r.

89. AHN, Inquisition, lib. 914, fol. 596r.

90. Christóbal Pellicer to Philip II, 14 Dec. 1581, ARV, Cartas a los Virreyes, carpeta 78.

91. Haliczer, *Inquisition and Society*, 256; auto de fe of 12 Mar. 1570, AHN, Inquisition, lib. 937, fol. 52v. Cardona administered a cluster of lands in the sierra south of Castellón de la Plana, as well as the important community of Benaguacil, located farther up the river Turia to the west of Valencia city; "Relación de las casas," in Boronat y Barrachina, *Los moriscos*, 1:433–34. "Confirmó que todos los moriscos de su rectoria vivían como moros y confirmó que la mezquita de Adzaneta se había repuesto por orden del almirante"; trial of Cardona, in Boronat y Barrachina, *Los moriscos*, 1:446.

92. AHN, Inquisition, lib. 934, fols. 150r–53v. In 1572 the seigneur of Ayodar similarly permitted his moriscos to bring in a notorious alfaqui to settle a land dispute; cases handled after the public auto de fe of 3 May 1572, AHN, Inquisition, lib. 936, fol. 114v.

93. Castelvi confessed to the charges against him, pleading mercy on account of his age, illness, and ignorance. On 25 July 1571, he heard a penitential Mass in the cathedral, paid a fine of five hundred ducados, and began a ten-year period of banishment from morisco areas; AHN, Inquisition, lib. 934, fol. 153v.

94. According to one witness, Cardona stated his wish that the "Lutherans" of France mount an armed assault on Spain "so that with all the commotion the reformation of the moriscos would slacken, and they would be left to live in their sect"; trial of Cardona, in Boronat y Barrachina, *Los moriscos*, 1:447, 454–56.

95. AHN, Inquisition, lib. 934, fols. 36r–44r. Pallás's reclusion to a monastery prevented him from pursuing legal disputes in which his adversaries, ironically enough, included his own moriscos; AHN, Inquisition, lib. 934, fols. 42–44; Catalá Sanz and Pérez García, *Los moriscos*, 46–50.

96. "Dizen que no an tenido ni tienen Rectores que les enseñan y aunque es verdad que en algunos lugares no tienen rectores que residan en los mismos lugares, sino en los con vezinos que son christianos viejos, por no fiarse de ellos: pero entodos los lugares se dize misa y se enseña la doctrina christiana y no se admiten al matrimonio si no la saben, y si alguna vez se dexa de dezir, es porque ninguno de ellos acude a oyrla, poniendo excusas aparentes con que los rectores y alguaziles se an de venir por fuerça a contentar siendo solos y desfavorecidos de los otros ministros de justicia y algunas vezes amenazados si insisten mucho en esto"; CCC, I, 7, 8, Moriscos I, 28.

97. "En los señores temporales ay tan grande afición a esta gente . . . se espantaría de en-

tender la utilidad que con medios justos, e injustos sacan desta pobre gente y todo lo çufren ellos de muy buena gana atrueque de ser favorecidos en la conservación de sus costumbres"; Ribera to Quiroga, Alcoy, 16 July 1582, IVDJ, envío 91, fol. 330.

98. "Estériles fueron los esfuerzos de nuestros Padres, y después de muchas penalidades hubieron de volverse a Valencia y Gandía sin haber conseguido casi nada"; Astraín, *Historia*, 206.

99. Fernández Terricabras, *Felipe II*, 193–94.

100. Villajoyosa, 26 May 1577, Ribera, *Sermones*, 3:299; Villajoyosa, 28 May 1577, Ribera, *Sermones*, 3:388; Alcoy, 6 June 1577, Ribera, *Sermones*, 4:49.

101. "Seremos admitidos, y aun convidados"; Alcoy, 23 June 1577, Ribera, *Sermones*, 4:197.

102. "Negocio trabajoso es sembrar y con tanta incertidumbre. Dice cuánto le costó a Jesucristo N.S. predicar la doctrina y sembrar la semilla del Evangelio. Y a los predicadores, qué trabajoso oficio es éste y cuán incierto porque son pocos los buenos y los que quieren aprovechar de este gran beneficio"; Játiva, 1 Feb. 1579, Ribera, *Sermones*, 1:382.

103. "Dos cosas: la primera, cómo se muestra el amor en dar a su Hijo, lo segundo, lo que el hombre ha de hacer de su parte para emplear esa obra tan importante"; Bocairente, 4 June 1582, Ribera, *Sermones*, 3:383.

104. "Sean tantas las miserias del hombre, y sus necesidades, también fue menester acudir a quien nos las ha de remediar"; Xixona, 27 May 1582, Ribera, *Sermones*, 3:115.

105. "No os quiere Dios comprado, y forzado, sino alquilado y libre"; "Considerar lo que hacen los obreros de viña y señores de ella, quitarle todos los sarmientos y dejarle sólo el tronco. Eso han de hacer los ministros del Evangelio, que han de quitar de los malos todo lo que hay en ellos"; Játiva, 15 Feb. 1579, Ribera, *Sermones*, 1:405–15.

106. "A sarmiento compara Dios a los malos, *quoniam nulli usui aptus est*"; Játiva, 15 Feb. 1579, Ribera, *Sermones*, 1:405–15.

107. Aguilar, *El gran patriarcha*.

108. "Como antes vine de prisa / no me acorde de llevar / a la fuente la pollina"; "A la puerta de mi casa / me he dexado una camisa"; "Voy a casa del Señor, / que ha de harme una botija / de agua de cepas, que es buena / para el dolor de barriga"; Aguilar, *El gran patriarcha*, act 3.

109. "Advertid que aunque son malos / se han de tratar con amor"; ibid.

110. Ribera to Clement VIII, 1602, in Fonseca, *Relación*, 90–92.

111. Viceroy Aytona to Philip II, Valencia, 6 Mar. 1582, ARV, Cartas a los Virreyes, carpeta 14. The viceroy dismissed these rumors as inaccurate; see Benítez, *Heroicas decisiones*, 333.

112. Ribera evidently came to this conclusion on his own, but he was not the only one to interpret Andrea Doria's arrival in this manner. On 6 March 1582, a Valencian citizen named Jaime Beltrán wrote to Philip II, "Here it is held to be certain that Your Majesty has resolved to remove the moriscos from this kingdom." He asked to be excused from the delegation of nobles who had departed for the Court to try to dissuade the king from taking this measure, adding, "the nobles are taking this badly, and I sincerely fear that this news will cause the moriscos to revolt"; Jaime Beltrán to Philip II, Valencia, 6 Mar. 1582, IVDJ, envío 10, no. 499. This petition arrived at the Court with a letter from the historian Antonio de Herrera to Mateo Vázquez in defense of his former employer, Vespasiano de Gonzaga; ibid.

113. AHN, Inquisition, lib. 358, fols. 165–66.

114. "Estoy muy persuadido que ha ordenado Dios esta novedad"; AHN, Inquisition, lib. 358, fol. 166.

115. "Que un daño tan peligroso, se remedie de una vez con toda brevedad"; Quiroga to Ribera, Madrid, 31 Mar. 1582, AHN, Inquisition, lib. 358, fol. 80r.

116. "Lo primero digo que estando su magd resuelto de echar los los moros de toda españa no convendría hazerlo de una vez"; 20 Apr. 1582, AHN, Inquisition, lib. 358, fol. 109v.

117. AHN, Inquisition, lib. 358, fol. 110v.

118. "Sustentarnos hemos con lo que pudiesemos y, sino fuera tanto, será mas seguro, y no es poco con alguna pérdida redimir la ruyna total de los haziendas y personas que padescería el Reyno si estos se levantasen"; AHN, Inquisition, lib. 358, fol. 111.

119. "Bien veo señor Illmo. que muchos con apariencia de piedad querrán defender esta gente y yo, por la misericordia de nuestro señor, no conozco en mi ánimo tanta falta della que, juntándose a la que tengo el ser muchos destos mis feligreses, no podría moverme tanto como el que más"; AHN, Inquisition, lib. 358, fol. 112.

120. "Y si no se conoscen de cerca los ánimos tan obstinados desta gente y se veen las desverguenzas públicas que tratan en offensa de Dios y de su magd. no se puede dar voto en sus cosas. Publicamente ayunan y profesan su ley y publicamente se muestran vassallos del turco; en mi tiempo he visto que quando tuvo su magd. victoria con la armada de la liga hizieron demonstración de luto y quando se perdió la goleta, de alegría"; AHN, Inquisition, lib. 358, fol. 112.

121. "Siendo de mucho menos daño dexarlos yr al limbo que no dar occasión para que el nombre de Dios sea blasphemado por tanto número de herejes en midio de una provincia que nuestro señor por su misericordia ha guardado libre de ynfidelidad"; AHN, Inquisition, lib. 358, fol. 112.

122. AHN, Inquisition, lib. 937, fol. 247r.

CHAPTER 5. DISILLUSIONMENT AND ITS CONSEQUENCES

1. "Para que vea las muchas y muy buenas razones que V.S.I. da, para que sin dilación se remedia los daños, que se siguen, de la mala vezindad de los moriscos desse Reyno"; Quiroga to Ribera, Madrid 11 May 1582, AHN, Inquisición, lib. 358, fol. 85v. On 22 May 1582, Quiroga wrote to the Valencian tribunal, ordering them to compile an "información general contra los moriscos," focusing on their contacts with the Turks and their disrespect for the Sacrament; AHN, Inquisition, lib. 358, fol. 86v.

2. "Y quando pienso la experiencia que su Mt. tiene en este género de cosas, me persuado que no reparará (como algunos zelosos del servicio de Dios y de su Mt. temen) en los inconvenientes que se le han representado"; Ribera to Quiroga, Valencia, 17 May 1582, AHN, Inquisition, lib. 358, fol. 167v.

3. "Y si Dios no fuese servido (por nros peccados) de encaminar lo que agora se pretende, sería forçado acudir a esto, aunque no serviese demás que dar treguas a nros enemigos para que dispongan mejor sus cosas con vituperació de la religion Xana, y daño universal de las nras"; AHN, Inquisition, lib. 358, fol. 167v.

4. Boronat y Barrachina, *Los moriscos*, 1:299–300.

5. Benítez, *Heroicas decisiones*, 349.

6. José García Oro has contended that Cisneros does not deserve his reputation as "incauto, prepotente y antagónico en espíritu y método" by contrast to Talavera; García Oro, *Cisneros*, 113.

7. "Porque sabiendo tan poco el dicho Maldonado desta gente, y no pudiendo tener mas noticia de sus cosas, de la que le an dado algunos perticulares interesados en los pocos meses que a estado en Vala"; CCC, I, 7, 8, Moriscos I, 28. Benítez identifies Maldonado as the former "general de la orden de la Merced"; Benítez, *Heroicas decisiones*, 342.

8. "La persona eclesiástica que el virrey desea embiar se entiende quien es, y el fin que lleva en esta pretensión, tan different del bien del negocio quanto es la poca noticia que del tiene, así por aver residido poco tiempo en este reyno"; CCC, I, 7, 8, Moriscos I, 28.

9. "En este reyno de Vala se a conocido bien, que aver personas deputadas para sola la conversión desta gente es lo que menos conviene al bien de la dicha conversión"; CCC, I, 7, 8, Moriscos I, 28.

10. "Basta saber que la industria de estos en conservarse con sus eregías es grandíssima, e increyble para los que vemos la rudeza que tienen en todo lo otro, y así los que an de tratar de su remedio añ de ser personas a quien ni puedan corromper con dádivas aunque las ofrezcan largas como acostumbran, ni engañar con mentiras y falsas submissiones y promesas"; CCC, I, 7, 8, Moriscos I, 28.

11. "Lo mismo hazemos los ordinarios como parece en que no confesándose hombre de todos ellos, ni aviendo remedio de que reciban más sacramentos que el babtismo y matrimonio y estos por fuerça, no los castigamos por ello: lo que se les manda así por los ordinarios como por los inquisidores es que no hagan ceremonias de moros y aunque desto tienen sobrada noticia, e instructión es tanta su obstinación que quieren mas ser quemados que dexarlas"; CCC, I, 7, 8, Moriscos I, 28.

12. "Y después que saly de Vala que fue a ii de mayo e visitado muchos lugares que tienen cerca otros de moriscos y me dizen que con [crossed out:] aver entendido la plática de echarlos que enduve por Vala están más insolentes que antes y se conoce bien claramente en su manera de proceder. [Added:] las borrascas que a avido sobre sus negocios, están más insolentes que antes y mas libres en su manera de proceder"; CCC, I, 7, 8, Moriscos I, 28. Boronat elides this correction in his transcription of this document, thereby deleting the detail that dates the paper to after September 1582; Boronat y Barrachina, *Los moriscos*, 1:325–28. On Ribera's sermons in Bocairente and Xixona in May 1582, see Ribera, *Sermones*, 3:114–15, 263–65, 383–85.

13. "Dize pues que estos moriscos se levantarían por orden y con favor del turco, y que sería aviéndose levantado primero los de granada y no queriendo estos acudirles por la anticipación que los otros tuvieron y que lo causa del levantamiento deste reyno, sería un pecho que se les pondría para defensa y seguridad de la marina"; CCC, I, 7, 8, Moriscos I, 28.

14. In the opening of this second memorial, Ribera refers to his previous memorials, as well as to "aver pensado por spacio de xii años en este particular." Given that Ribera always dated his experience with the moriscos to 1570, this dates the memorial to late 1582 or early 1583; CCC, I, 7, 8, Moriscos I, 27(2).

15. "A dado a VM algunos memoriales antes y después del año de —— en el qual vesando sus reales manos le hablo muy en particular destos negocios, y aunque deseando y procurando

·después que se tomase resolución en ellos, no lo an permytido los muchos gravíssimos negocios que N Sr a permytido que se ofreciesen a VM"; CCC, I, 7, 8, Moriscos I, 27(2).

16. "Porque es deriso y menosprecio de su sancta ley y palabra y justicia que se haze los sacramentos derramar tan preciosa semylla en peñas, dado las cosas sanctas a los perros y las margaritas a los puercos"; CCC, I, 7, 8, Moriscos I, 27(2).

17. "Sizen de la mejor tierra que tiene españa donde en pocos días se multiplacaran en número y en riqueza, y tratando en tantos christianos vendrán a topar algunos a quyen [crossed out: hazer daño] pervertir principalmente, si se casan con mugeres de las nuestras"; CCC, I, 7, 8, Moriscos I, 27(2).

18. James Casey's demographic research suggests that apologists such as Fonseca and Bleda grossly exaggerated the elevated birth rate of the moriscos; Casey, *Kingdom of Valencia*, 25–26. According to a recent study, the Old Christian population fell stagnant after 1580, whereas the morisco population rose steadily up to 1609; Saavedra, "Cambios demográficos," 48. On marriage patterns in the Ribera Alta, see Vincent, "Élements de démographie morisque."

19. "En esto veo inclinar a personas doctas atento que antes que se compeliesen a ser christianos eran amigos nuestros y que los que quisiesen serlo se podrían sacar de entre ellos y enseñarlos y aun se podría creer que dexande los libres acudirán algos a nuestra santa fe cathólica, lo que agora como forçados aborrecen tanto"; CCC, I, 7, 8, Moriscos I, 27(2). Ribera would reiterate his opposition to this approach in a 1587 letter to Philip II: "If there is any form of tolerance of their ceremonies, it is certain that the moriscos will perform them as if we had sent them to Algiers for a couple of years"; Ribera to Philip II, 1587, CCC, I, 7, 8, Moriscos I, 27(5).

20. "Que se dexassen yr antes se les mandase que se fuesen a tierra de moros como se hizo de los judíos sin tanta necesidad como la ay de que estos se vayan"; CCC, I, 7, 8, Moriscos I, 27(2).

21. "En caso que ningún destas cosas pareciese se avía de proceder en el negocio por los termynos que están dichos"; CCC, I, 7, 8, Moriscos I, 27(2).

22. "Que se les hazía agravio en averles baptizado por fuerza y que assí no eran cristianos y que les quebravan los privilegios del Emperador y que querían appellar a su Magestad y, si menester fuere, a su Santidad"; quoted in Benítez, *Heroicas decisiones*, 220.

23. "Que áun guardan sus leyes y costumbres de vivir y se consiente á los caballeros que los tengan. Algunas veces manifiestan el ódio con que persiguen á los christianos, de tal suerte que dan señales á los moros y sus espías y se juntan con ellos y roban los lugares"; Cock, *Relacion del viaje*, 206–7.

24. Ibid., 225.

25. "Pues a lo que se conjecturá por todas las personas que los an tratado están tan obstinadas en sus errores que ninguna humana industria bastará para reducirlos y assí nos abremos de contentar con aver hecho de nra. parte lo que se pueda y debe conforme a reglas de prudencia christiana"; Ribera to Philip II, 1587, "Instructión a su magestad para eregir el colegio de los nuevos convertidos," CCC, I, 7, 8, Moriscos I, 37. Included in Ribera's three letters of 1587 was a four-page "Instruction to Your Majesty" in which he called for a new seminary to teach Old Christian priests to speak Arabic, and yet he undermined the proposed seminary by banning moriscos and raising doubts as to its effectiveness; Ribera to Philip II, 1587, "Instruc-

tión a su magestad," CCC, I, 7, 8, Moriscos I, 37. In another memorandum, on the reforma-tion of the moriscos, submitted at the request of Philip II in June 1587, Ribera hinted at the negative repercussions that a continued campaign of instruction could have upon the Church; "Memorial sobre la reformación de los moriscos," CCC, I, 7, 8, Moriscos I, 23. The third re-port of 1587, beginning "La dificultad que (a mi parecer) se offrece en el nego de la instruc-ción de los moriscos," justified a program of heavy fines on the basis of morisco apostasy; CCC, I, 7, 8, 27(5). See also Boronat y Barrachina, *Los moriscos*, 1:369–78.

26. "Y en este punto a reparado, y repara siempre el Arçobispo, pareciéndole que es menor daño el dexarlos estar, que no emprender de burlas su remedio; porque si a la expectación que ellos tienen desta reformación, y al temor que an concebido de ella, no se satisfaze con buena, y bastante execución, será desacreditar el negocio, y los ministros del"; Ribera to Philip II, 1587, "Memorial sobre la reformación," CCC, I, 7, 8, Moriscos I, 23.

27. In those years when the total payments amounted to less than the allocated sum of 2,050 L, Ribera's treasurer simply rolled the surplus over into the following year. Given the rel-ative balance between the archiepiscopal annuity and the yearly payments, this account did not increase or decrease appreciably over time.

28. In the first few years of its existence, the account was used for a series of disbursements to silversmiths, tailors, notaries, and friars; Ribera to Philip II, 1587, "Instructión a su mages-tad," CCC, I, 7, 8, Moriscos I, 37.

29. These figures are taken from CCC, Quenta aparte, fol. 1, 6–32, and "Pensión apos-tólica," 1581–95, CCC, I, 7, 8, Resúmenes de pagas. In 1594 Ribera decided to create a new account under the direction of Jerónimo Nadal for these payments to morisco parishes, al-though the *cuenta aparte* (separate account) continued to contribute the requisite sums in an-nual installments. After an initial payment of 973 L, 19 s, 8 to Nadal's account on 23 Septem-ber 1594, the account recorded additional deposits to Nadal as "receptor de la nueva tassa;" CCC, Quenta aparte, fol. 30.

30. Ribera contributed 3,780 L annually, and in 1584–87 he authorized three *censales*, or loans, of 10,000 L, 10,000 L, and 12,000 L to the city of Valencia. In the ten years before the city paid all of the money back in 1591–94, the separate account collected an annual *pensión*, or interest payment, of 6.67 percent.

31. This figure is from Philip II's letter of 16 February 1596, written in response to a letter of Ribera's outlining the financial dimension of the parochial reorganization. This roughly matches my own estimate of the running total of the cuenta aparte in 1596, derived from sub-tracting the total expenditures as recorded in "Pensión apostólica" (CCC, I, 7, 8, Resúmenes de pagas) from the total deposits recorded in "Cargo" (CCC, I, R,) of 84,617 L.

32. "Y lo que más huviere corrido, se den a censo sobre ciudades, villas, y universidades Reales desse reyno a veynte mil el millar porque al dicho precio se hallaron las mejores situa-ciones del Reyno"; CCC, I, 7, 3.

33. CCC, Quenta aparte, fols. 65–69, 87–97; "Cargo," 1599–1606, CCC, I, R. In a letter dated 16 February 1596, Philip II criticized Ribera for allowing the separate account to grow "in excess." "A las ochenta y quatro mil setecientas y ochenta libras, que están en la Tabla, dessa me ciudad de Valencia, de lo procedido de la pensión, que se impuso, sobre el Arçobis-pado para la dotación de las Rectorias, por no haberse empleado en ellas lo haveis hecho, con fin de dar priessa a que se beneficien, los corridos"; CCC, I, 7, 3.

34. "El licenciado Sebastián de Covarrubias con acuerdo el Rte. Nun. el se assessor cobrará las primeras pagas de los que están obligados a contribuir en la dotación de las Retorias de esse Arçobispado como lo haveis pedido y para eso solamente ha quedado ahí"; Philip II to Ribera, 23 May 1599, CCC, I, 7, 3. In a letter dated 4 November 1595, Philip had lamented the continued apostasy of the moriscos and instructed Ribera "to order that in all the churches of your diocese, prayers be offered both in public and in secret, supplicating Our Father to guide and direct these souls to recognize their errors and to want to be saved"; CCC, I, 7, 3.

35. Covarrubias and the papal nuncio Camillo Caetano ordered the implementation of Gregory XIII's brief of 16 June 1576 concerning the endowment of the morisco parishes and authorized Juan Agorreta, Ribera's treasurer, to assess this "new tax"; document notarized by Juan Cristóbal Ferrer in Valencia, 1 Mar. 1597, BGUV, MS 697, doc. 9.

36. On 13 May 1598, Ribera ordered Jerónimo Nadal to pay the scribe Pedro de Lyerta 14 L, 15 s "por la copia del libro de las dismembraciones nuevamente hechas que contiene ciento y ochenta ojas"; notarial document dated Valencia, Jan. 1598, CCC, I, 7, 8, Resúmenes de pagas. Ribera appointed Ferrer as the *receptor* of this new tax and directed him to deposit these revenues into the regular account for payments to priests in morisco areas; CCC, Quenta aparte, fol. 48.

37. CCC, Quenta aparte, fols. 54, 56, 77, 79, 80. These contributions were much more irregular than the interest payments on the loans from the separate account. Of the thirty-four institutions and communities represented in the tax records, eleven made only one payment, and only three made every payment between 1597 and 1604; CCC, Quenta aparte, fols. 49–86.

38. Clark, *European Crisis*; Hamilton, *American Treasure*.

39. The Madrid council of 1587 reiterated the proposal of a committee in 1564 that the parishes of Orihuela, Segorbe, and Tortosa be endowed at 100 L, and during Ribera's episcopate the archdiocese made progress in these areas; Benítez, *Heroicas decisiones*, 316, 351–52.

40. "Uno para que a falta de clérigos idoneos del Reyno de Valencia proveyesen el Arzobispo y Prelados del las rectorías de los lugares de nuevos convertidos en extranjeros, y el otro para que a falta de unos y otros nombrasen frailes o religiosos de lo Compañia de Jesus con las declaraciones de que no obstante sus votos de clausura y pobreza pudiesen vivir fuera de sus monasterios y gozar de la renta de las cien libras"; Boronat y Barrachina, *Los moriscos*, 1:333.

41. Philip II to Ribera, Aceca, 6 Apr. 1596, CCC, I, 7, 3. On 28 June 1598, Prince Philip responded to the provincial of the Augustinians in Aragon, who had written on behalf of five other provinciales requesting to be excused from contributing priests. Philip denied their request and ordered them to provide as many friars as Ribera wanted, when he wanted them; CCC, I, 7, 3.

42. "Pensión apostólica," CCC, I, 7, 8, Resúmenes de pagas; Robres Lluch, "Catálogo."

43. The Franciscan convent of Murviedro, for example, staffed the parish of Benifairó from 1583 to 1586. Fray Gaspar de Ayala, of the Alcantarine monastery of San Onofre in Játiva, began his journey in the Vall de Ebo sometime before 1592, before moving to Estivella (1593–94), back to Vall de Ebo (1595), on to Benisivá (1599–1601), and finally, on the eve of expulsion, to Barcheta (1608).

44. The records for the period after 1580 are reasonably complete for twenty parishes. Francisco Juan Ripollés served in Benimarfull from 1586 to 1598; Robres Lluch, "Catálogo."

45. Fonseca, *Justa expulsion*, 34.

46. Pérez de Ayala, *Synodus diocesana valentiae*, 1566; Austria and Ramírez de Haro, *Les instructions*.

47. Ribera, *Synodus diocesana valentiae*, 1594.

48. The Valencian group sent a petition to the council in Madrid, which discussed it on 5 January 1600; Boronat y Barrachina, *Los moriscos*, 2:17n27. On the edict of grace, see Madrid, junta of 10 May 1599, ibid., 1:669.

49. "Y en particular le advertiréys de las personas que hubiere en vuestro lugar mas acceptas y reputadas entre las de esse pueblo: pues si estos tales se rindiessen y reduxessen a la obediencia del Evangelio, podrían causar mucho provecho, y atraer con su exemplo y admoniciones a los demás"; "Carta para los curas y retores de Moriscos," reprinted in Escrivá, *Vida*, 468–69.

50. "Tengamos esta obra por muy difícil (como lo es en realidad de verdad) pero no por imposible"; ibid., 474.

51. "Pero no sólo las palabras de ellos, sino también el sentido y significación de las palabras, de manera que se hagan capaces de lo que deven creer y obrar"; ibid., 490.

52. "Es pues necessario el certificarles de la voluntad de su Magd, para que sepan que no nos hemos de contentar con palabras, sino que las obras han de ser las que han de valer ante su Real acatamiento"; ibid., 481–82.

53. "Lo mismo digo quanto al hallarse con ellos en alguna cosa de plazer, como sería bayle, caça, o otros semejantes, los quales son indecentes, e incompatibles con el oficio de sal, luz, y antorcha"; ibid., 489.

54. "Obra es la que se emprende de grandíssima dificultad, porque se ha de contrastar con gente de que somos aborrecidos, por diversidad de decendencia, por discordia perpetua entre Moros y Christianos, por la poca amistad y charidad que en general usamos con ella: y assí tienen por proverbio, que los tratamos como a esclavos"; ibid., 476.

55. "En caso que nuestra industria no fuere de provecho, por la pertinacia y dureza de los oyentes, se conseguirá general utilidad en España: porque su Magd. avrá de cuydar de limpiarla de infieles, siendo su Real apellido Cathólico, y nosotros nos hallaremos no sólo descargados, pero enriquecidos"; ibid., 480.

56. Giménez, *Un catecismo*, 54–61; Kamen, *Phoenix and the Flame*, 363.

57. "Resolvióse assimismo que se hagan dos cathecismos para enseñar la doctrina christiana un en Romance y otro en lengua valenciana y que se ven el que commenço a hazer en latín Don Martín de Ayala Arcopo que fue de Valencia, para si estuviese como convenga que aquel se traduzga y ponga en perfectión"; BL, Egerton MS 1511, fol. 111. This passage proves that Ribera did not use Pérez de Ayala's *Doctrina christiana*, as has sometimes been asserted, as the basis for his catechism but rather a partial document in Latin, which does not survive.

58. 28 Aug. 1587, BL, Egerton MS 1511, fol. 110; 2 Sept. 1587, BL, Egerton MS 1511, fol. 111.

59. Boronat y Barrachina, *Los moriscos*, 1:660.

60. "Os encargo que señaleis personas graves en letras, buen zelo, y que tengan experiencia deste ministerio para que con vra. intervención reconozcan el dicho cathecismo y añadireis y quitareis del lo que a vos y a las dichas personas os parecera"; Philip II to Ribera, El Pardo, 4 Nov. 1595, CCC, I, 7, 3.

61. "La secta de los philósophos," junta of Madrid, 24 July 1597, Boronat y Barrachina, *Los moriscos*, 1:668.

62. "Le parecía que el libro primero no se devía permitir que anduviesse en romance sino en latín, por que no lo leyesse gente vulgar ni ydiota"; Boronat y Barrachina, *Los moriscos*, 1:668.

63. "Pues es manifiesto el [daño] que ha causado en Alemania y otras partes el haverse escrito en Romance libros de theología"; Philip II to Ribera, San Lorenzo, 13 Aug. 1597, CCC, I, 7, 3.

64. "Ninguno por rudo e ignorante que sea dexa de tener noticia [added: porque contra los gentiles se trata; crossed out: como es] ser dios uno, tener prudencia, en que consistan la virtud y el pecado, contra los judíos, ser xo. n sr. el verdadero messías prometido en la ley"; rough draft of a letter from Ribera to Philip II, CCC, I, 7, 8, Moriscos I, 29.

65. "La persona que se introduze no es philósopho ni alfaqui sino un simmple herbolario y asi las preguntas y réplicas que haze al maestro son [crossed out: las que a qualquiera ignorante y rústico se ofrecen y] proporcionadas al discurso que suelen tener los de aql oficio"; CCC, I, 7, 8, Moriscos I, 29.

66. "En todos los capítulos deste primer libro, en el qual ay veynte y cinco diálogos, y con ser todos copiosos de doctrina, no son veynte las preguntas, o razones de dudar que en todos ellos haze el discípulo, por donde se conoce que no se pretende tener argumentos ni réplicas sino dar tan solamente introductión y occasión para asentar la doctrina cathólica"; CCC, I, 7, 8, Moriscos I, 29. In this way Ribera argued that his *Catechismo* had been designed as a false dialogue, or a monologue in disguise; Cox, *Renaissance Dialogue*, 2–3.

67. "Las [dudas] que se ofrecen naturalmente como es en la materia de los philósophos puros, o que las avían oido dezir vulgarmente como son los desparates de los judíos y moros de los quales ninguno ay que no sepa algunas generalidades"; CCC, I, 7, 8, Moriscos I, 29.

68. "Quarto se dize en defensa del dicho catechismo, ser muy usado y estar en costumbre aprobada por los consejos supremos de su Mt., imprimirse diálogos doctrinales en los quales ay preguntas sin comparación mas subtiles y scholásticas que las que se contienen en este catechismo"; CCC, I, 7, 8, Moriscos I, 29.

69. "Se tratan por diálogos materias muy subtiles así contra los ereges, como contra gentiles y judíos"; CCC, I, 7, 8, Moriscos I, 29.

70. "Advirtiese que en la regla viii general del dicho catálogo se dize [added: prohibense tanbién las disputas y controversias en cosas de religion entre cathólicos y hereges y las confutaciones del acoran de mahoma en lengua vulgar. Se añade, no aviendo para ello licencia expressa in scriptis de los inquisidores por donde claro consta que no se pretendió cerrar la puerta a esta manera de libros, sino tan solamente excluir los que carecen de las partes convenientes y esto se conoce claro par las licencias que después desta prohibición se an dado.]" CCC, I, 7, 8, Moriscos I, 29.

71. "Discípulo. Dios os salve padre mío.

Maestro. Y el sea también contigo hermano. De donde bueno por esta tierra, que me pareces estrangero en el hábito habla?

D. Si soy, aunque algún tiempo ha que trato en esta costa del Andaluzía, y reyno de Granada: especialmente he negociado con salvo conducto en Málaga, y Gibraltar.

M. Según esso de allende deves ser.

D. Si, de Berveria soy, de un lugar de aql cabo de Tituán, que está bien veynte leguas apartado de la costa de Africa.

M. Pues a que propósito has entrado yan adentro en estos reynos?

D. El dessio de ser Christiano me trae principalmente." Ribera, *Catechismo*, 1–2.

72. "Y aún la Ceneti, que (como tu bien sabes) es mas bárbara y obscura"; Ribera, *Catechismo*, 6.

73. On the eve of the expulsion, Ribera again rejected a recommendation by Don Jaime Palafox (seigneur of Cotes de Blanes), the Jesuit Ignacio de las Casas, and John Creswell (the English Jesuit envoy in Madrid) that chairs of Arabic be founded in Spanish universities to promote the art of preaching to the moriscos in their own language; junta of 1608, CCC, I, 7, 8, Moriscos I, 29(2).

74. "En ninguna manera conviene ponerlos por el grandísimo daño que podrían hacer si prevaricasen y los que tienen las calidades necesarias lo primero que hacen es olvidar de todo punto la lengua y correrse"; Ribera to Philip II, 1587, "Instrución a su magestad," CCC, I, 7, 8, Moriscos I, 37. In his second memorial of 1587 Ribera also argued against morisco justices, bailiffs, and town councilors, even in areas with few Old Christians; Ribera to Philip II, 1587, "Memorial sobre la reformación," CCC, I, 7, 8, Moriscos I, 23.

75. "No es de los maestros que han de tener ni de las cosas que se les han de enseñar, ni tampoco de las que se se an de prohibir, por que esto esta todo muy bien sabido. . . . Toda la difficultad consiste en el camino que se ha de tomar, para que esta gente quiera ser instruyida"; Ribera to Philip II, 1587, "La difficultad que (a mi parecer) se offrece en el nego de la instrucción de los moriscos," CCC, I, 7, 8, Moriscos I, 27(5).

76. Ricardo García Cárcel has argued that the catechism's emphasis on *razón natural* versus the irrationalism of Islam reflects the influence of the anti-Muslim polemical tradition dating back to Lull; García Cárcel, "Estudio crítico del *catecismo* de Ribera-Ayala," 165.

77. Ribera, *Catechismo*, 85, 107–08.

78. "Y en fin si lees toda su vida, verás un exemplo puro de hombre brutal, y todo hecho bestia: que es verguença pensar que en cuerpo tan hediondo y carnal habitasse espíritu de prophecía"; ibid., 90–91.

79. Ibid., 107–9.

80. "Todas las personas que viven rectamente, agora sean Iudíos, agora Christianos, qualesquier que quisieredes, aunque dexen su ley, y vayan a otra, si hazen buenas obras serán salvos undubitadamente"; ibid., 121.

81. "Y si el Alcorán anduviesse traduzido en lengua vulgar, para que todos viessen las burlerías que en el hay, tendría lástima de las que de tan foez y bestial doctrina se dexan governar; ellos mesmos se avergonzarían dello"; ibid., 159.

82. Ibid., 114–17.

83. "Se paga de solo el coraçón"; ibid., 132–39.

84. "Impiamente pios"; ibid., 98–101.

85. Ribera to Philip II, 5 June 1590, ARV, Cartas a los Virreyes, carpeta 89.

86. "Por un memorial del Patriarcha Arçopo de Valencia se suplico a VS Illma fuesse servido mandar que los domingos y fiestas los moriscos penitenciados del sto offo no fuessen a la iglesia mayor a oyr sermon y missa, por ser tanta quantidad dellos y perturbar los officios

sino que en otra iglesia de alguna cofradía se an destinados por un clérigo que el arcopo les dará a su costa. y allí oygan missa"; Girón and Cortázar to the Council of Inquisition, Valencia, 9 Jan. 1592, AHN, Inquisition, lib. 917, fol. 403r.

CHAPTER 6. JUSTIFYING THE EXPULSION

1. Informe de Martín González de Cellorigo, quoted in Boronat y Barrachina, *Los moriscos*, 1:366–67. Cellorigo recommended distributing the moriscos in maritime areas throughout Castile.

2. Figueroa alluded to the retention of the baptized Jews under King Egica in 694 A.D. and their eventual assimilation through both confiscation of goods and intermarriage with Christians. "Este es un exemplar muy al vivo para estos moriscos"; Figueroa to Philip III, 1604, reprinted in Boronat y Barrachina, *Los moriscos*, 2:431–40.

3. Gómez Canseco, *El humanismo*, 234–41.

4. According to Bleda, on his second visit to his church he was so appalled by the laughter and scorn of the moriscos that he immediately mounted his horse and rode to Valencia, to beg Ribera to relieve him of his post; Bleda, *Corónica*, 938–40.

5. Later published as *Defensio fidei in causa neophytorum*. In the five years after 1604, Bleda continued to write letters to the king warning him of potential morisco uprisings and promoting expulsion, with such fervor that his order attempted to quiet him down by confining him to Valencia; Peset and Hernández, "De la justa expulsión," 234–36.

6. On 25 February 1598, Prince Philip wrote a letter to Ribera concerning the loans issued from the separate account, and in 1599 he followed up on his father's plans to send Covarrubias to Valencia to administer the new tax, order the publication of the catechism, and secure a papal brief authorizing the endowment of the morisco parishes; Prince Philip to Ribera, 25 Feb. 1598 and 22 July 1598, and Philip III to Ribera, 8 Jan. 1599 and 23 May 1599, CCC, I, 7, 3.

7. When Philip III and Lerma visited Valencia for the royal wedding in 1599, their tight schedule of social engagements attested to Lerma's close ties with the Valencian nobility, the principal opponents of expulsion; Gauna, *Relación*. Lerma had also served as viceroy of Valencia in 1595–98; Carreres Zacarés, *Libre de memories*, 1024.

8. García-Arenal and Ángel de Bunes, *Los españoles*, 122–27.

9. In a carefully choreographed liturgy, Ribera and the papal legate Caetano presided over a double wedding between Philip and Margarita and the infanta Isabella and the Archduke Albert of Austria; Consaloniero, *Relacion*.

10. "Temo que si V Mt no manda tomar resolución en este caso, aprovechándose de estas inspiraciones, he de ver en mis días perdida a España"; Ribera to Philip III, Dec. 1601, CCC, I, 7, 8, Moriscos I, 27(4).

11. "No te fies jamás (dize) de tus enemigos. . . . No le tengas cerca de ti, ni le pongas en buen lugar; porque sin duda te quitará a ti del tuyo, y se sentará en tu silla, y entenderás, que yo te aconsejava bien, y te afligirás sin provecho, de no aver tomado mi consejo"; CCC, I, 7, 8, Moriscos I, 27(4). Compare to "Non credas inimico tuo in aeternum sicut enim aeramentum eruginat nequitia illius et si humiliatus vadat curvus adice animum tuum et custodi te ab illo non statuas illum penes te nec sedeat ad dexteram tuam ne conversus stet in

loco tuo ne forte conversus in locum tuum inquirat cathedram tuam et in novissimo cognoscas verba mea et in sermonibus meis stimuleris"; Sirach 12:10–12, in *Biblia Sacra Vulgata*, 1044.

12. Gaspar de Córdoba to Ribera, Valladolid, 14 Dec. 1602, reprinted in Guadalajara, *Memorable expulsion*, 81–82. Philip III noted, "If I was not certain of your zeal and prudence, what you have said in this matter proves both"; Philip III to Ribera, 31 Dec. 1601, CCC, I, 7, 3. Lerma called Ribera's paper "the best I have seen; I see that it addresses the most important matter facing us today"; Lerma to Ribera, 8 Feb. 1602, reprinted in Guadalajara, *Memorable expulsion*, 82.

13. Benítez, *Heroicas decisiones*, 362–63.

14. Allen, *Philip III*. On Philip II's foreign policy, see Parker, *Grand Strategy*.

15. Feros, *Kingship and Favoritism*, 202.

16. "Vienen a ser la esponja de toda la riqueza de España, y assí es sin duda que ay grandíssima cantidad de oro y plata en su poder"; CCC, I, 7, 8, Moriscos I, 27(3), fol. 5. "Y esto todo lo hazen con mayor comodidad de los que compran, o alquilan, por ser ellos tan parcos y avarientos, que ni comen, ni beven, ni visten"; CCC, I, 7, 8, Moriscos I, 27(3), fols. 5–6. In his "Instrucción" to Philip II in 1587, Ribera cited the moriscos' prompt compliance with his own requirement that they build churches as evidence of their hidden wealth; Ribera to Philip II, 1587, "Instrución a su magestad," CCC, I, 7, 8, Moriscos I, 37.

17. "Para proveer sus galeras, o para embiar a las minas de las Indias, sin escrúpulo alguno de conciencia; lo que también será de no poca utilidad"; CCC, I, 7, 8, Moriscos I, 27(3), fol. 18.

18. CCC, I, 7, 8, Moriscos I, 27(3), fol. 10.

19. The expulsion of 1609–14 led to a population distribution much more in keeping with the arability of the land, as the remaining Old Christians avoided the interior; Ardit, *Els homes i la terra*, 33–34. See also Casey, *Kingdom of Valencia*.

20. Catalá Sanz and Pérez García, *Los moriscos*.

21. ARV, Gobernación, procesos criminales, nos. 1300, 1587. Morisco litigants also appealed sentences handed down by their seigneurs, as did the man who denied that he had stolen grain from his lord's castle in Petres; ARV, Real Audiencia, procesos criminales, sig. 440.

22. ARV, Gobernación, procesos criminales, nos. 1221, 1585. Two moriscos from Petres, arrested and jailed for stealing two cartloads of grapes from a vineyard in Murviedro (Sagunto), protested that they had received a license to harvest the grapes from an agent of the landowner. The lieutenant of criminal justice in Murviedro arrested them, they said, purely on account of his "great enmity" for the people of Petres, whose seigneurs famously insisted on supreme jurisdiction within their lands; ARV, Gobernación, procesos criminales, nos. 1437, 1593.

23. Barceló Torres, *Minorías islámicas*, 69.

24. AHN, Inquisition, lib. 329, fol. 225v; AHN, Inquisition, lib. 917, fol. 1r; AHN, Inquisition, lib. 934, fols. 233–34. The alfaqui of Alazquer allegedly held a meeting with Muslims from Argel to plan a fiery attack upon the Christian monuments of Valencia on Maundy Thursday, with the goal of taking over amid the chaos; AHN, Inquisition, lib. 935, fols. 89–90.

25. AHN, Inquisition, lib. 934, fols. 273–75. Valencian moriscos periodically fled by boat in collaboration with foreign Muslims; ARV, Real Audiencia, procesos criminales, sig. 414, sig. 421.

26. Several convicts also appealed to the secular courts, contending that their "excessive" galley sentences violated their rights; Real Audiencia, procesos criminales, sig. 544; ARV, Gobernación, procesos criminales, nos. 1774, 1605.

27. AHN, Inquisition, lib. 934, fol. 293.

28. AHN, Inquisition, lib. 913, fol. 583.

29. Moriscos did occasionally survive terms in the galleys; one from Benisano swam ashore after a shipwreck in a storm, only to be arrested as a fugitive upon his return home; ARV, Real Audiencia, procesos criminales, sig. 513.

30. AHN, Inquisition, lib. 935, fols. 59r–v. An eighty-year-old morisco from Oliva, who refused to confess to having prepared meat in the Islamic manner despite nine turns of the ropes around his arms, suffered one hundred lashes but escaped the galleys through a payment of two hundred ducats; the inquisitors agreed to this comparatively low sum on account of the defendant's old age and infirmity; AHN, Inquisition, lib. 934, fols. 426–30.

31. AHN, Inquisition, lib. 935, fols. 122–30.

32. "Aunque es cierto según la doctrina de todos los doctores, que para ser uno ereje es necessario saber que su opinión es contraria a la fe, pero también es muy cierto que para que no lo sea a de tener ánimo prompto de obedecer a la iglesia"; Ribera to Philip II, 1587, CCC, I, 7, 8, Moriscos I, 27(5).

33. "Porque la experiencia nos ha mostrado, que por descontento que tienen con sus padres, o maridos, o por otros respectos humanos, dizen que quieren ser Christianos, no pensándolo hazer"; Ribera to Philip III, Dec. 1601, CCC, I, 7, 8, Moriscos I, 27(4).

34. Ribera to Philip III, Jan. 1602, CCC, I, 7, 8, Moriscos I, 27(3), fol. 23.

35. "Árboles revegidos, llenos de nudos de heregias." "El remedio que piden los grandes males, assí espirituales como corporales, es arrancarlos de rayz, porque no puedan dañar ellos, ni sus rayzes echar nuevos pimpollos que en breve tiempo crezcan en árboles"; CCC, I, 7, 8, Moriscos I, 27(3), fols. 20, 1.

36. "O por dexarse llevar de la opinión que algunos personajes graves (per mal instruidos) han tenido, pareciéndoles que ganan gracia con ellos"; Ribera to Philip III, Jan. 1602, CCC, I, 7, 8, Moriscos I, 27(3), fols. 20–21.

37. AHN, Inquisition, lib. 935, fols. 88–92, 95r–v.

38. AHN, Inquisition, lib. 935, fols. 100–101, 110.

39. In several cases, women acted as guardians of Arabic and aljamiado literature, perhaps in the often mistaken hope that they would not be searched. In 1606 an official ransacked the house of Angela Quatrella in Picasent, where he found a book written in Arabic hidden in her bedclothes. Quatrella "became very agitated, and offered the official money to return the book, kissing his hands and begging him," though without success; AHN, Inquisition, lib. 935, fol. 75. See also Surtz, "Morisco Women," 433.

40. María Çaida of Algimia, to cite one example, confessed that she had persuaded a Granadan morisca and others to "live as moros"; AHN, Inquisition, lib. 935, fol. 30. On circumcision, see AHN, Inquisition, lib. 934, fol. 476.

41. AHN, Inquisition, lib. 935, fol. 54.

42. Along the same lines, a morisca from Mislata, arrested for claiming that "morisco burial in virgin soil was better than a Christian burial," demonstrated a solid knowledge of morisco rituals and prayers. Although she evidently had abandoned these rites five years earlier, be-

cause "she did not want her mother-in-law, who lived as a Christian, to see her doing them," she did not mention the issue at all in her regular confessions to her priest; AHN, Inquisition, lib. 934, fol. 442; AHN, Inquisition, lib. 935, fols. 38–39.

43. "Que los moriscos de Teruel tenían una bolsa para gastos del aljama e pedían limosna cada semana para ella y dava limosna para la dicha aljama como mora como la davan los demas moriscos de la calle"; AHN, Inquisition, lib. 934, fol. 480.

44. To cite but one example of the potential consequences of arguing about religion in the inquisitorial age, the morisca Angela Rabaza underwent torture after disagreeing with Old Christians about the virginity of Mary; AHN, Inquisition, lib. 935, fols. 104r–v.

45. One silk weaver claimed not to know that Gali was descended from moriscos, "perque ell dit testimoni no ha conegut ni vist ab aquell coses que sabessen ni fes guardassen a crestians nous"; ARV, Real Audiencia, procesos criminales, sig. 157.

46. "Hec ab eclesia parrochiali sancti Nicolai civitatis valentiae cum aliis etiam extra eam collocatis domibus disiuncta ac separata fuit: eiusque ecclesia sub invocatione sancti Michaelis fuit in parrochialem erecta"; BL, Egerton MS 1510, fol. 217.

47. They lost their case, and Philip II assigned a portion of these now royal revenues to the morisco convert Lorenzo Polo of Teruel, whose denunciations of his former coreligionists led to the prosecution of dozens of moriscos in the 1580s; 27 Mar. 1593, ARV, Cartas a los Virreyes, carpeta 106.

48. "Estos dos colegios fueron de ningún provecho, antes se ha visto que los que han salido del de los mochachos son mucho peores que los otros"; Ribera to Prada, Valencia, 9 Sept. 1609, CCC, I, 7, 8, Moriscos I, 12.

49. The viceroy recommended Nadal and another promising morisco student to Philip II for benefices, "as they are under your protection"; 26 Dec. 1594, ARV, Cartas a los Virreyes, carpeta 26. Gaspar de Gali, a morisco expelled from the school in 1593 for falling behind in his studies, wrote to Philip II to request his reinstatement; 5 June 1593, ARV, Cartas a los Virreyes, carpeta 97; schoolmaster to Philip II, 3 Jan. 1582, ARV, Cartas a los Virreyes, carpeta 79.

50. Seeking greater funding from the king in 1582, the schoolmaster lamented his inability to support more than a few students beyond the ten in residence, even though "many others asked urgently to be admitted to the college to be instructed in the holy Christian faith"; 3 Jan. 1582, ARV, Cartas a los Virreyes, carpeta 79. Philip II ordered the foundation of a similar college in Orihuela; 30 May 1597, ARV, Cartas a los Virreyes, carpeta 104.

51. Procurados fiscals contra Miquel Castellano, llaurador, Joan Ruxech, justícia, Esteve Maymó, morisc, i altres veins de Cárcer, desaparició de J. Castellano, 1595; ARV, Real Audiencia, procesos criminales, sig. 455.

52. "[Gomes, the witness] entengue que loy dix per tractar com tracta ab molta familiaritat ab xpians vells, y tractarse com den com a xpian verdader perque es casat ab xpiana vella, y perque los moriscos en veure que un xpia nou tracta ab xpans vells ab familiaritat tantct se creusen quels acusa"; ARV, Real Audiencia, procesos criminales, sig. 455.

53. Hernández Ruano, *Historia*, 93–96. Ruano argues that the moriscos of Xivert were representative of a broader assimilated population along the Catalan coast.

54. Císcar Pallarés, "La vida cotidiana."

55. Bartolomé Joly, *Voyage en Espagne*, cited in Casey, *Kingdom of Valencia*, 206. Many dispossessed people found a niche in Valencia's underworld as hired thugs, carrying out un-

pleasant tasks for the noble and ecclesiastical godfathers hidden behind the scenes. In the early 1560s, for example, the ongoing feud between the Figuerola (allied with the Duke of Segorbe) and the Pardo de la Casta (servants of the Duke of Gandía) led to a series of brutal murders; Sanchis Guarner, *La ciutat de València*, 258.

56. "Están cada día más atrevidos, más orgullosos, y más desvergonzados en declararse por Moros. Y assí no embargante la mucha diligencia y solicitud, que se pone por el Virrey deste Reyno, suceden cada día casos y muertes, y los Christianos Viejos que viven en comarca dellos no osan salir de noche de sus lugares"; Ribera to Philip III, Jan. 1602, CCC, I, 7, 8, Moriscos I, 27(3), fol. 27.

57. The bishop of Segorbe, among others, evoked this idea in 1587: "Parescer de Don Martín de Salvatierra," Madrid, 30 July 1587, in Boronat y Barrachina, *Los moriscos*, 1:626.

58. Ribera claimed that after eleven months in office there had only been one murder by night in the city, and in this case the killer was caught; Ribera to Philip III, 19 Nov. 1603, CCC, I, 7, 5, 10. On public punishments in Valencia, see Salavert and Graullera, *Professió*, 234.

59. ARV, Real Audiencia, procesos criminales, sig. 397.

60. As Teófilo Ruiz has argued, "Not all forms of banditry (piracy, crime, vagrancy) were reactions to the state or to class disparity. In many cases, bandits sided with noble interests and fought not *against* but *for* the state"; Ruiz, *Spanish Society*, 201.

61. The royal prohibition notwithstanding, the moriscos did not have great difficulty acquiring weapons; an Old Christian in a neighboring town knew that "the greater part of the moriscos of Ayodar have shotguns in their houses, because they fire them off every night"; ARV, Real Audiencia, procesos criminales, sig. 460.

62. ARV, Real Audiencia, procesos criminales, sig. 494.

63. ARV, Real Audiencia, procesos criminales, sig. 362. In a similar case, two brothers from Benifayo captured half of a herd of goats from a boy tending them in a common area. Upon their arrest, they maintained that they had not stolen the goats but remitted them to the seigneur of Benifayo as payment for pasturage on his lands; ARV, Gobernación, procesos criminales, nos. 1326, 1588.

64. Meyerson, *Muslims of Valencia*, 232–48.

65. ARV, Real Audiencia, procesos criminales, sig. 390.

66. ARV, Real Audiencia, procesos criminales, sig. 445. In another murder arising from an argument, two moriscos traveling with an associate on business murdered him in the wake of a heated argument over who would take the smallest rooms at a roadside inn; ARV, Gobernación, procesos criminales, nos. 1107, 1578.

67. "Y mataren la matexa nit los tres moltons ab una llum que tenien apart de manolls despart y un de aquells guardava a ell testimoni per que nols ves ad aquells, dient li y amenesant lo que sils mirava lo matarien en lo mateix part y no sab ell testimoni ahon anaren ni per hon sols sab que dexaren alli los tres caps dels moltons y les tripes"; ARV, Gobernación, procesos criminales, nos. 1380, 1590.

68. Along the same lines, Joan Ageig, a morisco from Alzira, fell into the hands of the law quickly after committing a robbery on the highway. Under questioning he claimed to be a day laborer, but his reputation as a thief and as an enforcer for a prostitute in the local brothel led to his conviction; ARV, Gobernación, procesos criminales, nos. 1914, 1609.

69. "Y porque publicamente hechava cada vez maldiciones a los que salían a rebato con-

tra Abiaix"; 7 Jan. 1588, ARV, Cartas a los Virreyes, carpeta 18. See also the trial of Joan Charcot, ARV, Real Audiencia, procesos criminales, sig. 402. Abiaix reappeared in 1606, when he ambushed an old friend in a melon orchard near Picasent, leaving him in a pool of blood; ARV, Real Audiencia, procesos criminales, sig. 542.

70. Shot in the neck in the ensuing firefight, the bailiff bled so much that "a hundred cloths would not stop it," while his attackers fled; ARV, Real Audiencia, procesos criminales, sig. 536.

71. In a raid the next day, the bailiff (*alguazil*) discovered the gang in the home of an accomplice, surrounded by stolen food and livestock; ARV, Real Audiencia, procesos criminales, sig. 564. Bandits could also serve as scapegoats: the alfaqui in Algar reportedly murdered two merchants who refused to "turn moro" and bribed the local judges to convict a known bandit in their place; AHN, Inquisition, lib. 935, fols. 88–92, 95r–v.

72. Ruiz, *Spanish Society*, 181–82.

73. Meyerson, *Muslims of Valencia*, 248.

74. During the manhunt of 1587, the viceroy expressed his frustration with the seigneur of Otonel's "great fondness for Abiaix," illustrating that even the Old Christians could respond to morisco bandits with admiration; 22 Oct. 1587, ARV, Cartas a los Virreyes, carpeta 17.

75. CCC, I, 7, 8, Moriscos I, 27(3), fol. 11.

76. "Pues los Iudios no eran hereges, ni tenían Reyes de su secta, a quien acudir por favor, ni eran naturalmente belicosos, ni enemigos nuestros"; CCC, I, 7, 8, Moriscos I, 27(3), fol. 12.

77. CCC, I, 7, 8, Moriscos I, 27(3), fol. 4; Ribera to Philip III, Dec. 1601, CCC, I, 7, 8, Moriscos I, 27(4).

78. As Ribera expressed the idea in a 1587 letter to Philip II, "To attempt to persuade them of the truth through reason will not work, because of their natural coarseness and because of the multitude of grave sins and blasphemies pressed into their souls"; Ribera to Philip II, 1587, CCC, I, 7, 8, Moriscos I, 27(5).

79. Ribera to Philip III, 13 May 1608, BN, MS 1492.

80. "Ni se puede dezir que incluye injusticia el condenarlos sin oyrlos: porque la notoriedad y evidencia del hecho y derecho suple esse defecto, y lo supliera, aunque llegara la pena a ser capital"; CCC, I, 7, 8, Moriscos I, 27(3), fol. 9.

81. "Por la qual se puede creer, que nuestro Señor ha querido reservar esta obra tan digna de pecho Real para V. Magestad, como reservó la libertad de su pueblo para Moyses, la entrada de la tierra de Promisión para Iosue, la vengança de la injuria antigua de los Amalechitas para Saul, y la victoria de los Philisteos para David"; Ribera to Philip III, Dec. 1601, CCC, I, 7, 8, Moriscos I, 27(4).

82. "De la misma estima que pudiera tener, el conquistar y ganar de nuevo a españa"; CCC, I, 7, 8, Moriscos I, 27(3), fol. 27.

83. "El único remedio es echarlos de España, sin que pueda esperarse buen sucesso de otro alguno"; CCC, I, 7, 8, Moriscos I, 27(3), fol. 3 (underlined in the original). Benítez observes that Ribera, who previously supported beginning the expulsion in Valencia, may have shifted his position to avoid earning a reputation among the Valencian nobility as the instigator of the expulsion decree; Benítez, *Heroicas decisiones*, 364.

84. The committee of theologians met as an adjunct to a larger Valencian committee convened on 22 November 1608, which included the viceroy Caracena, several bishops and in-

quisitors, and the chronicler Gaspar Escolano; Boronat y Barrachina, *Los moriscos*, 2:130; Ximeno, *Escritores*, 1:282.

85. "Que se cometía sacrilegio baptizándolos"; CCC, I, 7, 8, Moriscos I, 29(2).

86. As Ribera expressed it in a letter to Sobrino, "We cannot deliver lambs to the wolves, nor dispense holy baptism upon those whom moral evidence has shown will trample it" (No podemos entregar los corderos a los lobos ni dispensar el santo babtismo a quien con evidencia moral lo a de acoçear); CCC, I, 7, 8, Moriscos II, 63, no. 24.

87. "Porque era indexenxia de nuestra santa religión ponerla en disputa con gente tan torpe y obstinada"; CCC, I, 7, 8, Moriscos I, 29(2).

88. In a lengthy memorial to Philip III in September 1608, Sobrino demonstrated a firm grasp of the practical difficulties involved in instruction, including the geographical isolation of the moriscos, their hatred of the Christians, and the "tyrannical dominion and maltreatment of the barons and seigneurs, who treat the moriscos like slaves"; treatise by Antonio Sobrino, AGS, Estado, leg. 218. Sobrino's journal, which includes internal correspondence and copies of the documents under review, is housed in the Colegio de Corpus Christi, I, 7, 8, Moriscos II, 63.

89. CCC, I, 7, 8, Moriscos II, 63, no. 12. Sobrino further noted that if the moriscos truly were heretics, "the Church could not tolerate them, nor the Holy Office fail to punish them as such"; CCC, I, 7, 8, Moriscos II, 63, no. 6.

90. "Que de parte dellas no sea superficial, fingida y por cumplimiento, como hasta aquí, sino muy de coraçon y de rayz, necessario será que ellos sepan que pueden con seguridad comunicar todas las dudas y llagas de sus consciencias con los ministros que les fueren embiados para su instrucción"; CCC, I, 7, 8, Moriscos II, 63, no. 6.

91. "Porque si en contradición de los Principes infieles, los predicadores del Evangelio hazen tanto fruto en los Reynos estraños; que no podemos esperar de las puertas adentro de nuestras cosas favoreciendo la querella el proprio Rey?" BGUV, MS 697, doc. 4; Spanish translation from Latin in Guadalajara, *Memorable expulsion*, 97–98.

92. The council consisted of the constable of Castile, the commander of León, the Counts of Chinchón and Alba de Liste, the Dukes of Lerma and Infantado, the cardinal of Toledo, and Fray Jerónimo Javierre, the royal confessor. Danvila includes excerpts of the minutes in his *Conferencias*, 267–69.

93. Feros, *Kingship and Favoritism*, 202–5.

94. Ribera's support became especially important after the committee of theologians disappointed Philip III by failing to give him its blessing to expel the moriscos. On Paul V and the expulsion, see Pérez Bustamente, "El pontífice Paulo V."

95. Sánchez, *Women and Power*, 115. Sánchez underscores the growing power of Habsburg women in shifting Philip's attention to the central European context over the course of his reign.

96. Domínguez Ortiz and Vincent, *Historia*, 171–75; Tueller, *Good and Faithful Christians*, 142–46.

97. Feros, *Kingship and Favoritism*, 200.

98. Philip III's instructions to Mejía, AGS, Estado, leg. 2638 bis, fols. 16–19.

99. ARV, Real Audiencia, procesos criminales, sigs. 561, 562, 572; García Martínez, "Notas."

100. In this respect my conclusions differ from those of Márquez Villanueva, *El problema morisco*, and Domínguez Ortiz and Vincent, *Historia*, 178–79.

101. "This resolution will bring great sorrow to the realm, because we do not see the same order executed in Castile and Aragon"; Ribera to Prada, Valencia, 23 Aug. 1609, CCC, I, 7, 8, Moriscos I, 15. In retrospect, Ribera's lack of confidence that the king would proceed to exile the moriscos of Castile may seem unfounded, but it is worth noting that royal policy toward the moriscos—from the forced baptisms in Castile (1501) and Aragon (1521–28) to the dispersion of the Granadan moriscos (1570)—had not been characterized by any consistency on the national level.

102. "Sería de ninguna importancia lo que aquí se haze, sino se hiziesse lo mismo en toda España"; Ribera to Lerma, 1 Sept. 1609, CCC, I, 7, 8, Moriscos I, 22(1). Ribera had made a similar argument in a letter of December 1608: "El effecto que ha de resultar de la instrutión que se trata el tiempo lo mostrará y lo tiene mostrado la experiencia de lo pasado, pero no por esto se ha de dexar de tratar de ella con toda diligencia y cuydado"; Ribera to Prada, Valencia, 19 Dec. 1608, CCC, I, 7, 8, Moriscos I, 11.

103. "He resuelto que se saqùen todos los Moriscos desse Reyno, y que se echen en Berbería"; bandos de expulsión, Valencia, 22 Sept. 1609, reprinted in García-Arenal, *Los moriscos*, 251–55.

104. "Las diligencias que se han hecho para intruyllos en nuestra santa Fee, lo poco que todo ello ha aprovechado"; García-Arenal, *Los moriscos*, 251.

105. "Pero aviendo sabido, que los desse, y los de Castilla passavan adelante con su dañado intento: y he entendido por avisos ciertos y verdaderos, que continuando su apostasia y prodición, han procurado y procuran por medio de sus Embaxadores, y por otros caminos el daño y perturbación de nuestros Reynos"; ibid., 252.

106. "Que ningún Christiano viejo sea osado a tratar mal de obra, ni de palabra, ni llegar a sus haziendas a ninguno de los dichos Moriscos. . . . Que ansi mismo no les oculten en sus casas, encubran, ni den ayuda para ello"; ibid., 254.

107. The frequency and level of detail of the entries addressing the expulsion in Cabrera de Córdoba's *Relaciones* reflect the decrease in apprehension as the expulsion progressed across the peninsula.

108. Domínguez Ortiz and Vincent, *Historia*, 179.

109. Domínguez Ortiz and Vincent base their estimate upon the figures compiled by Lapeyre, *Historia*, 200.

110. "Los que se entendiere que biven como christianos [in the margin: o reciben el Sto sacramento por orden de su prelado] no han de ser desterrados: destos no hay en este Arçobispado hombre alguno, ni mas mugeres de las que están entretenidas por mi en esta ciudad; y lo mismo dixeron los Prelados de Tortosa, Segorbe y Orihuela que pasava en sus Obispados"; Ribera to Philip III, 27 Aug. 1609, CCC, I, 7, 8, Moriscos I, 24.

111. "La copia de carta inclusa que escrivio al dho Duque el Patriarca de Valencia, que trata de los inconvenientes que tiene el dexar ningún rastro de Moriscos en aquel reyno"; Council of State, 1 May 1610, AGS, Estado, leg. 228.

112. AHN, Inquisition, lib. 333, fols. 37r–v; Council of State, 19 June 1610, AGS, Estado, leg. 228.

113. "Que se queden en el cosa de 700 que ay agora para industriar en las cosas del campo

a los christianos viejos cultivar y conservar los fructos de aquel reyno. Pues de mas de lo dicho son estos muy buenos christianos"; Council of State, 29 May 1610, AGS, Estado, leg. 228.

114. Philip III did stipulate that if the moriscos were good Christians they should be sent to Christian lands outside the Spanish Empire; Council of State, 22 May 1610, AGS, Estado, leg. 228.

115. "No ay en el dicho reyno sino cosa de 500 hombres y otras tantas mugeres de mayor edad. . . . Advierte que con licencia de los perlados de aquel reyno quedan por buenos y catolicos xpianos mas de ochenta o 100 personas"; Council of State, 19 June 1610, AGS, Estado, leg. 228.

116. "Relación de los Moriscos que quedan en el Obispado de Origuela hecha por mandado de su Magd. por el Obispo Fr. Andres Balaguer a 25 de agosto año 1610 dividese en quatro partes"; AGS, Estado, leg. 224.

117. Flores Arroyuelo, *Los últimos moriscos*; García Pedraza, "La asimilación"; Perry, "Moriscas and the Limits of Assimilation"; Tueller, *Good and Faithful Christians*.

118. "Estos sres. virreyes son muy grandes christianos, y el virrey merece la merced que su Mt. y Va. Exa. [Lerma] le hazen. An concebido que es piedad christiana disimular, y admitir pareceres de personas interesadas, o deseosas de complecerles, o mal informadas, con lo qual se a venido, a dificultar lo que al principio fue muy fácil"; Ribera to Lerma, Valencia, 7 Sept. 1610, AGS, Estado, leg. 225, doc. 134.

119. "De los que estavan repartidos entre christianos viejos, se an huydo algunos y juntadose con los que están en la sierra"; AGS, Estado, leg. 225, doc. 134.

120. "Para evitar mayores males como son las muertes de muchos christianos viejos, el impedimiento de poblarse las lugares comarcanos, robos, sacrilegios en las iglesias y otros muchos, lícito es permitir que estos bivan entre nosotros algun tiempo con ánimo de echarlos quando pareciere que conviene. . . . Si no se toma este medio gastará Su Mt. mucho, sin provecho y que cada día serán ellos más, y los daños mayores"; AGS, Estado, leg. 225, doc. 134.

121. "Aunque sus padres los pidan: porque por el mismo caso que los padres son apostatas, deven ser apartados de ellos para que no caygan en los mismos errores"; CCC, I, 7, 8, Moriscos I, 24.

122. "Entre christianos viejos, officiales, o ciudadanos, con obligación de servirles hasta XXV o XXX años por solo el comer y vestir"; CCC, I, 7, 8, 24.

123. Consulta del Consejo de Estado, 1 Sept. 1609, in Boronat y Barrachina, *Los moriscos*, 2:524–26; Sobrino to Ribera, undated, CCC, I, 7, 8, Moriscos I, 20; Ribera to Prada, 9 Sept. 1609, CCC, I, 7, 8, Moriscos I, 12.

124. Ribera estimated that the children under the age of ten numbered between forty thousand and sixty thousand, of a total morisco population of three hundred thousand in Spain; Martínez, "Les enfants morisques."

125. Among the points the panel had been assigned to consider, Ribera and Bleda included separate entries asking whether it was licit to retain those aged ten and under and those aged four and under; parecer of Miguel Salon and Juan Sotelo, CCC, I, 7, 8, Moriscos I, 30; the final report of the committee, CCC, I, 7, 8, Moriscos I, 32. On Bleda, see Peset and Hernández, "De la justa expulsión," 250.

126. "Todas estas consideraciones y la piedad que a primera vista trae consigo el dexar los mochachos entre nosotros me han movido a escoger aquel camino como el mas seguro. Pero

aviendolo considerado mejor y perdido muchas horas de sueño me ha parecido que lo que parece piedad para los personas destos es crueldad para las nuestras, a las quales según regla de charidad bien ordenada, tenemos obligación en primer lugar"; Ribera to Prada, Valencia, 14 Sept. 1609, CCC, I, 7, 8, Moriscos I, 13.

127. As Sotelo warned Philip III of the moriscos, "No hay sperança de su correctión, antes justo rezelo y temor que bolverán a inficionar el Reyno"; CCC, I, 7, 8, Moriscos I, 30. Sobrino dissented on this point, arguing for the retention of the older children even after 1609; CCC, I, 7, 8, Moriscos II, 63, no. 44.

128. "Que los mochachos y mochachas menores de quatro años de edad, que quisieren quedarse, y sus padres, o curadores (siendo huérfanos) lo tuvieran por bien, no serán expelidos." The decree also made an exception for children aged six or under with Old Christian fathers and morisca mothers; García-Arenal, *Los moriscos*, 254–55.

129. Epalza, *Los moriscos*, 127.

130. Council of State, 25 Feb. 1610, AGS, Estado, leg. 228.

131. "Ha me parecido que para el buen effecto de los Colegios de moriscos y moriscas, que V.Md. manda se continuen en esta ciudad, conviene tener resolución de los cabos que van apuntados en el papel que será con esta"; Ribera to Philip III, Valencia, 3 May 1610, AGS, Estado, leg. 228.

132. On 27 April 1610, the Council of State ordered the dispersal of all Valencian moriscos in Castile under the age of seven, but the opposition of Caracena created delays for months; consulta of 27 Apr. 1610, AGS, Estado, leg. 228; consulta of 16 Sept. 1610, on delays, AGS, Estado, leg. 225; Ribera to his clergy, Valencia, 3 Aug. 1610, AGS, Estado, leg. 224.

133. Philip III to the Consejo de Aragón, 12 Sept. 1610, AGS, Estado, leg. 225.

134. Ribera to Philip III, Valencia, 9 Nov. 1610, AGS, Estado, leg. 220.

135. "Porque los amos, porque no se los quemase la Inquisición, pondrían diligencia en que supiesen y guardasen nra. Sta. Religion. Sería beneficio temporal: porque los amos, porque no los ahorcasen, procurarían corregirlos, açoralos y hecharlos hierros para reprimirlos, y los amarían y enseñarían con todo cuydado, por su provecho y utilidad"; AGS, Estado, leg. 220.

136. "Y tengo por sin duda, que si estos quedan libres, dentro de pocos años serán muchos dellos salteadores, y muchas de ellas malas mugeres"; AGS, Estado, leg. 220.

137. "El Reyno ganaría mucho: Porque así no se casarían los hombres, ni las mugeres, y cesaría la propagación de esta mala casta en estos Reynos"; AGS, Estado, leg. 220.

138. "Toda la esperança que se puede tener, moralmente, de que estos niños se olvidaran de la secta de Mahoma, consiste en que estén apartados unos de otros, y en que no haya quien les acuerde que sus padres son moros, y así será de grande perjuycio quedar los que fueren mayores de la edad que he dicho"; AGS, Estado, leg. 220.

139. Al-Hajari, *Supporter of Religion*, 62.

140. The painting, "Embarque de los Moriscos en el Grau de Valencia," by Pere Oromig, is reproduced in *La expulsión de los moriscos del reino de Valencia*.

141. The Revised Standard Version translates this verse as "I wish those who unsettle you would mutilate themselves!" In his rendering of "Utinam abscindantur qui vos conturbant," Ribera somewhat conveniently neglects the context in which this line was uttered, a debate

over circumcision; sermon preached in Valencia, 27 Sept. 1609, reprinted in Escrivá, *Vida*, 407–38.

142. "No os parece que he dicho con razón, que es esta la mayor hazaña que hemos visto de nuestros tiempos, ni leydo de los passados?"; ibid., 247.

143. "Verse rico hoy, y mañana pobre, y tomarlo con paciencia y alegría por el servicio de Dios y de su Rey, gran hazaña y digna de ser agradecida y recompensada"; ibid., 429.

144. Ibid., 438.

145. "O señor mio y que sermón predicó V.S.I. en su yglesia y lo que sus mgtes han estimado la doctrina y la gran prudenzia con que V.S.I. conprehendió quanto convenya dezir a ese reyno sobre la espulsión y materias de estas encaminandolo todo con tales termynos al punzar de nosa. edificacion del pueblo general y particularmente no se ha huido tal cosa y assí lo asuman quantos le leen"; Lerma to Ribera, Madrid, Dec. 1609, CCC, I, 7, 4, 243.

146. "Entendido se ha que havéys hecho publicar excomuniones contra las personas que tubieron Moriscos encubiertos y no los manifestaren; agradezcoos mucho el zelo con que tratáis desto"; Philip III to Ribera, San Lorenzo, 26 Oct. 1610, CCC, I, 7, 3, 92.

147. "Olvidad, os ruego, la lengua destos malditos, si hay alguien que la sepa"; Escrivá, *Vida*, 437.

CONCLUSION. THE IDEAL BISHOP AND THE END OF SPANISH ISLAM

1. Pedro de Ribadeneira, coordinator of the initiative in Spain, wrote two letters to Ribera in 1606–7, one soliciting information and one thanking him for his prompt cooperation; *Monumenta Historica Societatis Iesu*, 60:236–40.

2. "Item. Si saben o han ohido dezir que al siervo de Dios desde su tierna edad le començo Dios nro Sr. a hazer grandes mercedes y favores, previniéndole con muchas bendiciones, dones, y gracias naturales y sobrenaturales, guardándole de los lazos que el enemigo le armava para impedirle los servicios que havía de hazer a Dios nro Sr. en su yglesia con su dotrina y santidad"; "Los testigos que se han de recibir en el proceso," CCC, I, 7, 9, 7.

3. Escrivá was the son of Don Jerónimo Escrivá, a former *maestre racional*, and Doña Angela Mercader y Zapata, a woman praised by Juan Luis Vives and others for her erudition and knowledge of ancient languages. Francisco Escrivá studied theology under Ambrosio de Morales at the University of Alcalá before returning to Valencia, where he received a canonry in the cathedral. In 1570 he entered the Society of Jesus, and over the next forty years he served Ribera as counsel and confessor; Ximeno, *Escritores*, 1:278–79.

4. CCC, I, 7, 10, 1.

5. "Aunque reforme algo de las moralidades no sea tanto que la historia quede desnuda porque realmente me parecen mui bien las moralidades porque aunque no las haia menester el Pd. Bartolome Perez ni otros doctos somos maior número los indoctos"; Clavero to Escrivá, Madrid, 1 Feb. 1612, CCC, I, 7, 10, 13.

6. "De grandeza, de riqueza, de lindeza"; Escrivá, *Vida*, 184.

7. "Y el desseo de que fuesse venerado, honrrado, ensalçado, quanto fuesse possible de los fieles, en tiempo que era tan despreciado, y abatido, y ultrajado de los herejes"; ibid., 189.

8. As late as 1606, Paul V had issued a brief calling for a new campaign of instruction.

When he reviewed the work of another apologist, Damián Fonseca, the pope ordered two corrections, one insisting that he had never authorized the expulsion and another denying that he had refused to receive the moriscos in the papal states; Pérez Bustamente, "El pontífice Paulo V," 232.

9. "No hicieron más mella en ellos que si fueran unas piedras"; Escrivá, *Vida*, 456.

10. In the short term, Escrivá evidently failed to prove his case. In 1752 Benedict XIV declared that Ribera's counsel to Philip III with regard to the moriscos would not constitute an impediment to his beatification—suggesting that this had, in fact, been the key obstacle up until that point; Robres Lluch, *San Juan de Ribera*, 497.

11. "Esto pareció a todos de mucho inconveniente, y contra lo que se ha juzgado generalmente por hombres graves y pios, y de intelligencia y experiencia particular en estas materias: y asi se resolvió, que no solo sería útil para la instructión de la fe christiana, pero que causaría en los dichos moriscos nueva reputación y estimación de su secta, y que los actuaría más en sus errores"; report of the Valencian junta of 22 Nov. 1608, CCC, I, 7, 8, Moriscos I, 29(2).

12. Brown, *Painting in Spain*, 96.

13. Cárcel Ortí, *Historia*, 1:226–28.

14. AHN, Inquisition, lib. 935, fols. 168–77.

Bibliography

MANUSCRIPT COLLECTIONS

Archivo del Ayuntamiento. Valencia, Spain
   Cartas reales
      Vol. h3-5: 1559–72
      Vol. h3-6: 1572–95
      Vol. h3-7: 1594–1627
   Lletres misives, G 3, vols. 53–54: 1570–78
   Manuals de Consells
      93 A: 1569
      94 A. 1569–70
      95 A: 1570–71
      96 A: 1571–72
      110 A: 1585–86
      113 A: 1588
      114 A: 1588–89
      124 A: 1597–98
      125 A: 1598–99
      126 A: 1599–1600
      127 A: 1600
      129 A: 1602–3
Archivo del Reino de Valencia. Valencia, Spain
   Cartas a los Virreyes: Viceregal correspondence, 1521–1603
   Gobernación, procesos criminales: 49 criminal cases, 1530–1609
   Real 253: Royal letters, 1543–73
   Real Audiencia, procesos criminales: 60 criminal cases, 1526–1609
Archivo General de Simancas. Simancas, Spain
   Estado, legajos 208, 210, 211, 212, 213, 218, 220, 224, 225, 228: Council of State, 1608–10
   Estado, legajos 329, 334: Council of Aragon, 1562–73
   Estado, legajos 2636, 2638, 2638 bis, 2639, 2640, 2641: Council of State, 1598–1610
Archivo Histórico Nacional. Madrid, Spain
   Inquisition, libros 325, 326, 327, 328, 329, 330, 331, 332, 333: Letters from the Council of Inquisition, 1567–1613

Inquisition, libros 356, 357, 358, 359, 360, 361: Letters from the Inquisitor General, 1569–1618

Inquisition, libros 911, 912, 913, 914, 915, 916, 917, 918, 919: Letters from the Valencian tribunal, 1568–1615

Inquisition, libros 934, 935: Méritos de reos penitenciados, Valencia, 1581–1674

Inquisition, libros 936, 937, 938: Relaciones de causa, Valencia, 1550–96

Archivo Zabálburu. Madrid, Spain

Carpeta 248: Letters from Prince Philip, 1553–54

Biblioteca General de la Universidad de Valencia. Valencia, Spain

MS 697: Pragmáticas reales

MS 529: Jerónimo Pradas, *Libro de memorias de algunas cosas pertenecientes al Convento de Predicadores de Valencia que an sucedido desde el año 1603, hasta el de 1628.*

Juan Bautista Pérez, "Parecer sobre las Planchas de plomo que se han hallado en Granada"

Biblioteca Nacional. Madrid, Spain

MS 287: Libro de trece curiosos y diversos tratados recopilado en el anno 1614

MS 721: Papeles tocantes a inquisicion

MS 1492: Letter from Ribera to Philip III, 13 May 1608

MS 1750: Papeles tocantes a Phe II, vol. 2

MS 1778: Correspondencia de Perafán de Ribera

Bodleian Library. Oxford University, Oxford, England

Adderton MS A141

British Library. London, England

Egerton MSS 1510, 1511, 1832, 1833

Colegio de Corpus Christi. Valencia, Spain

Archivo del Patriarca

I, 4, 5: Varios

I, 5: Procesos difamatorios contra D. Juan de Ribera I

I, 5: Procesos difamatorios contra D. Juan de Ribera II

I, 6, 2: Gastos

I, 6, 10: Cartas de los agentes del R. Colegio en Madrid y Roma

I, 7, 3: Cartas reales

I, 7, 4: Asuntos Familiares del Santo Patriarca

I, 7, 5: Arzobispado y Virreynato

I, 7, 6: Varios (Cartas y documentos muy interesantes)

I, 7, 8: Moriscos I

I, 7, 8: Moriscos II

I, 7, 8: Resúmenes de pagas (apocas)

I, 7, 9: Beatificación I

I, 7, 10: Beatificación II

I, 7, A: Colegio de Corpus Christi

I, 7, B: Testament of Ribera

I, 8, 2: Reliquias

I, R: Moriscos, Colegio, Varios

Asientos de criados, 1575–92

Asientos de criados, 1592–97

Biblioteca del Fundador: Apuntos escolares, 9 vols.

Correspondencia santo

Época del Santo en Badajoz, I–II

Inventario de Procesos con sus fichas correspnd

Libro mayor, 1579–80

Libro mayor, 1587–88

Libro mayor, 1592–1600

Libro mayor, 1601–9

Moriscos, Colegio, Varios

Procesos, siglos XVI–XVII

Quenta aparte. Rectorias moriscos, 1591–1605

Varios de S. Juan de Ribera y del R. C-S. de C. CH. Valencia. 3 vols.

Colección Gregorio Mayans

  Vol. 585: Varios

  Vol. 633: Varios

  Vol. 677: Provisiones reales

Henry Charles Lea Collection. University of Pennsylvania, Philadelphia.

  MS 20: Informacio super conversione sarracenorum

Instituto de Valencia de Don Juan. Madrid, Spain

  Envío 10: Correspondence of viceroy Gonzaga

  Envíos 89, 91: Asuntos Ecclesiásticos

Real Academia de la Historia. Madrid, Spain

  Salazar y Castro, vol. 5, asig. 9/49: Letters to Bernardo de Bolea, vicechanciller del Consejo de Aragon

  Salazar y Castro, vol. 19, asig. 9/344: Varios históricos y genealógicos

  Salazar y Castro, vol. 20, asig. 9/425: Memoria de cosas diferentes

  Salazar y Castro, vol. 22, asig. 9/586: Letters from Ribera to Philip III

  Salazar y Castro, vol. 24, asig. 9/634: Papeles de Estado y Gobierno

  Salazar y Castro, vol. 26, asig. 9/673: Papeles pertenecientes al Reino de Aragón

  Salazar y Castro, vol. 27, asig. 9/759: Papeles varios, vol. 4

PRINTED SOURCES

Abulafia, David. "The Apostolic Imperative: Religious Conversion in Lull's *Blanquerna*." In *Religion, Text, and Society in Medieval Spain and Northern Europe*, edited by Thomas E. Burman, Mark D. Meyerson, and Leah Shopkow, 105–21. Toronto: Pontifical Institute, 2002.

Aguilar, Gaspar de. *Fiestas nupciales que la ciudad y reyno de Valencia han hecho en el felicissimo casamiento del Rey don Phelipe nuestro señor III deste nombre, con doña Margarita de Austria Reyna y señora nuestra.* Valencia: Pedro Patricio Mey, 1599.

———. *El gran patriarcha Don Juan de Ribera.* In *Norte de poesía española, illustrado del sol de doze comedias.* Valencia: Felipe Mey, 1616.

Ahlgren, Gillian. *Teresa of Avila and the Politics of Sanctity.* Ithaca: Cornell UP, 1996.

Al-Hajari, Ahmad ibn Qasim. *The Supporter of Religion against the Infidels*. Madrid: Consejo Superior de Investigaciones Científicas, 1997.

Allen, Paul C. *Philip III and the Pax Hispanica, 1598–1621*. New Haven: Yale UP, 2000.

Alonso Acero, Beatriz. "Cristiandad *versus* Islam en el gobierno de Maximiliano y María (1548–1551)." In *Carlos V: Europeísmo y universalidad*, edited by Juan Luis Castellano Castellano and Francisco Sánchez-Montes González, 3:15–28. Granada: Sociedad Estatal para la Conmemoración de los Centenarios de Felipe II y Carlos V, 2001.

Altman, Ida. *Emigrants and Society: Extremadura and America in the Sixteenth Century*. Berkeley: U of California P, 1989.

Amelang, James. *Honored Citizens of Barcelona*. Princeton: Princeton UP, 1986.

Andrés Martín, Melquiades. "Pensamiento teológico y vivencia religiosa en la reforma española (1400–1600)." In *Historia de la iglesia en España*, edited by Ricardo García Villoslada, 3:2:269–361. Madrid: Editorial Católica, 1980.

Antist, Vicente Justiniano. *Adiciones a la historia del Santo Fr. Luis Bertran*. Valencia: Pedro Patricio, 1593.

———. *Verdedera relacion de la vida y muerte del P. Fr. Luis Bertran*. Zaragoza: Juan de Alterach, 1583.

———. *La vida y historia del apostolico predicador sant Vincente Ferrer*. Valencia: Pedro de Huete, 1575.

Ardit, Manuel. *Els homes i la terra del País Valencià (segles XVI–XVIII)*. Barcelona: Curial, 1993.

Arias, Ricardo. *The Spanish Sacramental Plays*. Boston: Twayne Publishers, 1980.

Arroyas Serrano, Magín, and Vicent Gil Vicent. *Revuelta y represión en los moriscos castellonenses: El proceso inquisitorial de Pedro Amán, morisco vecino de Onda*. Onda: Ajuntament d'Onda, 1995.

Astraín, Antonio. *Historia de la Compañía de Jesús en la asistencia de España*. Madrid: Razón y Fe, 1925.

Aubin, Paul. *Le problème de la "conversion."* Paris: Beauchesne, 1963.

Austria, Jorge de, and Antonio Ramírez de Haro. *Les instructions e ordinacions per als novament convertits del regne de Valencia*. Valencia: Gabriel Ribas, 1594.

Barceló Torres, María del Carmen. *Minorías islámicas en la país valenciano: Historia y dialecto*. Valencia: Universidad de Valencia, 1984.

Barrio, Maximiliano. *Los obispos de Castilla y León durante el antiguo régimen*. Castilla y León: Junta de Castilla y León, 2000.

Bataillon, Marcel. *Erasmo y España*. Mexico City: Fondo de Cultura Económica, 1966.

Batllori, Miquel. "La santidad aliñada de Juan de Ribera (1532–1611–1960)." *Razón y Fe* 162 (1960): 9–18.

Baumgartner, Frederic. *Change and Continuity in the French Episcopate*. Durham: Duke UP, 1986.

Belenguer, Earnest. *Cortes del reinado de Fernando el Católico*. Valencia: Universidad de Valencia, 1972.

Benítez, Rafael. "Arbitrio del Dr. Mancebón para la reforma de la ermita de Nuestra Señora de las virtudes de Villena y creación de un colegio para niños moriscos (1587–88)." In *Hom-

enatge al Doctor Sebastià Garcia Martínez, 287–99. Valencia: Generalitat Valenciana, 1988.

——. "El arzobispo Tomás de Villanueva y los moriscos valencianos: Juntas, memoriales, y mixtificaciones." In *Política, religión e inquisición en la España moderna*, 107–28. Madrid: Universidad Autónoma de Madrid, 1996.

——. "Carlos V: La Inquisición y la conversión de los morisco valencianos." In *Carlos V: Europeísmo y universalidad*, edited by Juan Luis Castellano Castellano and Francisco Sánchez-Montes González, 4:45–75. Granada: Sociedad Estatal para la Conmemoración de los Centenarios de Felipe II y Carlos V, 2001.

——. "Control político y explotación económica de los moriscos: Régimen señorial y 'protección.'" *Chronica Nova* 20 (1990): 9–26.

——. "Las duras negociaciones de la concordia de 1571 entre los moriscos y la inquisición." In *Conflictos y represiones en el Antiguo Régimen*, 113–55. Valencia: Universidad de Valencia, 2000.

——. *Heroicas decisiones: La monarquía Católica y los moriscos valencianos*. Valencia: Institució Alfons el Magnànim, 2001.

——. "El patriarca Ribera y la inquisición ante el conflicto universitario." In *Homenaje a D. Ignacio Valls*, 321–49. Valencia: Universidad de Valencia, Facultad de Teología San Vicente Ferrer, 1990.

——. "La política de Felipe II ante la minoría morisca." In *Felipe II y el Mediterráneo*, edited by Ernest Belenguer, 2:503–36. Madrid: Sociedad Estatal para la Conmemoración de los Centenarios de Felipe II y Carlos V, 1999.

——. "La provisión del virreinato de Valencia en los años 70 y el gobierno de Felipe II." In *Homenaje a Antonio de Bethencourt Massieu*, 189–209. Gran Canaria: Ediciones del Cabildo Insular, 1995.

Benito Domenech, Fernando. *La arquitectura del Colegio del Patriarca y sus artífices*. Valencia: Federico Domenech, 1981.

——. *Pinturas y pintores en el Real Colegio de Corpus Christi*. Valencia: Federico Domenech, 1980.

Benlloch Poveda, Antonio. "Sínodos valentinos y reforma a finales del siglo XVI." In *Corrientes espirituales en la Valencia del siglo XVI (1550–1600): Actas del II Symposio de Teología Histórica*, 169–82. Valencia: Universidad de Valencia, Facultad de Teología San Vicente Ferrer, 1983.

Berenguer, Isidro Albert. *Bibliografía de la diócesis de Orihuela*. Alicante: Comisión Provincial de Monumentos, 1957.

Berger, Philippe. *Libro y lectura en la Valencia del Renacimiento*. Valencia: Institució Alfons el Magnànim, 1987.

Bergin, Joseph. *Cardinal de la Rochefoucauld*. New Haven: Yale UP, 1987.

——. *The Making of the French Episcopate, 1589–1661*. New Haven: Yale UP, 1996.

Bernal Díaz de Luco, Juan. *Aviso de curas*. Alcalá, 1543.

Beuter, Anton. *Primera parte de la coronica general de toda España, y especialmente del Reyno de Valencia*. Valencia: Pedro Patricio Mey, 1604.

Biblia Sacra Vulgata. Stuttgart: Deutsche Bibelgesellschaft, 1969.

Bilinkoff, Jodi. *The Avila of Santa Teresa*. Ithaca: Cornell UP, 1989.

——— . "A Saint for a City: Mariana de Jesús and Madrid, 1565–1624." *Archive for Reformation History* 88 (1997): 322–37.

Bireley, Robert. *Religion and Politics in the Age of the Counterreformation*. Chapel Hill: U of North Carolina P, 1981.

Bleda, Jaime. *Corónica de los moros de España*. Valencia, 1618.

——— . *Defensio fidei in causa neophytorum*. Valencia: Ioannem Chrysostomum Garriz, 1610.

——— . *Quatrocientos milagros*. Valencia: Pedro Patricio Mey, 1600.

Boer, Wietse de. *The Conquest of the Soul: Confession, Discipline, and Public Order in Counter-Reformation Milan*. Leiden: Brill, 2001.

Boix, Vicente. *Historia de la ciudad y reino de Valencia*. Valencia: Benito Monfort, 1845.

Bordes, José, and Enrique Sanz. "El protagonismo mudéjar en el comercio entre Valencia y el norte de África durante el siglo XV: Intercambio de culturas." In *Simposio Internacional de Mudejarismo: De mudéjares a moriscos: Una conversión forzada*, 1:275–82. Teruel: Instituto de Estudios Turolenses, Centro de Estudios Mudéjares, 2002.

Boronat y Barrachina, Pascual. *El B. Juan de Ribera y el R. Colegio de Corpus Christi*. Valencia: Francisco Vives y Mora, 1904.

——— , ed. *Los moriscos españoles y su expulsion*. 2 vols. Valencia: Francisco Vives y Mora, 1901.

Boruchoff, David A. "Cervantes y las leyes de reprehensíon cristiana." *Hispanic Review* 63 (1995): 39–55.

Bossy, John. *Christianity in the West, 1400–1700*. Oxford: Oxford UP, 1985.

Bouillard, Henri. *Conversion et grace chez S. Thomas d'Aquin*. Paris: Aubier, 1944.

Boussel, Patrice. *Des reliques et leur bon usage*. Paris: Balland, 1971.

Bouza Alvarez, José Luis. *Religiosidad contrarreformista y cultura simbólica del barroco*. Madrid: Consejo Superior de Investigaciones Científicas, 1990.

Braudel, Fernand. *The Mediterranean and the Mediterranean World in the Age of Philip II*. New York: Harper Collins, 1992.

Brilioth, Yngve. *A Brief History of Preaching*. Philadelphia: Fortress, 1965.

Bronseval, Claude de. *Viaje por la Valencia del siglo XVI*. Valencia: Ajuntament de València, 1993.

Brown, Jonathan. *Painting in Spain, 1500–1700*. New Haven: Yale UP, 1998.

Bueno Tárrega, Baltasar. *El Pare Sant Vicent Ferrer*. Valencia: Federico Domenech, 1995.

Bunes Ibarra, Miguel Angel de. *Los moriscos en el pensamiento histórico: Historiografía de un grupo marginado*. Madrid: Ediciones Cátedra, 1983.

Burns, Robert Ignatius. *The Crusader Kingdom of Valencia (1238–1276): A Study in the Organization of the Mediaeval Frontier*. Cambridge, Mass.: Harvard UP, 1967.

——— . *Islam under the Crusaders*. Princeton: Princeton UP, 1973.

——— . "Múdejars." In *Medieval Iberia: An Encyclopedia*, edited by E. Michael Gerli, 591–92. New York: Routledge, 2003.

——— . *Muslims, Christians, and Jews in the Crusader Kingdom of Valencia*. Cambridge: Cambridge UP, 1984.

Busquets Matoses, Jacinto. *Idea exemplar de prelados, dilineada en la vida y virtudes del venerable varón el Ilmo y Exmo Señor D. Juan de Ribera*. Valencia: Real Convento de Nuestra Señora del Carmen, 1683.

Cabrera de Córdoba, Luis. *Relaciones de las cosas sucedidas en la corte de España.* Madrid: J. Martín Alegria, 1857.

Calendar of State Papers. Vol. 9, *Foreign.* London: Eyre and Spottiswoode, 1890.

Candau Chacón, María Luisa. *Los moriscos en el espejo del tiempo.* Huelva: Universidad de Huelva, 1997.

Canet, José Luis, and Diego Romero, eds. *Crides, pragmàtiques, edictes, cartes i ordres per a l'administració i govern de la Cuitat i Regne de València en el segle XVI.* Vol. 2. Valencia: Universidad de Valencia, 2002.

Cárcel Ortí, María Milagros. *Las visitas pastorales de España (siglos XVI–XX).* Madrid : Asociación de Archiveros de la Iglesia en España, 2000.

Cárcel Ortí, María Milagros, and José Trenchs Odena. "Una visita pastoral del pontificado de San Juan de Ribera en Valencia (1570)." *Estudis* 8 (1979): 71–81.

Cárcel Ortí, Vicente. *Historia de la iglesia en Valencia.* 2d ed. Vol. 1. Valencia: Arzobispado de Valencia, 1987.

———. "El inventario de las bibliotecas de San Juan de Ribera en 1611." *Analecta Sacra Tarraconensia* 39 (1966): 319–79.

———. "Notas sobre la formación sacerdotal en Valencia desde el siglo XIII al XIX." *Hispania Sacra* 27 (1974): 151–99.

———. "Obras impresas del siglo XVI en la biblioteca de San Juan de Ribera." *Anales del Seminario de Valencia* 6 (1961): 117–383.

———. "Las visitas 'ad limina' de los arzobispos de Valencia." *Anales Valentinos* 4 (1978): 59–83.

Cárcel Ortí, Vicente, and María Milagros Cárcel Ortí, eds. *Relaciones sobre el estado de las diócesis valencianas.* Vol. 1, *Orihuela, Spain;* vol. 2, *Valencia;* vol. 3, *Segorbe, Spain.* Valencia: Conselleria de Cultura, Educació i Ciència, 1989.

Cardaillac, Louis. *Moriscos y cristianos: Un enfrentamiento polémico (1492–1640).* Madrid: Fondo de Cultura Económica, 1979.

Carleton, Kenneth. *Bishops and Reform in the English Church, 1520–1559.* Rochester, N.Y.: Boydell Press, 2001.

Caro Baroja, Julio. *Los moriscos del reino de Granada: Ensayo de historia social.* Madrid: Instituto de Estudios Políticos, 1957.

Carranza de Miranda, Bartolomé. *Controversia sobre la necesaria residencia personal de los obispos y de los otros pastores inferiores.* Edited by J. Ignacio Tellechea Idigoras. Madrid: Fundación Universitaria Española, 1993.

Carrasco, Juan, ed. *Historia de las Españas medievales.* Barcelona: Crítica, 2002.

Carrasco, Rafael. *Inquisición y represión sexual en Valencia: Historia de los sodomitas, 1565–1785.* Barcelona: Laertes, 1985.

Carreres Zacarés, Salvador, ed. *Libre de memories de diversos sucesos e fets memorables e de coses senyalades de la ciutat e regne de Valencia (1308–1644).* Valencia: Acción Bibliográfica Valenciana, 1930.

Casey, James. *The Kingdom of Valencia in the Seventeenth Century.* Cambridge: Cambridge UP, 1979.

Castañeda y Alcover, Vicente. *Sucesos en Valencia durante el reinado del emperador Carlos V y el virreinato del duque de Calabria, 1547–1551.* Valencia: Discurso Fundación del Instituto de España, 1963.

——, ed. *Coses evengudes en la ciutat y regne de Valencia: Dietario de Mosén Juan Porcar, capellán de San Martín (1589–1629)*. Madrid: Cuerpo Facultativo de Archiveros, Bibliotecarios, y Arqueólogos, 1934.

Castillo Mattasoglio, Carlos. *Libres para creer: La conversión según Bartolomé de las Casas en la Historia de las Indias*. Lima, Peru: Pontificia Universidad Católica del Peru, 1993.

Catalá de Valeriola, Bernardo. *Autobiografía y justas poéticas*. Valencia: Acción Bibliográfica Valenciana, 1929.

Catalá Sanz, Jorge, and Pablo Pérez García. *Los moriscos de Cortes y los Pallás: Documentos para su estudio*. Valencia: Universidad de Valencia, 2002.

Cebriá y Arazil, Fèlix. *Ceremonial de la ciudad de Valencia para la fiesta del Corpus*. Edited by Salvador Carreres Zacarés. Valencia: Ayuntamiento de Valencia, 1958.

Chejne, Anwar. *Islam and the West: The Moriscos, a Cultural and Social History*. Albany: State U of New York P, 1983.

Christian, William. *Apparitions in Late Medieval and Renaissance Spain*. Princeton: Princeton UP, 1981.

——. *Local Religion in Sixteenth-Century Spain*. Princeton: Princeton UP, 1981.

Cipres de Pobar, Silvio. *Origen y progresso de las pabordias de la sancta metropolitana iglesia de Valencia*. Rome: Camara Apostolica, 1641.

Císcar Pallarés, Eugenio. "'Algaravía' y 'algemía': Precisiones sobre la lengua de los moriscos in el reino de Valencia." *Al-Qantara* 15 (1994): 131–62.

——. "Mercaderes morsicos en la Valldigna (Valencia): Negocios, patrimonios y relaciones familiares." *Estudis* 21 (1995): 113–64.

——. *Moriscos, nobles y repobladores*. Valencia: Institució Alfons el Magnànim, 1993.

——. "La vida cotidiana entre cristianos viejos y moriscos en Valencia." In *Felipe II y el Mediterráneo*, edited by Ernest Belenguer, 2:569–91. Madrid: Sociedad Estatal para la Conmemoración de los Centenarios de Felipe II y Carlos V, 1999.

——, ed. *Las Cortes valencianas de Felipe III*. Valencia: Universidad de Valencia, 1974.

Clark, Peter, ed. *The European Crisis of the 1590s: Essays in Comparative History*. London: Allen and Unwin, 1985.

Cock, Henrique. *Relacion del viaje hecho por Felipe II en 1585*. Madrid: Aribau, 1876.

Colección de documentos inéditos para la historia de España. 113 vols. Madrid: Academia de la Historia, 1842–95.

Coleman, David. *Creating Christian Granada: Society and Religious Reform in an Old-World Frontier City, 1492–1600*. Ithaca: Cornell UP, 2003.

Confrontación de la teología y la cultura: Simposio de Teología Histórica. Valencia: Universidad de Valencia, Facultad de Teología San Vicente Ferrer, 1984.

Consaloniero, Juan Bautista. *Relacion del aparato que se hizo en la ciudad do Valencia*. Valencia: Pedro Patricio Mey, 1599.

Constable, Olivia Remie. *Trade and Traders in Muslim Spain*. Cambridge: Cambridge UP, 1994.

Corbató, Hermenegildo. *Los misterios del Corpus de Valencia*. Berkeley: U of California P, 1932.

Cordero, Martín. "Vida." In *Ensayo de un diccionario biográfico y bibliográfico*, edited by Francisco Martí Grajales, 128–77. Madrid: Revista de Archivos, Bibliotecas, y Museos, 1927.

Cornell, Vincent. "Fruit of the Tree of Knowledge." In *The Oxford History of Islam*, edited by John Esposito, 63–105. Oxford: Oxford UP, 1999.

Corrientes espirituales en la Valencia del siglo XVI (1550–1600): Actas del II Symposio de Teología Histórica. Valencia: Universidad de Valencia, Facultad de Teología San Vicente Ferrer, 1983.

Corteguera, Luis. *For the Common Good: Popular Politics in Barcelona, 1580–1640*. Ithaca: Cornell UP, 2002.

Covarrubias, Sebastián de. *Tesoro de la lengua castellana o española*. Madrid: Ediciones Turner, 1984.

Cox, Virginia. *The Renaissance Dialogue*. Cambridge: Cambridge UP, 1992.

Cruz, Anne J., and Mary Elizabeth Perry, eds. *Culture and Control in Counter-reformation Spain*. Minneapolis: U of Minnesota P, 1992.

Cubí, Manuel. *Vida del Beato Juan de Ribera*. Barcelona, 1912.

Danvila, Manuel. *La expulsión de los moriscos españoles: Conferencias pronunciadas en el Ateneo de Madrid*. Madrid: Libreria de Fernando Fé, 1889.

———. *Investigaciones histórico-críticos acerca de las Cortes y Parlamentos del antiguo reino de Valencia*. Madrid, 1905.

Diago, Francisco. *Anales del Reyno de Valencia*. Valencia: Paris-Valencia, 1981.

———. *Apuntamientos recogidos por Francisco Diago, O.P., para continuar los anales del Reyno de Valencia desde el rey Pedro III hasta Felipe II*. Vol. 2. Valencia: Acción Bibliográfica Valenciana, 1936–42.

Díaz Borrás, Andrés. *Los orígenes de la piratería Islámica en Valencia*. Barcelona: Consejo Superior de Investigaciones Científicas, 1993.

Diego, José R. de. "Una sentencia olvidada sobre el canon de las Escrituras." *Estudios Eclesiásticos* 41 (1966): 463–81.

Ditchfield, Simon, ed. *Christianity and Community in the West*. Aldershot, U.K.: Ashgate, 2001.

Domínguez Ortiz, Antonio. *Las clases privilegiadas en la España del antiguo régimen*. Madrid: Ediciones Istmo, 1973.

Domínguez Otriz, Antonio, and Bernard Vincent. *Historia de los moriscos: Vida y tragedia de una minoría*. Madrid: Revista de Occidente, 1978.

Dopico Black, Georgina. *Perfect Wives, Other Women: Adultery and Inquisition in Early Modern Spain*. Durham: Duke UP, 2001.

Duffy, Eamon. *The Voices of Morebath: Reformation and Rebellion in an English Village*. New Haven: Yale UP: 2001.

Duggan, Lawrence G. *Bishop and Chapter: The Governance of the Bishopric of Speyer to 1552*. New Brunswick: Rutgers UP, 1978.

Ehlers, Benjamin. "The Archbishop Juan de Ribera and the Jesuits of Valencia." Paper presented at the Sixteenth Century Studies Conference, Toronto, October 22–25, 1998.

———. "La esclava y el patriarca: Las visiones de Catalina Muñoz en la Valencia de Juan de Ribera." *Estudis* 23 (1997): 101–16.

———. "Juan Bautista Pérez and the *Plomos de Granada*: Spanish Humanism in the Late Sixteenth Century." *Al-Qantara, Revista de Estudios Árabes* 24 (2003): 427–48.

Eire, Carlos. *From Madrid to Purgatory: The Art and Craft of Dying in Sixteenth-Century Spain*. Cambridge: Cambridge UP, 1995.

Elliott, John. *The Revolt of the Catalans*. Cambridge: Cambridge UP, 1963.

——. *Spain and Its World, 1500–1700*. New Haven: Yale UP, 1989.

Enríquez, Fernando Afán de Ribera y. *Del título de la cruz de Christo*. Seville, 1619.

Enríquez de Ribera, Fadrique. *El viage de la Tierra Santa*. Madrid, 1748.

Epalza, Míkel de. *Los moriscos antes y después de la expulsión*. Madrid: Editorial Mapfre, 1992.

——. "Los voz oficial de los musulmanes hispanos, mudéjares y moriscos, a sus autoridades cristianas: Cuatro textos, en árabe, en castellano y en catalán-valenciano." *Sharq al-Andalus* 12 (1995): 279–97.

Epitome sive compendium constitutionem sanctae Metropolitanae Ecclesiae Valentinae. Valencia: Pedro Patricio Mey, 1582.

Escolano, Gaspar. *Década primera de la historia de Valencia*. 2 vols. Valencia: Pedro Patricio Mey, 1611.

Escrivá, Francisco. *Vida del illustrissimo y excellentissimo señor Don Juan de Ribera, patriarca de Antioquía y arçobispo de Valencia*. Valencia: Pedro Patricio Mey, 1612.

Esposito, John, ed. *The Oxford History of Islam*. Oxford: Oxford UP, 1999.

Evennett, H. Outram. *The Spirit of the Counter-Reformation*. Cambridge: Cambridge UP, 1968.

La expulsión de los moriscos del reino de Valencia. Valencia: Fundación Bancaja, 1997.

Falomir, Miguel. *La pintura y los pintores en la Valencia del renacimiento (1472–1620)*. Valencia: Generalitat Valenciana, 1994.

Felipo Orts, Amparo. "Control monárquico y oligarquía municipal en la Valencia de Felipe II." In *Felipe II y el Mediterráneo*, edited by Ernest Belenguer, 2:311–44. Madrid: Sociedad Estatal para la Conmemoración de los Centenarios de Felipe II y Carlos V, 1999.

——. "El rectorado de la universidad de Valencia durante el siglo XVI." *Estudis* 15 (1989): 67–92.

——. *La Universidad de Valencia durante el siglo XVI (1499–1611)*. Valencia: Universidad de Valencia, 1993.

Fernández, Juan, and Ramón López. "Los colegios jesuíticos valencianos: Datos para su historia." *Estudis* 16 (1990): 193–213.

Fernández Terricabras, Ignasi. *Felipe II y el clero secular: La aplicación del concilio de Trento*. Madrid: Sociedad Estatal para la Conmemoración de los Centenarios de Felipe II y Carlos V, 2000.

Feros, Antonio. *Kingship and Favoritism in the Spain of Philip III, 1598–1621*. Cambridge: Cambridge UP, 2000.

Ferrando Badía, Juan. *El histórico reino de Valencia y su organización foral*. Valencia: Generalitat Valenciana, 1995.

Ferraz, F. M. *El maestre racional y la hacienda foral valenciana*. Valencia: Tip. Moderna, 1913.

Ferror i Mallol, María Teresa. *La frontera amb l'Islam en el segle XIV: Cristians i sarraïns al País Valencià*. Barcelona: Consejo Superior de Investigaciones Científicas, 1988.

Fletcher, Richard. *Moorish Spain*. New York: Henry Holt, 1992.

——. *The Quest for El Cid*. London: Hutchinson, 1989.

Flores Arroyuelo, Francisco José. *Los últimos moriscos: Valle de Ricote, 1614*. Murcia: Academia Alfonso X El Sabio, 1989.

Fonseca, Damián. *Justa expulsión de los moriscos de España*. Rome, 1611.

——— . *Relación de la expulsión de los moriscos del reino de Valencia*. Valencia: Sociedad Valenciana de Bibliófilos, 1878.

Ford, Richard. *Manual para viajeros por los reinos de Valencia y Murcia*. Madrid: Ediciones Turner, 1982.

Forster, Marc R. *The Counter-Reformation in the Villages: Religion and Reform in the Bishopric of Speyer, 1560–1720*. Ithaca: Cornell UP, 1992.

Fray Francisco del Niño Jesús. *Diversas cartas del venerable hermano fray Francisco del Niño Jesús a D. Juan de Ribera*. Valencia: Joseph Garcia, 1732.

Fuente, Vicente de la. *Historia de las universidades en España*. Vol. 1. Frankfurt: Verlag, Sauer, and Auvermann, 1969.

Furio, Antoni. *Historia del pais Valencià*. Valencia: Institució Alfons el Magnànim, 1995.

Furió Ceriol, Fadrique. *El concejo y consejeros del Príncipe*. Valencia: Institució Alfons el Magnànim, 1952.

Furs de València. Valencia: Institut Valenciá d'Administració Pública, 1991.

Fuster, Joan. *Nosotros los valencianos*. Barcelona: Ediciones Península, 1976.

——— . *Poetas, moriscos y curas*. Madrid: Editorial Ciencia Nueva, 1969.

——— . *Rebeldes y heterodoxos*. Barcelona: Ediciones Ariel, 1972.

Galán Sánchez, Angel. *Una visión de la "decadencia española": La historiografía anglosajona sobre mudéjares y moriscos*. Málaga: Diputación Provincial de Málaga, 1991.

Gallego Salvadores, Jordán. "Provisión de cátedras en la Universidad de Valencia durante la primera mitad del siglo XVI." *Escritos del Vedat* 6 (1976): 165–201.

Gallego y Burín, Antonio. *Los moriscos del Reino de Granada, según el Sínodo de Cuadix de 1554*. Granada: Universidad de Granada, 1968.

García-Arenal, Mercedes. *Inquisición y moriscos: Los procesos del Tribunal de Cuenca*. Madrid: Siglo Veintiuno Editores, 1978.

——— . *Los moriscos*. Madrid: Editora Nacional, 1975.

——— , ed. *Islamic Conversions: Religious Identities in Mediterranean Islam*. Paris: Maisonneuve et Larose, 2001.

García-Arenal, Mercedes, and Miguel Ángel de Bunes. *Los españoles y el norte de África: Siglos XV-XVIII*. Madrid: Editorial Mapfre, 1992.

García Ballester, Luis. *Medicina, ciencia y minorías marginadas: Los moriscos*. Granada: Universidad de Granada, 1977.

García Cárcel, Ricardo. *Cortes del reinado de Carlos I*. Valencia: Universidad de Valencia, 1972.

——— . "Estudio crítico del *catecismo* de Ribera-Ayala." In *Les morisques et leurs temps*, edited by Louis Cardaillac, 159–68. Montpellier: Centre National de la Recherche Scientifique, 1983.

——— . *Las germanías de Valencia*. Barcelona: Ediciones Península, 1975.

——— . *Herejía y sociedad en el siglo XVI: La inquisición en Valencia, 1530–1609*. Barcelona: Ediciones Península, 1980.

——— . "Notas sobre población y urbanismo en la Valencia del siglo XVI." *Saitabi* 25 (1975): 133–55.

——— . "Las relaciones de la monarquía de Felipe II con la Compañía de Jesús." In *Felipe II y el Mediterráneo*, edited by Ernest Belenguer, 2:219–32. Madrid: Sociedad Estatal para la Conmemoración de los Centenarios de Felipe II y Carlos V, 1999.

García Martínez, Sebastián. *Bandolerismo, piratería y control de moriscos en Valencia durante el reinado de Felipe II*. Valencia: Universidad de Valencia, 1977.

———. "Notas sobre el primer trienio del marqués de Caracena en Valencia (1606–1609)." In *Homenaje al Dr. D. Juan Reglà*, 1:526–47. Valencia: Universidad de Valencia, 1975.

———. "El patriarca Ribera y la extirpación del erasmismo valenciano." *Estudis* 4 (1975): 69–104.

———. "San Juan de Ribera y la primera cuestión universitaria (1569–1572)." *Contrastes* [journal of the Department of Modern History, University of Murcia] (1985): 3–49.

García Mercadal, José. *Viajes de extranjeros por España y Portugal*. Madrid: Aguilar, 1952.

García Oro, José. *Cisneros: El Cardenal de España*. Barcelona: Editorial Ariel, 2002.

García Pedraza, Amalia. "La asimilación del morisco don Gonzalo Fernández el Zegrí: Edición y análisis de su testamento." *Al-Qantara: Revista de Estudios Árabes* 16 (1995): 39–58.

———. "El morisco ante la muerte: Algunas reflexiones sobre los testamentos otorgados por los moriscos granadinos (1500–1526)." In *Mélanges Louis Cardaillac*, edited by Abdeljelil Temimi, 1:338–52. Zaghouan, Tunisia: Fondation Temimi, 1995.

Garrido Aranda, Antonio. *Moriscos e indios: Precedentes hispánicos de la evangelización en México*. Mexico City: Universidad Autónoma de México, 1980.

Gauna, Felipe. *Relación de las fiestas celebradas en Valencia con motivo del casamiento de Felipe III*. Valencia: Acción Bibliográfica Valenciana, 1926.

Gavaston, Juan. *Tratado de la vida espiritual de nuestro padre S. Vicente Ferrer de la orden de predicadores: Traduzido de latin en romance, declarado, y comentado por el P. F. Iuan Gavaston Predicador general de la misma orden*. Valencia: Juan Chrysostomo Garriz, 1616.

Geary, Patrick. *Furta Sacra: Thefts of Relics in the Central Middle Ages*. Princeton: Princeton UP, 1978.

Giménez, José M. *Un catecismo para la iglesia universal*. Pamplona: Universidad de Navarra, 1987.

Glick, Thomas. *From Muslim Fortress to Christian Castle: Social and Cultural Change in Medieval Spain*. Manchester, U.K.: Manchester UP, 1995.

Gómez Canseco, Luis. *El humanismo después de 1600: Pedro de Valencia*. Seville: Universidad de Sevilla, 1993.

González, Vicente. *La personalidad artística del beato Juan de Ribera*. Valencia: Diputación Provincial de Valencia, 1948.

González González, Nicolas. *La teología de la predicación en Santo Tomás de Villanueva*. Madrid: Real Monasterio de el Escorial, 1959.

González Moreno, Joaquín. *Don Fadrique Enríquez de Ribera*. Seville: Imprenta Provincial, 1963.

González Navarro, Ramón. *Felipe II y las reformas constitucionales de la Universidad de Alcalá de Henares*. Madrid: Sociedad Estatal para la Conmemoración de los Centenarios de Felipe II y Carlos V, 1999.

Granada, Luis de. *Obras*. Edited by Justo Cuervo. Madrid: Gómez Fuentenebro, 1906–08.

Graullera, Vicente. *La esclavitud en Valencia en los siglos XVI y XVII*. Valencia: Institució Alfons el Magnànim, 1978.

Greyerz, Kaspar von, ed. *Religion and Society in Early Modern Europe, 1500–1800*. London: Allen and Unwin, 1984.

Guadalajara, Marco de. *Memorable expulsion y destierro de los moriscos de España.* Pamplona: Nicolas de Assiayn, 1613.

Guitarte Izquierdo, Vidal. *Obispos auxiliares en la historia del Arzobispado de Valencia.* Castellón de la Plana: Ayuntamiento de Castellón de la Plana, 1985.

Hale, John. *The Civilization of Europe in the Renaissance.* New York: Atheneum, 1994.

Haliczer, Stephen. *Inquisition and Society in the Kingdom of Valencia, 1478–1834.* Berkeley: U of California P, 1990.

Halperin Donghi, Tulio. *Un conflicto nacional: Moriscos y cristianos viejos en Valencia.* 2d ed. Valencia: Institució Alfons el Magnànim, 1980.

Hamilton, Earl J. *American Treasure and the Price Revolution in Spain.* Cambridge, Mass.: Harvard UP, 1934.

———. *Money, Prices, and Wages in Valencia, Aragon, and Navarre, 1351–1500.* Cambridge, Mass.: Harvard UP, 1936.

Harline, Craig, and Eddy Put. *A Bishop's Tale: Mathias Hovius among his Flock in Seventeenth-Century Flanders.* New Haven: Yale UP, 2000.

Harvey, L. P. *Islamic Spain, 1250–1500.* Chicago: U of Chicago P, 1990.

Hefner, Robert W., ed. *Conversion to Christianity.* Berkeley: U of California P, 1993.

Hegyi, Ottmar. *Cinco leyendas y otros relatos moriscos.* Madrid: Editorial Gredos, 1981.

Hembry, Phyllis M. *The Bishops of Bath and Wells, 1540–1640.* London: Athlone, 1967.

Hermann, Christian. *L'eglise d'Espagne sous le patronage royal, 1476–1834.* Madrid: Casa de Velázquez, 1988.

Hernández Parrales, Antonio, and Joaquín González Moreno. *El Beato Ribera y la Casa de Pilatos.* Seville: Peralto, 1960.

Hernández Ruano, Javier. *Historia de los moriscos valencianos de Xivert.* Alcalá de Xivert: Ayuntamiento de Alcalá de Xivert, 2003.

Herrera, José María, ed. *Historical Maps of the Town of Valencia.* Valencia: Valencia City Council, 1985.

Herzog, Tamar. "Private Organizations as Global Networks in Early Modern Spain and Spanish America." In *The Collective and the Public in Latin America,* edited by Luis Roniger and Tamar Herzog, 117–33. Brighton, U.K.: Sussex Academic Press, 2000.

Hess, Andrew C. *The Forgotten Frontier: A History of the Sixteenth-Century Ibero-African Frontier.* Chicago: U of Chicago P, 1978.

Hoffman, Philip T. *Church and Community in the Diocese of Lyon, 1500–1789.* New Haven: Yale UP, 1984.

Homza, Lu Ann. *Religious Authority in the Spanish Renaissance.* Baltimore: Johns Hopkins UP, 2000.

Hsia, R. Po-Chia. *Social Discipline in the Reformation: Central Europe 1550–1750.* New York: Routledge, 1989.

———. *The World of Catholic Renewal.* Cambridge: Cambridge UP, 1998.

Huerga, Alvaro, O.P. *Fray Luis de Granada.* Madrid: La Editorial Católica, 1988.

———. "Fray Luis de Granada y San Carlos Borromeo: Una amistad al servicio de la restauración católica." *Hispania Sacra* 11 (1958): 299–347.

———. *Historia de los alumbrados.* Vol. 1. Madrid: Fundación Universitario Española, 1978.

——. "La vida pseudomística y el proceso inquisitorial de sor Maria de la visitación ('la Monja de Lisboa')." *Hispania Sacra* 12 (1959): 35–130.

Hurtado de Mendoza, Diego. *Guerra de Granada.* Edited by Bernardo Blanco-González. Madrid: Castalia, 1970.

Las insignes reliquias de la capilla del real Colegio de Corpus Christi de Valencia. Valencia, 1948.

Janer, Florencio. *Condición social de los moriscos de España.* Barcelona: Alta Fulla, 1987.

Jedin, Hubert. *A History of the Council of Trent.* London: Thomas Nelson, 1957.

Jones, Martin D. W. *The Counter Reformation: Religion and Society in Early Modern Europe.* Cambridge: Cambridge UP, 1995.

Kagan, Richard L. "Prescott's Paradigm: American Historical Scholarship and the Decline of Spain." *American Historical Review* 101 (1996): 423–46.

——. *Students and Society in Early Modern Spain.* Baltimore: Johns Hopkins UP, 1974.

——, ed. *Spain in America: The Origins of Hispanism in the United States.* Urbana: U of Illinois P, 2002.

Kamen, Henry. *The Phoenix and the Flame: Catalonia and the Counter Reformation.* New Haven: Yale UP, 1993.

——. *The Spanish Inquisition: A Historical Revision.* New Haven: Yale UP, 1997.

Klingshern, William E. *Caesarius of Arles: The Making of a Christian Community in Late Antique Gaul.* Cambridge: Cambridge UP, 1994.

Labarta, Ana. *La onomástica de los moriscos valencianos.* Madrid: Consejo Superior de Investigaciones Científicas, 1987.

La Parra, Santiago. *Los Borja y los moriscos: (Repobladores y "terratenientes" en la Huerta de Gandía tras la expulsión de 1609).* Valencia: Institució Alfons el Magnànim, 1992.

Lapeyre, Henri. *Géographie de l'Espagne morisque.* Paris: SEVPEN, 1959.

Laredo, Bernardino de. *The Ascent of Mount Sion.* London: Faber and Faber, 1952.

Lea, Henry Charles. *The Moriscos of Spain: Their Conversion and Expulsion.* Philadelphia: Lea, 1901. Published in Spanish translation by the University of Alicante, 2001.

Lehfeldt, Elizabeth A. "Discipline, Vocation, and Patronage: Spanish Religious Women in a Tridentine Microclimate." *Sixteenth Century Journal* 30 (1999): 1009–30.

León-Portilla, Miguel, ed. *The Broken Spears: The Aztec Account of the Conquest of Mexico.* Boston: Beacon, 1992.

Llobregat Conesa, Enrique. *El corpus de Valencia.* Valencia: Tres i Quatre, 1978.

Longás Bartibás, Pedro. *Vida religiosa de los moriscos.* Madrid: E. Maestre, 1915.

Luebke, David M., ed. *The Counter-Reformation.* Malden, Mass.: Blackwell, 1999.

MacKay, Ruth. *The Limits of Royal Authority: Resistance and Obedience in Seventeenth-Century Castile.* Cambridge: Cambridge UP, 1999.

Magraner Rodrigo, Antonio. *La expulsión de los moriscos, sus razones jurídicas y consecuencias económicas para la región valenciana.* Valencia: Instituto Valenciano de Estudios Históricos, 1975.

Mármol Carvajal, Luis del. *Historia del rebelión y castigo de los moriscos de Granada.* In *Biblioteca de autores Españoles,* 21:123–365. Madrid: Atlas, 1852.

Márquez Villanueva, Francisco. *Personajes y temas del* Quijote. Madrid: Taurus, 1975.

———. *El problema morisco (desde otras laderas)*. Madrid: Ediciones Libertarias, 1998.

Martí, Antonio. *La preceptiva retórica española en el siglo de oro*. Madrid: Editorial Gredos, 1972.

Martí Mestre, Joaquim, ed. *El* Libre de antiquitats *de la Seu de Valencia*. Valencia: Institut Universitari de Filologia Valenciana, 1994.

Martín Ruiz, Francisco. *Economía y sociedad en el siglo XVI: Moriscos y cristianos en el partido de Marbella*. Málaga: F. Martín Ruiz, 1984.

Martínez, François. "Les enfants morisques de l'expulsion (1610–1621)." In *Mélanges Louis Cardaillac*, edited by Abdeljelil Temimi, 2:499–539. Zaghouan, Tunisia: Fondation Temimi, 1995.

Martínez Aloy, J. *La diputación de la generalidad del reino de Valencia*. Valencia: Hijo de F. Vives Mora, 1930.

Martorell, Joanot. *Tirant lo Blanch*. Barcelona: Edicions 62, 1983.

Mateu Ibars, J. *Los virreyes de Valencia*. Valencia: Ayuntamiento de Valencia, 1963.

McGinness, Frederick J. *Right Thinking and Sacred Oratory in Counter-Reformation Rome*. Princeton: Princeton UP, 1995.

McGrath, Alister E. *Reformation Thought*. Oxford: Blackwell, 1988.

Medina, Pedro de. *Libro de grandezas y cosas memorables de España*. Madrid: Consejo Superior de Investigaciones Científicas, 1944.

Menéndez y Pelayo, Marcelino. *Historia de los heterodoxos españoles*. Vol. 4, *Erasmistes y protestantes*. Madrid: Consejo Superior de Investigaciones Científicas, 1963. First ed. 1880.

Merimée, Henri. *El arte dramático en Valencia*. Valencia: Institució Alfons el Magnànim, 1985. First ed. 1913.

———. *Spectacles et comediens a Valencia (1580–1630)*. Toulouse: Edouard Privat-Auguste Picard, 1913.

Mestre, Antonio. *Despotismo e ilustración en España*. Barcelona: Ariel, 1976.

———. "Un documento desconocido del patriarca Ribera escrito en los momentos decisivos sobre la expulsión de los moriscos." *Estudios dedicados a Juan Peset Aleixandre*. Valencia: Universidad de Valencia, 1982.

———. "Jerarquía católica y oligarquía municipal ante el control de la Universidad de Valencia (el obispo Esteve y la cuestión de los pasquines contra el patriarca Ribera)." *Anales de la Universidad de Alicante Historia Moderna* 1 (1980): 9–35.

Mettam, Roger. *Power and Faction in Louis XIV's France*. Oxford: Blackwell, 1988.

Meyerson, Mark. *The Muslims of Valencia in the Age of Ferdinand and Isabel: Between Coexistence and Crusade*. Berkeley: U of California P, 1991.

Miller, Kathryn. "Muslim Minorities and the Obligation to Emigrate to Islamic Territory." *Islamic Law and Society* 7 (2000): 256–88.

Miralles Vives, Francisca. "Nuevos documentos para la historia de la Universidad: Los desórdenes de 1580–1590." *Saitabi* 35 (1985): 111–25.

Monter, William. *Frontiers of Heresy: The Spanish Inquisition from the Basque Lands to Sicily*. Cambridge: Cambridge UP, 1990.

Monumenta Historica Societatis Iesu. Vol. 60. Rome: Institutum historicum Societatis Iesu, 1894.

Muir, Edward. *Ritual in Early Modern Europe*. Cambridge: Cambridge UP, 1997.

Mulcahy, Rosemarie. *The Decoration of the Royal Basilica of El Escorial*. Cambridge: Cambridge UP, 1994.

Muñoz, Jerónimo. *Libro del nuevo cometa*. Edited by Víctor Navarro Brotóns. Valencia: Pedro de Huete, 1573. Reprint, Valencia: Hispaniae Scientia, 1981.

Münzer, Jerónimo. *Viaje por España y Portugal (1494–1495)*. Madrid: Ediciones Polifemo, 1991.

Nalle, Sara. *God in La Mancha: Religious Reform and the People of Cuenca, 1500–1650*. Baltimore: Johns Hopkins UP, 1992.

——— . *Mad for God: Bartolomé Sánchez, the Secret Messiah of Cardenete*. Charlottesville: U of Virginia P, 2001.

Narbona Vizcaíno, Rafael. *El nou d'octubre: Ressenya històrica d'una festa valenciana (segles 14–20)*. Valencia: Generalitat Valenciana, 1997.

——— . *Valencia, municipio medieval: Poder político y luchas ciudadanas. 1239–1418*. Valencia: Ajuntament de València, 1995.

Nirenberg, David. *Communities of Violence*. Princeton: Princeton UP, 1996.

O'Callaghan, Joseph F. *Reconquest and Crusade in Medieval Spain*. Philadelphia: U of Pennsylvania P, 2003.

O'Connor, Isabel A. *A Forgotten Community: The Mudejar Aljama of Xàtiva, 1240–1327*. Leiden: Brill, 2003.

Olin, John. *Catholic Reform from Cardinal Ximenes to the Council of Trent, 1495–1563*. New York: Fordham UP, 1990.

Olmos y Canalda, Elias. *Los prelados valentinos*. Madrid: Instituto Jerónimo Zurita, 1949.

O'Malley, John. *The First Jesuits*. Cambridge, Mass.: Harvard UP, 1993.

——— . *Praise and Blame in Renaissance Rome: Rhetoric, Doctrine, and Reform in the Sacred Orators of the Papal Court, c. 1450–1521*. Vol. 3. Durham: Duke UP, 1979.

——— . "Saint Charles Borromeo and the Praecipuum Episcoporum Munus: His Place in the History of Preaching." In *Religious Culture in the Sixteenth Century*, article 6. Brookfield, Vt.: Variorum, 1993.

——— . *Trent and All That: Renaming Catholicism in the Early Modern Era*. Cambridge, Mass.: Harvard UP, 2000.

Ortega y Gasset, José. *Mission of the University*. London: Transaction Publishers, 1972.

Osuna, Francisco de. *The Third Spiritual Alphabet*. New York: Paulist Press, 1981.

Ozment, Steven. *The Reformation in the Cities*. New Haven: Yale UP, 1975.

Palacio, Marco Antonio. *Classis Salomonis paradoxon*. Orihuela: Ludovicum Berosium, 1613.

Pardo Molero, Juan Francisco. "Imperio y cruzada: La política mediterránea de Carlos V vista desde Valencia." In *Carlos V: Europeísmo y universalidad*, edited by Juan Luis Castellano Castellano and Francisco Sánchez-Montes González, 3:359–78. Granada: Sociedad Estatal para la Conmemoración de los Centenarios de Felipe II y Carlos V, 2001.

Parker, Geoffrey. *The Grand Strategy of Philip II*. New Haven: Yale UP, 1998.

Pastor, Ludwig von. *The History of the Popes*. London: Kegan Paul, 1929.

Patrouch, Joseph F. *A Negotiated Settlement: The Counter-Reformation in Upper Austria under the Habsburgs*. Boston: Humanities Press, 2000.

Peñarroja Torrejòn, Leopoldo. *Cristianos bajo el Islam*. Madrid: Gredos, 1993.

———. *Moriscos y repobladores en el Reino de Valencia: La Vall de Uxó (1525–1625)*. Valencia: Del Cenia al Segura, 1984.

Pérez de Ayala, Martín. "Discurso de la vida." In *Autobiografías y memorias*, edited by Manuel Serrano y Sanz, 211–37. Madrid: Bailly, Bailliére e hijos, 1905.

———. *Doctrina christiana en lengua arábiga y castellana*. Valencia: Ioan Mey, 1566.

———. *Sínodo de la diócesis de Guadix y de Baza*. Granada: Archivum, 1994.

———. *Synodus diocesana valentiae, 1566*. Valencia: Gabriel Ribas, 1594.

Pérez Boyero, Enrique. *Moriscos y cristianos en los señoríos del Reino de Granada (1490–1568)*. Granada: Universidad de Granada, 1997.

Pérez Bustamente, Ciriaco. "El pontífice Paulo V y la expulsión de los moriscos." *Boletín de la Real Academia de la Historia* 129 (1951): 219–37.

Perry, Mary Elizabeth. "Moriscas and the Limits of Assimilation." In *Christians, Muslims and Jews in Medieval and Early Modern Spain*, edited by Mark D. Meyerson and Edward D. English, 274–89. Notre Dame: U of Notre Dame P, 1999.

Peset, Mariano, and Telesforo M. Hernández. "De la justa expulsión de los moriscos de España." *Estudis* 20 (1994): 231–52.

Pezzi, Elena. *Los moriscos que no se fueron*. Almería: Editorial Cajal, 1991.

Pike, Ruth. *Aristocrats and Traders: Sevillian Society in the Sixteenth Century*. Ithaca: Cornell UP, 1972.

Pilar Valero, María. "Impresión de libros sobre las obras del Mo. Vitoria." In *Documentos para la historia de la universidad de Salamanca*, 129–31. Cáceres: Universidad de Extremadura, 1989.

Piles, Leopoldo. *Estudio documental sobre el bayle general de Valencia, su autoridad y jurisdicción*. Valencia: Institució Alfons el Magnànim, 1970.

Pons Fuster, Francisco. "El iluminismo en Valencia: Siglos XVI y XVII." Ph.D. diss., University of Valencia, 1988.

———. *Místicos, beatas y alumbrados: Ribera y la espiritualidad valenciana del s. XVII*. Valencia: Institució Alfons el Magnànim, 1991.

Poole, Stafford. *Pedro Moya de Contreras*. Berkeley: U of California P, 1987.

Poska, Allyson M. "From Parties to Pieties: Redefining Confraternal Activity in Seventeenth-Century Ourense (Spain)." In *Confraternities and Catholic Reform in Italy, France, & Spain*, edited by John Patrick Donnelly and Michael W. Maher, 215–31. Kirksville, Mo.: Thomas Jefferson UP, 1999.

———. *Regulating the People: The Catholic Reformation in Seventeenth Century Spain*. Leiden: Brill, 1998.

Prades, Jaime. *Historia de la adoración y uso de las santas imagenes, y de la imagen de la fuente de la salud*. Valencia: Felipe Mey, 1597.

"Pragmàtica de Carlos V restringint la llibertad dels moriscos," Valencia 1541. In *Crides, pragmàtiques, edictes, cartes i ordres per a l'administració i govern de la Cuitat i Regne de València en el segle XV*, edited by Jose Luís Canet and Diego Romero, 1:84–91. Valencia: Universidad de Valencia, 2002.

Prodi, Paolo. *The Papal Prince*. Cambridge: Cambridge UP, 1987.

Rahner, Karl. *Bishops: Their Status and Function*. Baltimore: Helicon, 1965.

Ramírez Martínez, Santos. *Los moriscos de la vilanova de Mislata 1525–1609*. Mislata: Ajuntament de Mislata, 1994.

Ranke, Leopold von. *The History of the Popes*. Philadelphia: Lea and Blanchard, 1844.

Rawlings, Helen. *Church, State and Society in Early Modern Spain*. London: Palgrave, 2002.

Redondo, Agustín. *Antonio de Guevara (1480?-1545) et l'Espagne de son temps*. Geneva: Librairie Droz, 1976.

Reglà, Joan. *Aproximació a la història del país Valencià*. Valencia: Eliseu Climent, 1984.

———. *Estudios sobre los moriscos*. Valencia: Universidad de Valencia, 1971.

Reilly, Bernard. *The Medieval Spains*. Cambridge: Cambridge UP, 1993.

"Relación de las casas de christianos viejos y nuevos que ay en las ciudades, villas y lugares deste Reino de Valencia y de la parte de lebante y los señores dellas." In *Los moriscos españoles y su expulsion*, edited by Pascual Boronat y Barrachina, 1:428–42. Valencia: Francisco Vives y Mora, 1901.

Ribadeneyra, Pedro de. *Vida del P. Francisco de Borja*. Madrid: P. Madrigal, 1592.

Ribera, Juan de. "Al lector." In *La venerable setabense Sor Margarita Agullona Terciaria Franciscana: Su vida y escritos*, by Jaime Sanchis, 9–19. 2d ed. Valencia: Játiva, 1921. First ed. Valencia: Juan Chrisóstomo Garriz, 1607; 2d ed., Játiva, 1921.

———. *Catechismo para instruccion de los nuevamente convertidos de moros*. Valencia: Pedro Patricio Mey, 1599.

———. *Constituciones de la Capilla del Colegio y Seminario de Corpus Christi*. Valencia, 1896.

———. *Constituciones del Colegio y Seminario de Corpus Christi*. Valencia, 1896.

———. *Regla y constituciones dadas a las religiosas del convento de S. Gregorio de la ciudad de Valencia*. Valencia: Benito Monfort, 1834.

———. *Sermones: Edición crítica*. Edited by Ramón Robres Lluch. 6 vols. Valencia: Ediciones Corpus Christi, 1987–2001.

———. *Synodus diocesana valentiae*, 1578. Valencia: Gabriel Ribas, 1594.

———. *Synodus diocesana valentiae*, 1584. Valencia: Gabriel Ribas, 1594.

———. *Synodus diocesana valentiae*, 1590. Valencia: Gabriel Ribas, 1594.

———. *Synodus diocesana valentiae*, 1594. Valencia: Gabriel Ribas, 1594.

———. *Synodus diocesana valentiae*, 1599. Valencia: Pedro Patricio Mey, 1599.

Robinson, Francis. "Knowledge." In *The Cambridge Illustrated History of the Islamic World*, edited by Francis Robinson, 208–49. New York: Cambridge UP, 1996.

Robles, Laureano. "Las 'constituciones' valencianas de 1568 (evangelización y castellanización de los moriscos)." In *Los sínodos diocesanos del pueblo de Dios: Actas del V Simposio de Teología Histórica (24–26 octubre 1988)*, 273–300. Valencia: Universidad de Valencia, Facultad de Teología San Vicente Ferrer, 1998.

Robres Lluch, Ramón. "Catálogo y nuevas notas que fueron de los moriscos en el arzobispado de Valencia, y su repoblación (1527–1663)." *Anthologica Annua* 10 (1962): 143–91.

———. "San Carlos Borromeo y sus relaciones con el episcopado ibérico postridentino." *Anthologica Annua* 8 (1960): 83–141.

———. *San Juan de Ribera*. Barcelona: Juan Flors, 1960.

———. "La visita 'ad limina' durante el pontificado de sixto V (1585–1590)." *Anthologica Annua* 7 (1959): 147–213.

Robres Lluch, Ramón, and José Ramón Ortolá. *La monja de Lisboa: Epistolario inédito entre Fr. Luis de Granada y el patriarca Ribera*. Castellón de la Plana: Sociedad Castellonense de Cultura, 1947.

Roig, Jaime. *Libre de les dones, o spill*. Barcelona: Editorial Barcino, 1928.

Rosselló, Vivenç M., ed. *Les vistes valencianes d'Anthonie van den Wijngaerde*. Valencia: Generalitat Valenciana, 1990.

Royo Martínez, José. *Las visitas pastorales del pontificado de San Juan de Ribera en Picanya (1570–1600)*. Picanya: Ajuntament de Picanya, 1996.

Ruiz, Teofilo. *Spanish Society 1400–1600*. New York: Longman, 2001.

Saavedra, Pegerto. "Cambios demográficos y sociales en la España mediterránea durante el reinado de Felipe II." In *Felipe II y el Mediterráneo*, edited by Ernest Belenguer, 1:41–63. Madrid: Sociedad Estatal para la Conmemoración de los Centenarios de Felipe II y Carlos V, 1999.

Sainz de Zuñiga, Cándido. *Historia de las universidades hispánicas*. Vol. 2. Avila: Centro de Estudios e Investigaciones, 1957.

Salavert, Vicent, and Vicent Graullera. *Professió, ciència i societat a la València del segle XVI*. Barcelona: Curial, 1990.

Salvador Estaban, Emilia. *Cortes valencianas del reinado de Felipe II*. Valencia: Universidad de Valencia, 1973.

———. *La economía valenciana en el siglo XVI (comercio de importación)*. Valencia: Universidad de Valencia, 1972.

———. *Felipe II y los moriscos valencianos: Las repercusiones de la revuelta granadina (1568–1570)*. Colección Síntesis 6, 1987. Valladolid: Universidad de Valladolid.

Sánchez, Magdalena. *The Empress, the Queen, and the Nun: Women and Power at the Court of Philip III of Spain*. Baltimore: Johns Hopkins UP, 1998.

Sanchis, Jaime. *La venerable setabense Sor Margarita Agullona Terciaria Franciscana: Su vida y escritos*. First ed. Valencia: Juan Chrisóstomo Garriz, 1607; 2d ed., Játiva, 1921.

Sanchis Guarner, Manuel. *La ciutat de València: Síntesi d'història i de geografia urbana*. 2d ed. Valencia: Ajuntament de València, 1983.

———. *La processó valenciana del Corpus*. Paterna: Vicent García, 1978.

Sanchis y Sivera, José. *Nomenclator geográfico-eclesiástico de los pueblos de la diócesis de Valencia*. Valencia: M. Gimeno, 1922.

Sandoval, Prudencio de. *Historia de la vida y hechos del emperador Carlos V*. Vols. 80–82 of *Biblioteca de autores Españoles*. Madrid: Atlas, 1955–56.

Santos Hernández, Angel, S.J. *Jesuitas y obispados: La Compañía de Jesús y las dignidades eclesiásticas*. Madrid: Comillas, 1998.

Segui Cantos, Jose. "Poder político, iglesia y cultura en Valencia." Ph.D. diss., University of Valencia, 1990.

Sentandreu Benavent, Juan B. *El archivo de protocolos del Colegio de Corpus Christi*. Valencia: Hijo de F. Vives Mora, 1935.

Serrano y Sanz, Manuel. *Pedro de Valencia: Estudio biográfico-crítico*. Badajoz, 1910.

———, ed. *Autobiografías y memorias*. Madrid: Bailly, Bailliére e hijos, 1905.

Smith, Colin. *Christians and Moors in Spain*. 3 vols. Warminster, U.K.: Aris and Phillips, 1989.

Sobrino, Antonio. *Vida espiritual, y perfeccion christiana*. Valencia: Iuan Chrysostomo Garriz, 1612.

Soergel, Philip M. *Wondrous in His Saints: Counter-Reformation Propaganda in Bavaria*. Berkeley: U of California P, 1993.

Starr-LeBeau, Gretchen. *In the Shadow of the Virgin: Inquisitors, Friars, and* Conversos *in Guadalupe, Spain*. Princeton: Princeton UP, 2003.

Strasser, Ulrike. "Bones of Contention: Cloistered Nuns, Decorated Relics, and the Contest over Women's Place in the Public Sphere of Counter-Reformation Munich." *Archive for Reformation History* 90 (1999): 255–88.

Surtz, Ronald. "Morisco Women, Written Texts, and the Valencia Inquisition." *Sixteenth Century Journal* 32 (2001): 421–33.

Tallada, Tomás Cerdán de. *Visita de la carcel, y de los presos*. Valencia: Pedro de Huete, 1574.

Tanner, Norman, ed. *Decrees of the Ecumenical Councils*. Vol. 2. Washington, D.C.: Georgetown UP, 1990.

Tapia Sánchez, Serafín de. *La comunidad morisca de Avila*. Salamanca: Universidad de Salamanca, 1991.

Tárrega, Francisco. *Relacion de las fiestas que el señor arzobispo y su cabildo, hicieron en la translacion de la reliquia del glorioso S. Vicente Ferrer a la santa iglesia de Valencia*. Valencia: Pedro Patricio Mey, 1600.

Taylor, Larissa. *Soldiers of Christ: Preaching in Late Medieval and Reformation France*. Oxford: Oxford UP, 1992.

Tejado y Ramiro, Juan. *Colección de canones y de todos los concilios de la iglesia española*. Madrid: Pedro Montero, 1855.

Tellechea, José Ignacio. "Declaración inédita del santo patriarca sobre las consideraciones de Juan de Valdés." *Hispania Sacra* 12 (1959): 455–63.

———. *El obispo ideal en el siglo de la reforma*. Rome: Iglesia Nacional Española, 1963.

Teresa of Avila. *Interior Castle*. New York: Image Books, 1961.

Thomas, Keith. *Religion and the Decline of Magic*. London: Weidenfeld and Nicolson, 1971.

Tramoyeres, L. *Instituciones gremiales, su origen y organización en Valencia*. Valencia: Imp. Domenech, 1889.

Tueller, James B. "The Assimilating Morisco: Four Families in Valladolid Prior to the Expulsion of 1610." *Mediterranean Studies* 7 (1997): 167–77.

———. *Good and Faithful Christians: Moriscos and Catholicism in Early Modern Spain*. New Orleans: UP of the South, 2002.

Usher, Brett. *William Cecil and Episcopacy, 1559–1577*. London: Ashgate, 2003.

Vallés Borràs, Vicent. *La germanía*. Valencia: Institució Alfons el Magnànim, 2000.

Valls Pallares, Ignacio. *Don Martín Pérez de Ayala, teólogo-apologista y arzobispo de Valencia*. Valencia: Montepio del Clero Valentino, 1954.

Vega Carpio, Lope de. *Fiestas de Denia*. Valencia: Diego de le Torre, 1599.

Viciana, Martin de. *Libro tercero de la Chronyca de la inclita y coronada ciudad de Valencia y de su reyno*. Valencia: Joan Navarro, 1564.

Vidal y Micò, Francisco. *Historia de la portentosa vida de S. Vicente Ferrer*. Valencia: Joseph Estevan Dolz, 1735.

Vila Moreno, Alfonso. *La lengua valenciana en la administración parroquial (Siglos XVII a XIX)*. Valencia: Del Cenia al Segura, 1983.

Villalmanzo Cameno, Jesús, ed. *La expulsión de los moriscos del Reino de Valencia*. Valencia: Fundación Bancaja, 1997.

Villalonga, Ignacio. *Los jurados y el consejo: Régimen municipal foral valenciano*. Valencia: A. C. de Miguel Gimeno, 1916.

Vincent, Bernard. "Élements de démographie morisque." In *La Corona de Aragón y el Mediterráneo, siglos XV–XVI*, edited by Esteban Sarasa and Eliseo Serrano, 145–52. Zaragoza: Institución Fernando el Católico, 1997.

———. "La guerre del Alpujarras et l'islam méditerranéen." In *Felipe II y el Mediterráneo*, edited by Ernest Belenguer, 4:267–75. Madrid: Sociedad Estatal para la Conmemoración de los Centenarios de Felipe II y Carlos V, 1999.

Vizuete Mendoza, J. Carlos. *La iglesia en la edad moderna*. Madrid: Editorial Sintesis, 2000.

Williams, Diane S. "De Moriscos Padres Engendrada: Ana Félix and Morisca Self-(Re)presentation." In *Brave New Words: Studies in Spanish Golden Age Literature*, edited by Edward H. Friedman and Catherine Larson, 135–44. New Orleans: UP of the South, 1996.

Ximénez, Juan. *Vida del Beato Juan de Ribera*. Valencia, 1798.

Ximeno, Vicente. *Escritores del reyno de Valencia*. Vol. 1. Valencia: Joseph Estevan Dolz, 1749.

Index

Abiaix, Miquel, 139
Acquaviva, Claudius, 152
Adzaneta, 98
Aguilar, Gaspar de, 101–102
Agullona, Margarita, 68–72, 154
Albrecht V (duke of Bavaria), 66
Alcalá de Xivert, 136–137
Alcodar, 96
Alcoy, 100
Alfonso the Magnanimous (king of Aragon), 13
Alfonso XI (king of Castile), 1
Algiers, 128, 132, 137
Al-Hajari, 148
Aliaga, Isidoro (archbishop of Valencia), 156
Alicante, 144
aljamas, 11
aljamiado literature, 33
Alzira, 11, 95
Angeles, Bartolomé de los, 18
Antist, Justiniano, 87–88
Aquinas, Saint Thomas, 82
Arabic: linguistic studies, xiii; spoken colloquial
    Arabic, 89, 98; use in Christian evangelization,
    12, 18, 20, 119–123, 155; use in letters, 132; use in
    morisco ceremonies, 30–34, 96
Aragon: Aragonese Cortes, 111; bandits, 20, 139;
    immigrants to Valencia, 104; king Ferdinand II,
    14; king James I, 10–11, 41; moriscos of, 106;
    Mudejar rebellion, 12
Austria, Jorge de (archbishop of Valencia), 19, 86,
    117
Avalos, Alonso de, 77
Avila, Teresa of, 78

Badajoz, 2–6
Balaguer, Andrés (bishop of Orihuela), 145

Bautista Pérez, Juan, 181n124
Benaguacil, 98, 116, 138
Benavente, Count of (viceroy of Valencia), 25, 43,
    49
Bertrán, Saint Luis, 67–68
bishops: appointment of, 6–7; powers, 38–40, 154
Bleda, Jaime, 126, 146
Bocairente, 100
Borja, Saint Francisco de, 42
Boronat y Barrachina, Pascual, xii, 153
Borromeo, Saint Carlo (archbishop of Milan), x,
    58, 63, 87
Bossy, John, xi
Botero, Giovanni, 143
Braudel, Fernand, xiii
Buñol, 23, 30–33, 97

Calderón, Soto: university visitation of 1570, 45,
    48, 53, 55
Caracena, Marquis of (viceroy of Valencia), 143–146
Cárcer, 131, 136
Cardona, Margarita de, 74
Cardona, Sancho de, 98, 116
Carlet, 98
Caro, Juan Bautista, 47, 85
Carroz, Jerónimo: enemy of Juan de Ribera, 52,
    54; sacristan of the cathedral, 56, 60
Casa de Pilatos, 1–2, 82
Casas, Bartolomé de las, 88
Casey, James, 197n18
Castelvi, Francisco de, 98
Castile: moriscos of, 32, 106, 140–141, 143–145, 147;
    Mudejar rebellion, 12; political appointees in
    Valencia, 25, 41–42, 53, 78; popular religion, xi;
    queen Isabella I, 14; resistance to royal author-
    ity, 37

Catalá de Valeriola, Bernardo, 26, 70

Catalonia: Aragonese Cortes, 111; popular religion, 81; rebellions, 13; reconquest of Valencia, 10–11, 41; reform of the church, 43; resistance to royal authority, 26, 37; viceroyalty of Per Afán de Ribera, 2

Catholic Reformation: canonization of saints, 151–152; catechisms, 119–123; conversion of moriscos, 82–83; historiography, xi–xii; policy of Philip II, 2–3; popular religion, 81–82; reform of cathedrals, 59–61; reform of the clergy, 40; relics, 73–77, 154; seminaries, 62–63. *See also* bishops; mysticism; Trent, Council of

Celaya, Joan de, 42–43

Cerdán de Tallada, Tomás, 94

Cervantes, Miguel de, *Don Quijote*, 131, 133, 148

Charles V: appointment of bishops, 2; forced baptism of Muslims, 14–17; Mediterranean policy, 20

Chelva, 93

Chiva, 96, 139

Christian, William, xi

El Cid, 10

Ciruana, Miquel, 33–34

Cisneros, Francisco Jiménez de (archbishop of Toledo), 107–108

Clavero, Diego, 152

Clement VIII (pope), 75–76

Cocentaina, 14, 33

Cock, Hendrik, 111–112

Colegio de Corpus Christi: campaign to canonize Juan de Ribera, 151–153; center for reform, 77, 154–157; chapel of Margarita Agullona, 71–72, 154; finances, ix–x, 147; foundation, 62–66, 107–108; library, 87–88; purity of blood statutes, 65, 122

Constantino Ponce de la Fuente, 6

Cordero, Juan Martín, 27

Córdoba, 99

Corpus Christi procession, 22–30, 78

Cortes, 93, 98

Cortés, Hernán, 17

Council of Aragon, 43, 49–50, 55

Council of State, 106, 143, 145–146

Covarrubias, Sebastián de, 115–117

Cuenca: cathedral, 115; Jesuit colleges in, 43; moriscos of, 94–95; popular religion, 81; reform of the clergy, 40

Denia, 137–138, 144

Diago, Francisco, 88

Doblet, Damián, 23, 31–33

Don Quijote (Cervantes), 131, 133, 148

Eça of Fansara, 34

England: raid on Cádiz, 128; restrictions on English residents in Spain, 6; rumors of aid to moriscos, 83; Spanish armada, 112; truce with Spain, 129, 140–141; Vincent Ferrer in, 88

Enríquez de Ribera, Fadrique, 1

Erasmus, Desiderius, 6, 88

Escolano, Gaspar, 22, 25, 75–77

Escrivá, Francisco: ally of Juan de Ribera, 44, 61; campaign to canonize Ribera, 152–153

Espinosa, Diego de, 48, 53, 55

Espinosa, Miguel de, 61, 77

Espinosa, Tomás de, 77

Evennett, H. Outram, xi

Ferdinand II (king of Aragon), 14, 25

Feros, Antonio, 204n15

Ferrer, Saint Vincent: relics, 73–75, 154; sermons, 87–88

Figueroa, Feliciano de (bishop of Segorbe), 61, 126

Fonseca, Damián, 117

France: burial site of Vincent Ferrer, 73–75; Huguenots in Valencia, 140–141; rumors of aid to moriscos, 128, 143; truce with Spain, 129; universities in, 43

Franco, Francisco, 153

Gali, Fernando de, 29, 136

Galicia: confraternities, 26; popular religion, 81; reform of the clergy, 40

Gandía: *germanías* in, 14–15; moriscos of, 80, 97, 131, 137–138

Gandía, Duke of, 132

Gea, 92–93, 95–96

germanías, 14–17

La Goleta, 104

Gombau, Jerónimo, 60

Gonzaga, Vespasiano, 42

González de Cellorigo, Martín, 126

Granada: forced baptism of Muslims, 107–108; *plomos* of Granada, 123; Revolt of the Alpujarras, 21–22, 83, 89, 110

Granada, Luis de, 68, 87, 121
Granero, Diego, 119–120
Gregory XIII (pope), 94, 116, 124
Guadalest, 98, 116
Guevara, Fernando Niño de (archbishop of
   Toledo), 75–76

Haedo, Diego de, 92–93
Hattstein, Marquard von, 4
Hernández Ruano, Javier, 206n53
Hovius, Mathius (archbishop of Mechelen), 87

Inquisition of Valencia: commissioners, 17–19,
   108–109, 115–117; morisco treaty of 1526, 16–18;
   morisco treaty of 1571, 83–84, 91–94; prosecution of moriscos, 91–94, 132–137
Isabella I (queen of Castile), 14

James I (king of Aragon), 10–11, 41
Játiva: germanías in, 14–15; home of Margarita
   Agullona, 69–70; morería, 132; sermons in,
   89–90, 100–101, 109
Jesuits: College of San Pablo, 42–43, 152; sermons
   in morisco parishes, 88, 99; university reform,
   46–47
Jews: expulsion of 1492, 14, 63, 111, 140; Jewish law,
   80, 100, 120–122; purity of blood statutes, 47, 65;
   sermons of Vincent Ferrer, 87–88; Spanish Inquisition and, 17
John XXIII (pope), 153

Klingshern, William, 190n39

Laredo, Bernardino de, 5
Lea, Henry Charles, xii–xiii
León, Luis de, 121
Lepanto, Battle of, 83, 104, 107
Lerma, Duke of: morisco policy, 128–129, 143, 145,
   149–150; patron of Bernardo de Rojas y San-
   doval, 7; veneration of Vincent Ferrer, 75
Lipsius, Justus, 143
Loaces, Fernando de (archbishop of Valencia), 6
Loyola, Ignatius of, 43, 78
Lull, Ramón, 12
Luther, Martin, 17
Luviela, Miguel Juan: imprisonment, 45–46, 48–
   50; Valencian local identity, 42

Margarita of Austria, 128
Mármol Carvajal, Luis de, xii
Martínez, Miguel, 157
Matarana, Bartolomé, 64
Maurus, Saint, 76
Medina, Pedro de, 28, 121
Mejía, Agustín, 143–144
Mendoza, Diego Hurtado de (d. 1536), 14
Mendoza, Diego Hurtado de (d. 1575), xi
Meyerson, Mark, 208n73
Miedes, Bernardo Gómez de, ally of Juan de Ri-
   bera, 44, 54, 61
Mijavila, Juan Joaquín: imprisonment, 45–46,
   48–50; preacher of the city of Valencia, 56;
   Valencian local identity, 42
Miranda, Gregorio de, 18
Moncofa, 144
Monzón, Pedro: arrest of, 36; imprisonment, 45,
   47, 53–56; Valencian local identity, 42
moriscos: expulsion from Spain, 141–148; forced
   baptisms, 14–17; historiography, xii–xiii; inquisitorial treaty of 1526, 16–18; inquisitorial
   treaty of 1571, 83–84, 91–94; paintings of the expulsion, 148–149; population, 29, 110–111, 130–
   133; prosecution by the Inquisition, 91–94, 132–
   133; religious instruction, 116–123; religious
   practices, 30–34, 94–99, 133–137, 155; school
   for children, ix, 115, 136, 146–148; violence, 20–
   22, 137–141, 144
Mozarabic Christians, 13
Muça, Miguel, 96
Mudejars, 11–15, 92
Muñoz, Catalina, 68, 154
Münzer, Jerónimo, 170n112
mysticism: in Badajoz, 5–6; in Valencia, 68–72

Naples, 2
Netherlands: bishop Mathius Hovius, 87; Dutch
   revolt, 112; truce with Spain, 129, 143

Olivares, Count of, 75, 116
Orihuela, 117, 145
Ortega y Gasset, José, 181n125
Ottoman Turks: rivalry with Charles V, 16, 18, 20;
   rivalry with Philip II, 107, 128; rivalry with
   Philip III, 128; threat of invasion of Spain, 41,
   110–111, 131–132, 137; treatment of Christians,
   98

Pallás, Luis, 98–99

papacy: Clement VIII, 75–76; Gregory XIII, 94, 116, 124; John XXIII, 153; Paul III, 3; Paul V, 142–143, 152; Pius V, 6

Parcent, 95

Paul III (pope), 3

Paul V (pope), 142–143, 152

Pérez, Bartolomé, 152

Pérez de Ayala, Martín (archbishop of Valencia): morisco policy, 117, 119; reform program, 19–20

Pérez de Chinchón, Bernardino, 121

Philip II (king of Spain): appointment of Juan de Ribera to Valencia, 6–7; authorization of Colegio de Corpus Christi, 62–63; church reform, 2–4; correspondence with Ribera on moriscos, 103–113, 124–125; disarmament of moriscos, 21; foreign policy, 106–107, 112–113, 128; university reform, 44–45, 48–50

Philip III (king of Spain): correspondence with Juan de Ribera on moriscos, 126–130; expulsion of moriscos, 143–150; foreign policy, 128–129; patron of Colegio de Corpus Christi, 65

Picanya, 81

Pineda, Antonio, 36, 54

Pius V (pope), 6

Porcar, Joan, 74

Poska, Allyson, 170n101

Prades, Jaime, 72

Quiroga, Gaspar de (archbishop of Toledo): church reform, 7; correspondence with Juan de Ribera, 99, 103–106; morisco treaty of 1571, 83–84

Quran: in catechism of 1599, 122–123; in morisco religious practices, 31–32, 89, 95–96, 128, 134–135; in Muslim Spain, 13

Ramírez de Haro, Antonio, 18–19, 117

Ranke, Leopold von, xi

Relics, 73–77, 154

Ribalta, Francisco, 64, 156–157

Ribera, Per Afán de: death of, 39; education of Juan de Ribera, 6; father of Juan de Ribera, 46; political career, 2

Ribera, Saint Juan de (archbishop of Valencia): acquisition of relics, 73–76; bishop of Badajoz, 2–6; catechism of 1599, 119–123; Colegio de Corpus Christi, ix–x, 62–66, 77, 154; Corpus Christi procession, 24–30, 78; correspondence with Philip II on moriscos, 103–113, 124–125; correspondence with Philip III on moriscos, 127–130; death of, 151; early life, 1–2; episcopal powers, 38–40, 153–156; expulsion of moriscos, 104, 106, 141–150; library, 87–88; morisco policy, 81–83, 90–92, 107–113, 154–156; patronage of mystics, 5–6, 68–72; petition of 1602 on moriscos, 130–141; reform of cathedral, 59–61, 124–125; reform of morisco parishes, 84–86, 94–99, 113–119; resistance to reforms of, 51–55; sermons, 86–90, 99–101; university visitation of 1570, 44–48, 153

Robres, Ramón, 153

Roca, Francisco Juan: ally of Juan de Ribera, 44, 54; reform of morisco parishes, 85

Rojas, Juan de: prosecution of moriscos, 93; university visitation of 1570, 45, 53, 55

Rojas y Sandoval, Bernardo de (archbishop of Toledo), 7

Rojas y Sandoval, Cristóbal de (bishop of Córdoba), 61

Ruiz, Teofilo, 208n72

Sans, 138

Santander, Luis, 46–47, 54

Sariñena, Juan, 64, 68

Sebastian I (king of Portugal), 91

Segorbe: diocese of, 117, 145; moriscos of, 93, 131, 133–135

Segorbe, Duke of, 21, 112

Simó, Francisco, 156–157

Sobrino, Antonio, 142, 146, 148

Talavera, Hernando de (archbishop of Granada), 107–108

Teruel, 135

Tortosa, 145

Trent, Council of: decrees, 3–4, 152; episcopal authority, 37, 48, 70, 73; justification, 100; preaching, 86–87

Valencia: Aragonese Cortes, 111; Corpus Christi procession, 22–30, 78; Dominican monastery, 74; economy, 12–13; local identity, 58–59, 76–78; *morería*, 132; reconquest of, 10–11, 140–141; town council, 25–26, 41–45, 49–51, 55–56, 60, 63–64, 73–76

Valencia, cathedral of, 27, 59–61, 124–125

Valencia, Pedro de, 126

Valencia, University of: history, 41–42; visitation of 1570, 44–48

Vall de Uxó, 112

Vich, Miguel: ally of Juan de Ribera, 44, 54; reform of morisco parishes, 85

Vilanova, Jerónimo, 152

Villanueva, Saint Tomás de (archbishop of Valencia), 19

Vinaròs, 144

Vitoria, Francisco de, 2

Ximénez, Juan, 153

Xixona, 101

Zenequi, Francisco, 80, 105